A
TOUR
IN
SCOTLAND;
MDCCLXIX.

TROS TYRIUSQUE *mihi nullo discrimine agetur.*

THIRD EDITION.

WARRINGTON,
Printed by W. Eyres,
MDCCLXXIV.

This edition published by Melven Press, 176 High Street, Perth, Scotland.

PRESS

1979

ISBN 0 9505884 9 0

INTRODUCTION

An Introduction and memoir to Thomas Pennant's First Tour of Scotland in 1769.

Thomas Pennant's first tour of Scotland began at Chester in 1769. On horseback he progressed at a leisurely pace, keenly observing the landscape through which he passed, and with great perception noting details of his experiences in a journal later to be expanded into an account of his travels. Of gentle birth, inheritor of considerable estates, he could afford to indulge his great passion for travel. By this time his other great passion for natural history had already brought him acclaim following the publication of his three volume work BRITISH ZOOLOGY begun in 1761. This was a work he favoured with several new editions and which in 1767 was instrumental in his being elected a Fellow of the Royal Society.

Scotland in the mid eighteenth century was virtually *terra incognita* to the southerner. The era of the tourist was yet to come, although Martin Martin's notable account of the Western Isles which he visited at the end of the previous century must have been read by Pennant. The book will probably have inspired him to visit Scotland as it did Doctor Johnson to visit the Hebrides in 1773. Perhaps this era was heralded by Pennant's sojourn since he reported wryly that he had proved North Britain could be visited with safety, adding with cynicism that ever since, it had been inundated with southern visitants. He recalled in his autobiography that 1769 had been 'a very active one. I had the hardiness to venture on a journey to the remotest part of North Britain, a country almost as little known to its southern brethren as Kamschatska.' The first edition sold out immediately, to be followed quickly by a second which proved equally successful. It went to prove that 'a candid account of Scotland was a novelty,' to quote again from his autobiography.

This tour was the cause of a violent dispute between Johnson and Bishop Percy who had disparaged Pennant's accuracy. 'A carrier who goes alongside Loch Lomond could describe it better.' Johnson retorted 'He's a Whig sir, sad dog. But he's the best traveller I ever read; he observes more things than anyone else does.' Of the later tour in Scotland Johnson made the comment that the author had 'a greater variety of inquiry than almost any man' though Boswell wrote it off as 'superficial.' Clearly this Welshman possessed wit, an eye for detail, historical acumen and a scientist's analytical mind. And yet he complained that his education had been somewhat neglected.

Pennant was born at the family seat of Downing near Holywell in Flintshire on 14th June 1726. His father David Pennant had succeeded to the estate two years before under the will of a distant relative. This is not the place to set out the long and distinguished lineage of the author. It is appropriate to mention that he was very much aware of his own family history and in particular of his descent from the Welsh patriot

Tudor Trevor, the first to settle on the neighbouring estate of Bychton.

Shortly afterwards his parents indulged in the Welsh custom of placing their child into the hands of a foster parent of low social rank. In the memoir which appears in his edition of A TOUR IN WALES, 1883, Professor John Rhys writes that this may well be the last recorded instance of the practice, also once common in Scandinavian countries, and testifies to its antiquity. So, Thomas Pennant spent his first years in a neighbouring farmhouse with foster parents who esteemed it a great honour to do their master this service. The practice had some advantages. A person of gentle birth who would spend much of his life mixing with others of his class might be better equipped to learn sympathy for the wants and hardships of the working class. And, as Rhys was most emphatic to point out, it would foster a knowledge of the Welsh language which at this time enjoyed a prestige sadly lacking today.

He progressed from Rev. W. Lewis's school in Wrexham to another in Fulham, but details of his life during this period are scant and one may only assume that he may have received some assistance from his uncle, the Rev. John Pennant in Hadley near Enfield Chase, with whom he often stayed. This period of his life was largely spent in or near London where in 1744 at the age of 18 he witnessed his mother's death. In the same year he entered the University of Oxford matriculating at Queen's College as a commoner. In his autobiography Pennant again remains silent about his university career. Perhaps he took no liking to study for he left after a couple of years without taking a degree. It was during his short career as an undergraduate that he made his first recorded tour — to

Cornwall — where he was encouraged, by Doctor Borlase of Ludgvan, in the study of minerals and fossils. He was certainly under no compulsion to train for a profession. But it seems his indulgence earned him little wealth since he admits that at the time of his marriage with Elizabeth Falconer in 1759 his circumstances were 'very narrow'. After his marriage he settled down at Whiteford and in 1761 served in the office of High Sheriff of Flintshire. But Natural History was his current interest, first inspired, so he tells us, by the gift at the age of twelve of a book called Willoughby's Ornithology.

A life of inactive leisure was anathema to him. He took much pride in his health, to quote 'I had a great share of health during the literary part of my days, much of this owing to the riding exercise of my extensive tours, to my manner of living and my temperance. I go to rest at ten, rise winter and summer at seven, and shave regular(sic) at the same hour. I avoid the meal of excess, a supper.' Two hundred years on and that philosophy touches a familiar chord and is certainly not the testimony of the idle rich as another self portrait agrees: 'when not pursuing my activity as an author I was father of a family, landlord of a small but numerous tenantry and a not inactive magistrate.' And in addition to these serious pursuits he never neglected the company of friends or convivial society.

His first extensive tour was made in Ireland in 1754, but his diary was woefully incomplete, his excuse being 'such was the conviviality of the country.' It was not until after the untimely death of his first wife in 1764 that he truly indulged his wanderlust. In 1765 his travels brought him into contact with several great men of his time. He remembers with warmth meeting the French naturalist and scientist Buffon, and was only a little irritated that the great man had failed to acknowledge the source of some illustrations he had sent for inclusion in his masterpiece HISTOIRE NATURELLE. He was probably rather mollified by some favourable comment on his efforts in volume fifteen, at that time nearing completion, since his opinion is tempered to (there being) 'only small faults in a great character.'

He bearded Voltaire in his den, 'that wicked wit', as he termed him, who so greatly disdained the curtailment of his studies for the alternative of needless conversation. He recorded the whole of his conversation with Voltaire at Ferney, 'extremely witty and amusing, descending to a disfigurement of oaths and curses with which he was pleased to demonstrate his scant acquaintance of English.' Doctor Johnson consulted Voltaire before undertaking his tour of the Hebrides. Johnson recalls that 'he looked at me as if I had talked of going to the North Pole and said: "You do not insist on my coming with you?" No sir. "Then I am very willing that you should go."

He corresponded for many years with the eminent Swedish naturalist Linnaeus until the latter was forced to desist by reason of his failing health. In 1757, before his endeavours were widely known, Pennant was elected a member of the Royal Society of Uppsala on the recommendation of Linnaeus who clearly recognised the man's blossoming genius. Thomas Pennant always considered this the greatest of all his honours since it carried the distinction of being awarded so early in his career. It pre-empted the Doctor of Laws conferred by the University of Oxford in full convocation when after a laudatory speech he was presented to the Vice Chancellor. But this was in 1771 a long time after he had published his fine work BRITISH ZOOLOGY, and in the same year in which he published BRITISH QUADRUPEDS. Both were to see additions and improvements in later years, and in fact he tinkered with the former for more than fifteen years.

The first tour of Scotland in 1769 was soon followed by a second, longer tour whose results were published in two volumes 1774/75. This time he visited the Hebrides, and concentrated on the western areas of the country. He failed to visit the northernmost extremities and left it to a Rev. Low of Birsay in Orkney to supply details for a concluding volume. This gentleman's endeavours did not, it seems, appeal to Pennant as 100 years were to elapse before a local publisher put the matter into print.* However some of the material was included in ANTIQUITIES AND SCENERY OF THE NORTH OF SCOTLAND published in 1780 by Rev. C. Cordiner, Episcopal minister of Banff.

Pennant tells us little about the reception of these later volumes, only to say they were equally successful. In comment on the first he gives his reasons for making the tour at all: 'In this tour, as in all the succeeding, I laboured earnestly to conciliate the affections of the two nations, so wickedly and studiously set at variance by evil designing people.' It is clear he had in mind the disastrous attempts made in the first half of that century to restore the Stuart line, and John Rhys makes it clear that his sympathies lay with the Hanoverian dynasty. Pennant comments on the battle of Culloden which had been fought only twenty three years previously: 'let a veil be flung over a few excesses (presumably the bloody reprisals carried out at the instigation of the Duke

*A Tour Through the Islands of Orkney and Schetland 1774, reprinted by Melven Press: 1978

of Cumberland) consequential of a day productive of so much benefit to the united kingdoms.'

In the edition we republish are included the plates executed from drawings by his prodigy Moses Griffith. The man deserves more than a mere mention as an example of the author's magnanimity and sincere generosity.

Moses Griffith accompanied Pennant on all his tours except the first. He recorded the landscape faithfully and his sketches today are a priceless memorial of the times. But, he was quite untrained and entirely self taught. He was of humble parentage in the remote district of Llŷn and joined the author in 1749, in his own words 'I acquired that treasure Moses Griffith.' Pennant's will set out many small legacies for the benefit of friends and acquaintances. Moses Griffith was no exception and £200 p.a. was given for his daughter and son.

Between the years 1763 and 1764 Pennant went through a period of much personal distress. His father died in 1763, and in 1764, after five years of happy marriage, came the death of his wife Elizabeth, leaving him two children, David and Arabella. David succeeded his father in Downing and himself led a distinguished career. It is noteworthy that most of Pennant's tours were undertaken between the death of his first wife and his marriage with Ann Mostyn in 1777. She was the sister of his close friend Sir Roger Mostyn and gave him two children, Sarah and Thomas. Pennant never fully revovered from the shock and grief felt at the death of his daughter at the age of fourteen. His son Thomas became rector at Weston Turville in Buckinghamshire and married without issue.

Perhaps Pennant's most intriguing work was that from which several quotations are made above, published in 1793 under the title LITERARY LIFE OF THE LATE THOMAS PENNANT BY HIMSELF, suggesting it was to be published posthumously, but his 'authorial existence' (as he termed it) is implied rather than his life. It is a descriptive and often witty resume of his literary career and as such is sadly lacking in personal reminiscence. It directs his sons not to publish most of the manuscripts on which he was working up to the time of his death under the general title OUTLINES OF THE GLOBE. These describe an imaginary tour of the world, the detail gathered from books, conversation with travellers and illustrated from descriptions and pictures from many sources. Right to the end he was a traveller in spirit if not in fact and that is truly how we remember him best today. Let Professor John Rhys have the last words: 'His character was one of rare occurrence uniting the greatest application with the most disinterested love of literature for he held a station in society which rendered him above the daily duties of professional authorship. Whatever he touched he beautified; either by the elegance of his diction, the historical illustrations he introduced or the popular charm he gave to things well known before.'

Thomas Pennant died after a short and painful illness at Downing in December 1798 at the age of 72.

BARRY KNIGHT

TO

SIR ROGER MOSTYN, BAR[T].

OF

MOSTYN, FLINTSHIRE.

DEAR SIR,

A GENTLEMAN well known to the political world in the beginning of the present century made the tour of *Europe*, and before he reached *Abbeville* discovered that in order to see a country to best advantage it was infinitely preferable to travel by day than by night.

I CANNOT help making this applicable to myself, who, after publishing three volumes of the *Zoology* of GREAT BRITAIN, found out that to be able to speak with more precision of the subjects I treated of, it was far more prudent to visit the whole than part of my country: struck therefore with the reflection of having never seen SCOTLAND, I instantly ordered my baggage to be got ready, and in a reasonable time found myself on the banks of the *Tweed*.

As soon as I communicated to you my resolution, with your accustomed friendship you wished to hear from me: I could give but a partial performance of my promise, the attention of a traveller being so much taken up as to leave very little room for epistolary duties; and I flatter myself you will find this tardy execution of my engagement more satisfactory than the hasty accounts I could send you on my road. But this is far from being the sole motive of this address.

I HAVE irresistible inducements of public and of a private nature: to you I owe a most

free

free enjoyment of the little territories Providence had beſtowed on me; for by a liberal and equal ceſſion of fields, and meads and woods, you connected all the divided parts, and gave a full ſcope to all my improvements. Every view I take from my window reminds me of my debt, and forbids my ſilence, cauſing the pleaſing glow of gratitude to diffuſe itſelf over the whole frame, inſtead of forcing up the imbittering ſigh of *Oh! ſi angulus ille!* Now every ſcene I enjoy receives new charms, for I mingle with the viſible beauties, the more pleaſing idea of owing them to you, the worthy neighbor and firm friend, who are happy in the calm and domeſtic paths of life with abilities ſuperior to oſtentation, and goodneſs content with its own reward: with a ſound judgement and honeſt heart you worthily diſcharge the ſenatorial truſt repoſed in you, whoſe unprejudiced vote aids to ſtill the madneſs of the People, or aims to check the preſumption of the Miniſter. My happineſs in being from your earliest life your neighbor, makes me confident in my observation; your increasing and discerning band of friends discovers and confirms the justice of it: may the reasons that attract and bind us to you ever remain, is the most gratefull wish that can be thought of, by,

DEAR SIR,

Your obliged,

and affectionate Friend,

DOWNING,
October 20th, 1771.

THOMAS PENNANT.

ADVERTISEMENT.

THE considerable additions and corrections in the present edition, are owing to the liberal ſpirit of communication among the Gentlemen of the Northern parts of this Kingdom, in my Tours of the years 1772 and 1773.

BY means of their friendly ſtrictures, this edition is freed from ſome errors that muſt unavoidably attend the performance of a rapid traveller, notwithſtanding all his wiſhes to be accurate.

FROM the ſame ſources are drawn very conſiderable additions, which are inſerted in their proper places; together with variety of remarks on the characters of the ſeveral perſonages whoſe reſemblances have been delivered down to us on canvas. Out of theſe I have cauſed the heads of the venerable Counteſs of *Deſmond*, and the Admirable CRICHTON, to be engraven by the ingenious Mr. *Aliamet*,

and

and the celebrated Mr. *Hall.* All the Plates of the former editions are ſuppreſſed; and a ſet of new ſubjects added, of places eminent in hiſtory, or diſtinguiſhed by their beauty. Mr. *Mazel* has exerted himſelf in the execution.

I MUST return particular thanks to the ſeveral Gentlemen who have favored me with informations; and beg that the following, un-mentioned in the courſe of the work, would accept my beſt acknowlegements.

WILLIAM CONSTABLE, Eſq. of BURTON CONSTABLE, *Yorkſhire.*
Doctor RAMSAY, EDINBURGH.
Mr. GEORGE PATON, *ibid.*
Profeſſor OGILVIE, Old ABERDEEN.
Doctor SAUNDERS, BAMFF.
Rev. Mr. LAUTIE, Miniſter of FORDYCE.
Rev. Mr. ALEXANDER GRANT, Miniſter of DAVIOT.
Rev. Mr. SUTHERLAND, Miniſter of DORNOCH.
Rev. Mr. MAC-INTYRE, Miniſter of GLENORCHIE.
Rev. Mr. FARISH, CARLISLE.
Mr. HARRISON, Surgeon, PENRITH.
JOSEPH NICHOLSON, Eſq. HAWKESDALE.

AND,

The Rev. Doctor BURN, of ORTON, *Weſtmoreland.*

I MUST

I MUST in particular acknowlege the liberal turn of thoſe Gentlemen who freely permit me to anticipate ſome paſſages in their Hiſtory of CUMBERLAND and WESTMORELAND, which they intend ſoon to favor the Public with.

A select bibliography

British Zoology	1761
British Zoology — second ed.	1768
British Zoology — Vol III (Fishes)	1769
Indian Zoology	1769
Tour of Scotland 1 vol 8vo	1771
Tour of Scotland 2nd ed.	1772
A History of Quadrupends	1771
A Tour of Scotland 3rd ed.	1774
Voyage to the Hebrides	1774
Second Tour of Scotland vol I	1774
vol II	1775
British Zoology n.e. in 3 vols	1776
Tour in Wales vol I	1778
Tour in Wales vol II	1781
Tour in Wales vol I, n.e.	1783
Tour in Wales, two vols in one	1784
Arctic Zoology	1785
Literary Life of the Late Thos. Pennant by Himself	1793
History of Whiteford and Holywell	1796

APPENDIX.

		Page
No. I.	OF SCOTCH PINES,	265.
II.	Of ELGIN and the Shire of MURRAY,	269.
III.	Of the ADMIRABLE CRICHTON,	295.
IV.	Of the MURDER of an INNES,	311.
V.	Of CATHNESS, STRATHNAVER, and SUTHERLAND,	318.
VI.	MEMOIRS of SIR EWEN CAMERON,	347.
VII.	Of the MASSACRE of the COLQUHOUNS,	365.
VIII.	ITINERARY,	367.

TO avoid ſwelling this Book to an unreaſonable ſize, the Appendix of the former Editions is omitted: but being referred to, it is proper for the ſatisfaction of the curious Reader to add a Liſt of the Articles he may wiſh to conſult.

No. I. Of the Conſtitution of the CHURCH of SCOTLAND.
II. Of the FASTING WOMAN of ROSS-SHIRE.
III. Of the PARALLEL ROADS in GLEN-ROY.
IV. GALIC PROVERBS, TRANSLATIONS, &c.
V. Order of Council relating to the Removal of Venereal Perſons from EDINBURGH to INCH-KEITH.
VI. Of the COLUMNS in PENRITH CHURCH-YARD.
VII. RECAPITULATION of the ANIMALS mentioned in the TOUR, &c.

The greateſt part of the two laſt Articles are inſerted in the text of the preſent Edition.

PLATES.

P L A T E S.

Page

ROWS in BRIDGE-STREET, CHESTER; with a VIEW of ST. PETER's CHURCH, 1

BURTON CONSTABLE, the Seat of WILLIAM CONSTABLE, Efq. HOLDERNESS, *Yorkshire,* 14

The BASS ISLE, taken from TANTALLON CASTLE, and LOCH-LEVEN CASTLE; from SKETCHES by Profeffor OGILVIE, of Old ABERDEEN, 46

EDINBURGH CASTLE, from GREY FRIERS Church-Yard, 51

DUPPLIN, the Seat of the Earl of KINNOULL, 72

HEAD of the old Countefs of DESMOND, 74

DUNKELD cathedral 80

TAYMOUTH, the Seat of the Earl of BREADALBANE, 82

Cafcade near TAYMOUTH 87

The BROTCHE and WALKING-STAFF at Col. CAMPBEL'S, of GLEN-LION, 90

VIEW near BLAIR 103

YORKE CASCADE, near BLAIR of ATHOL, 105

P L A T E S.

	Page
FASKALLY,	106
BRAE MAR caftle	109
The BRIDGE of DON,	128
URN, FLINT ARROW-HEAD, &c.	139
A VIEW of a HOUSE, fuppofed to be that of CASTLE GORDON when complete; taken from an old PRINT, infcribed BOG-IN-GIGHT,	142
VIEW of ELGIN,	146
INVERNESS	160
FRESWICK caftle	177
Upper fall of FYERS	199
KILCHURN CASTLE,	216
INVERARAY,	218
The ancient CASTLE of INVERARAY, from an old PRINT,	220
STERLING caftle	238

ANTIQUITIES at NETHERBY. *No.* I. A GAULISH DEITY. II. Another. III. A third, NEHALENNIA, the Goddefs of the Chalk Diggers, as appears by an infcription preferved by *Heinefius*, p. 190.

DEÆ *NEHALENNIÆ*
OB MERCES RITE CONSERVATAS
M. SECUNDUS SILVANUS
NEGOTTOR ☉ RETARIUS
BRITANNICIANUS
V. S. L. M.

Page

The Chalk trade was very confiderable in this ifland: *Pliny** defcribes the manner of working, which agrees with the prefent; and adds, that it was a manure that would laft eighty years. As it fo greatly promoted fertility, it is not without reafon that the lap of the Goddefs is filled with fruits.

No. IV. DEÆ MATRES V. An antient SHOE, 249

*Lib. xvii. c. 8.

ARTHUR's ROUND TABLE, and MAYBOROUGH, 256

SHAP ABBY, 257

TAIL PIECE, *vide* p. 250.

ADMIRABLE CRICHTON, 295

ERRATA.

Page	Line				
56,	13,	*for*	cæmeteries	*read*	cemeteries.
81,	6,		ædifice		edifice.
157,	11,		a gofpel		as gofpel.
163,	17,		Lord *Fortrofe*		Earl of *Seaforth.*
183,	3 from the bottom,		*Edrachilis*		*Reay.*
231,	11,		two others are		another is.
249,	16,		*Nehalenia*		*Nehalennia.*
258,	1,		*Vetevipont*		*Veteripont.*

ADDITIONS.

Page

95. *Struan*'s lands were originally granted to an Anceftor of his, as a reward for taking *Robert Graham,* the ruffian who murdered *James* I. They were then valued at 100 marks. He was alfo permitted to ufe, as his coat of arms, a *Graham* bound in chains.

162. The Barony of *Lovat* came into that family by the marriage of a *Frazier* with the Heirefs of a Lord *Biffet,* who had great poffeffions in thofe parts.

Moses Griffiths del

P. Mazell sculp

ROWS IN BRIDGE STREET, CHESTER.

A
TOUR
IN
SCOTLAND,
MDCCLXIX.

ON *Monday* the 26th of JUNE take my departure from CHESTER, a city without parallel for the ſingular ſtructure of the four principal ſtreets, which are as if excavacated out of the earth, and ſunk many feet beneath the ſurface; the carriages drive far beneath the level of the kitchens, on a line with ranges of ſhops, over which on each ſide of the ſtreets paſſengers walk from end to end, in galleries open in front, ſecure from wet or heat. The back courts of all theſe houſes are level with the ground, but to go into any of theſe four ſtreets it is neceſſary to deſcend a flight of ſeveral ſteps. CHESTER.

The *Cathedral* is an antient ſtructure, very ragged on the outſide,

from

from the nature of the red friable ſtone* with which it is built: the tabernacle work in the choir is very neat; but the beauty and elegant ſimplicity of a very antique gothic chapter-houſe, is what merits a viſit from every traveller.

The *Hypocauſt* near the *Feathers* Inn, is one of the remains of the *Romans* †, it being well known that this place was a principal ſtation. Among many antiquities found here, none is more ſingular than the rude ſculpture of the *Dea Armigera Minerva*, with her bird and her altar, on the face of a rock in a ſmall field near the *Welch* end of the bridge.

The caſtle is a decaying pile. The walls of the city, the only complete ſpecimens of antient fortifications, are kept in excellent order, being the principal walk of the inhabitants: the views from the ſeveral parts are very fine; the mountains of *Flintſhire*, the hills of *Broxton*, and the inſulated rock of *Beeſton*, form the ruder part of the ſcenery; a rich flat forms the ſofter view, and the proſpect up the river towards *Boughton* recalls in ſome degree the idea of the *Thames* and *Richmond* hill.

Paſſed thro' *Tarvin*, a ſmall village; in the church-yard is an epitaph in memory of Mr. *John Thomaſen*, an excellent penman, but particularly famous for his exact and elegant imitation of the *Greek* character.

Delamere, which *Leland* calls a faire and large foreſt, with plenty of redde deere and falow, is now a black and dreary waſte; it feeds a few rabbets, and a few black *Terns* ‡ ſkim over the ſplaſhes that water ſome part of it.

* Saxum arenarium friabile rubrum *Da Coſta foſſils.* I. 139.

† This city was the *Deva* and *Devana* of *Antonine*, and the ſtation of the *Legio viceſima victrix.*

‡ *Br. Zool.* II. 430.

A few

A few miles from this heath lies *Northwich*, a ſmall town, long famous for its rock ſalt, and brine pits. Some years ago I viſited one of the mines; the ſtratum of ſalt lies about forty yards deep; that which I ſaw was hollowed into the form of a temple. I deſcended thro' a dome, and found the roof ſupported by rows of pillars, about two yards thick, and ſeveral in height; the whole was illuminated with numbers of candles, and made a moſt magnificent and glittering appearance. Above the ſalt is a bed of whitiſh clay*, uſed in making the *Liverpool* earthen-ware; and in the ſame place is alſo dug a good deal of the *Gypſum*, or plaiſter ſtone. The foſſil ſalt is generally yellow, and ſemipellucid, ſometimes debaſed with a dull greeniſh earth, and is often found, but in ſmall quantities, quite clear and color-leſs. SALT PITS.

The road from this place to *Macclesfield* is thro' a flat, rich, but unpleaſant country. That town is in a very flouriſhing ſtate; is poſſeſſed of a great manufacture of mohair and twiſt buttons; has between twenty and thirty ſilk mills, and a very conſiderable copper ſmelting houſe, and braſs work.

Here lived in great hoſpitality at his manour houſe† *Henry Stafford* Duke of *Buckingham*, a moſt powerful Peer, the ſad inſtrument of the ambition of *Richard* III. He was at once rewarded by that monarch ‡ with a grant of fifty caſtles and manours; but ſtruck with remorſe at being acceſſary to ſo many crimes, fell from his allegiance, and by a juſt retribution, ſuffered on a ſcaffold by the mere *fiat* of his unfeeling maſter.

In the church is the ſepulchral chapel, and the magnificent mo-

* Argilla cærula-cinerea *Da Coſta foſſils.* I. 48.

† *King*'s Vale Royal. 86. ‡ *Dugdale*'s Baronage I. 168.

numents of the family of the *Savages:* and on a braſs plate on the wall this comfortable advertiſement of the price of remiſſion of ſins in the other life: it was to be wiſhed that the expence of obtaining ſo extenſive a charter from his holineſs in this world had likewiſe been added.

Theſe are the words.

The Pdon for ſaying of 5 *Pater noſt* and 5 *aves* and a creed is 26 thouſand yeres and 26 dayes of Pardon.

In the chapel belonging to the *Leghs* of *Lyme* is another ſingular inſcription and its hiſtory.

Here lyeth the body of *Perkin a Legh*
That for King *Richard* the death did die,
Betrayed for righteouſneſs,
And the bones of Sir *Peers* his ſonne
That with king *Henrie* the fift did wonne
in *Paris*.

'This *Perkin* ſerved king *Edward* the third and the *black Prince* 'his ſonne in all their warres in *France* and was at the battel of '*Creſſie* and had *Lyme* given him for that ſervice; and after their 'deathes ſerved king *Richard* the ſecond, and left him not in his 'troubles but was taken with him and beheaded at *Cheſter* by king '*Henrie* the fourthe. and the ſayd Sir *Peers* his ſonne ſerved king '*Henrie* and was ſlaine at the battel of *Agencourt*.

'In their memorie Sir *Peter Legh* of *Lyme* knight deſcended from 'them finding the ſayd ould verſes written upon a ſtone in this 'Chappel did reedifie this place *An° Dni* 1620.

After leaving this town, the country almoſt inſtantly changes and becomes very mountanous and barren, at leſt on the ſurface; but

but the bowels compenſate for the external ſterility, by yielding ſufficient quantity of coal for the uſe of the neighboring parts of *Cheſhire*, and for the burning of lime: vaſt quantity is made near *Buxton*, and being carried to all parts for the purpoſes of agriculture, is become a conſiderable article of commerce.

The celebrated warm bath of BUXTON * is ſeated in a bottom, amidſt theſe hills, in a moſt chearleſs ſpot, and would be little frequented, did not *Hygeia* often reſide here, and diſpenſe to her votaries the chief bleſſings of life, eaſe and health. With joy and gratitude I this moment reflect on the efficacious qualities of the waters; I recollect with rapture the return of ſpirits, the flight of pain, and re-animation of my long, long crippled rheumatic limbs. But how unfortunate is it, that what Providence deſigned for the general good, ſhould be rendered only a partial one, and denied to all, except the opulent; or I may ſay to the (comparatively) few that can get admittance into the houſe where theſe waters are impriſoned? There are other ſprings (*Cambden* ſays nine) very near that in the *Hall*, and in all probability of equal virtue. I was informed that the late Duke of *Devonſhire*, not long before his death, had ordered ſome of theſe to be incloſed and formed into baths. It is to be hoped that his ſucceſſor will not fail adopting ſo uſeful and humane a plan; that he will form it on the moſt enlarged ſyſtem, that they may open not ſolely to thoſe whom miſuſed wealth hath rendered invalids, but to the poor cripple, whom honeſt labor hath made a BUXTON.

* The *Romans*, who were remarkably fond of warm baths, did not over-look theſe agreeable waters: they had a bath, incloſed with a brick wall, adjacent to the preſent St. *Anne*'s well, which Dr, *Short*, in his eſſay on mineral waters, ſays was razed in 1709.

burden

burden to himſelf and his country; and to the ſoldier and ſailor, who by hard ſervice have loſt the uſe of thoſe very limbs which once were active in our defence. The honor reſulting from ſuch a foundation would be as great, as the ſatisfaction ariſing from a conſciouſneſs of ſo benevolent a work would be unſpeakable. The charms of diſſipation would then loſe their force; and dull and taſteleſs would every human luxury appear to him, who had it in his power thus to lay open theſe fountains of health, and to be able to exult in ſuch pathetic and comfortable ſtrains as theſe: *When the ear heard me, then it bleſſed me, and when the eye ſaw me it gave witneſs to me;*

Becauſe I delivered the poor that cried, and the fatherleſs, and him that had none to help him.

The bleſſing of him that was ready to periſh came upon me, and I cauſed the widow's heart to ſing for joy.

I was eyes to the blind, and feet was I to the lame.

After leaving *Buxton*, paſſed thro' *Middleton* dale, a deep narrow chaſm between two vaſt cliffs, which extend on each ſide near a mile in length: this road is very ſingular, but the rocks are in general too naked to be beautiful. At the end is the ſmall village of *Stoney Middleton*; here the proſpect opens, and at *Barſly Bridge* exhibits a pretty view of a ſmall but fertile vale, watered by the *Derwent*, and terminated by *Chatſworth*, and its plantations. Arrived and lay at

Cheſterfield; an ugly town. In this place is a great manufacture of worſted ſtockings, and another of a brown earthen-ware, much of which is ſent into *Holland*, the country which, within leſs than half a century ago, ſupplied not only theſe kingdoms but half of

Europe

Europe with that commodity. The clay is found near the town, over the baſs or cherty* ſtratum, above the coal. The ſteeple of *Cheſterfield* church is a ſpire, covered with lead, but by a violent wind ſtrangely bent, in which ſtate it remains.

In the road ſide, about three miles from the town, are ſeveral pits of iron ſtone, about nine or ten feet deep. The ſtratum lies above the coal, and is two feet thick. I was informed that the adventurers pay ten pounds per annum to the Lord of the Soil, for liberty of raiſing it; that the laborers have ſix ſhillings per load for getting it: each load is about twenty ſtrikes or buſhels, which yields a tun of metal. Coal, in theſe parts, is very cheap, a tun and a half being ſold for five ſhillings. JUNE 27.

Changed horſes at *Workſop* and *Tuxford*; croſſed the *Trent* at *Dunham-Ferry*, where it is broad but ſhallow: the ſpring tides flow here, and riſe about two feet, but the common tides never reach this place. Paſs along the *Foſs-Dike*, or the canal opened by *Henry* I.† to form a communication between the *Trent* and the *Witham*. It was opened‡ in the year 1121, and extends from *Lincoln* to *Torkeſey*; its length is eleven miles three quarters, the breadth between dike and dike at the top is about ſixty feet, at bottom twenty-two: veſſels from fifteen to thirty-five tuns navigate this canal,

* Or flinty.

† *Dugdale* on embanking, 167.

‡ I make uſe of this word, as Doctor *Stukely* conjectures this canal to have been originally a *Roman* work; and that another of the ſame kind (called the *Carſ-dike*) communicated with it, by means of the *Witham*, which began a little below *Waſhenbro'*, three miles from *Lincoln*, and was continued thro' the fens as far as *Peterborough*. *Stukely*'s *Carauſius*. 129. ſeqq. Ejuſd. *Account of Richard of Cirenceſter*. 50.

nal, and by its means a conſiderable trade in coals, timber, corn and wool, is carried on. In former times, the perſons who had landed property on either ſide were obliged to ſcower it whenever it was choaked up, and accordingly we find preſentments were made by juries in ſeveral ſucceeding reigns for that purpoſe. Reach

LINCOLN, an antient but ill-built city, much fallen away from its former extent. It lies partly on a plain, partly on a very ſteep hill, on whoſe ſummit are the cathedral and the ruins of the caſtle. The firſt is a vaſt pile of gothic architecture; has nothing remarkable on the outſide, but within is of matchleſs beauty and magnificence: the ornaments are exceſſively rich, and in the fineſt gothic taſte; the pillars light, the centre lofty, and of a ſurpriſing grandeur. The windows at the N. and S. ends are very antient, but very elegant; one repreſents a leaf with its fibres, the other conſiſts of a number of ſmall circles. There are two other antient windows on each ſide the great iſle: the others, as I recollect, are modern. This church was, till of late years, much out of repair, but has juſt been reſtored in a manner that does credit to the Chapter. There is indeed a ſort of arch near the W. end, that ſeems placed there (for the ſame purpoſe as *Bayes* tells us he wrote one of his ſcenes) meerly to ſet off the reſt.

The proſpect from this eminence is very extenſive, but very barren of objects; a vaſt flat as far as the eye can reach, conſiſting of plains not the moſt fertile, or of fens* and moors: the laſt are far leſs

* The fens, naked as they now appear, were once well wooded. Oaks have been found buried in them, which were ſixteen yards long, and five in circumference; fir trees from thirty to thirty-five yards long, and a foot or eighteen inches ſquare.

leſs extenſive than they were, many being drained, and will ſoon become the beſt land in the country. But ſtill much remains to be done: the fens near *Reveſby Abby* *, eight miles beyond *Horncaſtle*, are of vaſt extent; but ſerve for little other purpoſe than the rearing great numbers of geeſe, which are the wealth of the fenmen.

During the breeding ſeaſon, theſe birds are lodged in the ſame houſes with the inhabitants, and even in their very bed-chambers: in every apartment are three rows of coarſe wicker pens placed one above another; each bird has its ſeparate lodge divided from the other, which it keeps poſſeſſion of during the time of ſitting. A perſon, called a *Gozzard* †, attends the flock, and twice a day drives the whole to water; then brings them back to their habitations, helping thoſe that live in the upper ſtories to their neſts, without ever miſplacing a ſingle bird. GEESE.

The geeſe are plucked five times in the year; the firſt plucking is at *Lady-Day*, for feathers and quills, and the ſame is renewed, for feathers only, four times more between that and *Michaelmas*. The old geeſe ſubmit quietly to the operation, but the young ones are very noiſy and unruly. I once ſaw this performed, and obſerved that goſlins of ſix weeks old were not ſpared; for their tails were

ſquare. Theſe trees had not the mark of the ax, but appeared as if burnt down by fire applied to their lower parts. Acorns and ſmall nuts have alſo been found in great quantities in the ſame places. *Dugdale* on embanking, 141.

* *Reveſby Abby* was founded 1142, by *W. de Romara*, Earl of *Lincoln*, for *Ciſtercian* monks, and granted by *H.* VIII. an. 30. to *Ch.* Duke of *Suffolk*. The founder turning monk was buried here. *Tanner*. 263.

† i. e. Gooſe-herd.

plucked, as I was told, to habituate them early to what they were to come to. If the ſeaſon proves cold, numbers of geeſe die by this barbarous cuſtom*.

Vaſt numbers are driven annually to *London*, to ſupply the markets; among them, all the ſuperannuated geeſe and ganders (called here *Cagmags*) which ſerve to fatigue the jaws of the good Citizens, who are ſo unfortunate as to meet with them.

FEN BIRDS.

The fen called the *Weſt Fen*, is the place where the Ruffs and Reeves reſort to in the greateſt numbers †; and many other ſorts of water fowl, which do not require the ſhelter of reeds or ruſhes, migrate here to breed; for this fen is very bare, having been imperfectly drained by narrow canals, which interſect it for great numbers of miles. Theſe the inhabitants navigate in moſt diminutive ſhallow boats; they are, in fact, the roads of the country.

The *Eaſt Fen* is quite in a ſtate of nature, and gives a ſpecimen of the country before the introduction of drainage: it is a vaſt tract of moraſs, intermixed with numbers of lakes, from half a mile to two or three miles in circuit, communicating with each other by narrow reedy ſtraits: they are very ſhallow, none are above four or five feet in depth; but abound with fiſh, ſuch as Pike, Perch, Ruff, Bream, Tench, Rud, Dace, Roach, Burbot, Sticklebacks and Eels. It is obſervable, that once in ſeven or eight years, immenſe ſhoals of Sticklebacks appear in the *Welland* below *Spalding*,

* It was alſo practiſed by the antients. *Candidorum alterum vectigal: Velluntur quibuſdam locis bis anno.* Plinii lib. x. c. 22.

† *Br. Zool.* II. 363. *Suppl. tab.* XV. *p.* 22.

and

and attempt coming up the river in form of a vaſt column. They are ſuppoſed to be the collected multitudes waſhed out of the fens by the floods of ſeveral years; and carried into ſome deep hole, when over-charged with numbers, they are obliged to attempt a change of place. They move up the river in ſuch quantities as to enable a man, who was employed in taking them, to earn, for a conſiderable time, four ſhillings a day, by ſelling them at a half-penny per buſhel. They were uſed to manure land, and attempts have been made to get oil from them. The fen is covered with reeds, the harveſt of the neighboring inhabitants, who mow them annually; for they prove a much better thatch than ſtraw, and not only cottages, but many very good houſes are covered with them. Stares, which during winter reſort in myriads to rooſt in the reeds, are very deſtructive, by breaking them down by the vaſt numbers that perch on them. The people are therefore very diligent in their attempts to drive them away, and are at great expence in powder to free themſelves of theſe troubleſome gueſts. I have ſeen a ſtock of reeds harveſted and ſtacked worth two or three hundred pounds, which was the property of a ſingle farmer.

The birds which inhabit the different fens are very numerous: I never met with a finer field for the Zoologiſt to range in. Beſides the common Wild-duck, of which an account is given in another place *, wild Geeſe, Garganies, Pochards, Shovelers and Teals, breed here. I have ſeen in the *Eaſt Fen* a ſmall flock of the tufted

* *Br. Zool.* II. 462. In general, to avoid repetition, the reader is referred to the four *Octavo* volumes of *Britiſh* Zoology, for a more particular account of animals mentioned in this Tour.

Ducks; but they ſeemed to make it only a baiting place. The Pewit Gulls and black Terns abound; the laſt in vaſt flocks almoſt deafen one with their clamors: a few of the great Terns, or Tickets, are ſeen among them. I ſaw ſeveral of the great creſted Grebes on the *Eaſt Fen*, called there *Gaunts*, and met with one of their floating neſts with eggs in it. The leſſer creſted Grebe, the black and duſky Grebe, and the little Grebe, are alſo inhabitants of the fens; together with Coots, Water-hens, ſpotted Water-hens, Water-rails, Ruffs, Redſhanks, Lapwings or Wipes, Red-breaſted Godwits and Whimbrels. The Godwits breed near *Waſhenbrough*; the Whimbrels only appear for about a fortnight in *May* near *Spalding*, and then quit the country. Oppoſite to *Foſſdyke Waſh*, during ſummer, are great numbers of *Avoſettas*, called there *Yelpers*, from their cry: they hover over the ſportſman's head like the Lapwing, and fly with their necks and legs extended.

Knots are taken in nets along the ſhores near *Foſſdyke* in great numbers during winter; but they diſappear in the ſpring.

The ſhort-eared owl, *Br. Zool.* I. 156. viſits the neighbourhood of *Waſhenbrough*, along with the Woodcocks, and probably performs its migrations with thoſe birds, for it is obſerved to quit the country at the ſame time: I have alſo received ſpecimens of them from the *Daniſh* dominions, one of the retreats of the Woodcock. This owl is not obſerved in this country to perch on trees, but conceals itſelf in long old graſs; if diſturbed, takes a ſhort flight, lights again, and keeps ſtaring about, during which time its horns are very viſible. The farmers are fond of the arrival of theſe birds, as they clear the fields of mice, and will even fly in ſearch of prey during day, provided the weather is cloudy and miſty.

But

But the greateſt curioſity in theſe parts is the vaſt Heronry at Creſſi-Hall, ſix miles from *Spalding*. The Herons reſort there in *February* to repair their neſts, ſettle there in the ſpring to breed, and quit the place during winter. They are numerous as Rooks, and their neſts ſo crouded together, that myſelf and the company that was with me counted not fewer than eighty in one tree. I here had opportunity of detecting my own miſtake, and that of other Ornithologiſts, in making two ſpecies of Herons; for I found that the creſted Heron was only the male of the other: it made a moſt beautiful appearance with its ſnowy neck and long creſt ſtreaming with the wind. The family who owned this place was of the ſame name with theſe birds, which ſeems to be the principal inducement for preſerving them. HERONRY.

In the time of *Michael Drayton*,

Here ſtalk'd the ſtately crane, as though he march'd in war.

But at preſent this bird is quite unknown in our iſland; but every other ſpecies enumerated by that obſervant Poet ſtill are found in this fenny tract, or its neighborhood.

Viſited *Spalding*, a place very much reſembling, in form, neat- JUNE 28.
neſs, and ſituation, a *Dutch* town: the river *Welland* paſſes through SPALDING.
one of the ſtreets, a canal is cut through another, and trees are planted on each ſide. The church is a handſome ſtructure, the ſteeple a ſpire. The churches in general, throughout this low tract, are very handſome; all are built of ſtone, which muſt have been brought from places very remote, along temporary canals; for, in many inſtances, the quarries lie at leſt twenty miles diſtant.

But

But the edifices were built in zealous ages, when the benedictions or maledictions of the church made the people conquer every difficulty that might obstruct these pious foundations. The abby of *Crowland*, seated in the midst of a shaking fen *, is a curious monument of the insuperable zeal of the times it was erected in; as the beautiful tower of *Boston* church, visible from all parts, is a magnificent specimen of a fine gothic taste.

JUNE 29. SWINESHEAD-ABBY. Passed near the site of *Swineshead-Abby*, of which there are not the left remains. In the walls of a farm house, built out of the ruins, you are shewn the figure of a Knight Templar, and told it was the monk who poisoned King *John*; a fact denied by our best historians.

Returned thro' *Lincoln*; went out of town under the *Newport-Gate*, a curious *Roman* work; passed over part of the heath; changed horses at *Spittle*, and at *Glanford Bridge*; dined at the ferry-house on the banks of the *Humber*; and after a passage of about five miles, with a brisk gale, landed at *Hull*, and reached that night *Burton-Constable*, the seat of Mr. *Constable*, in that part of *Yorkshire* called *Holderness*; a rich flat country, but excellent for producing large cattle, and a good breed of horses, whose prices are near doubled since the *French* have grown so fond of the *English* kind.

Made an excursion to *Hornsea*, a small town on the coast, re-

* This monastery was founded by *Ethelbald* king of *Mercia*, A. D. 716. The ground being too marshy to admit a weighty building of stone, he made a foundation, by driving into the ground vast piles of oak; and caused more compact earth to be brought in boats nine miles off to lay on them, and form a more sound foundation.

markable

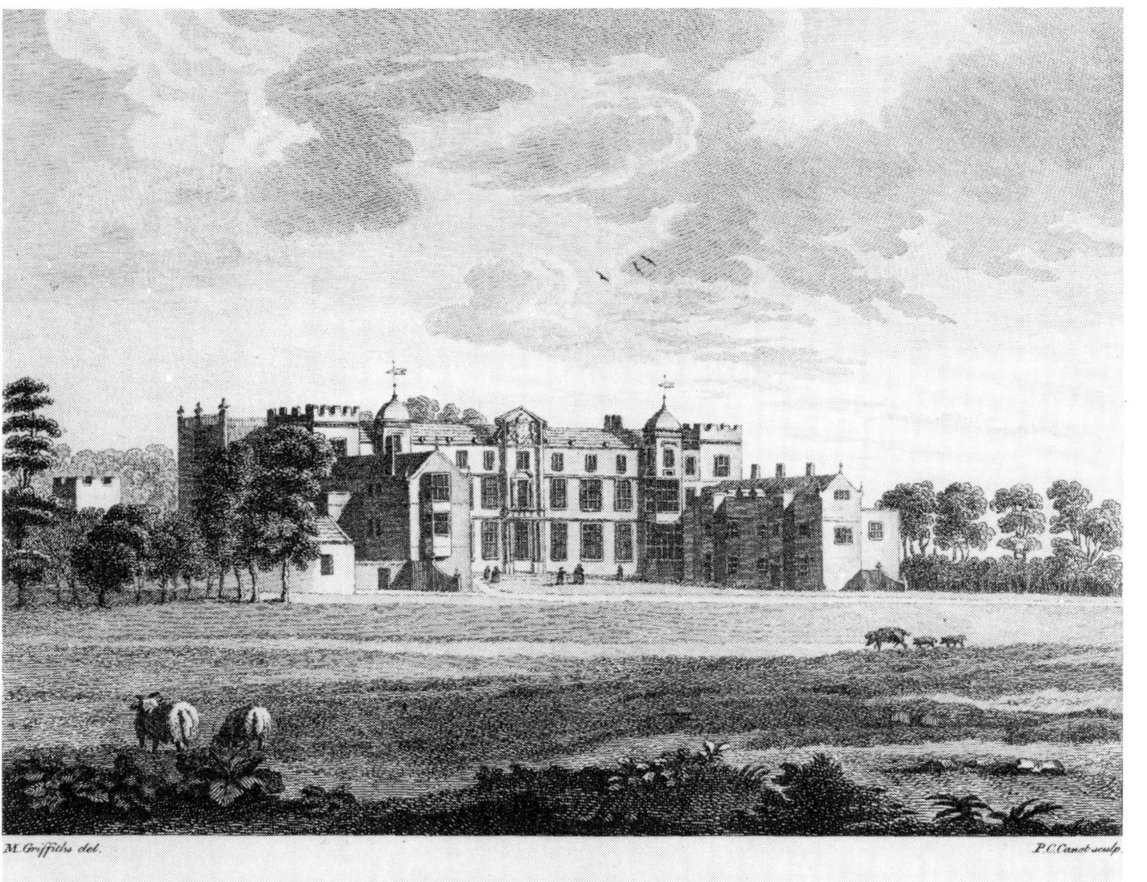

M. Griffiths del. P.C. Canot sculp.

BURTON CONSTABLE.

markable only for its mere, a piece of water about two miles long, and one broad, famous for its pike and eels; it is divided from the ſea by a very narrow bank, ſo is in much danger of being ſome time or other loſt.

The cliffs on the coaſt of *Holderneſs* are high, and compoſed of clay, which falls down in vaſt fragments. Quantity of amber is waſhed out of it by the tides, which the country people pick up and ſell: it is found ſometimes in large maſſes, but I never ſaw any ſo pure and clear as that from the *Baltic*. It is uſually of a pale yellow color within, and prettily clouded; the outſide covered with a thin coarſe coat. AMBER.

After riding ſome miles over a flat grazing country, paſſed through the village of *Skipſey*, once under the protection of a caſtle founded by *Drugon* or *Drugan*, a valiant *Flandrian*, who came over at the time of the conqueſt. The Conqueror gave him in marriage one of his near relations; and as a portion made him Lord of *Holderneſs*. *Drugon* by ſome unlucky accident killed his ſpouſe; but having his wits about him, haſtened to the King, and informing his Majeſty that his Lady and he had a great deſire to viſit their native country, requeſted a ſum of money for that purpoſe: the Conqueror immediately ſupplied the wants of *Drugon*; who had ſcarcely embarked, when advice was brought from *Skipſey* of the death of the Lady: purſuit was inſtantly made, but in vain; the artful *Flandrian* evaded all attempts to bring him to account *. JULY 2.

Near this village is a conſiderable camp; but I paſſed it too haſtily to determine, of what nation.

* M. S. at *Burton-Conſtable*.

A few

A few miles farther is *Burlington Quay*, a ſmall town cloſe to the ſea. There is a deſign of building a pier, for the protection of ſhipping; at preſent there is only a large wooden quay, which projects into the water, from which the place takes its name. From hence is a fine view of the white cliffs of *Flamborough-Head*, which extends far to the Eaſt, and forms one ſide of the *Gabrantuicorum ſinus portuoſus* of *Ptolomy*, a name derived from the *Britiſh Gyfr*, on account of the number of goats found there, according to the conjecture of *Cambden*.

A mile from hence is the town of *Burlington*. The body of the church is large, but the ſteeple, by ſome accident, has been deſtroyed: near it is a large gateway, with a noble gothic arch, poſſibly the remains of a priory of black canons, founded by *Walter de Gant*, in the beginning of the reign of *Henry* I.

This coaſt of the kingdom is very unfavorable to trees, for, except ſome woods in the neighborhood of *Burton-Conſtable*, there is a vaſt nakedneſs from the *Humber*, as far as the extremity of *Cathneſs*, with a very few exceptions, which ſhall be noted in their proper places.

JULY 3. FLAMBOROUGH-HEAD. Went to *Flamborough-Head*. The town is on the North ſide; conſiſts of about one hundred and fifty ſmall houſes, entirely inhabited by fiſhermen, few of whom, as is ſaid, die in their beds, but meet their fate in the element they are ſo converſant in. Put myſelf under the direction of *William Camidge*, Cicerone of the place, who conducted me to a little creek at that time covered with fiſh, a fleet of cobles having juſt put in. Went in one of thoſe little boats to view the *Head*, coaſting it for upwards of two miles. The

The cliffs are of a tremendous height, and amazing grandeur; beneath are ſeveral vaſt caverns, ſome cloſed at the end, others are pervious, formed with a natural arch, giving a romantic paſſage to the boat, different from that we entered. In ſome places the rocks are inſulated, are of a pyramidal figure, and ſoar up to a vaſt height: the baſes of moſt are ſolid, but in ſome pierced thro', and arched; the color of all theſe rocks is white, from the dung of the innumerable flocks of migratory birds, which quite cover the face of them, filling every little projection, every hole that will give them leave to reſt; multitudes were ſwimming about, others ſwarmed in the air, and almoſt ſtunned us with the variety of their croaks and ſcreams. I obſerved among them Corvorants, Shags in ſmall flocks, Guillemots, a few Black Guillemots very ſhy and wild, Auks, Puffins, Kittiwakes *, and Herring Gulls. Landed at the ſame place, but before our return to *Flamborough*, viſited *Robin Leith*'s hole, a vaſt cavern, to which there is a narrow paſſage from the land ſide; it ſuddenly riſes to a great height, the roof is finely arched, and the bottom is for a conſiderable way formed in broad ſteps, reſembling a great but eaſy ſtair-caſe; the mouth opens to the ſea, and gives light to the whole.

ITS BIRDS.

Lay at *Hunmandby*, a ſmall village above *Filey Bay*, round which are ſome plantations that thrive tolerably well, and ought to be an encouragement to gentlemen to attempt covering theſe naked hills.

Filey Brig is a ledge of rocks running far into the ſea, and often fatal to ſhipping. The bay is ſandy, and affords vaſt quantities of

* Called here *Petrels*. *Br. Zool. Suppl. tab.* xxiii. *p.* 26.

fine fiſh, ſuch as Turbot, Soles, &c. which during ſummer approach the ſhore, and are eaſily taken in a common ſeine or dragging-net.

JULY 4. Set out for *Scarborough*; paſſed near the ſite of *Flixton*, a hoſpital founded in the time of *Athelſtan*, to give ſhelter to travellers from the *wolves*, *that they ſhould not be devoured by them* *; ſo that in thoſe days this bare tract muſt have been covered with wood, for thoſe ravenous animals ever inhabit large foreſts. Theſe *hoſpitia* are not unfrequent among the *Alps*; are either appendages to religious houſes, or ſupported by voluntary ſubſcriptions. On the ſpot where *Flixton* ſtood is a farm-houſe, to this day called the *Spital Houſe*. Reach

SCARBOROUGH, a large town, built in form of a creſcent on the ſides of a ſteep hill; at one extremity are the ruins of a caſtle, ſeated on a cliff of a ſtupendous height, from whence is a very good view of the town. In the caſtle-yard is a barrack for one hundred and fifty men, but at preſent untenanted by ſoldiery. Beneath, on the ſouth ſide, is a large ſtone pier, (another is now building) which ſhelters the ſhipping belonging to the town. It is a place abſolutely without trade, yet owns above 300 ſail of ſhips, which are hired out for freight: in the late war the Government had never leſs than 100 of them in pay.

The number of inhabitants belonging to this place are above 10,000, but as great part are ſailors, nothing like that number are reſident, which makes one church ſufficient for thoſe who live on ſhore. It is large, and ſeated almoſt on the top of the hill. The

* *Cambden. Brit.* II. 902.

range

range of buildings on the *Cliff* commands a fine view of the caſtle, town, and of innumerable ſhipping that are perpetually paſſing backward and forward on their voyages. The ſpaw* lies at the foot of one of the hills, S. of the town; this and the great conveniency of ſea-bathing, occaſion a vaſt reſort of company during ſummer; it is at that time a place of great gayety, for with numbers health is the pretence, but diſſipation the end.

The ſhore is a fine hard ſand, and during low water is the place where the company amuſe themſelves with riding. This is alſo the fiſh market; for every day the cobles, or little fiſhing boats, are drawn on ſhore here, and lie in rows, often quite loaden with variety of the beſt fiſh. There was a fiſherman, on the 9th of *May*, 1767, brought in at one time,

20 Cods,

14 Lings,

17 Skates,

8 Holibuts, beſides a vaſt quantity of leſſer fiſh; and ſold the whole for 3 l. 15 s. It is ſuperfluous to repeat what has been before mentioned, of the methods of fiſhing, being amply deſcribed, *Vol.* III. p. 193, of the *Britiſh Zoology*; yet it will be far from impertinent to point out the peculiar advantages of theſe ſeas, and the additional benefit this town might experience, by the augmentation of its fiſheries. For this account, and for numberleſs civilities, I

* The waters are impregnated with a purgative ſalt, (*Glauber*'s) a ſmall quantity of common ſalt, and of ſteel. There are two wells, the fartheſt from the town is more purgative, and its taſte more bitter; the other is more chalybeate, and its taſte more briſk and pungent. D. H.

think myſelf much indebted to Mr. *Travis*, ſurgeon, who communicated to me the following Remarks:

" *Scarborough* is ſituated at the bottom of a bay, formed by *Whitby* rock on the North, and *Flamborough-Head* on the South; the town is ſeated directly oppoſite to the centre of the W. end of the *Dogger* bank; which end, (according to *Hammond*'s chart of the North Sea) lies S. and by W., and N. and by E., but by a line drawn from *Tinmouth* caſtle, would lead about N. W. and S. E. Tho' the *Dogger* bank is therefore but 12 leagues from *Flamborough-Head*, yet it is 16 and a half from *Scarborough*, 23 from *Whitby*, and 36 from *Tinmouth* caſtle. The N. ſide of the bank ſtretches off E. N. E. between 30 and 40 leagues, until it almoſt joins to the *Long-Bank*, and *Jutt*'s Riff.

" It is to be remarked, that the fiſhermen ſeldom find any Cod, Ling, or other round fiſh upon the *Dogger* bank itſelf, but upon the ſloping edges and hollows contiguous to it. The top of the bank is covered with a barren ſhifting ſand, which affords them no ſubſiſtence; and the water on it, from its ſhallowneſs, is continually ſo agitated and broken, as to allow them no time to reſt. The flat fiſh do not ſuffer the ſame inconvenience there; for when diſturbed by the motion of the ſea, they ſhelter themſelves in the ſand, and find variety of ſuitable food. It is true, the *Dutch* fiſh upon the *Dogger* bank; but it is alſo true they take little except Soles, Skates, Thornbacks, Plaiſe, &c. It is in the hollows between the *Dogger* and the *Well-Bank*, that the Cod are taken which ſupply *London* market.

" The ſhore, except at the entrance of *Scarborough* pier, and ſome few other places, is compoſed of covered rocks, which abound with

with Lobſters and Crabs, and many other ſhell fiſh; (no Oyſters) thence, after a ſpace covered with clean ſand, extending in different places from one to five or ſix miles. The bottom, all the way to the edge of the *Dogger* banks, is a ſcar; in ſome places very rugged, rocky, and cavernous; in others ſmooth, and overgrown with variety of ſubmarine plants, Moſſes, Corallines, &c.* Some parts again are ſpread with ſand and ſhells; others, for many leagues in length, with ſoft mud and ooz, furniſhed by the diſcharge of the *Tees* and *Humber*.

"Upon an attentive review of the whole, it may be clearly inferred, that the ſhore along the coaſt on the one hand, with the edges of the *Dogger* bank on the other, like the ſides of a decoy, give a direction towards our fiſhing grounds to the mighty ſhoals of Cod, and other fiſh, which are well known to come annually from the Northern ocean into our ſeas; and ſecondly, that the great variety of fiſhing grounds near *Scarborough*, extending upwards of 16 leagues from the ſhore, afford ſecure retreats and plenty of proper food for all the various kinds of fiſh, and alſo ſuitable places for each kind to depoſite their ſpawn in.

"The fiſhery at *Scarborough* only employs 105 men, and brings in about 5250 l. per annum, a trifle to what it would produce, was there a canal from thence to *Leeds* and *Mancheſter*; it is probable it would then produce above ten times that ſum, employ ſome thouſands of men, give a comfortable and cheap ſubſiſtence to our manufacturers, keep the markets moderately reaſonable, enable our

* I met with on the ſhores near *Scarborough*, ſmall fragments of the true red coral.

manu-

manufacturing towns to underſell our rivals, and prevent the hands, as is too often the caſe, raiſing inſurrections, in every year of ſcarcity, natural or artificial."

On diſcourſing with ſome very intelligent fiſhermen, I was informed of a very ſingular phænomenon they annually obſerve about the ſpawning of fiſh *. At the diſtance of 4 or 5 leagues from ſhore, during the months of *July* and *Auguſt*, it is remarked, that at the depth of 6 or 7 fathom from the ſurface, the water appears to be ſaturated with a thick jelly, filled with the *Ova* of fiſh, which reaches 10 or 12 fathoms deeper: this is known by its adhering to the ropes the cobles anchor with when they are fiſhing; for they find the firſt 6 or 7 fathom of rope free from ſpawn, the next 10 or 12 covered with ſlimy matter, the remainder again free to the bottom. They ſuppoſe this gelatinous ſtuff to ſupply the new-born fry with food, and that it is alſo a protection to the ſpawn, as being diſagreeable to the larger fiſh to ſwim in.

There is great variety of fiſh brought on ſhore. Beſides thoſe deſcribed as *Britiſh* fiſh, were two ſpecies of Rays: the Whip-Ray has alſo been taken here, and another ſpecies of Weever; but theſe are ſubjects more proper to be referred to a *Fauna*, than an Itinerary, for a minute deſcription.

JULY 10.

ALUM WORKS.

Left *Scarborough*, paſſed over large moors to *Robin Hood*'s *Bay*. On my road, obſerved the vaſt mountains of alum ſtone, from which that ſalt is thus extracted: It is firſt calcined in great heaps, which continue burning by its own phlogiſton, after being well ſet

* Mr. *Oſbeck* obſerved the ſame in *S. Lat.* 35, 36, in his return from *China*. The ſeamen call it the flowering of the water. *Vol.* II. 72.

on

on fire by coals, for ſix, ten, or fourteen months, according to the ſize of the heap, ſome being equal to a ſmall hill. It is then thrown into pits and ſteeped in water, to extract all the ſaline particles. The liquor is then run into other pits, where the vitriolic ſalts are præcipitated by the addition of a ſolution of the *ſal ſodæ*, prepared from kelp; or by the volatile *alkali* of ſtale urine. The ſuperfluous water being then evaporated duely by boiling in large furnaces, the liquor is ſet to cool; and laſtly, is poured into large caſks, to cryſtallize.

The alum works in this country are of ſome antiquity: they were firſt diſcovered by Sir *Thomas Chaloner*, in the reign of Queen *Elizabeth*, who obſerving the trees tinged with an unuſual color, made him ſuſpicious of its being owing to ſome mineral in the neighborhood. He found out that the ſtrata abounded with an aluminous ſalt.

At that time, the *Engliſh* being ſtrangers to the method of managing it, there is a tradition that Sir *Thomas* was obliged to ſeduce ſome workmen from the *Pope*'s alum-works near *Rome*, then the greateſt in *Europe*. If one may judge from the curſe which his Holineſs thundered out againſt Sir *Thomas* and the fugitives, he certainly was not a little enraged; for he curſed by the very form that *Ernulphus* * has left us, and not varied a tittle from that moſt comprehenſive of imprecations.

The firſt pits were near *Giſborough*, the ſeat of the *Chaloners*, who ſtill flouriſh there, notwithſtanding his Holineſs's *anathema*. The works were ſo valuable as to be deemed a royal mine. Sir *Paul*

* Vide *Triſtram Shandy*.

Pindar,

Pindar, who rented them, payed annually to the King 12,500 l., to the Earl of *Mulgrave* 1,640 l., to Sir *William Pennyman* 600 l.; kept 800 workmen in pay, and ſold his alum at 26 l. per tun. But this monopoly was deſtroyed on the death of *Charles* I. and the right reſtored to the proprietors.

JET.

In theſe alum rocks are frequently found *cornua ammonis*, and other foſſils, lodged in a ſtony nodule. Jet is ſometimes met with in thin flat pieces, externally of the appearance of wood. According to *Solinus*, *Britain* was famous for this foſſil *.

The ſands near *Robin Hood*'s village were covered with fiſh of ſeveral kinds, and with people who met the cobles in order to purchaſe their cargo: the place ſeemed as if a great fiſh fair had been held there; ſome were carrying off their bargains, others buſied in curing the fiſh; and a little out at ſea was a fleet of cobles and five-men boats, and others arriving to diſcharge the capture of the preceding tides †. There are 36 of the firſt belonging to this little place. The houſes here make a groteſque appearance, are ſcattered over the face of a ſteep cliff in a very ſtrange manner, and fill every projecting ledge, one above another, in the ſame manner as thoſe of the peaſants in the rocky parts of *China*. *Sand's End*, *Runwick*, and *Staithes*, three other fiſhing-towns on this coaſt, are (as I am told) built in the ſame manner.

* GAGATES *hic plurimus optimuſque eſt lapis: ſi decorem requiras, nigro gemmeus: ſi naturam aquá ardet, oleo reſtinguitur: ſi poteſtatem attritu calefactus applicita detinet, atque ſuccinum.* C. xxiv.

† From hence the fiſh are carried in machines to *Derby*, *Litchfield*, *Birmingham*, and *Worceſter*: the towns which lie beyond the laſt are ſupplied from the Weſt of *England*.

The

The country through this day's journey was hilly, the coaſt high. Reach

Whitby, called by the *Saxons*, *Streaneſhalch*, or bay of the light-houſe, a large town, oddly ſituated between two hills, with a narrow channel running through the middle, extending about a mile farther up the vale, where it widens, and forms a bay. The two parts of the town are joined by a good draw-bridge, for the conveniency of letting the ſhipping paſs. From this bridge are often taken the viviparous Blenny, whoſe back-bone is as green as that of the Sea Needle. The river that forms this harbour is the *Eſk*, but its waters are very inconſiderable when the tide is out. Here is a pretty briſk trade in ſhip-building; but except that, a ſmall manufacture of ſail-cloth, and the hiring of ſhips as at *Scarborough*, like that town it has ſcarce any commerce. It is computed there are about 270 ſhips belonging to this place. Of late, an attempt has been made to have a ſhare in the *Greenland* fiſhery; four ſhips were ſent out, and had very good ſucceſs. There are very good dry docks towards the end of the harbour; and at the mouth a moſt beautiful pier. At this place is the firſt ſalmon-fiſhery on the coaſt.

St. Hilda's Church.

On the hill above the S. ſide of the town is a fine ruin of St. *Hilda*'s church. The ſite was given to that ſaint by *Oſwy*, king of *Northumberland*, about A. D. 657; poſſibly in conſequence of a vow he made to found half a dozen monaſteries, and make his daughter a nun, ſhould heaven favor his arms. St. *Hilda* founded a convent here for men and women, dedicated it to St. *Peter*, and put it under the direction of an abbeſs. This eſtabliſhment was ruined by the excurſions of the *Danes*; but after the conqueſt it

E was

was rebuilt, and filled with *Benedictines*, by *Walter de Percy*. In less enlightened times it was believed that not a wild goose dared to fly over this holy ground, and if it ventured was sure to fall precipitate and perish in the attempt.

Went about two miles along the shore, then turned up into the country, a black and dreary moor; observed on the right a vast artificial mount, or *Tumulus*, called *Freeburgh* Hill, a monument, in all probability, the work of the *Danes*, whose custom it was to fling up such *Tumuli* over the graves of their kings or leaders; or in memory of the slain in general, upon the spot where they had obtained any great victory. It is possible that this mount owed its rise to the victory gained by *Ivar*, a *Danish* prince, over *Ella*, king of *Bernicia*, who was on his way from the North to succour *Osbert*; for we are told that *Ivar*, after defeating the last, went from *York* to meet *Ella*, and fought and slew him on his march.

At the end of this moor, about three miles from *Gisborough*, is a beautiful view over the remaining part of *Yorkshire*, towards *Durham*, *Hartlepool*, and the mouth of the *Tees*, which meanders through a very rich tract. The country instantly assumes a new face; the road lies between most delightful hills finely wooded, and the little vales between them very fertile: on some of the hills are the marks of the first alum works, which were discovered by Sir *Thomas Chaloner*.

GISBOROUGH.

GISBOROUGH, a small town, pleasantly situated in a vale, surrounded at some distance by hills, and open on the east to the sea, which is about five miles distant. It is certainly a delightful spot; but I cannot see the reason why *Cambden* compares it to *Puteoli*. Here was once a priory of the canons of the order of St. *Austin*,

founded

founded by *Robert de Brus*, 1129, after the diſſolution granted by *Edward* VI. to the *Chaloners*: a very beautiful eaſt window of the church is ſtill remaining. The town has at preſent a good manufacture of ſail-cloth.

The country continues very fine quite to the banks of the *Tees*, a conſiderable river, which divides *Yorkſhire* from the biſhoprick of *Durham*. After travelling 109 miles in a ſtrait line through the firſt, enter *Durham*, croſſing the river on a very handſome bridge of arches, the battlements neatly pannelled with ſtone; and reach

STOCKTON, lying on the *Tees* in form of a creſcent. A handſome town; the principal ſtreet is remarkably fine, being 165 feet broad; and ſeveral leſſer ſtreets run into it at right angles. In the middle of the great ſtreet are neat ſhambles, a town-houſe, and large aſſembly-room. There is beſides a large ſquare. About a century ago, according to *Anderſon*, it had ſcarce a houſe that was not made of clay and thatch; but is now a flouriſhing place. Its manufacture is ſail-cloth; and great quantities of corn, and lead, (from the mineral parts of the country) are ſent off from hence by commiſſion. As the river does not admit of large veſſels ſo high as the town, thoſe commodities are ſent down to be ſhipped.

The ſalmon fiſhery here is neglected, for none are taken beyond what is neceſſary to ſupply the country. Smelts come up the river in the winter time. On the weſt ſide of the town ſtood the caſtle; what remained of it is at preſent converted into a barn. The country from hence to *Durham* is flat, very fertile, and much incloſed. Towards the weſt is a fine view of the highlands of the country: thoſe hills are part of that vaſt ridge which commence in

 the

the north, and deeply divide this portion of the kingdom; and on that account are called by *Cambden* the *Appennines* of *England.*

DURHAM. The approach to DURHAM is romantic, through a deep hollow, cloathed on each ſide with wood. The city is pretty large, but the buildings old. Part are on a plain, part on the ſide of a hill. The abby, or cathedral, and the caſtle, where the Biſhop lives when he reſides here, are on the ſummit of a cliff, whoſe foot is waſhed on two ſides by the river *Were.* The walks on the oppoſite banks are very beautiful, flagged in the middle and paved on the ſides, and are well kept. They are cut through the wood, impend over the river, and receive a venerable improvement from the caſtle and antient cathedral which ſoar above.

The laſt is very old*; plain without, and ſupported within by maſſy pillars, deeply engraved with lozenge-like figures, and zigzag furrows: others are plain. The ſkreen to the choir is wood covered with a coarſe carving. The choir neat, but without ornament.

The chapter-houſe ſeems very antient, and is in the form of a theatre. The cloiſters large and handſome. All the monuments are defaced, except that of Biſhop *Hatfield.* The Prebendal houſes are very pleaſantly ſituated, and have a fine view backwards.

There are two handſome bridges over the *Were* to the walks; and a third covered with houſes, which join the two parts of the town. This river produces Salmon, Trout, Roach, Dace, Minow,

* Begun in 1093, by Biſhop *William de Carilepho.*

Loche,

Loche, Bulhead, Sticklebacks, Lamprey, the leſſer Lamprey, Eels, Smelts, and Samlet. The laſt, before they go off to ſpawn, are obſerved to be covered with a white ſlime: they are called here *Rack-riders*, becauſe they appear in winter, or bad weather; *Rack*, in the *Engliſh* of *Shakeſpear*'s days, ſignifying the driving of the clouds by tempeſts, a word ſtill retained here.

> That which is now a horſe, even with a thought
> The *Rack* diſlimns, and makes it indiſtinct
> As water is in water.
>
> *Antony and Cleopatra*. Act iv.

There is no inconſiderable manufacture, at *Durham*, of ſhalloons, tammies, ſtripes and callamancoes. I had heard on my road many complaints of the eccleſiaſtical government this county is ſubject to; but, from the general face of the country, it ſeems to thrive wonderfully under them.

Saw *Cokin*, the ſeat of Mr. *Car*; a moſt romantic ſituation, layed out with great judgment: the walks are very extenſive, principally along the ſides or at the bottom of deep dells, bounded with vaſt precipices, finely wooded; and many parts of the rocks are planted with vines, which I was told bore well, but late. The river *Were* winds along the hollows, and forms two very fine reaches at the place where you enter theſe walks. Its waters are very clear, and its bottom a ſolid rock. The view towards the ruins of *Finchal*-Abbey is remarkably great; and the walk beneath the cliffs has a magnificent ſolemnity, a fit retreat for its monaſtic inhabitants. This was once called the Deſert, and was the rude ſcene of the auſterities of St. *Godric*, who carried them to the moſt JULY 12.

ſenſeleſs

ſenſeleſs extravagance *. A ſober mind may even at preſent be affected with horror at the proſpect from the ſummits of the cliffs into a darkſome and ſtupendous chaſm, rendered ſtill more tremendous by the roaring of the waters over its diſtant bottom.

Paſſed through *Cheſter-le-Street*, a ſmall town, near which is *Lumley-Caſtle*, the ſeat of the Earl of *Scarborough*; a place, as I was told, very well worth ſeeing; but unfortunately it proved a public day, (i. e. a day when the whole country is admitted, and the inquiſitive traveller who may never paſs that road again, alone excluded) and ſo I loſt ſight of it. The tract from *Durham* to *Newcaſtle* was very beautiful; the riſings gentle, and prettily wooded, and the views agreeable; that on the borders remarkably fine, there being, from an eminence not far from the capital of

* St. *Godric* was born at *Walpole* in *Norfolk*, and being an itinerant merchant, got acquainted with St. *Cuthbert* at *Farn Iſland*. He made three pilgrimages to *Jeruſalem*; at length, was warned by a viſion to ſettle in the deſert of *Finchal*. He lived an hermitical life there during 63 years, and practiſed unheard-of auſterities: he wore an iron ſhirt next his ſkin, day and night, and wore out three: he mingled aſhes with the flour he made his bread of; and, leaſt it ſhould then be too good, kept it three or four months before he ventured to eat it. In winter, as well as ſummer, he paſſed whole nights, up to his chin in water, at his devotions. Like St. *Antony*, he was often haunted by fiends in various ſhapes; ſometimes in form of beautiful damſels, ſo was viſited with evil concupiſcence, which he cured by rolling naked among thorns and briars: his body grew ulcerated; but, to encreaſe his pain, he poured ſalt into the wounds: wrought many miracles, and died 1170. *Britannia ſacra*, 304. About ten years after his deceaſe, a *Benedictine* priory of thirteen monks was founded there in his honor, by *Hugh Pudſey*, Biſhop of *Durham*.

Northumberland, an extenſive view of a rich country, watered by the coaly *Tyne*. Reach

NEWCASTLE, a large town, divided into two unequal parts by the river, and both ſides very ſteep: the lower parts, very dirty and diſagreeable, are inhabited by Keelmen and their families, a mutinous race; for which reaſon this town is always garriſoned: in the upper parts are ſeveral handſome well-built ſtreets. NEWCASTLE.

The great buſineſs of the place is the coal trade. The collieries lie at different diſtances, from five to eighteen miles from the river; and the coal is brought down in waggons along rail roads, and diſcharged from covered buildings at the edge of the water into the keels or boats that are to convey it on ſhipboard. Theſe boats are ſtrong, clumſy and round, will carry about 25 tuns each; ſometimes are navigated with a ſquare ſail, but generally are worked with two vaſt oars. No ſhips of large burthen come up as high as *Newcaſtle*, but are obliged to lie at *Shields*, a few miles down the river, where ſtage coaches go thrice every day for the conveniency of paſſengers. This country is moſt remarkably populous; *Newcaſtle* alone contains near 40,000 inhabitants; and there are at leſt 400 ſail of ſhips belonging to that town and its port. The effect of the vaſt commerce of this place is very apparent for many miles round; the country is finely cultivated, and bears a moſt thriving and opulent aſpect.

Left *Newcaſtle*; the country in general flat; paſſed by a large ſtone column with three dials on the capital, with ſeveral ſcripture texts on the ſides, called here *Pigg*'s Folly, from the founder. JULY. 13.

A few miles further is *Stannington* Bridge, a pleaſant village. *Morpeth*, a ſmall town with a neat town-houſe, and a tower for the bell

bell near it. The caſtle was on a ſmall eminence, but the remains are now very inconſiderable. Some attempt was made a few years ago to introduce the *Mancheſter* manufacture, but without ſucceſs. There is a remarkable ſtory of this place, that the inhabitants reduced their own town to aſhes, on the approach of King *John*, A. D. 1215, out of pure hatred to their monarch, in order that he might not find any ſhelter there.

This place gave birth to *William Turner*, as Dr. *Fuller* expreſſes it, an excellent *Latiniſt*, *Græcian*, *Oratour*, and *Poet*; he might have added polemic divine, champion and ſufferer in the proteſtant cauſe, phyſician and naturaliſt. His botanic writings are among the firſt we had, and certainly the beſt of them; and his criticiſms on the birds of *Ariſtotle* and *Pliny* are very judicious. He was the firſt who flung any light on thoſe ſubjects in our iſland; therefore clames from a naturaliſt this tribute to his memory *.

Felton, a pleaſant village on the *Coquet*, which, ſome few miles lower, diſcharges itſelf into the ſea, oppoſite to a ſmall iſle of the ſame name, remarkable for the multitudes of water-fowl which reſort there to breed.

ALNWICK CASTLE.

At *Alnwick*, a ſmall town, the traveller is diſappointed with the ſituation and environs of the caſtle, the reſidence of the *Percies*, the antient Earls of *Northumberland*. You look in vain for any marks of the grandeur of the feudal age; for trophies won by a family eminent in our annals for military prowess and deeds of chivalry; for halls hung with helms and hauberks, or with the ſpoils of the chace; for extenſive foreſts, and venerable oaks. You look in vain

* He was born in the reign of *Henry* VIII. died in 1568.

for

for the helmet on the tower, the antient ſignal of hoſpitality to the traveller, or for the grey-headed porter to conduct him to the hall of entertainment. The numerous train, whoſe countenances gave welcome to him on his way, are now no more; and inſtead of the diſintereſted uſher of the old times, he is attended by a *valet* eager to receive the fees of admittance.

There is vaſt grandeur in the appearance of the outſide of the caſtle; the towers magnificent, but injured by the numbers of rude ſtatues crouded on the battlements. The apartments are large, and lately finiſhed in the gothic ſtyle with a moſt incompatible elegance. The gardens are equally inconſiſtent; trim to the higheſt degree, and more adapted to a *villa* near *London*, than the antient ſeat of a great Baron. In a word, nothing, excepting the numbers of uninduſtrious poor that ſwarm at the gate, excites any one idea of its former circumſtances.

A ſtage further is *Belford*, the ſeat of *Abraham Dixon*, Eſq; a modern houſe; the front has a moſt beautiful ſimplicity in it: the grounds improved as far as the art of huſbandry can reach; the plantations large and flouriſhing: a new and neat town, inſtead of the former wretched cottages; and an induſtrious race, inſtead of an idle poor, at preſent fill the eſtate.

BAMBOROUGH CASTLE.

On an eminence on the ſea coaſt, about four miles from *Belford*, is the very antient caſtle of *Bamborough*, built by *Ida*, firſt king of the *Northumbrians*, A. D. 548. But, according to the conjecture of an antiquarian I met with there, on the ſite of a *Roman* fortreſs. It was alſo his opinion, that the ſquare tower was actually the work of the *Romans*. It had been of great ſtrength; the hill it is founded on is exceſſively ſteep on all ſides, and acceſſible only by flights of ſteps on the ſouth eaſt. The ruins are ſtill conſiderable, but many of them now filled with ſand, caught up by the winds which rage here with great violence, and carried to very diſtant places. The remains of a great hall are very ſingular; it had been warmed by two fire-places of a vaſt ſize, and from the top of every window ran a flue, like that of a chimney, which reached the ſummits of the battlements. Theſe flues ſeem deſigned as ſo many ſupernumerary chimnies, to give vent to the ſmoke that the immenſe fires of thoſe hoſpitable times filled the rooms with: halls ſmoky, but filled with good cheer, were in thoſe days thought no inconvenience. Thus my brave countryman *Howel ap Rys*, when his enemies had fired his houſe about his ears, told his people to riſe and defend themſelves like men, for ſhame, *for he had knowne there as greate a ſmoake in that hall upon a Chriſtmas even* *.

Bp. Crew's Charity.

This caſtle, and the manour belonging to it, was once the property of the *Forſters*; but purchaſed by Lord *Crew*, Biſhop of *Durham*, and with other conſiderable eſtates, left veſted in Truſtees, to be applied to unconfined charitable uſes. Three of theſe Truſtees are a majority: one of them makes this place his reſidence, and bleſſes the coaſt by his judicious and humane application of the Prelate's generous bequeſt. He has repaired and rendered habitable the great ſquare tower: the part reſerved for himſelf and family is a large hall and a few ſmaller apartments; but the reſt of the ſpacious edifice is allotted for purpoſes which make the heart to glow with joy when thought of. The upper part is an ample granary; from whence corn is diſpenced to the poor without

* *Hiſt. Gwedir family*, 118.

diſtinction,

diſtinction, even in the deareſt time, at the rate of four ſhillings a buſhel; and the diſtreſſed, for many miles round, often experience the conveniency of this benefaction.

Other apartments are fitted up for the reception of ſhipwrecked ſailors; and bedding is provided for thirty, ſhould ſuch a number happen to be caſt on ſhore at the ſame time. A conſtant patrole is kept every ſtormy night along this tempeſtuous coaſt, for above eight miles, the length of the manour, by which means numbers of lives have been preſerved. Many poor wretches are often found on the ſhore in a ſtate of inſenſibility; but by timely relief, are ſoon brought to themſelves.

It often happens, that ſhips ſtrike in ſuch a manner on the rocks as to be capable of relief, in caſe numbers of people could be ſuddenly aſſembled: for that purpoſe a cannon * is fixed on the top of the tower, which is fired once, if the accident happens in ſuch a quarter; twice, if in another; and thrice, if in ſuch a place. By theſe ſignals the country people are directed to the ſpot they are to fly to; and by this means, frequently preſerve not only the crew, but even the veſſel; for machines of different kinds are always in readineſs to heave ſhips out of their perillous ſituation.

In a word, all the ſchemes of this worthy Truſtee have a humane and uſeful tendency: he ſeems as if ſelected from his brethren for the ſame purpoſes as *Spenſer* tells us the firſt of his ſeven *Beadſmen* in the houſe of *holineſſe* was.

* Once belonging to a *Dutch* frigate of 40 guns; which, with all the crew, was loſt oppoſite to the caſtle, about ſixty years ago.

The firſt of them, that eldeſt was and beſt,
Of all the houſe had charge and government,
As guardian and ſteward of the reſt:
His office was to give entertainement
And lodging unto all that came and went:
Not unto ſuch as could him feaſt againe
And doubly quite for that he on them ſpent;
But ſuch as want of harbour did conſtraine;
Thoſe, for God's ſake, his dewty was to entertaine *.

Farn Isles. Oppoſite to *Bamborough* lie the *Farn* iſlands, which form two groupes of little iſles and rocks to the number of ſeventeen, but at low water the points of others appear above the ſurface; they all are diſtinguiſhed by particular names. The neareſt iſle to the ſhore is that called the *Houſe Iſland*, which lies exactly one mile 68 chains from the coaſt: the moſt diſtant is about ſeven or eight miles. They are rented for 16 l. *per annum:* their produce is Kelp, ſome few Feathers, and a few Seals, which the tenant watches and ſhoots for the ſake of the oil and ſkins. Some of them yield a little graſs, and ſerve to feed a cow or two, which the people are deſperate enough to tranſport over in their little boats.

July 15. Viſited theſe iſlands in a coble, a ſafe but ſeemingly hazardous ſpecies of boat, long, narrow, and flat-bottomed, which is capable of going thro' a high ſea, dancing like a cork on the ſummits of the waves.

Touched at the rock called the *Meg*, whitened with the dung of Corvorants which almoſt covered it; their neſts were large, made of tang, and exceſſively fœtid.

* The Rev. *Thomas Sharpe*, B. D.

Rowed

Rowed next to the *Pinnacles*, an iſland in the fartheſt groupe; ſo called from ſome vaſt columnar rocks at the ſouth end, even at their ſides, and flat at their tops, and entirely covered with Guillemots and Shags: the fowlers paſs from one to the other of theſe columns by means of a narrow board, which they place from top to top, forming a narrow bridge, over ſuch a horrid gap that the very ſight of it ſtrikes one with horror.

EIDER DUCKS.

Landed at a ſmall iſland, where we found the female *Eider* ducks * at that time ſitting: the lower part of their neſts was made of ſea plants; the upper part was formed of the down which they pull off their own breaſts, in which the eggs were ſurrounded and warmly bedded: in ſome were three, in others five eggs, of a large ſize and pale olive color, as ſmooth and gloſſy as if varniſhed over. The neſts are built on the beach, among the looſe pebbles, not far from the water. The Ducks ſit very cloſe, nor will they riſe till you almoſt tread on them. The Drakes ſeparate themſelves from the females during the breeding ſeaſon. We robbed a few of their neſts of the down, and after carefully ſeparating it from the tang, found that the down of one neſt weighed only three quarters of an ounce, but was ſo elaſtic as to fill the crown of the largeſt hat. The people of this country call theſe St. *Cuthbert's* Ducks, from the ſaint of the iſlands †.

* Vide *Br. Zool.* II. 454. I have been informed that they alſo breed on *Inſh-Colm*, in the *Firth* of *Forth*.

† I muſt here acknowledge my obligations to *Joſeph Banks*, Eſq; who, previous to his circumnavigation, liberally permitted my artiſt to take copies of his valuable collection of Zoologic drawings; amongſt others, thoſe of the *Eider* Ducks.

Beſides

Besides these birds, I observed the following:

Puffins, called here *Tom Noddies*,
Auks, here *Skouts*,
Guillemots,
Black Guillemots,
Little Auks,
Shiel Ducks,
Shags,
Corvorants,
Black and white Gulls,
Brown and white Gulls,
Herring Gulls, which I was told fed sometimes on eggs of other birds,
Common Gulls, here *Annets*,
Kittiwakes, or Tarrocks,
Pewit Gulls,
Great Terns,
Sea Pies,
Sea Larks, here *Brokets*,
Jackdaws, which breed in rabbet-holes,
Rock Pidgeons,
Rock Larks.

The Terns were so numerous, that in some places it was difficult to tread without crushing some of the eggs.

The last isle I visited was the *House Island*, the sequestered spot where St. *Cuthbert* passed the two last years of his life. Here was afterwards established a priory of *Benedictines* for six or eight Monks subordinate

ſubordinate to *Durham*. A ſquare tower, the remains of a church, and ſome other buildings, are to be ſeen there ſtill; and a ſtone coffin, which, it is pretended, was that of St. *Cuthbert*. At the north end of the iſle is a deep chaſm, from the top to the bottom of the rock, communicating to the ſea; through which, in tempeſtuous weather, the water is forced with vaſt violence and noiſe, and forms a fine *jet d'eau* of ſixty feet high: it is called by the inhabitants of the oppoſite coaſt the *Churn*.

Reached ſhore through a moſt turbulent rippling, occaſioned by the fierce current of the tides between the iſlands and the coaſt.

Purſued my journey northward. Saw at a diſtance the *Cheviot* hills; on which, I was informed, the green Plovers breed; and that, during winter, flocks innumerable of the great Bramblings, or Snow-flakes, appear; the moſt ſouthern place of their migration, in large companies. JULY 17.

The country almoſt woodleſs, there being but one wood of any conſequence between *Belford* and *Berwick*. Saw on the left an antient tower, which ſhewed the character of the times, when it was unhappily neceſſary, on theſe borders, for every houſe to be a fortreſs.

On the right, had a view of the ſea, and, not remote from the land, of *Lindesfarn*, or *Holy* Iſland, once an epiſcopal ſeat, afterwards tranſlated to *Durham*. On it are the ruins of a caſtle and a church. In ſome parts are abundance of *Entrochi*, which are called by the country people St. *Cuthbert*'s beads.

After a few miles riding, have a full view of *Berwick*, and the river *Tweed* winding weſtward for a conſiderable way up the country;

country; but its banks were without any particular charms*, being almoſt woodleſs. The river is broad; and has over it a bridge of ſixteen very handſome arches, eſpecially two next the town.

BERWICK is fortified in the modern way; but is much contracted in its extent to what it was formerly; the old caſtle and works now lying at ſome diſtance beyond the preſent ramparts. The barracks are large, conſiſt of a center and two wings. The church was built by *Cromwel*, and, according to the ſpirit of the builder, without a ſteeple. Even in *Northumberland*, (towards the borders) the ſteeples grow leſs and leſs, and as it were forewarned the traveller that he was ſpeedily to take leave of epiſcopacy. The town-houſe has a large and handſome modern tower to it: the ſtreets in general are narrow and bad, except that in which the town-houſe ſtands.

Abundance of wool is exported from this town: eggs in vaſt abundance collected through all the country, almoſt as far as *Carliſle:* they are packed up in boxes, with the thick end downwards, and are ſent to *London* for the uſe of ſugar refiners. I was told that as many are exported as bring in annually the ſum of fourteen thouſand pounds.

SALMON FISHERY.

The ſalmon fiſheries here are very conſiderable, and likewiſe bring in vaſt ſums: they lie on each ſide the river, and are all private property, except what belongs to the Dean and Chapter of *Durham*, which, in rent and tythe of fiſh, brings in 450 l. *per ann.*, for all the other fiſheries are liable to tythe. The common rents of

* I was informed that the beautiful banks of the *Tweed* verify the old ſong at the paſſage at *Coldſtream*.

those

thoſe are 50 l. a year, for which tenants have as much ſhore as ſerves to launch out and draw their nets on ſhore: the limits of each are ſtaked; and I obſerved that the fiſhers never failed going as near as poſſible to their neighbour's limits. One man goes off in a ſmall flat-bottomed boat, ſquare at one end, and taking as large a circuit as his net admits, brings it on ſhore at the extremity of his boundary, where others aſſiſt in landing it. The beſt fiſhery is on the ſouth ſide *: very fine ſalmon trout are often taken here, which come up to ſpawn from the ſea, and return in the ſame manner as the ſalmon do. The chief import is timber from *Norway* and the *Baltic*.

Almoſt immediately on leaving *Berwick*, enter

SCOTLAND,

in the ſhire of *Merch*, or *Mers* †. A little way from *Berwick*, on the weſt, is *Halydon* hill, famous for the overthrow of the *Scots* under the regent *Douglas*, by *Edward* III. on the attempt of the former to raiſe the ſiege of the town. A cruel action blaſted the

* For a fuller account of this fiſhery, vide *Britiſh Zoology*, III. 241. To it may alſo be added, that in the middle of the river, not a mile weſt of the town, is a large ſtone, on which a man is placed, to obſerve what is called the *reck* of the ſalmon coming up.

† *Boethius* ſays, that in his time buſtards were found in this county; but they are now extirpated: the hiſtorian calls them *Guſtardes*. *Deſc. Scot.* xiii.

laurels of the conqueror: *Seton*, the deputy governor *, ſtipulated to ſurrender in fifteen days, if not relieved in that time, and gave his ſon as hoſtage for the performance. The time elapſed; *Seton* refuſed to execute the agreement, and with a *Roman* unfeelingneſs beheld the unhappy youth hung before the walls.

The entrance into *Scotland* has a very unpromiſing look; for it wanted, for ſome miles, the cultivation of the parts more diſtant from *England:* but the borders were neceſſarily neglected; for, till the acceſſion of *James* VI. and even long after, the national enmity was kept up, and the borderers of both countries diſcouraged from improvement, by the barbarous inroads of each nation. This inattention to agriculture continued till lately; but on reaching the ſmall village of *Eytown*, the ſcene was greatly altered; the wretched cottages, or rather hovels of the country, were vaniſhing; good comfortable houſes ariſe in their ſtead; the lands are incloſing, and yield very good barley, oats, and clover; the banks are planting: I ſpeak in the preſent tenſe; for there is ſtill a mixture of the old negligence left amidſt the recent improvements, which look like the works of a new colony in a wretched impoveriſhed country.

Soon after the country relapſes; no arable land is ſeen; but for four or five miles ſucceeds the black joyleſs heathy moor of

COLDINGHAM. *Coldingham:* happily, this is the whole ſpecimen that remains of the many miles, which, not many years ago, were in the ſame dreary unprofitable ſtate. Near this was the convent of that name immortalized by the heroiſm of its Nuns; who, to preſerve them-

* *Keith*, the Governor, having a little before left the place, in order to excite *Archibald Douglas*, Regent of *Scotland*, to attempt to raiſe the ſiege.

ſelves

ſelves inviolate from the *Danes*, cut off their lips and noſes; and thus rendering themſelves objects of horror, were, with their abbeſs *Ebba* *, burnt in the monaſtery by the diſappointed ſavages.

At the end of the moor came at once in ſight of the *Firth* † of *Forth*, the *Boderia* of *Ptolemy*; a moſt extenſive proſpect of that great arm of the ſea, of the rich country of *Eaſt Lothian*, the *Baſs Iſle*; and at a diſtance, the iſle of *May*, the coaſt of the county of *Fife*, and the country as far as *Montroſe*.

After going down a long deſcent, dine at *Old Cambus*, at a mean houſe, in a poor village; where I believe the Lord of the ſoil is often execrated by the weary traveller, for not enabling the tenant to furniſh more comfortable accommodations, in ſo conſiderable a thoroughfare.

The country becomes now extremely fine; bounded at a diſtance, on one ſide, by hills; on the other, by the ſea: the intervening ſpace is as rich a tract of corn land as I ever ſaw; for *Eaſt Lothian* is the *Northamptonſhire* of *North Britain:* the land is in many places manured with ſea tang; but I was informed, that the barley produced from it is much lighter than barley from other manure.

* A. D. 870.

† *Bodotria* of *Tacitus*, who deſcribes the two Firths of *Clyde* and *Forth*, and the intervening Iſthmus, with much propriety; ſpeaking of the fourth ſummer *Agricola* had paſſed in *Britain*, and how convenient he found this narrow tract for ſhutting out the enemy by his fortreſſes, he ſays, *Nam* Glota (Firth of *Clyde) et* Bodotria, *diverſi maris æſtu per immenſum revecti, anguſto terrarum ſpatio dirimuntur.* Vit. Agr.

On the ſide of the hills, on the left, is Sir *John Hall's*, of *Dunglas*; a fine ſituation, with beautiful plantations. Paſs by *Broxmouth*, a large houſe of the *Duke* of *Roxborough*, in a low ſpot, with great woods ſurrounding it. Reach

DUNBAR.

DUNBAR: the chief ſtreet broad and handſome; the houſes built of ſtone; as is the caſe with moſt of the towns in *Scotland*. There are ſome ſhips ſent annually from this place to *Greenland*, and the exports of corn are pretty conſiderable. The harbour is ſafe, but ſmall; its entrance narrow, and bounded by two rocks. Between the harbour and the caſtle is a very ſurpriſing ſtratum of ſtone, in ſome reſpects reſembling that of the *Giant's Cauſeway* in *Ireland*: it conſiſts of great columns of a red grit ſtone, either triangular, quadrangular, pentangular, or hexangular; their diameter from one to two feet, their length at low water thirty, dipping or inclining a little to the ſouth.

COLUMNAR ROCKS.

They are jointed, but not ſo regularly, or ſo plainly, as thoſe that form the *Giant's Cauſeway*. The ſurface of ſeveral that had been torn off, appear as a pavement of numbers of convex ends, probably anſwering to the concave bottoms of other joints once incumbent on them. The ſpace between the columns was filled with thin ſepta of red and white ſparry matter; and veins of the ſame pervaded the columns tranſverſely. This range of columns faces the north, with a point to the eaſt, and extends in front about two hundred yards. The breadth is inconſiderable: the reſt of the rock degenerates into ſhapeleſs maſſes of the ſame ſort of ſtone, irregularly divided by thick ſepta. This rock is called by the people of *Dunbar*, the *Iſle*.

Oppoſite

Oppofite are the ruins of the caftle, feated on a rock above the fea; underneath one part is a vaft cavern, compofed of a black and red ftone, which gives it a moft infernal appearance; a fit reprefentation of the pit of *Acheron*, and wanted only to be peopled with witches to make the fcene complete: it appears to have been the dungeon, there being a formed paffage from above, where the poor prifoners might have been let down, according to the barbarous cuftom of war in early days. There are in fome parts, where the rock did not clofe, the remains of walls; for the openings are only natural fiffures; but the founders of the caftle taking advantage of this cavity, adding a little art to it, rendered it a moft complete and fecure prifon.

On the other fide are two natural arches, through which the tide flowed; under one was a fragment of wall, where there feems to have been a portal for the admiffion of men or provifions from fea: through which, it is probable that *Alexander Ramfay*, in a ftormy night, reinforced the garrifon, in fpite of the fleet which lay before the place, when clofely befieged by the *Englifh*, in 1337, and gallantly defended for nineteen weeks by that heroine *black Agnes*, Countefs of *March* *.

Through one of thefe arches was a moft picturefque view of the *Bafs Ifle*, with the fun fetting in full fplendor; through the other of the *May* ifland, gilt by its beams.

* *Buchanan*, *lib.* ix. c. 25. The *Englifh* were obliged to defift from their enterprize. *Agnes* was eldeft daughter of Sir *Thomas Randal*, of *Stradown*, Earl of *Murray*, and nephew to *Robert Bruce*. She was called black *Annes*, fays *Robert Lindefay*, becaufe fhe was black-fkinned.

Over

Over the ruins of a window were the three legs, or arms of the Iſle of *Man*, a lion rampant, and a St. *Andrew*'s croſs.

In the church is the magnificent monument of Sir *George Hume*, Earl of *Dunbar*, the worthieſt and beſt *Scotch* Miniſter of *James* VI. till he choſe his favorites for their perſonal, inſtead of their intellectual accompliſhments: moderate, prudent, and ſucceſsfull in the management of the *Scotch* affairs: and, as *Spotſwood* remarks, 'a 'man of deep wit, few words, and in his Majeſty's ſervice no leſs 'faithfull than fortunate: the moſt difficile affairs he compaſſed 'without any noiſe; and never returned when he was employed 'without the work performed that he was ſent to do:' to his honor, he recommended the temperate, firm, and honeſt *Abbot* to the ſee of *Canterbury*, and by his aſſiſtance gave peace to the Church of *Scotland*, too ſoon interrupted by their deaths. *Dunbar*'s merit is evident; for the weakneſſes and the infamy of his Maſter's reign did not commence during the period of his power.

The monument is a large and beautifull ſtructure of marble, decorated with arms, figures, and fluted pillars. The Earl is repreſented in armour, kneeling; with a cloak hanging looſely on him. The inſcription imports no more than his titles and the day of his death, *January* 29th, 1610.

Near this town were fought two battles fatal to the *Scots*. The firſt in 1296; when the Earls of *Surry* and *Warwick*, Generals of *Edward* I. defeated the army of *Baliol*, took the caſtle, and delivered the nobility they found in it to the *Engliſh* monarch, who, with his uſual cruelty, devoted them all to death.

The other was the celebrated victory of *Cromwel*, in 1650; when the covenanting army choſe to fight rather under the direction

of

LOCH LEVEN CASTLE.

THE BASS ISLE FROM TANTELLON CASTLE.

Moses Griffiths del. P. Mazell sculp.

of the Miniſters than the commmand of their Generals: and the event was correſpondent. Theſe falſe prophets gave the troops aſſurance of victory; and many of them fell in the fight with the lying ſpirit in their mouths. *Cromwel* had the appearance of enthuſiaſm; they the reality: for when the artfull uſurper ſaw their troops deſcend from the heights from whence they might without a blow have ſtarved the whole *Engliſh* army, he with a well-founded confidence, exclamed, THE LORD HATH DELIVERED THEM INTO OUR HANDS.

But the caſtle has been the ſcene of very different tranſactions. In 1567 it was in poſſeſſion of the infamous Earl *Bothwell*, who here committed the ſimulated outrage on the perſon of the fair *Mary Stuart*: ſhe certainly ſeems to have had foreknowledge of the violence; and the affront ſhe ſuſtained, was but a *pignus direptum male pertinaci*. Here alſo the Earl retreated, after being given up by his miſtreſs at the capitulation of Carberry hill; and from hence he took his departure for his long but merited miſery.

In this town was a convent of *Mathurines*, founded by *Patrick* Earl of *Dunbar* and *March*, in 1218; and another of *Carmelites* or white friers, in 1263.

Rode within ſight of *Tantallon* caſtle, now a wretched ruin; once the ſeat of the powerfull *Archibald Douglas*, Earl of *Angus*, which for ſome time reſiſted all the efforts of *James* V. to ſubdue it. JULY 18.

A little further, about a mile from the ſhore, lies the *Baſs* Iſland, or rather rock, of a moſt ſtupendous height; on the ſouth ſide the top appears of a conic ſhape, but the other over-hangs the ſea in a moſt tremendous manner. The caſtle, which was once the ſtate priſon of *Scotland*, is now neglected: it lies cloſe to the BASS ISLE.

edge

edge of the precipice, facing the little village of *Caſtleton*; where I took boat, in order to viſit this ſingular ſpot; but the weather proved unfavorable, the wind blew ſo freſh, and the waves ran ſo high, that it was impoſſible to attempt landing; for even in calmer weather it cannot be done without hazard, there being a ſteep rock to aſcend, and commonly a great ſwell, which often removes the boat, while you are ſcaling the precipice; ſo, in caſe of a falſe ſtep, there is the chance of falling into a water almoſt unfathomable.

GANNETS.

Various ſorts of water fowl repair annually to this rock to breed; but none in greater numbers than the *Gannets*, or *Soland* geeſe, multitudes of which were then ſitting on their neſts near the ſloping part of the iſle, and others flying over our boat: it is not permitted to ſhoot at them, the place being farmed principally on account of the profit ariſing from the ſale of the young of theſe birds, and of the *Kittiwake*, a ſpecies of gull, ſo called from its cry. The firſt are ſold at *Edinburgh* * for twenty-pence apiece, and ſerved up roaſted a little before dinner. This is the only kind of proviſion whoſe price has not been advanced; for we learn from Mr. *Ray*, that it was equally dear above a century ago †. It is unneceſſary

* SOLAN GOOSE.

There is to be ſold, by JOHN WATSON, Jun. at his Stand at the Poulty, *Edinburgh*, all lawful days in the week, wind and weather ſerving, good and freſh *Solan* Geeſe. Any who have occaſion for the ſame may have them at reaſonable rates.

Aug. 5. 1768. EDINBURGH ADVERTISER.

† *Ray's Itineraries*, 192.

to

to ſay more of this ſingular bird, as it has been very fully treated of in the ſecond volume of the *Britiſh Zoology*.

With much difficulty landed at *North Berwick*, three miles diſtant from *Caſtleton*, the place we intended to return to. The firſt is a ſmall town, pleaſantly ſeated near a high conic hill, partly planted with trees: it is ſeen at a great diſtance, and is called the *Law* of *Berwick*; a name given to ſeveral other high hills in this part of the iſland.

PRESTON PANS.

Paſs through *Abberladie* and *Preſton Pans*: the laſt takes its name from its ſalt-pans, there being a conſiderable work of that article; alſo another of vitriol. Saw at a ſmall diſtance the field of battle, or rather of carnage, known by the name of the battle of *Preſton Pans*, where the Rebels gave a leſſon of ſeverity, which was more than retaliated, the following ſpring, at *Culloden*. Obſerved, in this day's ride, (I forget the ſpot) *Seaton*, the once princely ſeat of the Earl of *Wintoun*, now a ruin; judiciouſly left in that ſtate, as a proper remembrance of the ſad fate of thoſe who engage in rebellious politicks. There are great marks of improvement on approaching the capital; the roads good, the country very populous, numbers of manufactures carried on, and the proſpect embelliſhed with gentlemen's ſeats. Reach

EDINBURGH.

EDINBURGH*.

A city that poſſeſſes a boldneſs and grandeur of ſituation beyond any that I had ever ſeen. It is built on the edges and ſides of a

* Known throughout the Highlands by the name of *Dun-edin*.

vaſt ſloping rock, of a great and precipitous height at the upper extremity, and the ſides declining very quick and ſteep into the plain. The view of the houſes at a diſtance ſtrikes the traveller with wonder; their own loftineſs, improved by their almoſt aerial ſituation, gives them a look of magnificence not to be found in any other part of *Great Britain.* All theſe conſpicuous buildings form the upper part of the great ſtreet, are of ſtone, and make a handſome appearance: they are generally ſix or ſeven ſtories high in front; but, by reaſon of the declivity of the hill, much higher backward; one in particular, called *Babel,* has about twelve or thirteen ſtories. Every houſe has a common ſtaircaſe, and every ſtory is the habitation of a ſeparate family. The inconvenience of this particular ſtructure need not be mentioned; notwithſtanding the utmoſt attention, in the article of cleanlineſs, is in general obſerved. The common complaint of the ſtreets of *Edinburgh* is now taken away, by the vigilance of the magiſtrates *, and their ſeverity againſt any that offend in any groſs degree †. It muſt be obſerved, that this unfortunate ſpecies of architecture aroſe from the turbulence of the times in which it was in vogue: every body was deſirous of getting as near as poſſible to the protection of the caſtle;

* The ſtreets are cleaned early every morning. Once the City payed for the cleaning; at preſent, it is rented for four or five hundred pounds *per annum.*

† In the cloſes, or allies, the inhabitants are very apt to fling out their filth, &c. without regarding who paſſes; but the ſufferer may call every inhabitant of the houſe it came from to account, and make them prove the delinquent, who is always puniſhed with a heavy fine.

the

Moses Griffiths del. P. Mazell sculp.

EDINBURGH CASTLE FROM GREY FRIARS CHURCH YARD.

the houſes were crouded together, and I may ſay, piled one upon another, merely on the principle of ſecurity.

The caſtle is antient, but ſtrong, placed on the ſummit of the hill, at the edge of a very deep precipice. Strangers are ſhewn a very ſmall room, in which *Mary* Queen of *Scots* was delivered of *James* VI. CASTLE.

From this fortreſs is a full view of the city and its environs; a ſtrange proſpect of rich country, with vaſt rocks and mountains intermixed. On the ſouth and eaſt are the meadows, or the public walks, *Herriot*'s hoſpital, part of the town overſhadowed by the ſtupendous rocks of *Arthur*'s ſeat and *Saluſbury*'s *Craigs*, the *Pentland* hills at a few miles diſtance, and at a ſtill greater, thoſe of *Muirfoot*, whoſe ſides are covered with verdant turf.

To the north is a full view of the *Firth* of *Forth*, from *Queen*'s *Ferry* to its mouth, with its ſouthern banks covered with towns and villages. On the whole, the proſpect is ſingular, various and fine.

The reſervoir of water * for ſupplying the city lies in the *Caſtle-ſtreet*, and is well worth ſeeing: the great ciſtern contains near two hundred and thirty tuns of water, which is conveyed to the ſeveral conduits, that are diſpoſed at proper diſtances in the principal ſtreets; theſe are conveniences that few towns in *North Britain* are without. RESERVOIR.

On the ſouth ſide of the *High-ſtreet*, is the Parlement Cloſe, a ſmall ſquare, in which is the Parlement Houſe, where the courts

* It is conveyed in pipes from the *Pentland* hills, five miles diſtant.

ADVOCATE'S LIBRARY.

of juſtice are held. Below ſtairs is the Advocate's library, founded by Sir *George Mackenzie*, and now contains above thirty thouſand volumes, and ſeveral manuſcripts: among the more curious are the four Evangeliſts, very legible, notwithſtanding it is ſaid to be ſeveral hundred years old.

St. *Jerome*'s Bible, wrote about the year 1,100.

A *Malabar* book, written on leaves of plants.

A *Turkiſh* manuſcript, illuminated in ſome parts like a miſſal. *Elogium in ſultan Morad filium filii Soliman Turcici. Script. Conſtantinopoli. Anno Hegiræ.* 992.

A Cartulary, or records of the monaſteries, ſome very antient.

A very large Bible, bound in four volumes; illuſtrated with ſcripture prints, by the firſt engravers, paſted in, and collected at a vaſt expence. There are beſides great numbers of antiquities, not commonly ſhewn, except enquired after.

The *Luckenbooth* row, which contains the *Tolbooth*, or city priſon, and the weighing-houſe, which brings in a revenue of 500l. *per annum*, ſtands in the middle of the *High-ſtreet*, and, with the guard-houſe, contributes to ſpoil as fine a ſtreet as moſt in *Europe*, being in ſome parts eighty feet wide, and finely built.

The exchange is a handſome modern building, in which is the cuſtom-houſe: the firſt is of no uſe, in its proper character; for the merchants always chuſe ſtanding in the open ſtreet, expoſed to all kinds of weather.

The old cathedral is now called the New Church, and is divided into four places of worſhip; in one the Lords of the Seſſions attend: there is alſo a throne and a canopy for his Majeſty, ſhould he viſit this capital, and another for the Lord Commiſſioner. There is no muſic either in this or any other of the *Scotch* churches, for *Peg* ſtill faints at the ſound of an organ. This is the more ſurprizing, as the *Dutch*, who have the ſame eſtabliſhed religion, are extremely fond of that ſolemn inſtrument; and even in the great church of *Geneva* the Pſalmody is accompanied with an organ.

The ſame church has a large tower, oddly terminated with a ſort of crown.

On the front of a houſe in the *Nether Bow*, are two fine profile heads of a man and woman, of *Roman* ſculpture, ſuppoſed to be thoſe of *Severus* and *Julia*: but, as appears from an inſcription* made by the perſon who put them into the wall, were miſtaken for *Adam* and *Eve*. ROMAN HEADS.

Near the *Trone* church are the remains of the houſe once inhabited by *Mary Stuart*; now a tavern.

At the end of the *Cannongate-ſtreet* ſtands *Holy-Rood* palace, originally an abby founded by *David* I. in 1128. The towers on the N. W. ſide were erected by *James* V. together with other buildings, for a royal reſidence: according to the editor of *Cambden*, great part, except the towers above-mentioned, were burnt by *Cromwel*; but the other towers, with the reſt of this magnificent palace, as it now ſtands, were executed by Sir *William Bruce*, by the directions of *Charles* II.; within is a beautifull ſquare, with piazzas on every ſide. It contains great numbers of fine apart- HOLY-ROOD HOUSE.

* *In ſudore vultus tui veſceris pane.* Anno 1621. Theſe heads are well engraven in *Gordon*'s Itinerary, *tab.* iii.

ments;

ments; ſome, that are called the King's, are in great diſorder; the reſt are granted to ſeveral of the nobility.

In the Earl of *Breadalbane*'s, are ſome excellent portraits, particularly three full lengths, remarkably fine, by *Vandyck*, of

Henry Earl of *Holland*,

William Duke of *Newcaſtle*,

Charles Earl of *Warwick* *;

And by Sir *Peter Lely*, the Duke and Dutcheſs of *Lauderdale*, and *Edward* Earl of *Jerſey*. There is beſides a very good head of a boy, by *Morrillio*, and ſome views of the fine ſcenes near his Lordſhip's ſeat at *Taymouth*.

At Lord *Dunmore*'s lodgings is a very large piece of *Charles* I. and his Queen going to ride, with the ſky ſhowering roſes on them; a Black holds a grey horſe; the celebrated *Jeffery Hudſon* † the dwarf with a ſpaniel in a ſtring, and ſeveral other dogs ſporting round: the Queen is painted with a love-lock, and with browner hair and complection, and younger, than I ever ſaw her drawn. It is a good piece, and was the work of *Mytens*, predeceſſor in fame to *Vandyck*. In the ſame place are two other good portraits of *Charles* II. and *James* VII.

The gallery of this palace takes up one ſide, and is filled with coloſſal portraits of the Kings of *Scotland*.

* I am informed that the portraits of the Earls of *Holland* and *Warwick* are now removed to *Taymouth*.

† For a further account of this little hero, conſult Mr. *Walpole*'s Anecdotes of Painting, II. p. 8.

In

In the old towers are ſhewn the apartments where the murther of *David Rizzo* was committed.

That beautiful piece of *gothic* architecture, the church, or chapel, of *Holy-Rood Abby*, is now a ruin, the roof having fallen in, by a moſt ſcandalous neglect, notwithſtanding money had been granted by Government to preſerve it entire. Beneath the ruins lie the bodies of *James* II. and *James* V. *Henry Darnly*, and ſeveral other perſons of rank: and the inſcriptions on ſeveral of their tombs are preſerved by *Maitland*. A gentleman informed me, that ſome years ago he had ſeen the remains of the bodies, but in a very decayed ſtate; the beards remained on ſome; and that the bones of *Henry Darnly* proved their owner, by their great ſize, for he was ſaid to be ſeven feet high. CHAPEL.

Near this palace is the *Park*, firſt incloſed by *James* V.; within are the vaſt rocks *, known by the names of *Arthur*'s Seat and *Saluſbury*'s *Craigs*; their fronts exhibit a romantic and wild ſcene of broken rocks and vaſt precipices, which from ſome points ſeem to over-hang the lower parts of the city. Great columns of ſtone, from forty to fifty feet in length, and about three feet in diameter, regularly pentagonal, or hexagonal, hang down the face of ſome of theſe rocks almoſt perpendicularly, or with a very ſlight dip, and form a ſtrange appearance. Conſiderable quantities of ſtone from the quarries have been cut and ſent to *London* for paving the ſtreets, its great hardneſs rendering it excellent for that purpoſe. Beneath theſe hills are ſome of the moſt beautifull walks about *Edinburgh*, commanding a fine proſpect over ſeveral parts of the country. PARKS.

* According to *Maitland*, their perpendicular height is 656 feet.

On

On one ſide of the *Park* are the ruins of St. *Anthony*'s chapel, once the reſort of numberleſs votaries.

The ſouth part of the city has ſeveral things worth viſiting.

HERRIOT'S HOSPITAL.

Herriot's hoſpital is a fine old building, much too magnificent for the end propoſed, that of educating poor children: it was founded by *George Herriot*, jeweller to *James* VI. who followed that monarch to *London*, and made a large fortune. There is a fine view of the caſtle, and the ſloping part of the city, from the front: the gardens were once the reſort of the gay; and there the *Scotch* poets often laid, in their comedies, the ſcenes of intrigue.

In the church-yard of the Grey Friers, is the monument of Sir *George Mackenzie*, a rotunda; with a multitude of other tombs. This is one of the few cæmeteries to this populous city; and from it is a very fine view of the caſtle, and the lofty ſtreet that leads to that fortreſs.

COLLEGE.

The college is a mean building; it contains the houſes of the Principal and a few of the Profeſſors: the Principal's houſe is ſuppoſed to be on the ſite of that in which *Henry Darnly* was murdered, then belonging to the Provoſt of the *Kirk* of *Field*. The ſtudents of the univerſity are diſperſed over the town, and are about ſix hundred in number; but wear no academic habit. The ſtudents are liable to be called before the Profeſſors, who have power of rebuking or expelling them: I cannot learn that either is ever exerted; but, as they are for the moſt part volunteers for knowledge, few of them deſert her ſtandards. There are twenty-two Profeſſors of different ſciences, moſt of whom read lectures: all the chairs are very ably filled; thoſe in particular which relate to the ſtudy of medicine, as is evident from the number of ingenious phyſicians,

physicians, *eleves* of this university, who prove the abilities of their masters. The *Musæum* had, for many years, been neglected; but, by the assiduity of the present Professor of natural history, bids fair to become a most instructive repository of the *naturalia* of these kingdoms.

The royal infirmary is a spatious and handsome edifice, capable of containing two hundred patients. The operation-room is particularly convenient, the council-room elegant, with a good picture in it of Provost *Drummond*. From the cupola of this building is a fine prospect, and a full view of the city. INFIRMARY.

Not far from hence are twenty-seven acres of ground, designed for a square, called *George Square:* a small portion is at present built, consisting of small but commodious houses, in the *English* fashion. Such is the spirit of improvement, that within these three years sixty thousand pounds have been expended in houses of the modern taste, and twenty thousand in the old.

Watson's hospital should not be forgot: a large good building, behind the Grey Friers church; an excellent institution for the educating and apprenticing the children of decayed merchants; who, after having served their time with credit, receive fifty pounds to set up with.

The *meadows*, or public walks, are well planted, and are very extensive: these are the mall of *Edinburgh*, as *Comely Gardens* are its *Vauxhall*.

The *Cowgate* is a long street, running parallel with the *High-street*, beneath the steep southern declivity of the city, and terminates in the *Grass-market*, where cattle are sold, and criminals executed. On several of the houses are small iron crosses, which, I was informed, denoted that they once belonged to the Knights of St. *John*.

On the north ſide of the city lies the new town, which is planned with great judgment, and will prove a magnificent addition to *Edinburgh*; the houſes in St. *Andrew*'s ſquare coſt from 1800l. to 2000l. each, and one or two 4000 or 5000l. They are all built in the modern ſtyle, and are free from the inconveniences attending the old city.

Theſe improvements are connected to the city by a very beautifull bridge, whoſe higheſt arch is ninety-five feet high.

In the walk of this evening, I paſſed by a deep and wide hollow beneath *Calton* Hill, the place where thoſe imaginary criminals, witches and ſorcerers, in leſs enlightened times, were burnt; and where, at feſtive ſeaſons, the gay and gallant held their tilts and tournaments. At one of theſe, it is ſaid that the Earl of *Bothwell* made the firſt impreſſion on the ſuſceptible heart of *Mary Stuart*, having galloped into the ring down the dangerous ſteeps of the adjacent hill; for he ſeemed to think that

> Women, born to be control'd,
> Stoop to the forward and the bold.

Theſe deſperate feats were the humour of the times of chivalry: *Brantome* relates, that the *Duc de Nemours* galloped down the ſteps of the *Sainte Chappel* at *Paris*, to the aſtoniſhment of the beholders. The men cultivated every exerciſe that could preſerve or improve their bodily ſtrength; the ladies, every art that tended to exalt their charms: *Mary* is reported to have uſed a bath of white wine; a cuſtom ſtrange, but not without precedent. *Jaques du Fouilloux*, enraptured

enraptured with a country girl, enumerating the arts which ſhe ſcorned to uſe to improve her perſon, mentions this:

Point ne portoit de ce linge ſemelle
Pour amoindrir ſon ſeing et ſa mammelle.
Vaſquine nulle, ou aucun peliçon
Elle ne portoit, ce n'eſtoit ſa façon.
Point ne *prenoit vin blanc pour ſe baigner*,
Ne drogue encore pour ſon corps alleger *.

At a ſmall walk's diſtance from *Calton* Hill, lies the new botanie garden †, conſiſting of five acres of ground, a green-houſe fifty feet long, two temperate rooms, each twelve feet, and two ſtoves, each twenty-eight: the ground riſes to the north, and defends the plants from the cold winds: the ſoil a light ſand, with a black earth on the ſurface. It is finely ſtocked with plants, whoſe arrangement and cultivation do much credit to my worthy friend Dr. *Hope*, Profeſſor of Botany, who planned and executed the whole. It was begun in 1764, being founded by the munificence of his preſent Majeſty, who granted fifteen hundred pounds for that purpoſe.

During this week's ſtay at *Edinburgh*, the prices of proviſions were as follow:

* *L'Adoleſcence de Jaques du Fouilloux*, 88.

† The old botanic garden lies to the eaſt of the new bridge: an account of it is to be ſeen in the *Muſeum Balfourianum*.

Beef, from 5d. to 3d. ½.
Mutton, from 4d. to 3d. ½.
Veal, from 5d. to 3d.
Lamb, 2d. ½.
Bacon, 7d.
Butter, in summer, 8d. in winter, 1s.
Pigeons, *per* dozen, from 8d. to 5s.
Chickens, *per* pair, 8d. to 1s.
A fowl, 1s. 2d.
Green goose, 3s.
Fat goose, 2s. 6d.
Large turkey, 4s. or 5s.
Pig, 2s.
Coals, 5d. or 6d. *per* hundred, delivered.

Many fine excursions may be made at a small distance from this city. *Leith*, a large town, about two miles north, lies on the *Firth*, is a flourishing place, and the port of *Edinburgh*. The town is dirty and ill built, and chiefly inhabited by sailors; but the pier is very fine, and is a much-frequented walk. The races were at this time on the sands, near low-water mark: considering their vicinity to a great city and populous country, the company was far from numerous; a proof that dissipation has not generally infected the manners of the *North Britons*.

LEITH.

Craigmellar castle is seated on a rocky eminence, about two miles south of *Edinburgh*; is square, and has towers at each corner. Some few apartments are yet inhabited; but the rest of this great pile is in ruins.

Newbottle,

Newbottle, the ſeat of the Marquiſs of *Lothian*, is a pleaſant ride of a few miles from the capital. It was once a *Ciſtercian* abby, founded by *David* I. in 1140; but, in 1591, was erected into a lordſhip, in favour of Sir *Mark Ker*, ſon of Sir *Walter Ker*, of *Ceſsford*. The houſe lies in a warm bottom, and, like moſt other of the houſes of the *Scotch* nobility, reſembles a *French Chateau*, by having a village or little paltry town adjacent. The ſituation is very favorable to trees, as appears by the vaſt ſize of thoſe near the houſe; and I was informed, that fruit ripens here within ten days as early as at *Chelſea*.

The *Marquiſs* poſſeſſes a moſt valuable collection of portraits, many of them very fine, and almoſt all very inſtructive. A large half-length of *Henry Darnly* repreſents him tall, aukward and gauky, with a ſtupid, inſipid countenance; moſt likely drawn after he had loſt, by intemperance and debauchery, thoſe charms which captivated the heart of the amorous *Mary*.

A head of her mother, *Marie de Guiſe*; not leſs beautifull than her daughter.

A head of *Madame Monpenſier*, and of ſeveral other illuſtrious perſons, who graced the court of *Louis* XIII.

Prince *Rupert* and Prince *Maurice*, in one piece.

Some ſmall portraits, ſtudies of *Vandyck*; among which is one of *William* Earl of *Pembroke*, of whom Lord *Clarendon* gives ſo advantageous a character.

A beautifull half-length of *Henrietta*, Queen of *Charles* I. Her charms almoſt apologize for the compliances of the uxorious monarch.

His daughter, the Dutcheſs of *Orleans*.

The

The wife of *Philip* the bold, inſcribed *Marga Mala, Lodo Mala.*

Head of *Robert Car*, Earl of *Somerſet*; the countenance effeminate, ſmall features, light flaxen or yellowiſh hair, and a very ſmall beard: is an original of that worthleſs favorite, and proves that the figure given as his among the illuſtrious heads is erroneous, the laſt being repreſented as a robuſt black man. A print I have of him by *Simon Paſs*, is authentic: the plate is of octavo ſize, repreſents him in hair curled to the top; and in his robes, with the George pendent.

His father, Sir *Robert Car* of *Fernihurſt.*

An Earl of *Somerſet?* of whom I could get no account; handſome; with long light hair inclining to yellow: a head.

A full length of *James* I. by *Jameſon.* Another of *Charles* I. when young, in rich armour, black and gold: a capital piece.

Lady *Tufton*; a fine half-length.

Earl *Morton*, regent: half-length; a yellow beard.

A head of General *Ruthven*, Sir *Patrick Ruthven*, a favorite of *Guſtavus Adolphus*; knighted in his Majeſty's tent in preſence of the whole army at *Darſaw* in *Pruſſia*, on the 23d of *September* 1627. As potent in the campaigns of *Bacchus* as of *Mars*, and ſerviceable to his great maſter in both. He vanquiſhed his enemies in the field; and by the ſtrength of his head, and goodneſs of underſtanding, could in convivial hours extract from the miniſters of unfriendly powers, ſecrets of the firſt importance. He paſſed afterwards into the ſervice of *Charles* I. and behaved with the ſpirit and integrity that procured him the honors of Earl of *Forth* in *Scotland*, and afterwards Earl of *Brentford* in *England*; and died in a very advanced age in 1651.

Two

Two very curious half-lengths on wood: one of a man with a long forked black beard; his jacket ſlaſhed down in narrow ſtripes from top to bottom, and the ſtripes looſe: the other with a black full beard; the ſame ſort of ſtripes, but drawn tight by a girdle.

The Doge of *Venice*, by *Titian*.

Three by *Morillio*; boys and girls in low life.

A remarkable fine piece of our three firſt circum-navigators, *Drake*, *Hawkins*, and *Candiſh*; half-length.

The heads of *Mark* Earl of *Lothian*, and his lady, by Sir *Antonio More*.

Mark Ker, prior of *Newbottle*, who, at the reformation, complied with the times, and got the eſtate of the abby.

SUBTERRANEOUS ROOMS.

In the woods adjacent to this ſeat are ſome ſubterraneous apartments and paſſages cut out of the live rock: they ſeem to have been excavacated by the antient inhabitants of the country either as receptacles for their proviſions, or a retreat for themſelves and families in time of war, in the ſame manner, as *Tacitus* relates, as was cuſtomary with the old *Germans* *.

DALKEITH.

Two or three miles diſtant from *Newbottle* is *Dalkeith*, a ſmall town, adjoining to *Dalkeith* Houſe, the ſeat of the Duke of *Buccleugh*: originally the property of the *Douglaſes*; and was, when in form of a caſtle, of great ſtrength; and, during the time of the Regent *Morton*'s retreat, ſtyled the *Lion's Den*.

* *Solent et ſubterraneos ſpecus aperire, eoſque multo inſuper fimo onerant, ſuffugium hiemi, et receptaculum frugibus, quia rigorem frigorum ejuſmodi locis molliunt: et ſi quando hoſtis advenit aperta populatur: Abdita autem et defoſſa, aut ignorantur, aut eo ipſa fallunt, quod quærenda ſunt.* De Moribus Germanor. c. 16.

The

The portraits at *Dalkeith* are numerous, and ſome good: among others, the

Firſt Duke of *Richmond* and his Dutcheſs.

The Dutcheſs of *Cleveland*.

Counteſs of *Buccleugh*, mother to the Dutcheſs of *Monmouth*, and Lady *Eglington*, her ſiſter.

The Dutcheſs and her two ſons: the Dutcheſs of *York*; her hand remarkably fine: the Dutcheſs of *Lenox*.

Mrs. *Lucy Waters*, mother of the Duke of *Monmouth*, with his picture in her hand.

Dutcheſs of *Cleveland* and her ſon, an infant; ſhe in character of a *Madonna*: fine.

The Duke of *Monmouth*, in character of a young St. *John*.

Lord *Strafford* and his Secretary; a ſmall ſtudy of *Vandyck*.

Henry VIII. and Queen *Catherine*, with the divorce in her hand; two ſmall pieces, by *Holbein*. *Anna Bullein*, by the ſame, dreſſed in a black gown, large yellow netted ſleeves, in a black cap, peaked behind.

Lady *Jane Gray*, with long hair, black and very thick; not handſome; but the virtues and the intellectual perfections of that ſuffering innocent, more than ſupplied the abſence of perſonal charms.

A large ſpirited picture of the Duke of *Monmouth* on horſeback. The ſame in armour. All his pictures have a handſome likeneſs of his father.

Dutcheſs of *Richmond*, with a bow in her hand, by Sir *Peter Lely*.

A fine head of the late Duke of *Ormond*.

A beau-

A beautifull head of *Mary Stuart*; the face ſharp, thin and young; yet has a likeneſs to ſome others of her pictures done before miſfortunes had altered her; her dreſs a ſtrait gown, open at the top and reaching to her ears, a ſmall cap, and ſmall ruff, with a red roſe in her hand.

In this palace is a room entirely furniſhed by *Charles* II. on occaſion of the marriage of *Monmouth* with the heireſs of the houſe *.

At *Smeton*, another ſeat of the Duke of *Buccleugh*, a mile diſtant from the firſt, is a fine half-length of General *Monk* looking over his ſhoulder, with his back towards you: he reſided long at *Dalkeith*, when he commanded in *Scotland*.

Nell Gwinne, looſely attired.

A fine marriage of St. *Catherine*, by *Vandyck*.

Left *Edinburgh*, and paſs'd beneath the caſtle, whoſe height and ſtrength, in my then ſituation, appeared to great advantage. The country I paſt through was well cultivated, the fields large, but moſtly incloſed with ſtone walls; for hedges are not yet become univerſal in this part of the kingdom: it is not a century ſince they were known here. Reach the JULY 24.

South-Ferry, a ſmall village on the banks of the *Firth*, which ſuddenly is contracted to the breadth of two miles by the jutting out of the land on the north ſhore; but almoſt inſtantly widens towards the weſt, into a fine and extenſive bay. The proſpect on each ſide is very beautifull; a rich country, frequently

* Since this, I have been informed that not far from *Dalkeith*, at *Roſslyn*, is a moſt beautifull and entire chapel of gothic architecture, well worth a viſit from a curious Traveller.

diversified with towns, villages, castles, and gentlemen's seats *. There is beside a vast view up and down the *Firth*, from its extremity, not remote from *Sterling*, to its mouth near *May* isle; in all, about sixty miles. To particularize the objects of this rich view: from the middle of the passage are seen the coasts of *Lothian* and *Fife*; the isles of *Garvie* and *Insh-Colm*; the town of *Dumfermline*; S. and N. *Queen's-Ferries*; and *Burrowstoness* smoaking at a distance from its numerous salt-pans and fire-engines. On the south side are *Hopetoun* house, *Dundass* castle, and many other gentlemen's seats; with *Blackness* castle potently garrisoned. On the north side, *Rosythe* castle, *Dunibrissel*, and at a distance the castle and town of *Brunt-Island*; with the road of *Leith* often filled with ships, and a magnificent distant view of the castle of *Edinburgh* on the south.

This Ferry is also called *Queen's-Ferry*, being the passage much used † by *Margaret*, Queen to *Malcolm* III. and sister to *Edgar Etheling*; her residence being at *Dumfermline*. Cross over in an excellent boat; observe midway the little isle called *Insh-Garvey*, with the ruin of a small castle. An *arctic* Gull flew near the boat, pursued by other Gulls, as birds of prey are: this is the species that persecutes and pursues the lesser kinds, till they mute through fear, when it catches up their excrements e'er they reach the water: the boatmen, on that account, styled it the dirty *Aulin*.

* Such as *Seith* castle, *Dumfermline* town, Lord *Morris's*, Lord *Hopetoun's*, Captain *Dundass's*.

† Or, as others say, because she, her brother and sister, first landed there, after their escape from *William* the Conqueror.

Landed

Landed in the ſhire of *Fife* *, at *North-Ferry*, near which are the great granite quarries, which help to ſupply the ſtreets of *London* with paving ſtones; many ſhips then waiting near, in order to take their lading. The granite lies in great perpendicular ſtacks; above which is a reddiſh earth filled with friable micaceous nodules. The granite itſelf is very hard, and is all blaſted with gun-powder: the cutting into ſhape for paving coſts two ſhillings and eight-pence per tun, and the freight to *London* ſeven ſhillings. GRANITE QUARRY.

The country, as far as *Kinroſs*, is very fine, conſiſting of gentle riſings; much corn, eſpecially *Bear*; but few trees, except about a gentleman's ſeat, called *Blair*, where there are great and flouriſhing plantations. Near the road are the laſt collieries in *Scotland*, except the inconſiderable works in the county of *Sutherland*.

Kinroſs is a ſmall town, ſeated in a large plain, bounded by mountains; the houſes and trees are ſo intermixed, as to give it an agreeable appearance. It has ſome manufactures of linnen and cutlery ware. At this time was a meeting of juſtices, on a ſingular occaſion: a vagrant had been, not long before, ordered to be whipped; but ſuch was the point of honor among the common people, that no one could be perſuaded to go to *Perth* for the executioner, who lived there: to preſs, I may ſay, two men for that ſervice, was the cauſe of the meeting; ſo Mr. *Boſwell* may rejoice to find the notion of honor prevale in as exalted a degree among his own countrymen, as among the virtuous *Corſicans* †.

* Part of the antient *Caledonia*.

† *Hiſt. Corſica*, p. 285, of the third edition.

Not far from the town is the houſe of *Kinroſs*, built by the famous architect Sir *William Bruce*, for his own reſidence, and was the firſt good houſe of regular architecture in *North Britain*. It is a large, elegant, but plain building: the hall is fifty-two feet long; the grounds about it well planted; the fine lake adjacent; ſo that it is capable of being made as delightfull a ſpot as any in *North Britain*.

Loch-Leven, a magnificent piece of water, very broad, but irregularly indented, is about twelve miles in circumference, and its greateſt depth about twenty-four fathoms: is finely bounded by mountains on one ſide; on the other, by the plain of *Kinroſs*; and prettily embelliſhed with ſeveral groves, moſt fortunately diſpoſed. Some iſlands are diſperſed in this great expanſe of water; one of which is large enough to feed ſeveral head of cattle: but the moſt remarkable is that diſtinguiſhed by the captivity of *Mary Stuart*, which ſtands almoſt in the middle of the lake. The caſtle ſtill remains; conſiſts of a ſquare tower, a ſmall yard with two round towers, a chapel, and the ruins of a building, where, it is ſaid, the unfortunate Princeſs was lodged. In the ſquare tower is a dungeon with a vaulted room above, over which had been three other ſtories. Some trees are yet remaining on this little ſpot; probably coeval with *Mary*, under whoſe ſhade ſhe may have ſat, expecting her eſcape at length effected by the enamoured *Douglas* *. This caſtle had before been a royal reſidence, but not for captive monarchs;

LOCH-LEVEN CASTLE.

* Hiſtorians differ in reſpect to the cauſe that influenced him to aſſiſt in his ſovereign's eſcape: ſome attribute it to his avarice, and think he was bribed with jewels,

monarchs; having been granted from the crown by *Robert* III. to *Douglas*, Laird of *Loch-Leven*.

This caſtle underwent a ſiege in the year 1335; and the method attempted to reduce it was of a moſt ſingular kind. *John* of *Sterling*, with his army of *Angliciſed Scots*, ſat down before it; but finding from the ſituation that it was impoſſible to ſucceed in the common forms, he thought of this expedient. He ſtopped up the water of *Leven*, at its diſcharge from the lake, with a great dam, with ſtones, and every thing that would obſtruct its courſe, hoping by that means to raiſe the waters ſo high, as to drown the whole garriſon. But the watchfull governor, *Alan de Vipont*, took an opportunity of ſallying out in boats when the beſiegers were off their guard; and piercing the dam, releaſed the pent-up waters, and formed a moſt deſtructive deluge on all the plain below; ſtruck a panick into the enemy's army, put them to flight, and returned to his caſtle laden with the ſpoils of the camp *.

St. *Serf*'s iſle is noted for having been granted by *Brude*, laſt King of the *Picts*, to St. *Servan* and the *Culdees*; a kind of prieſts among the firſt Chriſtians of *North Britain*, who led a ſort of monaſtic life in cells, and for a conſiderable time preſerved a pure and uncorrupt religion: at length, in the reign of *David* I. were ſuppreſſed in favor of the church of *Rome*. The priory of *Port-moak* was on this iſle, of which ſome ſmall remains yet exiſt.

jewels, reſerved by *Mary*; others, that he was touched by a more generous paſſion: the laſt opinion is the moſt natural, conſidering the charms of the Queen, and the youth of her deliverer.

* *Sibbald*'s Hiſt. of *Fife* and *Kinroſs*. 108.

The

FISH AND BIRDS. The fiſh of this lake are Pike, ſmall Perch, fine Eels, and moſt excellent Trouts; the beſt and the reddeſt I ever ſaw; the largeſt about ſix pounds in weight. The fiſhermen gave me an account of a ſpecies they called the *Gally* Trout, which are only caught from *October* to *January*; are ſplit, ſalted and dried, for winter proviſion: by the deſcription. they certainly were our Char, only of a larger ſize than any we have in *England*, or *Wales*, ſome being two feet and a half long. The birds that breed on the iſles are Herring Gulls, Pewit Gulls, and great Terns, called here *Pictarnes*.

Lay at a good inn, a ſingle houſe, about half a mile North of *Kinroſs*.

JULY 25. RUMBLING BRIG. Made an excurſion about ſeven miles Weſt, to ſee the *Rumbling Brig* at *Glen-Devon*, a bridge of one arch, flung over a chaſm worn by the river *Devon*, about eighty feet deep, very narrow, and horrible to look down; the bottom, in many parts, is covered with fragments of rocks; in others, the waters are viſible, guſhing between the ſtones with great violence: the ſides, in many places, project, and almoſt lock in each other; trees ſhoot out in various ſpots, and contribute to encreaſe the gloom of the glen, while the ear is filled with the cawing of Daws, the cooing of Wood-Pigeons, and the impetuous noiſe of the waters.

CAWDRON LIN. A mile lower down is the *Cawdron Lin*. Here the river, after a ſhort fall, drops on rocks hollowed in a ſtrange manner into large and deep cylindric cavities, open on one ſide, or formed into great circular cavities, like cauldrons *: from whence the name of the

* In *Sweden*, and the North of *Germany*, ſuch holes as theſe are called *Giant's* Pots. *Kalm's Voy*. I. 121. and *Ph. Tranſ. abridg*. V. 165.

place.

place. One in particular has the appearance of a vaſt brewing-veſſel; and the water, by its great agitation, has acquired a yellow ſcum, exactly reſembling the yeſty working of malt liquor. Juſt beneath this, the water darts down about thirty feet in form of a great white ſheet: the rocks below widen conſiderably, and their clifty ſides are fringed with wood. Beyond is a view of a fine meadowy vale, and the diſtant mountains near *Sterling*.

Two miles North is *Caſtle Campbell*, ſeated on a ſteep peninſulated rock between vaſt mountains, having to the South a boundleſs view through a deep glen ſhagged with bruſh wood: for the foreſts that once covered the country, are now entirely deſtroyed. Formerly, from its darkſome ſituation, this pile was called the caſtle of *Gloom*; and all the names of the adjacent places were ſuitable: it was ſeated in the pariſh of *Dolor*, was bounded by the glens of *care*, and waſhed by the birns of *ſorrow*. This caſtle, with the whole territory belonging to the family of *Argyle*, underwent all the calamities of civil war in 1645; for its rival, the Marquis of *Montroſe*, carried fire and ſword through the whole eſtate. The caſtle was ruined; and its magnificent reliques exiſt, as a monument of the horror of the times. No wonder then that the *Marquis* experienced ſo woefull and ignominious a fate, when he fell into the power of ſo exaſperated a chieftain. CASTLE CAMPBELL.

Returned to my inn along the foot of the *Ochil* hills, whoſe ſides were covered with a fine verdure, and fed great numbers of cattle and ſheep. The country below full of oats, and in a very improving ſtate: the houſes of the common people decent, but moſtly covered with ſods; ſome were covered both with ſtraw and ſod. The

The inhabitants extremely civil, and never failed offering brandy, or whey, when I ſtopt to make enquiries at any of their houſes.

STRAITH-EARN.

In the afternoon croſſed a branch of the ſame hills, which yielded plenty of oats; deſcended into *Straith-Earn*, a beautifull vale, about thirty miles in length, full of rich meadows and corn fields, divided by the river *Earn*, which ſerpentines finely through the middle, falling into the *Tay*, of which there is a ſight at the Eaſt end of the vale. It is prettily diverſified with groves of trees and gentlemen's houſes; among which, towards the Weſt end, is *Caſtle Drummond*, the forfeited ſeat of the Earl of *Perth*.

DUPPLIN.

Dupplin *; the reſidence of the Earl of *Kinnoul*, ſeated on the North ſide of the vale, on the edge of a ſteep glen. Only a ſingle tower remains of the old caſtle, the reſt being modernized. The South front commands a pleaſing view of the vale: behind are plantations, extending ſeveral miles in length; all flouriſh greatly, except thoſe of aſh. I remarked in the woods, ſome very large cheſnuts, horſe-cheſnuts, ſpruce and ſilver firs, cedar and arbor vitæ. Broad-leaved *laburnum* thrives in this country greatly, grows to a great ſize, and the wood is uſed in fineering.

FRUIT.

Fruits ſucceed here very indifferently; even nonpareils require a wall to ripen: grapes, figs, and late peaches, will not ripen: the winters begin early, and end late, and are attended with very high

LABOR.

winds. I was informed that labor is dear here, notwithſtanding

* Near this place was the battle of *Dupplin*, 1332, between the *Engliſh*, under the command of *Baliol*, and the *Scots*. The laſt were defeated, and ſuch a number of the name of *Hay* ſlain, that the family would have been extinct, had not ſeveral of their wives been left at home pregnant.

it

Moses Griffith del. P. Mazell sculp.

DUPPLIN HOUSE.

it is only eight-pence a day; the common people not being yet got into a method of working, ſo do very little for their wages. Notwithſtanding this, improvements are carried on in theſe parts with great ſpirit, both in planting and in agriculture. Lord *Kinnoul* planted laſt year not fewer than eighty thouſand trees, beſides *Scotch* firs; ſo provides future foreſts for the benefit of his ſucceſſors, and the embelliſhment of his country. In reſpect to agriculture, there are difficulties to ſtruggle with; for the country is without either coal or lime-ſtone; ſo that the lime is brought from the eſtate of the Earl of *Elgin*, near *Dumfermline*, who, I was told, drew a conſiderable revenue from the kilns.

In *Dupplin* are ſome very good pictures; a remarkable one of *Luther*, *Bucer*, and *Catherine* the nun, in the characters of muſicians, by *Georgiani di Caſtel franco.*

A fine head of a ſecular prieſt, by *Titian.* St. *Nicholas* bleſſing three children. Two of cattle, by *Roſa di Tivoli.* A head of *Spencer.* *Rubens'* head, by himſelf. A fine head of *Butler*, by Sir *Peter Lely.* Mrs. *Tofts*, in the character of St. *Catherine*, by Sir *Godfrey Kneller.* Sir *George Haye*, of *Maginnis*, in armour, 1640; done at *Rome*, by *L. Ferdinand. Haye*, Earl of *Carliſle*, in *Charles* the Firſt's time; young and very handſome, by *Cornelius Janſen.* The ſecond Earl of *Kinnoul*, by *Vandyck.* Chancellor *Haye*, by *Mytens.* A good portrait of Lord Treaſurer *Oxford*, by *Richardſon.* And a beautifull miniature of Sir *John Earnly.*

But the moſt remarkable is a head of the celebrated Counteſs of *Deſmond*, whom the apologiſts for the uſurper *Richard* III. bring in as an evidence againſt the received opinion of his deformity. She was daughter of the *Fitzgeralds*, of *Drumana** in the county of *Waterford*; and married in the reign of *Edward* IV., *James* fourteenth Earl of *Desmond:* was in *England* in the same reign; and danced at court with his brother *Richard*, then Duke of *Gloucester*. She was then a widow, for Sir *Walter Raleigh* says they held her jointure from all the Earls of *Desmond* since that time †. She lived to the age of some years above a hundred and forty; and died in the reign of *James* I. It appears that she retained her full vigor in a very advanced time of life; for the ruin of the house of *Desmond* reduced her to poverty, and obliged her to take a journey quite from *Bristol* to *London*, to sollicit relief from the court, at a time she was above a hundred and forty ‡. She also twice or thrice renewed her teeth; for Lord *Bacon* assures us, in his Hist. of Life and Death, *ter per vices dentiisse*; and in his Natural History mentions that she did *dentire* twice or thrice, casting her old teeth, and others coming in their place §.

JULY 27.
HILL OF MONCRIEF.

Ascended the hill of *Moncrief*; the prospect from thence is the glory of *Scotland*, and well merits the eulogia given it for the variety and richness of its views. On the South and West appear *Straith-Earn*, embellished with the seats of Lord *Kinnoul*, Lord *Rollo*, and of several other gentlemen; the *Carse*, or rich plain of *Gowrie*; *Stormont* hills; and the hill of *Kinnoul*, whose vast cliff is

* *Smith*'s Hist. of *Cork*. II. 36.

† *Raleigh*'s Hist. of the World. Book I. Ch. V. Sect. V.

‡ Sir *W. Temple*'s Essay on Health and Long Life. *Vide* his Works, Folio Ed. I. 276.

§ Cent. VIII. Sect. 755.

remarkable

Alliamet Sculp

CATHERINE Countess of DESMOND.

remarkable for its beautifull pebbles. The meanders of the *Earn*, which winds more than any river I at this time had ſeen, are moſt enlivening additions to the ſcene. The laſt turn it takes forms a fine peninſula prettily planted; and juſt beyond it joins the *Tay*, whoſe æſtuary lies full in view; the ſea cloſing the proſpect on this ſide.

To the North lies the town of *Perth*, with a view of part of its magnificent bridge; which, with the fine woods called *Perth* Parks, the vaſt plain of *Straith-Tay*, the winding of that noble river, its iſlands, and the grand boundary, formed by the diſtant highlands, finiſh this matchleſs ſcene. The inhabitants of *Perth* are far from being blind to the beauties of their river; for with ſingular pleaſure they relate the tradition of the *Roman* army, when it came in ſight of the *Tay* *, burſting into the exclamation of, *Ecce Tiberim.*

On approaching the town are ſome pretty walks handſomely planted, and at a ſmall diſtance, the remains of ſome works of *Cromwel*'s, called *Oliver*'s Mount.

PERTH is large, and in general well-built; two of the ſtreets are remarkably fine; in ſome of the leſſer are yet a few wooden houſes in the old ſtyle; but as they decay, the magiſtrates prohibit the rebuilding them in the old way. There is but one pariſh, which has two churches, beſides meetings for ſeparatiſts, who are very numerous. One church, which belonged to a monaſtery, is very antient: not a veſtige of the laſt is now to be ſeen; for the diſciples of that rough apoſtle *Knox*, made a general deſolation of every edifice that had given ſhelter to the worſhippers of the church of *Rome:* PERTH.

* Taus, *Taciti vit. Agr.*

it being one of his maxims, to pull down the nefts, and then the Rooks would fly away.

The flourifhing ftate of *Perth* is owing to two accidents: the firft, that of numbers of *Cromwel*'s wounded officers and foldiers chufing to refide here, after he left the kingdom, who introduced a fpirit of induftry among the people: the other caufe was the long continuance of the Earl of *Mar*'s army here in 1715, which occafioned vaft fums of money being fpent in the place. But this town, as well as all *Scotland*, dates its profperity from the year 1745; the government of this part of *Great Britain* having never been fettled till a little after that time. The rebellion was a diforder violent in its operation, but falutary in its effects.

TRADE. The trade of *Perth* is confiderable. It exports annually one hundred and fifty thoufand pounds worth of linnen, from twenty-four to thirty thoufand bolls of wheat and barley to *London* and *Edinburgh*, and about the fame in cured falmon. That fifh is taken there in vaft abundance; three thoufand have been caught in one morning, weighing, one with another, fixteen pounds; the whole capture, forty-eight thoufand pounds. The fifhery begins at St. *Andrew*'s Day, and ends *Auguft* 26th, old ftyle. The rents of the fifheries amount to three thoufand pounds *per annum*.

I was informed that fmelts come up this river in *May* and *June*.

PEARL. There has been in thefe parts a very great fifhery of pearl, got out of the frefh-water mufcles. From the year 1761 to 1764, 10,000l. worth were fent to *London*, and fold from 10s. to 1l. 16s. *per* ounce. I was told that a pearl has been taken there that weighed 33 grains. But this fifhery is at prefent exhaufted, from the

the avarice of the undertakers: it once extended as far as *Loch-Tay*.

Gowrie Houſe is ſhewn to all ſtrangers; formerly the property and reſidence of the Earl of *Gowrie*, whoſe tragical end and myſterious conſpiracy (if conſpiracy there was) are ſtill freſh in the minds of the people of *Perth*. At preſent the houſe is occupied by ſome companies of artillery. I was ſhewn the ſtaircaſe where the unhappy nobleman was killed, the window the frighted monarch *James* roared out of, and that he eſcaped through, when he was ſaved from the fury of the populace, by Baily *Roy*, a friend of *Gowrie*'s, who was extremely beloved in the town. GOWRIE CONSPIRACY.

From the little traditions preſerved in the place, it ſeems as if *Gowrie* had not the leſt intent of murthering the King: on the day his Majeſty came to *Perth*, the Earl was engaged to a wedding-dinner with the Dean of *Guild:* when the account of the King's deſign reached him, he changed color, on being taken ſo unprovided; but the Dean forced him to accept the nuptial feaſt, which was ſent over to the Earl's houſe.

When the King fled, he paſſed by the ſeat of Sir *William Moncrief*, near *Earn-bridge*, who happening to be walking out at that time, heard from the mouth of his terrified majeſty the whole relation; but the Knight found it ſo marvellous and ſo disjointed, as plainly to tell the King, *that if it was a true ſtory, it was a very ſtrange one.*

Gowrie was a moſt accompliſhed gentleman. After he had finiſhed his ſtudies, he held the Profeſſor of Philoſophy's chair for two years, in one of the *Italian* univerſities.

Croſs

Croſs the *Tay* on a temporary bridge; the ſtone bridge, which is to conſiſt of nine arches, being at this time unfiniſhed: the largeſt arch is ſeventy-ſix feet wide; when complete, it promiſes to be a moſt magnificent ſtructure. The river here is very violent, and admits of ſcarce any navigation above; but ſhips of eighty or ninety tuns come as far as the town.

SCONE. *Scone* lies about a mile and half higher up, on the Eaſt bank of the river. Here was once an abby of great antiquity *, which was burnt by the reforming zealots of *Dundee*. The preſent palace was begun by Earl *Gowrie*; but, on his death, being granted by *James* VI. to his favorite, Sir *David Murray*, of *Goſpatrie*, was completed by him; who, in gratitude to the King, has, in ſeveral parts of the houſe, put up the royal arms. The houſe is built round two courts; the dining-room is large and handſome, has an antient but magnificent chimney-piece, the King's arms, with this motto,

Nobis hæc invicta miſerunt centum ſex Proavi.

Beneath are the *Murray* arms. In the drawing-room is ſome good old tapeſtry, with an excellent figure of *Mercury*. In a ſmall bed-chamber is a medly ſcripture-piece in needle-work, with a border of animals, pretty well done; the work of *Mary Stuart*, during her confinement in *Loch-Leven* caſtle: but the houſe in general is in a manner unfurniſhed.

The gallery is about a hundred and fifty-five feet long; the top arched, divided into compartments, filled with paintings, in water

* Founded by *Alexander* I. 1114, for canons regular of St. *Auguſtine*.

colors,

colors, of different sorts of huntings; and that *Nimrod*, *James* VI. and his train, appear in every piece.

Till the destruction of the abby, the Kings of *Scotland* were crowned here, sitting in the famous wooden chair, which *Edward* I. transported to *Westminster Abby*, much to the mortification of the *Scots*, who esteemed it as their palladium. *Charles* II. before the battle of *Worcester*, was crowned in the present chapel. The old Pretender resided at *Scone* for a considerable time in 1715, and his son made it a visit in 1745.

Re-passed the *Tay* at *Bullion*'s Boat; visited the field of *Loncarty*, celebrated for the great victory * obtained by the *Scots* over the *Danes*, by means of the gallant peasant *Hay*, and his two sons; who, with no other weapons than the yokes which they snatched from their oxen then at plough, first put a stop to the flight of their countrymen, and afterwards led them on to conquest. The noble families of *Hay* descend from this rustic hero, and in memory of the action, bear for their arms the instrument of their victory, with the allusive motto of *Sub jugo*. There are on the spot several *tumuli*, in which are frequently found bones deposited in loose stones, disposed in form of a coffin. Not remote is a spot which supplied me with far more agreeable ideas; a tract of ground, which in 1732 was a mere bog, but now converted into good meadows, and about fifty acres covered with linnen; several other parts with buildings, and all the apparatus of the linnen manufacture, extremely curious, and worth seeing, carried on by the industrious family of the *Sandimans*: and in the bleachery are annually whitened, LONCARTY.

* In the time of *Kenneth*, who began his reign in 976.

four

four hundred thouſand yards of linnen, the manufacture of this family, and of Mr. *Marſhall* and others from *Perth*.

The country is good, full of barley, oats, and flax in abundance; but after a few miles travelling, is ſucceeded by a black heath. Ride through a beautifull plantation of pines, and after deſcending an eaſy ſlope, the plain beneath ſuddenly contracts itſelf into a narrow glen. The proſpect before me ſtrongly marked the entrance into the *Highlands*, the hills that bounded it on each ſide being

BIRNAM WOOD.

lofty and rude. On the left was *Birnam* Wood, which ſeems never to have recovered the march which its anceſtors made to *Dunſinane*:

DUNSINANE.

I was ſhewn at a great diſtance a high ridge of hills, where ſome remains of that famous fortreſs (*Macbeth*'s caſtle) are ſaid yet to exiſt.

The paſs into the *Highlands* is awefully magnificent; high, craggy, and often naked mountains preſent themſelves to view, approach very near each other, and in many parts are fringed with wood, overhanging and darkening the *Tay*, that rolls with great rapidity beneath. After ſome advance in this hollow, a moſt beautifull knowl, covered with pines, appears full in view; and ſoon

DUNKELD.

after, the town of *Dunkeld*, ſeated under and environed by crags, partly naked, partly wooded, with ſummits of a vaſt height. Lay at *Inver* *, a good inn, on the Weſt ſide of the river.

JULY 28.

Croſſed it in a boat, attended by a tame ſwan, which was perpetually ſolliciting our favors by putting its neck over the ſides of the ferry-boat. Land in the Duke of *Athol*'s gardens, which are

* *Inver*, a place where a leſſer river runs into a greater; or a river into a lake or ſea, as *Aber* ſignifies in the *Britiſh*.

extremely

P. Sandby pinx.t P. Mazell sculp.t

Dunkeld Cathedral.

extremely pleasing, washed by the river, and commanding from different parts of the walks the most beautifull and picturesque views of wild and gloomy nature that can be conceived. Trees of all kinds grow here extremely well; and even so Southern a shrub as *Portugal* laurel flourishes greatly. In the garden are the ruins of the cathedral, once a magnificent ædifice, as appears by the beautifull round pillars still standing; but the choir is preserved, and at present used as a church. In the burial-place of the family is a large monument of the Marquis of *Athol*, hung with the arms of the numerous connections of the family. In another part is a tomb of an old bishop.

On the other side the river is a pleasing walk along the banks of the water of *Bran* *, a great and rapid torrent, full of immense stones. On a rock at the end of the walk is a neat building, impending over a most horrible chasm, into which the river precipitates itself with great noise and fury from a considerable height. The windows of the pavillion are formed of painted glass; some of the panes are red, which makes the water resemble a fiery cataract. About a mile further is another *Rumbling Brig*, like, but inferiour in grandeur, to that near *Kinross*.

The town of *Dunkeld* is small, and has a small linnen manufacture. Much company resorts here, in the summer months, for the benefit of drinking goats' milk and whey: I was informed here, that those animals will eat serpents; as it is well known that stags do.

* Rivers in *Scotland* are very frequently called *waters*.

After a ride of two miles along a narrow ſtrait, amidſt trees, and often in ſight of the *Tay*, was driven by rain into a fiſherman's hut, who entertained me with an account of his buſineſs: ſaid he paid ten pounds *per ann.* for the liberty of two or three miles of the river; ſold the firſt fiſh of the ſeaſon at three-pence a pound; after that, got three ſhillings *per* fiſh. The houſes in theſe parts began to be covered with broom, which laſts three or four years: their inſides mean, and very ſcantily furniſhed; but the owners civil, ſenſible, and of the quickeſt apprehenſions.

The ſtrait now widens into a vale plentifull in oats, barley and flax, and well peopled. On the right is the junction of the *Tay* and the *Tumel*: the channels of theſe rivers are wide, full of gravel, the mark of their devaſtation during floods. Due North is the road to *Blair* and *Fort Auguſtus*, through the noted paſs of *Killicrankie*; turn to the left; ride oppoſite to *Caſtle Menzies*: reach *Taymouth*, the ſeat of the Earl of *Breadalbane*.

JULY 29, &c. TAYMOUTH. *Taymouth** lies in a vale ſcarce a mile broad, very fertile, bounded on each ſide by mountains finely planted. Thoſe on the South are covered with trees, or with corn fields, far up their ſides. The hills on the North are planted with pines and other trees, and vaſtly ſteep, and have a very *alpine* look; but particularly reſemble the great ſlope oppoſite the *grande Chartreuſe* in *Dauphiné*. His Lordſhip's policy † ſurrounds the houſe, which ſtands in the park, and is one of the few in which fallow deer are ſeen.

* Its name, in old maps, is *Balloch*; i. e. the mouth of the Loch: *Bala* in the *Britiſh* language.

† This word here ſignifies improvements, or demeſne: when uſed by a merchant, or tradeſman, ſignifies their warehouſes, ſhops, and the like.

The

Moses Griffiths. del.

P. C. Canot sculp.

TAYMOUTH.

The ground is in remarkable fine order, owing to his Lordſhip's affiduity in clearing it from ſtones, with which it was once covered. A *Blaſter* was in conſtant employ to blaſt the great ſtones with gun-powder; for, by reaſon of their ſize, there was no other method of removing them. WALKS.

The *Berceau* walk is very magnificent, compoſed of great trees, forming a fine *gothic* arch; and probably that ſpecies of architecture owed its origin to ſuch vaulted ſhades. The walk on the bank of the *Tay* is fifty feet wide, and two and twenty hundred yards long; but is to be continued as far as the junction of the *Tay* and the *Lion*, which is about as far more. The firſt runs on the ſides of the walk with great rapidity, is clear, but not color-leſs, for its pellucidneſs is like that of brown cryſtal; as is the caſe with moſt of the rivers in *Scotland*, which receive their tinge from the bogs. The *Tay* has here a wooden bridge two hundred feet long, leading to a white ſeat on the ſide of the oppoſite hill, commanding a fine view up and down *Straith-Tay*. The rich meadows beneath, the winding of the river, the beginning of *Loch-Tay*, the diſcharge of the river out of it, the neat village and church of *Kinmore*, form a moſt pleaſing and magnificent proſpect.

The view from the temple of *Venus* is that of the lake, with a nearer ſight of the church and village, and the diſcharge of the river. The lake is about a mile broad, and fifteen long, bounded on each ſide by lofty mountains; makes three great bends, which adds to its beauty. Thoſe on the South are well planted, and finely cultivated high up; interſperſed with the habitations of the *Highlanders*, not ſingly, but in ſmall groupes, as if they loved ſo-ciety or clanſhip: they are very ſmall, mean, and without windows LOCH-TAY.

or chimnies, and are the disgrace of *North Britain*, as its lakes and rivers are its glory. *Loch-Tay* is, in many places, a hundred fathoms deep, and within as many yards of the shore, fifty-four.

Till of late, this lake was supposed to be as incapable of freezing as *Loch-Ness*, *Loch-Earn*, and *Loch-Each*; tho' *Loch-Rannoch*, and even *Loch-Fine*, an arm of the sea, often does. But in *March* 1771, so rigorous and uncommon was the cold, that about the 20th of that month this vast body of water was frozen over, in one part, from side to side, in the space of a single night; and so strong was the ice, as greatly to damage a boat which was caught in it.

Loch-Tay abounds with Pike, Perch, Eels, Salmon, Charr, and Trout; of the last, some have been taken that weighed above thirty pounds. Of these species, the *Highlanders* abhor Eels, and also Lampreys, fancying, from the form, that they are too nearly related to Serpents.

The North side is less wooded, but more cultivated. The vast hill of *Laurs*, with beds of snow on it, through great part of the year, rises above the rest, and the still loftier mountain of *Benmor* closes the view far beyond the end of the lake. All this country abounds with game, such as Grous, Ptarmigans *, Stags, and a

WHITE HARE.

peculiar species of Hare, which is found only on the summits of the highest hills, and never mixes with the common kind, which is frequent enough in the vales †: is less than the common Hare; its limbs more slender; its flesh more delicate: is very agile and

* *Br. Zool. illustr.* 21. *tab.* xiii.

† The same, *p.* 40. *tab.* xlvii.

full

full of frolick when kept tame; is fond of honey and carraway comfits, and prognosticates a storm by eating its own dung: in a wild state, does not run an end, but seeks shelter under stones as soon as possible. During summer its predominant color is grey: about *September* it begins to assume a snowy whiteness, the alteration of color appearing about the neck and rump, and becomes entirely white, except the edges and tips of the ears: in *April* it again resumes its grey coat.

PTARMIGANS.

The *Ptarmigans* inhabit the very summits of the highest mountains, amidst the rocks, perching among the grey stones, and during summer are scarcely to be distinguished from them, by reason of their color. They seldom take long flights, but fly about like pigeons; are silly birds, and so tame as to suffer a stone to be flung at them without rising. It is not necessary to have a dog to find them. They taste so like a Grous, as to be scarce distinguishable. During winter, their plumage, except a few feathers on the tail, are of a pure white, the color of the snow, in which they bury themselves in heaps, as a protection from the rigorous air.

BIRDS.

Royston Crows, called here Hooded Crows, and in the *Erse*, *Feannag*, are very common, and reside here the whole year. They breed in all sorts of trees, not only in the *Highlands*, but even in the plains of *Murray*: lay six eggs; have a shriller note than the common sort; are much more mischievous; pick out the eyes of lambs, and even of horses, when engaged in bogs; but, for want of other food, will eat cranberries, and other mountain berries.

Ring Ouzels breed among the hills, and in autumn descend in flocks to feed on the berries of the wicken trees.

Sea Eagles breed in ruined towers, but quit the country in winter? the black Eagles continue there the whole year.

It

It is very difficult to leave the environs of this delightfull place. Before I go within doors, I muſt recall to mind the fine winding walks on the South ſide of the hills, the great beech ſixteen feet in girth, the pictureſque birch with its long ſtreaming branches, the hermitage, the great cataracts adjacent, and the darkſome chaſm beneath. I muſt enjoy over again the view of the fine reach of the *Tay*, and its union with the broad water of the *Lion*: I muſt ſtep down to view the druidical circles of ſtones; and laſtly, I muſt viſit

TAY-BRIDGE. *Tay-bridge*, and, as far as my pen can contribute, extend the fame of our military countrymen, who, among other works worthy of the *Romans*, founded this bridge, and left its hiſtory inſcribed in theſe terms:

Mirare
viam hanc militarem
Ultra *Romanos* terminos
M. Paſſuum. CCL hac illac
extenſam;
Teſquis et paludibus inſultantem
per Montes rupeſque patefactam
et indignanti TAVO
ut cernis inſtratam:
Opus hoc arduuum ſuâ ſolertiâ,
Et decennali militum operâ,
A. Ær. Xnæ 1733. Poſuit G. WADE
Copiarum in SCOTIA Præfectus.
Ecce quantum valeant
Regis GEORGII II. Auſpicia.

Taymouth

Tomkyns pinx.t P. Mazell sculp.t

Cascade near Taymouth.

Taymouth is a large houſe, a caſtle modernized. The moſt remarkable part of its furniture is the works of the famous *Jameſon**, the *Scotch Vandyck*, an eleve of this family. That ſingular performance of his, the genealogical picture, is in good preſervation. The chief of the *Argyle* family is placed recumbent at the foot of a tree, with a branch; on the right is a ſingle head of his eldeſt ſon, Sir *Duncan Campbell*, Laird of *Lochou*; but on the various ramifications, are the names of his deſcendents, and along the body of the tree are nine ſmall heads, in oval frames, with the names on the margins, all done with great neatneſs: the ſecond ſon was firſt of the houſe of *Breadalbane*, which branched from the other about four hundred years ago. In a corner is inſcribed, *The Geneologie of the houſe of* Glenorquhie *Quhairof is deſcendit ſundrie nobil & worthie houſes.* Jameſon *faciebat.* 1635. Its ſize is eight feet by five. In the ſame room are about twenty heads of perſons of the family; among others, that of a lady, ſo very ugly, that a wag, on ſeeing it, with lifted hands pronounced, that ſhe was *fearfully and wonderfully made.* There are in the ſame houſe, ſeveral heads by *Jameſon*; but many of them unfortunately ſpoiled in the repairing.

JAMESON.

In the library is a ſmall book, called, from the binding, the *black book*, with ſome beautifull drawings in it, on vellum, of the *Breadalbane* family, in water colors. In the firſt page is old Sir

* Son of an architect at *Aberdeen*; ſtudied under *Rubens*, at *Antwerp*. *Charles* I. ſat to him, and preſented him with a diamond ring. He always drew himſelf with his hat on. His prices were 20l. *Scots*, or 1l. 13s. 4d. *Engliſh*, *per* head: was born in 1586; died at *Edinburgh*, 1644. For a further account, conſult Mr. *Walpole*'s Anecdotes of Painting.

Duncan,

Duncan, between two other figures; then follow ſeveral chiefs of the family, among whom is Sir *Colin*, Knight of *Rhodes*, who died 1480, aged 80. At the end is a manuſcript hiſtory of the family, ending, I think, in 1633.

JULY 30. Went to divine ſervice at *Kinmore** church, which, with the village, was re-built, in the neateſt manner, by the preſent Lord *Breadalbane:* they ſtand beautifully on a ſmall headland, projecting into the lake. His Lordſhip permits the inhabitants to live rent-free, on condition they exerciſe ſome trade, and keep their houſes clean: ſo that, by theſe terms, he not only ſaves the expence of ſending, on every trifling occaſion, to *Perth* or *Crief*, but has got ſome as good workmen, in common trades, as any in his Majeſty's dominions.

The church is a remarkably neat plain building, with a very handſome tower ſteeple. The congregation was numerous, decent, attentive, ſtill; well and neatly clad, and not a ragged or ſlovenly perſon among them. There were two ſervices, one in *Engliſh*, the other in *Erſe*. After the firſt, numbers of people, of both ſexes, went out of church, and ſeating themſelves in the church-yard, made, in their motly habits, a gay and picturesque appearance.

HIGHLAND CONGREGATION.

The devotion of the common people of *Scotland*, on the uſual days of worſhip, is as much to be admired, as their conduct at the ſacrament in certain places is to be cenſured. It is celebrated but once in a year †; when there are ſometimes three thouſand communi-

* Or the Great Head.

† Formerly the ſacrament was adminiſtered but once in two years.

cants,

cants, and as many idle ſpectators. Of the firſt, as many as poſſible crowd on each ſide of a long table, and the elements are ſometimes rudely ſhoven from one to another; and in certain places, before the day is at an end, fighting and other indecencies enſue. It has often been made a ſeaſon for debauchery; and to this day, *Jack* cannot always be perſuaded to eat his meat like a chriſtian *.

Every Sunday a collection is made for the ſick or neceſſitous; for poor's rates are unknown in every country pariſh in *Scotland*. Notwithſtanding the common people are but juſt rouzed from their native indolence, very few beggars are ſeen in *North Britain*: either they are full maſters of the leſſon of being content with a very little; or, what is more probable, they are poſſeſſed of a ſpirit that will ſtruggle hard with neceſſity before it will bend to the aſking of alms.

Viſited a pretty iſland in *Loch-Tay*, tufted with trees, and not far from the ſhore. On it are the ruins of a priory dependent on that at *Scone*; founded in 1122, by *Alexander* the Firſt; in which were depoſited the remains of his Queen *Sybilla*, natural daughter to *Henry* I.: it was founded by *Alexander* in order for the prayers of the Monks for the repoſe of his ſoul, and that of his royal conſort †. To this iſland the *Campbells* retreated, during the ſucceſſes of the Marquis of *Montroſe*, where they defended themſelves againſt

* *Tale of a Tub.*

† As appears from a grant made by that Monarch of the iſle in *Loch-Tay*. *Ut Eccleſia* DEI *ibi pro me et pro Anima* SYBILLÆ *Reginæ ibi defunctæ fabricetur*, &c.

that hero, which was one cauſe of his violent reſentment againſt the whole name.

JULY 31. Rode to *Glen-Lion*; went by the ſide of the river* that gives name to it. It has now loſt its antient title of *Duie*, or *Black*, given it on account of a great battle between the *Mackays* and the *Macgregors*; after which, the conquerors are ſaid to have ſtained the water with red, by waſhing in it their bloody ſwords and ſpears. On the right is a rocky hill, called *Shi-hallen*, or the Paps. Enter *Glen-Lion* through a ſtrait paſs: the vale is narrow, but fertile; the banks of the river ſteep, rocky, and wooded; through which appears the rapid water of the *Lion*. On the North is a round fortreſs, on the top of the hill; to which, in old times, the natives retreated, on any invaſion. A little farther, on a plain, is a ſmall *Roman* camp †, called by the Highlanders *Fortingal*, or the Fort of the Strangers: themſelves they ſtile *Na fian*, or deſcendents of

GREAT YEW. *Fingal*. In *Fortingal* church-yard are the remains of a prodigious yew-tree, whoſe ruins meaſured fifty-ſix feet and a half in circumference.

Saw at the houſe of Col. *Campbell* of *Glen-Lion*, a curious walking-ſtaff, belonging to one of his anceſtors: it was iron caſed in leather, five feet long; at the top a neat pair of extended wings, like a *caduceus*; but, on being ſhaken, a poniard, two feet nine inches long, darted out.

* This river freezes; but the *Tay*, which receives it, never does.

† It poſſibly might have been made during the expedition of *Severus*, who penetrated to the extremity of this iſland. It was the moſt Northern work of the *Romans* I had any intelligence of.

He

BROTCHE.

es Griffiths del. *P. Mazell sculp*

He alſo favored me with the ſight of a very antient brotche, which the *Highlanders* uſe, like the *fibula* of the *Romans*, to faſten their veſt: it is made of ſilver, is round, with a bar croſs the middle, from whence are two tongues to faſten the folds of the garments: one ſide is ſtudded with pearl, or coarſe gems, in a very rude manner; on the other, the names of the three kings of *Cologne*, CASPAR, MELCHIOR, BALTAZAR; with the word *conſummatim*. It was probably a conſecrated brotche, and worn not only for uſe, but as an amulet. *Keyſler*'s account of the virtues attributed to their names confirms my opinion. He ſays that they were written on ſlips of paper in this form, and worn as preſervatives againſt the falling-ſickneſs:

> *Gaſpar* fert Myrrham, Thus *Melchior*, *Balthazar* Aurum;
> Solvitur a morbo *Chriſti* pietate caduco.

Return South, and come at once in ſight of *Loch-Tay*. The day very fine and calm, the whole ſcene was moſt beautifully repeated in the water. I muſt not omit that on the North ſide of this lake is a moſt excellent road, which runs the whole length of it, leading to *Teindrum* and *Inveraray*, in *Argyleſhire*, and is the route which travellers muſt take, who make what I call the *petit tour* * of *Scotland*. This whole road was made at the ſole expence of the preſent

* Which comprehends the route I have deſcribed; adding to it, from *Taymouth*, along the road, on the ſide of the lake, to *Killin*, 16 miles; from thence to *Teindrum*, 20; *Glenorchie*, 12; *Inveraray*, 16; *Luſs*, on the banks of *Loch-Lomond*, 30; *Dunbarton*, 12; *Glaſgow*, 15; *Sterling*, 31; *Edinburgh*, by *Hopetoun* Houſe, 35; a tract unparalleled, for the variety and frequency of fine and magnificent ſcenery.

Lord *Breadalbane*; who, to facilitate the travelling, alſo erected thirty-two ſtone-bridges over the torrents that ruſh from the moun-
ROADS. tains into the lake. They will find the whole country excell in roads, partly military, partly done by ſtatute labor, and much by the munificence of the great men.

I was informed, that Lord *Breadalbane*'s eſtate was ſo extenſive that he could ride a hundred miles an end on it, even as far as the Weſt Sea, where he has alſo ſome iſlands. Theſe great properties are divided into diſtricts, called *Officiaries*: a ground officer preſides over each, and has three, four, or five hundred men under his care. He ſuperintends the duties due from each to their Lord, ſuch as fetching peat, bringing coal from *Crief*, &c. which they do, at their own expence, on horſes backs, travelling in ſtrings, the tail of one horſe being faſtened by a cord, which reaches to the head of the next: the horſes are little, and generally white or grey; and as the farms are very ſmall, it is common for four people to keep a plough between them, each furniſhing a horſe, and this is called a horſe-gang.

The North ſide of *Loch-Tay* is very populous; for in ſixteen ſquare miles are ſeventeen hundred and eighty-ſix ſouls: on the other ſide, about twelve hundred. The country, within theſe thirty years, manufactures a great deal of thread. They ſpin with rocks *, which they do while they attend their cattle on the hills; and, at the four fairs in the year, held at *Kinmore*, above ſixteen hundred pounds worth of yarn is ſold out of *Breadalbane* only:

* Their Lord gives among them annually a great number of ſpinning-wheels, which will ſoon cauſe the diſuſe of the rock.

which

which ſhews the great increaſe of induſtry in theſe parts, for leſs than forty years ago there was not the leſt trade in this article. The yarn is bought by perſons who attend the fairs for that purpoſe, and ſell it again at *Perth*, *Glaſgow*, and other places, where it is manufactured into cloth.

Much of this may be owing to the good ſenſe and humanity of the chieftain; but much again is owing to the abolition of the feudal tenures, or vaſſalage; for before that was effected, (which was done by the influence of a Chancellor *, whoſe memory *Scotland* gratefully adores for that ſervice) the Strong oppreſſed the Weak, the Rich the Poor. Courts indeed were held, and juries called; but juries of vaſſals, too dependent and too timid to be relied on for the execution of true juſtice.

Leave *Taymouth*; ford the *Lion*, and ride above it thro' ſome woods. On the left burſts out a fine caſcade, in a deep hollow, covered with trees: at a ſmall diſtance to the Weſt is *Caſtle Garth*, a ſmall caſtle ſeated like *Caſtle Campbell*, between two deep glens. Keep aſcending a ſteep hill, but the corn country continues for a while: the ſcene then changes for a wild, black, and mountainous heath. Deſcend into *Rannoch*, a meadowy plain, tolerably fertile: the lake of the ſame name extends from Eaſt to Weſt; is about eleven miles long, and one broad: the Northern bank appears very barren; part of the Southern finely covered with a foreſt of pine and birch, the firſt natural woods I had ſeen of pines: rode a good way in it, but obſerved no trees of any ſize, except a birch ſixteen

AUG. 1

RANNOCH.

PINE FOREST.

* Earl of *Hardwick*, who may be truly ſaid to have given to the *North Britons* their great charter of liberty.

feet

feet in circumference: the ground beneath the trees is covered with heath, bilberies, and dwarf arbutus, whoſe gloſſy leaves make a pretty appearance. This place gives ſhelter to black game, and

ROES. Roes. Theſe animals are found from the banks of *Loch-Lomond*, as far North as the entrance into *Cathneſs:* in ſummer their hair is ſhort, ſmooth, gloſſy, and red; at approach of winter grows long and hoary, and proves an excellent defence againſt the rigor of the *Highland* air. The weight of a full-grown Roe is 60 lb. The horns of the ſecond year are ſtrait, ſlender, and without any branch: in the third become bifurcated: in the fourth, trifurcated, and grow more ſcabrous and ſtronger, in proportion to their longevity. They feed during ſummer on graſs, and are remarkably fond of the *Rubus Saxatilis*, called in the *Highlands* on that account the *Roebuck Berry*. When the ground is covered with ſnow, they browze on the extreme branches of the pine and juniper. They bring two young at a time: the fawns elegantly ſpotted with white. It is extremely difficult to rear them; commonly eight out of ten dying in the attempt. The fleſh of the Roe is by ſome accounted a delicacy: to me it ſeemed very dry. They keep in ſmall families of five or ſix.

Near theſe woods is a ſaw-mill, which is rented from the Government; and the tenant is obliged to work 150 tuns of timber annually, paying eighteen ſhillings and ſix-pence *per* tun. The deal, which is the red ſort, is ſold in plank to different parts of the country, carried on horſes backs, for the trees are now grown ſo ſcarce as not to admit of exportation *.

* Some Pot-Aſh is alſo made of the Birch Wood.

The

The lake affords no other fiſh than Trouts, ſmall Chars, and Bull Trouts; the laſt, as I was informed, are ſometimes taken of the length of four feet and a half. Many water fowl breed in the birns or little ſtreams that trickle into the lake; among others, different ſort of Grebes, and Divers: I was told of one which the inhabitants call *Fur-bhuachaille*, that makes a great noiſe before ſtorms, and by their deſcription find it to be the ſpeckled Diver, *Br. Zool.* 2d. ed. II. 414. No rats have hitherto been obſerved in this country.

THE POET STRUAN.

This country was once the property of *Robertſon* of *Struan*, who had been in the rebellion of 1715; had his eſtate reſtored, but in 1745 rebelling a ſecond time, the country was burnt, and the eſtate annexed to the crown. He returned a few years after, and died as he lived, a moſt abandoned ſot; notwithſtanding which, he had a genius for poetry, and left behind him a volume of elegies, and other pieces, in ſome of which he elegantly laments the ravages of war among his vaſſals, and the loſs of his favorite ſcenes, and in particular his fountain *Argentine*.

SUPERSTITIONS.

The country is perfectly highland; and in ſpite of the intercourſe this and the neighboring parts have of late years had with the reſt of the world, it ſtill retains ſome of its antient cuſtoms and ſuperſtitions: they decline daily, but leaſt their memory ſhould be loſt, I ſhall mention ſeveral that are ſtill practiſed, or but very lately diſuſed in the tract I had paſſed over. Such a record will have this advantage when the follies are quite extinct, in teaching the unſhackled and enlightened mind the difference between the pure ceremonies of religion, and the wild and anile flights of ſuperſtition.

The

SPECTRES.

The belief in ſpectres ſtill exiſts; of which I had a remarkable proof while I was in the county of *Breadalbane.* A poor viſionary, who had been working in his cabbage-garden, imagined that he was raiſed ſuddenly into the air, and conveyed over a wall into an adjacent corn-field *; that he found himſelf ſurrounded by a crowd of men and women, many of whom he knew to have been dead ſome years, and who appeared to him ſkimming over the tops of the unbended corn, and mingling together like bees going to hive: that they ſpoke an unknown language and with a hollow ſound: that they very roughly puſhed him to and fro; but on his uttering the name of GOD, all vaniſhed but a female ſprite, who ſeizing him by the ſhoulder, obliged him to promiſe an aſſignation, at that very hour, that day ſevenight: that he then found that his hair was all tied in double knots, and that he had almoſt loſt the uſe of his ſpeech: that he kept his word with the ſpectre, whom he ſoon ſaw come floating thro' the air towards him: that he ſpoke to her, but ſhe told him at that time ſhe was in too much haſte to attend to him, but bid him go away, and no harm ſhould befall him; and ſo the affair reſted when I left the country. But it is incredible the miſchief theſe *Ægri Somnia* did in the neighborhood: the friends and relations of the deceaſed, whom the old Dreamer had named, were in the utmoſt anxiety at finding them in ſuch bad company in the other world: the almoſt extinct belief of the old idle tales began again to gain ground, and the good miniſter will have many a weary

* Theſe tales of ſpectral tranſportations are far from being new; Mr. *Aubrey*, in his Miſcellanies, p. 13, gives two ridiculous relations of almoſt ſimilar facts, one in *Devonſhire*, the other in the ſhire of *Murray*.

diſcourſe

diſcourſe and exhortation before he can eradicate the abſurd ideas this idle ſtory has revived.

In this part of the country the notion of witchcraft is quite loſt: it was obſerved to ceaſe almoſt immediately on the repeal of the witch act *; a proof what a dangerous inſtrument it was in the hands of the vindictive, or of the credulous.

Among the ſuperſtitious cuſtoms theſe are the moſt ſingular. A *Highlander* never begins any thing of conſequence on the day of the week on which the 3d of *May* falls, which he ſtyles *La Sheachanna na bleanagh*, or the diſmal day. UNLUCKY DAY.

On the 1ſt of *May*, the herdſmen of every village hold their *Bel-tein* †, a rural ſacrifice. They cut a ſquare trench on the ground, leaving the turf in the middle; on that they make a fire of wood, on which they dreſs a large caudle of eggs, butter, oatmeal and milk; and bring, beſides the ingredients of the caudle, plenty of beer and whiſky; for each of the company muſt contribute ſomething. The rites begin with ſpilling ſome of the caudle on the ground, by way of libation: on that, every one takes a cake of oatmeal, upon which are raiſed nine ſquare knobs, each dedicated to ſome particular being, the ſuppoſed preſerver of their flocks and herds, or to ſome particular animal, the real deſtroyer of them: each perſon then turns his face to the fire, breaks off a knob, and flinging it over his ſhoulders, ſays, *This I give to thee, preſerve thou* BEL-TEIN.

* Which was not till the year 1736.

† My account of this, and every other ceremony mentioned in this Journal, was communicated to me by gentlemen reſident on the ſpot where they were performed.

my horses; this to thee, preserve thou my sheep; and so on. After that, they use the same ceremony to the noxious animals: *This I give to thee, O Fox! spare thou my lambs; this to thee, O hooded Crow! this to thee, O Eagle!*

When the ceremony is over, they dine on the caudle; and after the feast is finished, what is left is hid by two persons deputed for that purpose; but on the next *Sunday* they re-assemble, and finish the reliques of the first entertainment *.

FUNERAL CUSTOMS.

On the death of a Highlander, the corps being stretched on a board, and covered with a coarse linnen wrapper, the friends lay on the breast of the deceased a wooden platter, containing a small quantity of salt and earth, separate and unmixed; the earth, an emblem of the corruptible body; the salt, an emblem of the immortal spirit. All fire is extinguished where a corps is kept; and it is reckoned so ominous for a dog or cat to pass over it, that the poor animal is killed without mercy.

* A custom, savoring of the *Scotch Bel-tein*, prevales in *Gloucestershire*, particularly about *Newent* and the neighboring parishes, on the twelfth day, or on the *Epiphany*, in the evening. All the servants of every particular farmer assemble together in one of the fields that has been sown with wheat; on the border of which, in the most conspicuous or most elevated place, they make twelve fires of straw, in a row; around one of which, made larger than the rest, they drink a chearful glass of cyder to their master's health, success to the future harvest, and then returning home they feast on cakes, made of carraways, &c. soaked in cyder, which they clame as a reward for their past labors in sowing the grain. This seems to resemble a custom of the antient *Danes*, who, in their addresses to their deities, emptied, on every invocation, a cup in honor of them. NIORDI *et* FREJÆ *memoria poculis recolebatur, annua ut ipsis contingeret felicitas, frugumque et reliquæ annonæ uberrimus proventus.* Worm. Monum. Dan. lib. 1. *p.* 28.

The

The *Late-wake* is a ceremony uſed at funerals. The evening after the death of any perſon, the relations and friends of the deceaſed meet at the houſe, attended by bagpipe or fiddle; the neareſt of kin, be it wife, ſon, or daughter, opens a melancholy ball, dancing and greeting, *i. e.* crying violently at the ſame time; and this continues till day-light; but with ſuch gambols and frolicks among the younger part of the company, that the loſs which occaſioned them is often more than ſupplied by the conſequences of that night *. If the corps remains unburied for two nights, the ſame rites are renewed. Thus, *Scythian*-like, they rejoice at the deliverance of their friends out of this life of miſery. LATE-WAKE.

The *Coranich*, or ſinging at funerals, is ſtill in uſe in ſome places: the ſongs are generally in praiſe of the deceaſed; or a recital of the valiant deeds of him, or his anceſtors. I had not the fortune to be preſent at any in *North Britain*, but formerly aſſiſted at one in the South of *Ireland*, where it was performed in the fullneſs of horror. The cries are called by the *Iriſh* the *'Ulogohne* and *Hûllulu*, two words extremely expreſſive of the ſound uttered on theſe occaſions, and being of *Celtic* ſtock, Etymologiſts would ſwear to be the origin of the ολολυγων of the *Greeks*, and *Ululatus* of the *Latins*. *Virgil* is very fond of uſing the laſt, whenever any of his females are diſtreſſ-ed; as are others of the *Roman* Poets, and generally on occaſions ſimilar to this. CORANICH.

* This cuſtom was derived from their Northern anceſtors. *Longè ſecurius moriendum eſſe arbitrantur, quam vivendum: puerperia luctu,* funeraque *feſtivo cantu, ut in plurimum concelebrantes.* OLAUS MAGNUS. 116.

It was my fortune to arrive at a certain town in *Kerry*, at the time that a perſon of ſome diſtinction departed this life: my curioſity led me to the houſe, where the funeral ſeemed conducted in the pureſt claſſical form.

Quodcunque aſpicerem luctus gemituſque ſonabant,
Formaque non taciti funeris intùs erat.

In ſhort, the *conclamatio* was ſet up by the friends in the ſame manner as *Virgil* deſcribes that conſequential of *Dido*'s death.

Lamentis gemituque et fæmineo ululatu
Tecta fremunt.

Immediately after this followed another ceremony, fully deſcribed by *Cambden*, in his account of the manners of the antient *Iriſh*; the earneſt expoſtulations and reproaches given to the deceaſed, for quitting this world, where ſhe enjoyed ſo many bleſſings, ſo good a huſband, ſuch fine children. This cuſtom is alſo of great antiquity, for *Euryalus*'s mother makes the ſame pathetic addreſs to her dead ſon.

Tune illa ſenectæ
Sera meæ requies? potuiſti relinquere ſolam
Crudelis?

But when the time approached for carrying out the corps, the cry was redoubled,

Tremulis ululatibus æthera complent;

a numerous band of females waiting in the outer court, to attend the hearſe, and to pay (in chorus) the laſt tribute of their voices. The habit of this ſorrowing train, and the neglect of their perſons, were admirably ſuited to the occaſion: their robes were black, and flowing,

flowing, resembling the antient *Palla*; their feet naked, their hair long and disheveled: I might truely say,

> *Vidi egomet nigra succinctam vadere palla*
> CANIDIAM; *pedibus nudis, passoque capillo,*
> *Cum* SAGANA *majore ululantem.*

Among these mourners were dispersed the females who sung the praises of the deceased, and were in the place of the *Mulieres Præficæ* of the *Romans*, and like them, a mercenary tribe. I could not but observe that they over-did their parts, as *Horace* acquaints us the hireling mourners of his days did.

> *Ut qui conducti plorant in funera, dicunt*
> *Et faciunt prope plura dolentibus ex animo.*

The corps was carried slowly along the verge of a most beautifull lake, the *ululatus* was continued, and the whole procession ended among the venerable ruins of an old abby. But to return to *North Britain.*

Midwives give new-born babes a small spoonfull of earth and whisky, as the first food they taste.

Before women bake their bannocks, or oatmeal cakes, they make a cross on the last.

The notion of second-sight still prevales in a few places: as does the belief of Fairies; and children are watched till the christening is over, least they should be stole, or changed. FAIRIES.

Elf-shots, *i. e.* the stone arrow-heads of the old inhabitants of this island, are supposed to be weapons shot by Fairies at cattle, to which are attributed any disorders they have: in order to effect a cure, the cow is to be touched by an elf-shot, or made to drink the water in which one has been dipped. The same virtue is said to be found in the crystal gems*, and in the adder-stone, our *Glein*

* *Woodward's* Method of Fossils, p. 30. See also Mr. *Aubrey's* Miscellanies, p. 128.

Naidr;

Naidr; and it is alſo believed that good fortune muſt attend the owner; ſo, for that reaſon, the firſt is called *Clach Bhuai*, or the powerfull ſtone. Captain *Archibald Campbell* ſhewed me one, a ſpheroid ſet in ſilver, which people came for the uſe of above a hundred miles, and brought the water it was to be dipt in with them; for without that, in human caſes, it was believed to have no effect.

Theſe have been ſuppoſed to be *magical* ſtones or gems uſed by the *Druids*, to be inſpected by a chaſte boy, who was to ſee in them an apparition informing him of future events. This impoſture, as we are told by Doctor *Woodward*, was revived in the laſt century by the famous Doctor *Dee*, who called it his *ſhew ſtone* and *holy ſtone*, and pretended, by its means, to foretell events. I find in *Montfaucon**, that it was cuſtomary in early times to depoſite Balls of this kind in urns or ſepulchers: thus twenty were found at *Rome* in an alabaſtrine urn: and one was diſcovered in 1653, in the tomb of *Childeric* at *Tournai*; he was King of *France*, and died A. D. 480.

AUG. 2. Left *Carrie*, the houſe of Mr. *Campbell*, factor for the *Struan* eſtate, where I had a very hoſpitable reception the preceding night. Went due Eaſt; paſſed over a bridge croſs the *Tumel*, which diſcharges itſelf out of *Loch-Rannoch*. Not far off were ſome neat ſmall houſes, inhabited by veteran ſoldiers, who were ſettled here after the peace of 1748; had land, and three pounds in money given, and nine pounds lent, to begin the world with. In ſome few places this plan ſucceeded; but in general, was fruſtrated by the diſſipation of theſe new coloniſts, who could by no means reliſh an induſtrious life; but as ſoon as the money was ſpent, which ſeldom laſted long, left their tenements to be poſſeſſed by the next comer.

* *Les Monumens de la Monarchie Françoiſe.*

Saw

P. Sandby pinx.t P. Mazell sculp.t

View near Blair.

Saw a ftamping-mill, calculated to reduce lime-ftome to a fine powder, in order to fave the expence of burning, for manure. The ftampers beat it into fmall pieces in a trough, which a ftream of water paffed through, carrying off the finer parts into a proper receptacle, the grofs ones being ftopped by a grate. I did not find that this project anfwered; but was told, that the benefit the land was to receive from it, would not appear till the third year.

On going up a fteep hill, have a fine view of the lake. Where the mountains almoft clofe, is *Mount Alexander*, where *Struan* once refided, and which he called his hermitage: it is a moft romantic fituation, prettily wooded, impending over a fine bafon, formed by the *Tumel*, in a deep hollow beneath. At the bottom of this hill is *Argentine*, a little fountain; to which he gave that name from the filvery *micæ* it flings up: near this are feveral rude but beautifull walks amidft the rocks and trees, among which, in clefts and chafms, I was fhewn the hard bed of the poor poet, when his difloyalty had made it penal for him to fhew his head. Near this the rocks almoft meet, and the river rufhes with vaft violence between. Some outlawed *M'Gregors* were once furprized on the precipice, and all killed; one, who made a defperate leap upon a ftone in the middle of the water, and another to the oppofite fide, had the hard fate to be fhot in climbing the rocky fteeps. ARGENTINE.

A mile lower are the falls of the *Tumel*: I have feen higher; but, except that of the *Rhine*, never faw one with more water.

Afcend a very fteep and high hill through a great birch wood; a moft picturefque fcene, from the pendent form of the boughs waving with the wind from the bottom to the utmoft fummits of the

the mountain. On attaining the top, had a view of the beautifull little *Straith*, fertile and prettily wooded, with the river in the middle, forming numbers of quick meanders, then ſuddenly ſwelling into a lake, that fills the vale from ſide to ſide; is about three miles long, and retains the name of the river. After riding along a black moor, in ſight of vaſt mountains, arrive at

Blair *, or *Athol* Houſe, ſeated on an eminence above a plain, watered by the *Gary*, an outrageous ſtream, whoſe ravages have greatly deformed the vally, by the vaſt beds of gravel which it has left behind. The houſe was once fortified, and held a ſiege againſt the Rebels in 1746; but at preſent is much reduced in height, and the inſide highly finiſhed by the noble owner. The moſt ſingular piece of furniture is a cheſt of drawers made of broom, moſt elegantly ſtriped in veins of white and brown. This plant grows to a great ſize in *Scotland*, and furniſhes pieces of the breadth of ſix inches.

GREAT BROOM-TREES

Near the houſe is a fine walk ſurrounding a very deep glen finely wooded, but in dry weather deficient in water at the bottom; but on the ſide of the walk on the rock is a ſmall cryſtalline fountain, inhabited at that time by a pair of *Naiads*, in form of golden fiſh. In a ſpruce fir was a hang-neſt of ſome unknown bird, ſuſpended at the four corners to the boughs; it was open at top, an inch and a half in diameter, and two deep; the ſides and bottom thick, the materials moſs, worſted, and birch bark, lined with hair and feathers. The ſtreams afford the *Parr*, a ſmall ſpecies of Trout,

HANG-NEST.

PARR.

* Or a level clear ſpot of ground, a fit place for an engagement.

ſeldom

P. Sandby del. P. Mazell sculp.

YORKE CASCADE.

ſeldom exceeding eight inches in length, marked on the ſides with nine large bluiſh ſpots, and on the lateral line with ſmall red ones *.

No traveller ſhould omit viſiting *Yorke Caſcade*, a magnificent cataract, amidſt moſt ſuitable ſcenery, about a mile diſtant from the houſe.

This country is very mountainous, has no natural woods except of birch; but the vaſt plantations that begin to cloath the hills will amply ſupply theſe defects. There is a great quantity of oats raiſed in this neighborhood, and numbers of black cattle reared, the reſources of the exhauſted parts of *South Britain*.

KILLICRANKIE.

Viſit the paſs of *Killicrankie*, about five miles South of *Blair*: near the Northern entrance was fought the battle between the Viſcount *Dundee* and General *Mackay*, in which the firſt was killed in the moment of victory. The paſs is extremely narrow, between high mountains, with the *Gary* running beneath in a deep, darkſome, and rocky channel, over-hung with trees, forming a ſcene of horrible grandeur. The road through this ſtrait is very fine, formed by the ſoldiery lent by the Government, who have ſix-pence *per* day from the country beſides their pay. About a mile beyond the paſs, Mr. *Robertſon*'s, of *Faſkally*, appears like fairy ground amidſt theſe wild rocks, ſeated in a moſt beautifull meadow, watered by the river *Tumel*, ſurrounded with pretty hills finely wooded.

The Duke of *Athol*'s eſtate is very extenſive, and the country populous: while vaſſalage exiſted, the chieftain could raiſe two or three thouſand fighting men, and leave ſufficient at home to take

* *Br. Zool. illuſtr.*

care of the ground. The forests, or rather chases, (for they are quite naked) are very extensive, and feed vast numbers of Stags, which range, at certain times of the year, in herds of five hundred. Some grow to a great size: I have heard of one that weighed 18 stone, *Scots*, or 314 lb. exclusive of head, entrails and skin. The hunting of these animals was formerly after the manner of an *Eastern* monarch. Thousands of vassals surrounded a great tract of country, and drove the Deer to the spot where the Chieftains were stationed, who shot them at their leisure. The magnificent hunt, made by an Earl of *Athol*, near this place, for the amusement of *James* V. and the Queen-mother, is too remarkable to be omitted; the relation is therefore given as described by Sir *David Lindsay* of the *Mount* *, who, in all probability, assisted at it.

GREAT HUNTINGS.

" The Earl of *Athole*, hearing of the King's coming, made great " provision for him in all things pertaining to a prince, that he was " as well served and eased, with all things necessary to his estate, " as he had been in his own palace of *Edinburgh*. For I heard say, " this noble Earl gart make a curious palace to the King, to his " Mother, and to the Embassador, where they were so honourably " eased and lodged as they had been in *England*, *France*, *Italy*, or " *Spain*, concerning the time and equivalent, for their hunting and " pastime; which was builded in the midst of a fair meadow, a fair " palace of green timber, wind with green birks, that were green " both under and above, which was fashioned in four quarters, and " in every quarter and nuik thereof a great round, as it had been a " block-house, which was lofted and gested the space of three house

* *Hist. Scotland*, 146.

" height;

Moses Griffith del. P. Mazell sculp.

FASKALLY.

" height; the floors laid with green ſcarets ſpreats, medwarts and " flowers, that no man knew whereon he zeid, but as he had been " in a garden. Further, there were two great rounds in ilk ſide of " the gate, and a great portculleis of tree, failing down with the " manner of a barrace, with a draw-bridge, and a great ſtank of " water of ſixteen foot deep, and thirty foot of breadth. And alſo " this palace within was hung with fine tapeſtry and arraſſes of ſilk, " and lighted with fine glaſs windows in all airths; that this palace " was as pleaſantly decored, with all neceſſaries pertaining to a " prince, as it had been his own palace-royal at home. Further, " this Earl gart make ſuch proviſion for the King, and his Mother, " and the Embaſſador, that they had all manner of meats, drinks, " and delicates that were to be gotten, at that time, in all *Scotland*, " either in burgh or land; that is to ſay, all kind of drink, as ale, " beer, wine, both white and claret, *malvery*, *muſkadel*, *Hippocras*, " *aquavitæ*. Further, there was of meats, wheat-bread, main-bread " and ginge bread; with fleſhes, beef, mutton, lamb, veal, veni-" ſon, gooſe, grice, capon, coney, cran, ſwan, partridge, plover, " duck, drake, briſſel-cock and pawnes, black-cock and muir-" fowl, cappercaillies: and alſo the ſtanks, that were round about " the palace, were full of all delicate fiſhes, as ſalmonds, trouts, " pearches, pikes, eels, and all other kind of delicate fiſhes that " could be gotten in freſh waters; and all ready for the banket. " Syne were there proper ſtewards, cunning baxters, excellent cooks " and potingars, with confections and drugs for their deſerts; and " the halls and chambers were prepared with coſtly bedding, veſſel " and napery, according for a king, ſo that he wanted none of his " orders more than he had been at home in his own palace. The

 " King

"King remained in this wildernefs, at the hunting, the fpace of "three days and three nights, and his company, as I have fhewn. "I heard men fay, it coft the Earl of *Athole*, every day, in ex-"pences, a thoufand pounds."

But hunting meetings, among the great men, were often the preludes to rebellion; for under that pretence they collected great bodies of men without fufpicion, which at length occafioned an act of parlement prohibiting fuch dangerous affemblies.

AUG. 3. GLEN-TILT.

Set out for the county of *Aberdeen*; ride Eaftward over a hill into *Glen-Tilt*, famous in old times for producing the moft hardy warriors; is a narrow glen, feveral miles in length, bounded on each fide by mountains of an amazing height; on the South is the great hill of *Ben y glo*, whofe bafe is thirty-five miles in circumference, and whofe fummit towers far above the others. The fides of many of thefe mountains is covered with fine verdure, and are excellent fheep-walks: but entirely woodlefs. The road is the moft dangerous and the moft horrible I ever travelled: a narrow path, fo rugged that our horfes often were obliged to crofs their legs, in order to pick a fecure place for their feet; while, at a confiderable and precipitous depth beneath, roared a black torrent, rolling through a bed of rock, folid in every part but where the *Tilt* had worn its antient way. Salmon force their paffage even as high as this dreary ftream, in fpite of the diftance from the fea, and the difficulties they have to encounter.

Afcend a fteep hill, and find ourfelves on an *Arrie*, or tract of mountain which the families of one or two hamlets retire to with their flocks for pafture in fummer. Here we refrefhed ourfelves with.

W. Tomkyns Pinx.t P. Mazell. sculp.t

Broe-mar Castle.

with ſome goats' whey, at a *Sheelin*, or *Bothay*, a cottage made of turf, the dairy-houſe, where the Highland ſhepherds, or graziers, live with their herds and flocks, and during the fine ſeaſon make butter and cheeſe. Their whole furniture conſiſts of a few horn-ſpoons, their milking utenſils, a couch formed of ſods to lie on, and a rug to cover them. Their food oat-cakes, butter or cheeſe, and often the coagulated blood of their cattle ſpread on their bannocks. Their drink milk, whey, and ſometimes, by way of indulgence, whiſky. Such dairy-houſes are common to moſt mountainous countries: thoſe in *Wales* are called *Vottys*, or Summer-houſes; thoſe on the *Swiſs Alps*, *Sennes*. SHEELINS.

Dined on the ſide of *Loch-Tilt*, a ſmall piece of water, ſwarming with Trouts. Continued our journey over a wild, black, moory, melancholy tract. Reached *Brae-mar* †; the country almoſt inſtantly changed, and in lieu of dreary waſtes, a rich vale, plenteous in corn and graſs, ſucceeded. Croſs the *Dee* near its head, which, from an inſignificant ſtream, in the courſe of a very few miles, increaſes to the ſize of a great river, from the influx of numbers of other waters: and is remarkable for continuing near fifty miles of its courſe, from *Invercauld* to within ſix miles of *Aberdeen*, without any ſenſible augmentation. The rocks of *Brae-mar*, on the Eaſt, are exceedingly romantic, finely wooded with pine. The cliffs are very lofty, and their front moſt rugged and broken, with vaſt pines growing out of their fiſſures. BRAE-MAR.

On the North ſide of the river lies *Dalmore*, diſtinguiſhed by the fineſt natural pines in *Europe*, both in reſpect to the ſize of the trees FOREST OF DALMORE.

* *Brae*, ſignifies a ſteep face of any hill.

and

and the quality of the timber. Single trees have been fold out of it for fix guineas: they were from eighty to ninety feet high, without a collateral branch, and four feet and a half in diameter at the lower end. The wood is very refinous, of a dark red color, and very weighty. It is preferable to any brought from *Norway*, and being fawn into plank on the fpot, brings annually to the proprietor a large revenue. On the oppofite fide of the river is the eftate of *Inverey*, noted alfo for its pines, but of a fize inferior to thofe of *Dalmore*. When the river is fwelled with rains, great floats of timber from both thefe eftates are fent down into the Low Countries.

This tract abounding with game, was, in old times, the annual refort of numbers of nobility, who affembled here to pafs a month or two in the amufements of the chace. Their huntings refembled campaigns; they lived in temporary cottages, called *Lonquhards*, were all dreffed in an uniform habit conformable to that of the country, and paffed their time with jollity and good chear, moft admirably defcribed by *John Taylor*, the water poet, who, in 1618, made there his *Pennileffe Pilgrimage*, and defcribes, in page 135, the rural luxury with all the glee of a *Sancho Pança*.

" I thank my good Lord *Erfkin*," (fays the Poet) " hee com-" manded that I fhould alwayes bee lodged in his lodging, the " kitchen being alwayes on the fide of a banke, many kettles and " pots boyling, and many fpits turning and winding, with great " variety of cheere: as venifon bak'd, fodden, roft and ftu'de beefe, " mutton, goates, kid, hares, frefh falmon, pidgeons, hens, capons, " chickens, partridge, moore-coots, heath-cocks, caperkellies, and " termagants:

" termagants; good ale, sacke, white and claret, tent (or Allegant) " and most potent *aquavitæ* *.

" All these, and more than these, we had continually, in super-" fluous abundance, caught by faulconers, fowlers, fishers, and " brought by my Lord's *(Mar)* tenants and purveyors, to victual " our campe, which consisted of fourteen or fifteen hundred men, " and horses. The manner of the hunting is this: five or six hun-" dred men doe rise early in the morning, and they doe disperse " themselves divers wayes, and seven, eight, or ten miles compasse, " they doe bring or chase in the deer in many heards (two, three, " or four hundred in a heard) to such or such a place, as the noble-" men shall appoint them; then when day is come, the lords and " gentlemen

* The *French*, during the reign of *Charles* IX. seemed not only to have made full as large sacrifices to *Diana* and *Bacchus*, but even thought their entertainment incomplete without the presence of *Venus*. *Jacques du Fouilloux*, a celebrated writer on hunting of that age, with much seriousness describes all the requisites for the chace, and thus places and equips the jovial crew: --- ' L'Assemblée se doit faire ' en quelque beau lieu soubs des arbres auprès d'une fontaine ou Ruisseau, là ' ou les veneurs se doiuent tous rendre pour faire leur rapport. Ce pendant le ' Sommelier doit venir avec trois bons chevaux chargez d'instrumens pour *arrouser le* ' *gosier*, comme coutrets, barraux, barils, flacons et bouteilles: lesquelles doiuent ' estre pleines de bon vin *d'Arbois*, *de Beaume*, *de Chaloce et de Graue*: luy estant ' descendu du cheval, les metra refraischir en l'eau, ou bien les pourra faire refro-' idir avec du Canfre: apres il estranda la nappe sur la verdure. Ce fait, le cuisi-' nier s'en viendra chargé de plusieurs *bons harnois de gueule*, comme jambons, lan-' gues de bœuf fumées, groins, et oreilles de pourceau, cervelats, eschinées, pieces ' de bœuf de Saison, carbonnades, jambons de *Mayence*, pastez, longes de veau ' froides couuertes de poudre blanche, et autres menus suffrages pour remplir le ' boudin lequel il metra sur la nappe.

' Lors

" gentlemen of their companies doe ride or goe to the ſaid places, " ſometimes wading up to the middles through bournes and rivers; " and then they being come to the place, doe lye down on the " ground till thoſe foreſaid ſcouts, which are called the *Tinckhell*, " doe bring down the deer; but, as the proverb ſays of a bad " cooke, ſo theſe *Tinckhell* men doe lick their own fingers; for, " beſides their bowes and arrows which they carry with them, wee " can heare now and then a harguebuſe, or a muſquet, goe off, " which doe ſeldom diſcharge in vaine: then after we had ſtayed " three houres, or thereabouts, we might perceive the deer appeare " on the hills round about us, (their heads making a ſhew like a " wood) which being followed cloſe by the *Tinckhell*, are chaſed " down

' Lors le Roy ou le Seigneur avec ceux de ſa table eſtrendront leurs manteaux ' ſur l'herbe, et ſe coucheront de coſté deſſus, beuuans, mangeans, rians et ' faiſans grand chere;' and that nothing might be wanting to render the entertainment of ſuch a ſet of merry men complete, honeſt *Jacques* adds, ' et s'il y a ' quelque femme de reputation en ce pays qui faſſe plaiſir aux compagnons, elle ' doit etre alleguée, et ſes paſſages et remuemens de feſſes, attendant le rapport a ' venir.'

But when the great man ſallies out to the chace of foxes and badgers, he ſeems not to leave ſo important an affair to chance, ſo ſets off thus amply provided in his triumphal car; ' Le Seigneur,' (ſays *Fouilloux)* ' doit avoir ſa petite charrette, ' là où il ſera dedans, avec la Fillette agée de ſeize a dix ſept ans, laquelle luy ' frottera la teſte par les chemins. Toutes les chevilles et paux de la charrette ' doiuent eſtre garnis de flaccons et bouteilles, et doit avoir au bout de la charrette ' un coffre de bois, plein de coqs d'inde froids, jambons, langues de Bœufs et ' autre bons harnois de gueule. Et ſi c'eſt en temps d'hiver, il pourra faire porter ' ſon petit pavillon, et faire du feu dedans pour ſe chauffer, ou bien donner un ' coup en robbe a la nymphe.' *p.* 35, 75.

" down into the valley where wee lay; then all the valley on each " ſide being way-laid with a hundred couple of ſtrong Iriſh grey- " hounds, they are let looſe, as occaſion ſerves, upon the heard of " deere, that with dogs, gunnes, arrows, durks and daggers, in " the ſpace of two houres fourſcore fat deere were ſlaine, which " after are diſpoſed of ſome one way and ſome another, twenty or " thirty miles, and more than enough left for us to make merry " withall at our rendevouze. Being come to our lodgings, there " was ſuch baking, boyling, roſting and ſtewing, as if Cook Ruf- " fian had been there to have ſcalded the Devill in his feathers." But to proceed.

Paſs by the caſtle of *Brae-mar*, a ſquare tower, built about a hundred and fifty years ago, to curb the diſcontented chieftains; but at preſent unneceſſarily garriſoned by a company of foot, being rented by the Government from Mr. *Farquharſon*, of *Invercauld*, whoſe houſe I reach in leſs than half an hour.

Invercauld is ſeated in the centre of the *Grampian* hills, in a fertile vale, waſhed by the *Dee*, a large and rapid river: nothing can be more beautifull than the different views from the ſeveral parts of it. On the Northern entrance, immenſe ragged and broken crags bound one ſide of the proſpect; over whoſe grey ſides and ſummits is ſcattered the melancholy green of the picturesque pine, which grows out of the naked rock, where one would think nature would have denied vegetation.

A little lower down is the caſtle above-mentioned; formerly a neceſſary curb on the little kings of the conntry; but at preſent ſerves ſcarce any purpoſe, but to adorn the landſcape.

The views from the ſkirts of the plain, near *Invercauld*, are very great; the hills that immediately bound it are cloathed with trees, particularly with birch, whoſe long and pendent boughs, waving a vaſt height above the head, ſurpaſs the beauties of the weeping willow.

The Southern extremity is pre-eminently magnificent; the mountains form there a vaſt theatre, the boſom of which is covered with extenſive foreſts of pines: above, the trees grow ſcarcer and ſcarcer, and then ſeem only to ſprinkle the ſurface; after which vegetation ceaſes, and naked ſummits * of a ſurprizing height ſucceed, many of them topped with perpetual ſnow; and, as a fine contraſt to the ſcene, the great cataract of *Garval-bourn*, which ſeems at a diſtance to divide the whole, foams amidſt the dark foreſt, ruſhing from rock to rock to a vaſt diſtance.

Some of theſe hills are ſuppoſed to be the higheſt part of *Great Britain*: their height has not yet been taken, but the conjecture is made from the deſcent of the *Dee*, which runs from *Brae-mar* † to the ſea, above ſeventy miles, with a moſt rapid courſe.

In this vale the Earl of *Mar* firſt ſet up the Pretender's ſtandard on the 6th of *September* 1715; and in conſequence drew to deſtruction his own, and ſeveral of the moſt noble families of *North Britain*.

Rode to take a nearer view of the environs; croſſed the *Dee* on a good ſtone-bridge, built by the Government, and entered on

* The higheſt is called *Ben y bourd*, under which is a ſmall *Loch*, which I was told had ice the latter end of *July*.

† The moſt diſtant from the ſea of any place in *North Britain*.

excellent

excellent roads into a magnificent foreſt of pines of many miles extent. Some of the trees are of a vaſt ſize; I meaſured ſeveral that were ten, eleven, and even twelve feet in circumference, and near ſixty feet high, forming a moſt beautifull column, with a fine verdant capital. Theſe trees are of a great age, having, as is ſuppoſed, ſeen two centuries *. Their value is conſiderable; Mr. *Farquharſon* informed me, that by ſawing and retailing them, he has got for eight hundred trees five-and-twenty ſhillings each: they are ſawed in an adjacent ſaw-mill, into plank ten feet long, eleven inches broad, and three thick, and ſold for two ſhillings apiece. PINE FOREST.

Near this antient foreſt is another, conſiſting of ſmaller trees, almoſt as high, but very ſlender; one grows in a ſingular manner out of the top of a great ſtone, and notwithſtanding it ſeems to have no other nouriſhment than what it gets from the dews, is above thirty feet high.

The proſpect above theſe foreſts is very extraordinary, a diſtant view of hills over a ſurface of verdant pyramids of pines.

This whole tract abounds with game: the Stags at this time were ranging in the mountains; but the little Roebucks † were perpetually bounding before us; and the black game often ſprung under our feet. The tops of the hills ſwarmed with *Grous* and *Ptarmigans*. Green Plovers, Whimbrels, and Snow-flecks ‡, breed STAGS. ROES. BIRDS.

* Vide Appendix.

† Theſe animals are reared with great difficulty; even when taken young, eight out of ten generally die.

‡ *Br. Zool. illuſtr.* 17. *tab.* xi.

here: the laſt aſſemble in great flocks during winter, and collect ſo cloſely in their eddying flight, as to give the ſportſman opportunity of killing numbers at a ſhot. Eagles *, Peregrine Falcons, and Goſhawks breed here: the Falcons in rocks, the Goſhawks in trees: the laſt purſues its prey an end, and daſhes through every thing in purſuit; but if it miſſes its quarry, deſiſts from following it after two or three hundred yards flight. Theſe birds are proſcribed; half a crown is given for an eagle, a ſhilling for a hawk, or hooded crow.

Foxes are in theſe parts very ravenous, feeding on roes, ſheep, and even ſhe goats.

Rooks viſit theſe vales in autumn, to feed on the different ſort of berries; but neither winter nor breed here.

I ſaw flying in the foreſts, the greater Bulfinch of Mr. *Edwards*, *tab.* 123, 124. the *Loxia enucleator* of *Linnæus*, whoſe food is the ſeed of pine cones; a bird common to the North of *Europe* and *America*.

BIRCH WOODS.

On our return paſſed under ſome high clifts; with large woods of birch intermixed. This tree is uſed for all ſorts of implements of huſbandry, roofing of ſmall houſes, wheels, fuel; the Highlanders alſo tan their own leather with the bark; and a great deal of excellent wine is extracted from the live tree. Obſerved among theſe rocks a ſort of projecting ſhelf, on which had been a hut, acceſſible only by the help of ſome thongs faſtened by ſome very

* The Ring-tail Eagle, called here the Black Eagle. I ſuſpect, from the deſcription, that the Dotrel breeds here. I heard alſo of a bird, called here *Snatach na cuirn*, but could not procure it.

expert

expert climbers, to which the family got, in time of danger, in former days, with their moſt valuable moveables.

COTTAGES.

The houſes of the common people in theſe parts are ſhocking to humanity, formed of looſe ſtones, and covered with clods, which they call *devols*, or with heath, broom, or branches of fir: they look, at a diſtance, like ſo many black mole-hills. The inhabitants live very poorly, on oatmeal, barley-cakes, and potatoes; their drink whiſky, ſweetened with honey. The men are thin, but ſtrong; idle and lazy, except employed in the chace, or any thing that looks like amuſement; are content with their hard fare, and will not exert themſelves farther than to get what they deem neceſſaries. The women are more induſtrious, ſpin their own huſbands' cloaths, and get money by knitting ſtockings, the great trade of the country. The common women are in general moſt remarkably plain, and ſoon acquire an old look, and by being much expoſed to the weather without hats, ſuch a grin, and contraction of the muſcles, as heightens greatly their natural hardneſs of features: I never ſaw ſo much plainneſs among the lower rank of females: but the *ne plus ultra* of hard features is not found till you arrive among the fiſh-women of *Aberdeen*.

Tenants pay their rent generally in this country in money, except what they pay in poultry, which is done to promote the breed, as the gentry are ſo remote from any market. Thoſe that rent a mill pay a hog or two; an animal ſo deteſted by the Highlanders, that very few can be prevaled on to taſte it, in any ſhape. Labor is here very cheap, the uſual pay being fifty ſhillings a year, and two pecks of oatmeal a week.

Purſued

Purſued my journey Eaſt, along a beautifull road by the river ſide, in ſight of the pine foreſts. The vale now grows narrow, and is filled with woods of birch and alder. Saw on the road ſide the ſeats of gentlemen, high built, and once defenſible. The peaſants cultivate their little land with great care to the very edge of the ſtony hills. All the way are vaſt maſſes of granite, the ſame which is called in *Cornwall*, Moor-ſtone.

PASS OF BOLLITIR.

The Glen contracts, and the mountains approach each other. Quit the *Highlands*, paſſing between two great rocks, called the Paſs of *Bollitir*, a very narrow ſtrait, whoſe bottom is covered with the tremendous ruins of the precipices that bound the road. I was informed, that here the wind rages with great fury during winter, and catching up the ſnow in eddies, whirls it about with ſuch impetuoſity, as makes it dangerous for man or beaſt to be out at that time. Rain alſo pours down ſometimes in deluges, and carries with it ſtone and gravel from the hills in ſuch quantity, that I have ſeen the effects of theſe *ſpates*, as they are called, lie croſs the roads, as the *avelenches*, or ſnow-falls, do thoſe of the *Alps*. In many parts of the *Highlands* were *hoſpitia* for the reception of travellers, called by the *Scotch*, *Spittles*, or hoſpitals: the ſame were uſual in *Wales*, where they are ſtyled *Yſpytty*; and, in both places, were maintained by the religious houſes: as ſimilar *Aſylums* are to this day ſupported, in many parts of the *Alps*.

This paſs is the Eaſtern entrance into the Highlands. The country now aſſumes a new face: the hills grow leſs; but the land more barren, and is chiefly covered with heath and rock. The edges of the *Dee* are cultivated, but the reſt only in patches, among which is generally a groupe of ſmall houſes. There is alſo a change a change of trees, oak being the principal wood, but even that is fcarce.

On the South fide of the river is *Glen-Muik*, remarkable for a fine cataract formed by the river *Muik*, which after running for a confiderable way along a level moor, at once falls down a perpendicular rock of a femicircular form, called the *Lin of Muik*, into a hole of fo great a depth worn by the weight of water, as to be fuppofed by the vulgar to be bottomlefs. LIN OF MUIK.

Refrefhed my horfes at a hamlet called *Tullich*, and looking Weft, faw the great mountain *Laghin y gair*, which is always covered with fnow.

Almoft oppofite to the village of *Tullich* is *Pananich*, noted for the mineral water difcovered a few years ago, and found to be very beneficial in rheumatic and fcrophulous cafes, and complaints of the gravel. During fummer great numbers of people afflicted with thofe diforders refort there to drink the waters; and for their reception, feveral commodious houfes have already been built. PANANICH SPAW.

A little below *Tullich* ride over the South corner of the hill of *Culbleen*, where foon after the Revolution a blood-lefs battle was fought between King *William's* forces under the command of General *Mackay*, and fome gentlemen of the country with their dependents. The laft made fuch an expeditious retreat, that in derifion it was called *the race of Tullich*. HILL OF CULBLEEN.

The Hill of *Culbleen* is the South-Weft extremity of a range of mountains which form a deep femicircle, and enclofe on all fides except the South a very fruitful bottom, and five parifhes, called *Cromar*. The foil, excepting fome moors and little hills, is good to the foot of the mountains, and produces the beft barley in the

county

county of *Aberdeen.* *Cromar* is the entrance into the Low Countries; the *Erse* language has been disused in it for many ages, yet is spoken at this time six miles West in *Glen-gairn.*

HILL OF MORVERN. One of the mountains to the West is styled the Hill of *Morvern*, is of a stupendous height, and on the side next to *Cromar* almost perpendicular. From the top, the whole country as far as *Aberdeen*, thirty computed miles, seems from this height as a plain; and the prospect terminates in the *German* ocean. The other great mountains appear to sink to a common size; and even *Laghin y gair* abates of its grandeur. About four miles below *Culbleen*, at *Charles-Town*, ride on a line with the Hill of *Coul*, the South-East extremity of the *Cromar* mountains.

A little North of *Charles-Town* stands *Aboyne* Castle, the seat of the Earl of *Aboyne*, amidst large plantations; but his Lordship's pines in the forest of *Glen-Tanner* yield to none in *Scotland* excepting those of *Dalmore.*

Observed several vast plantations of pines, planted by gentlemen near their seats: such a laudable spirit prevales in this respect, that in another half-century it never shall be said, that to spy the nakedness of the land you are come.

Dine at the little village of *Kincardine.* Hereabouts the common people cultivate a great deal of cabbage. The oat-fields are inclosed with rude low mounds of stone.

Lay at a mean house at *Banchorie.* The country, from *Bollitir* to this place, dull, unless where varied by the windings of the river, or with the plantations.

AUG. 7. The nearer to *Aberdeen*, the lower the country grows, and the greater

greater the quantity of corn: in general, oats and barley; for there is very little wheat ſown in thoſe parts. Reach

ABERDEEN.

ABERDEEN, a fine city, lying on a ſmall bay formed by the *Dee*, deep enough for ſhips of two hundred tuns. The town is about two miles in circumference, and contains thirteen thouſand ſouls, and about three thouſand in the ſuburbs; but the whole number of inhabitants between the bridges *Dee* and *Don*, which includes both the *Aberdeens*, and the interjacent houſes, or hamlets, is eſtimated at twenty thouſand. It once enjoyed a good ſhare of the tobacco trade, but was at length forced to reſign it to *Glaſgow*, which was ſo much more conveniently ſituated for it. At preſent, its imports are from the *Baltic*, and a few merchants trade to the *Weſt Indies* and *North America*. Its exports are ſtockings, thread, ſalmon, and oatmeal: the firſt is a moſt important article, as appears by the following ſtate of it. For this manufacture, 20,800 pounds worth of wool is annually imported, and 1600 pounds worth of oil. Of this wool is annually made 69,333 dozen pairs of ſtockings, worth, at an average, 1l. 10s. *per* dozen. Theſe are made by the country people, in almoſt all parts of this great county, who get 4s. *per* dozen for ſpinning, and 14s. *per* dozen for knitting; ſo that there is annually paid them 62,329l. 14s. And beſides, there is about 2000l. value of ſtockings manufactured from the wool of the county, which encourages the breed of ſheep much; for even as high as *Invercauld*, the farmer ſells his ſheep at twelve ſhillings apiece, and keeps them till they are four or five years old, for the ſake of the wool. About 200 combers are alſo employed conſtantly. The thread manufacture is another conſiderable article, tho' trifling in compariſon of the woollen.

STOCKING TRADE.

SALMON. The ſalmon fiſheries on the *Dee* and the *Don*, are a good branch of trade: about 46 boats, and 130 men, are employed on the firſt; and in ſome years, 167,000 ℔. of fiſh have been ſent pickled to *London*, and about 930 barrels of ſalted fiſh exported to *France*, *Italy*, &c. The fiſhery on the *Don* is far leſs conſiderable.

The town of *Aberdeen* is in general well built, with granite from the neighboring quarries. The beſt ſtreet, or rather *place*, is the Caſtle-ſtreet: in the middle is an octagon building, with neat bas relievos of the Kings of *Scotland*, from *James* I. to *James* VII. The Town-houſe makes a good figure, and has a handſome ſpire in the centre.

The Eaſt and Weſt churches are under the ſame roof; for the *North Britons* obſerve œconomy even in their religion: in one I obſerved a ſmall ſhip hung up; a votive offering frequent enough in *Popiſh* churches, but appeared very unexpectedly here. Some vindicate the practiſe, and ſay that the ſhip only denotes the right the mariners have to a ſitting place beneath; but perhaps much may be ſaid on both ſides.

ANDREW CANT. In the church-yard lies *Andrew Cant*, miniſter of *Aberdeen*, from whom the Spectator derives the word to *cant*; but, in all probability, *Andrew* canted no more than the reſt of his brethren, for he lived in a whining age *; the word therefore ſeems to be derived from *canto*, from their ſinging out their diſcourſes. The inſcription on his monument ſpeaks of him in very high terms, ſtyles him *vir ſuo ſeculo ſummus, qui orbi huic et urbi eccleſiaſtes, voce et vita inclinatam religionem ſuſtinuit, degeneres mundi mores refinxit, ardens*

* In *Charles* the Firſt's time.

et amans BOANERGES *et* BARNABAS, MAGNES *et* ADAMUS, &c. &c.

In the ſame place are multitudes of long-winded epitaphs; but the following, though ſhort, has a moſt elegant turn:

Si fides, ſi humanitas, multoque gratus lepore candor;
Si ſuorum amor, amicorum charitas, omniumque Benevolentia ſpiritum reducere poſſent,
Haud heic ſitus eſſet Johannes Burnet *a* Elrick. 1747.

The college is a large old building, founded by *George* Earl of *Marechal*, 1593. On one ſide is this ſtrange inſcription; probably alluding to ſome ſcoffers at that time: COLLEGE

They have ſeid,
Quhat ſay thay?
Let Yame ſay.

In the great room are ſeveral good pictures. A head of the Founder. The preſent Lord *Marechal* when young, and General *Keith*, his brother. Biſhop *Burnet* in his robes, as Chancellor of the Garter. A head of *Mary Stuart*, in black, with a crown in one hand, a crucifix in the other. *Arthur Jonſton*, a fine head, by *Jameſon*. *Andrew Cant*, by the ſame. *Gordon*, of *Strabloch*, publiſher of the maps; Doctor *Gregory*, author of the reflecting teleſcope; and ſeveral others, by *Jameſon*.

In the library is the alcoran on vellum, finely illuminated.

A *Hebrew* Bible, Manuſcript, with Rabbinical notes, on vellum.

Iſidori excerpta ex libro: a great curioſity, being a complete natural hiſtory, with figures, richly illuminated on ſquares of plated gold, on vellum.

 A Pa-

A Paraphrase on the Revelation, by *James* VI. with notes, in the King's own hand.

A fine missal.

There are about a hundred and forty students belonging to this college.

The convents in *Aberdeen* were; one of *Mathurines*, or of the order of the Trinity, founded by *William* the *Lion*, who died in 1214: another of *Dominicans*, by *Alexander* II.: a third of *Observantines*, a building of great length in the middle of the city, founded by the citizens, and Mr. *Richard Vaus*, &c.: and a fourth of *Carmelites*, or White Friers, founded by *Philip de Arbuthnot* in 1350. In the ruins of this was discovered a very curious silver chain, six feet long, with a round plate at one end, and at the other a pear-shaped appendage; which is still preserved in the library.

SCHOOL. The grammar-school is a low but neat building. *Gordon*'s

HOSPITAL. hospital is handsome; in front is a good statue of the founder: it maintains forty boys, children of the inhabitants of *Aberdeen*, who are apprenticed at proper ages.

The infirmary is a large plain building, and sends out between eight and nine hundred cured patients annually.

On the side of the Great Bleachery, which is common to the town, are the publick walks. Over a road, between the Castle-street and the Harbour, is a very handsome arch, which must attract the attention of the traveller.

On the East of the town is a work begun by *Cromwel*, from whence is a fine view of the sea: beneath is a small patch of ground, noted for producing very early barley, which was then reaping.

Prices

Prices of provifions in this town were thefe: Beef, (16 ounces to the pound) 2 d. ½. to 5 d.; mutton the fame; butter, (28 ounces to the pound) 6 d. to 8 d.; cheefe, ditto, 4 d. to 4 d. ½.; a large pullet, 6 d. or 10 d.; duck, the fame; goofe, 2 s. 3 d. PROVISIONS.

Crofs the harbour to the granite quarries that contribute to fupply *London* with paving-ftones. The ftone lies either in large nodules or in fhattery beds; are cut into fhape, and the fmall pieces for the middle of the ftreets are put on board for feven fhillings *per* tun, the long ftones at ten-pence *per* foot. GRANITE QUARRY.

The bridge of *Dee* lies about two miles S. of the town, and confifts of feven neat arches: before the building of that of *Perth* it was efteemed the fineft ftructure of the kind in *North Britain*. It was founded and is ftill fupported by funds deftined for that purpofe by Bifhop *Elphinfton*; and the following infcription on the buttrefs of a ruinous ifle in the cathedral of old *Aberdeen*, informs us of the architect: — '*Thomas* the fon of *Thomas French* mafter 'mafon who built the bridge of *Dee* and this ifle, is enterred at the 'foot hereof, who died *Anno* 1530.'

AUG. 8. OLD ABERDEEN.

Vifited old *Aberdeen*, about a mile North of the new; a poor town, feated not far from the *Don*. The college is built round a fquare, with cloifters on the South fide. The chapel is very ruinous within; but there ftill remains fome wood-work of exquifite workmanfhip. This was preferved by the fpirit of the Principal at the time of the reformation, who armed his people and checked the blind zeal of the Barons of the *Mearns*, who after ftriping the cathedral of its roof, and robbing it of the bells, were going to violate this feat of learning. They fhipped their facrilegious booty with

with an intention of expoſing it to ſale in *Holland* *; but the veſſel had ſcarcely gone out of port, but it periſhed in a ſtorm with all its ill gained lading.

The college was founded in 1494 by *William Elphinſton*, Biſhop of this place, and Lord Chancellor of *Scotland* in the reign of *James* III.; and Lord Privy Seal in that of *James* IV. He was a perſon of ſuch eminence, that his cotemporaries firmly believed that his death was preſaged by various prodigies, and that ſupernatural voices were heard at his interrment, as if Heaven more peculiarly intereſted itſelf in the departure of ſo great a character †.

The library is large. The moſt remarkable things are; *John Treviſa*'s tranſlation of *Higden's Polychronicon*, in 1387; the manuſcript excellently wrote, and the language very good, for that time. A very neat *Dutch* miſſal, with elegant paintings on the margin. Another, of the angels appearing to the ſhepherds, with one of the men playing on the bagpipes. A manuſcript catalogue of the old treaſury of the college.

Hector Boethius was the firſt Principal of the college, and ſent for from *Paris* for that purpoſe, on an annual ſalary of forty marks, *Scots*, at thirteen-pence each. The ſquare tower on the ſide of the college was built by contributions from General *Monk* and the Officers under him, then quartered at *Aberdeen*, for the reception of ſtudents; of which there are about a hundred belonging to the college, who lie in it.

* *Spotſwood's Hiſt. Church of Scotland.* 6.

† *Boethius*'s Hiſt. of the Biſhops of *Aberdeen*.

In Biſhop *Elphinſton*'s hall is a picture of Biſhop *Dunbar*, who finiſhed the bridge of *Dee*, and completed every thing elſe that the other worthy Prelate had begun. Beſides this are portraits of *Forbes*, Biſhop of *Aberdeen*, and Profeſſors *Sandiland* and *Gordon*, by *Jameſon*. The *Sybils*: ſaid to be done by the ſame hand, but ſeemed to me in too different a ſtyle to be his; but the *Sybilla Ægyptiaca* and *Erythræa* are in good attitudes.

The cathedral is very antient; no more than the two very antique ſpires and one iſle, which is uſed as a church, are now remaining. This Biſhoprick was founded in the time of *David* I. who tranſlated it from *Mortlick* in *Bamffſhire* to this place.

From a *tumulus*, called *Tillie dron*, now covered with trees, is a fine view of an extenſive and rich country; once a moſt barren ſpot, but by the induſtry of the inhabitants brought to its preſent ſtate. A pretty vale bordered with wood, the cathedral ſoaring above the trees, and the river *Don*, form all together a moſt agreeable proſpect. Theſe are comprehended in the pleaſure grounds of *Seaton*, the houſe of *George Middleton*, Eſq; which lies well ſheltered in the North-Weſt corner of the valley, and was probably the firſt villa built in the North of *Scotland* according to the preſent idea of elegance.

Beneath are ſome cruives, or wears, to take ſalmon in. The owners are obliged by law to make the rails of the cruives * of a certain width, to permit fiſh of a certain ſize to paſs up the river;

* Cruives, &c. ſhall have their heeke two inches wide, that the fry may paſs. *Rob.* I.

but

but as that is neglected, they pay an annual ſum to the owners of the fiſheries which lie above, to compenſate the loſs.

In the *Regiam Majeſtatem* are preſerved ſeveral antient laws relating to the ſalmon fiſheries, couched in terms expreſſive of the ſimplicity of the times.

From *Saturday* night till *Monday* morning, they were obliged to leave a free paſſage for the fiſh, which is ſtyled the *Saterdayes Sloppe* *.

Alexander I. enacted, 'That the ſtreame of the water ſal be in 'all parts ſwa free, that ane ſwine of the age of three zeares, well 'feed, may turne himſelf within the ſtreame round about, ſwa that 'his ſnowt nor taill ſall not touch the bank of the water.

'Slayers of reide fiſh or ſmoltes of ſalmond, the third time are 'puniſhed with death. And ſic like he quha commands the ſamine 'to be done.' *Jac.* IV. *parl.* 6. *ſtat. Rob.* III.

AUG. 9. Continue my journey: paſs over the bridge of *Don*; a fine gothic arch flung over that fine river, from one rock to the other; the height from the top of the arch to the water is ſixty feet; its width ſeventy-two. It was built by *Henry de Cheyn*, Biſhop of *Aberdeen* and nephew to *John Cummin* Lord of *Badenoch*, who ſuffering exile for his attachment to the faction of the *Cummins*, on his being reſtored to his ſee, applied all the profits that had accumulated during his abſence, towards this magnificent work †. Ride for ſome miles on the ſea ſands; paſs through *Newburgh*, a ſmall village, and at low water ford the *Ythen*, a river productive

* *Alex.* I.

† *Keith's Scotch Biſhops.* 65. This Prelate was living in 1333.

of

P. Mazell Sculp.

THE BRIDGE OF DON.

of the pearl muſcle: go through the pariſh of *Furvie*, now entirely overwhelmed with ſand, (except two farms) and about 500l. *per ann.* loſt to the *Errol* family, as appears by the oath of the factor, made before the court of ſeſſions in 1600, to aſcertain the miniſter's ſalary. It was at that time all arable land, now covered with ſhifting ſands, like the deſerts of *Arabia*, and no veſtiges remain of any buildings, except a ſmall fragment of the church.

INUNDATION OF SAND.

The country now grows very flat; produces oats; but the crops are conſiderably worſe than in the preceding country. Reach

Bowneſs, or *Buchaneſs*, the ſeat of the Earl of *Errol*, perched like a Falcon's neſt, on the edge of a vaſt cliff above the ſea. The drawing-room, a large and very elegant apartment, hangs over it; the waves run in wild eddies round the rocks beneath, and the ſea fowl clamor above and below, forming a ſtrange proſpect and ſingular chorus. The place was once defenſible, there having been a ditch and draw-bridge on the acceſſible ſide; but now both are deſtroyed.

Above five miles South is *Slains*, the remains of the old family caſtle, ſeated ſtrongly on a peninſulated rock; but demoliſhed in 1594, by *James* VI. on the rebellion of the Earl of *Huntly*. Near this place are ſome vaſt caverns, once filled with curious ſtalactical incruſtations, but now deſtroyed, in order to be burnt into lime; for there is none in this country, that uſeful commodity being imported from the Earl of *Elgin*'s works on the *Firth* of *Forth*.

Here the ſhore begins to grow bold and rocky, and indented in a ſtrange manner with ſmall and deep creeks, or rather immenſe and

BULLERS OF BUCHAN. horrible chaſms. The famous *Bullers* of *Buchan* lie about a mile North of *Bowneſs*, are a vaſt hollow in a rock, projecting into the ſea, open at top, with a communication to the ſea through a noble natural arch, through which boats can paſs, and lie ſecure in this natural harbour. There is a path round the top, but in ſome parts too narrow to walk on with ſatisfaction, as the depth is about thirty fathom, with water on both ſides, being bounded on the North and South by ſmall creeks.

Near this is a great inſulated rock, divided by a narrow and very deep chaſm from the land. This rock is pierced through midway between the water and the top, and in great ſtorms the waves ruſh through it with vaſt noiſe and impetuoſity. On the ſides, as well

KITTIWAKES. as thoſe of the adjacent cliffs, breed multitudes of *Kittiwakes* *. The young are a favorite diſh in *North Britain*, being ſerved up a little before dinner, as a whet for the appetite; but, from the rank ſmell and taſte, ſeem as if they were more likely to have a contrary effect. I was told of an honeſt gentleman who was ſet down for the firſt time to this kind of whet, as he ſuppoſed; but after demoliſhing half a dozen, with much impatience declared, that he had eaten *ſax*, and did not find himſelf a bit *more* hungry than before he began.

FISHERY OF SEA DOGS. On this coaſt is a great fiſhery of Sea Dogs †, which begins the laſt week of *July*, and ends the firſt in *September*. The livers are boiled for oil; the bodies ſplit, dried, and ſold to the common

* *Br. Zool. illuſtr.* 26. *tab.* xxiii.

† The picked Dog, *Br. Zool.* III. 77.

people,

people, who come from great diſtances for them. Very fine Turbots are taken on this coaſt; and towards *Peterhead* are good fiſheries of Cod and Ling. The Lord of the Manour has 3l. 6s. 8d. *per annum* from every boat, (a ſix-man boat) but if a new crew ſets up, the Lord, by way of encouragement, finds them a boat. Beſides theſe, they have little yawls for catching bait at the foot of the rocks. Muſcles are alſo much uſed for bait, and many boat's loads are brought for that purpoſe from the mouth of the *Ythen*. Of late years, a very ſucceſsful ſalmon fiſhery has been ſet up in the ſandy bays below *Slains*. This is performed by long nets, carried out to ſea by boats, a great compaſs taken, and then hawled on ſhore. It is remarked, theſe fiſh ſwim againſt the wind, and are much better taſted than thoſe taken in freſh waters.

Moſt of the labor on ſhore is performed here by the women: they will carry as much fiſh as two men can lift on their ſhoulders, and when they have ſold their cargo and emptied their baſket, will re-place part of it with ſtones: they go ſixteen miles to ſell or barter their fiſh; are very fond of finery, and will load their fingers with trumpery rings, when they want both ſhoes and ſtockings. The fleet was the laſt war ſupplied with great numbers of men from this and other parts of *Scotland*, as well as the army: I think near 70,000 engaged in the general cauſe, and aſſiſted in carrying our glory through all parts of the globe: of the former, numbers returned; of the latter, very few.

HOUSES.

The houſes in this country are built with clay, tempered in the ſame manner as the *Iſraelites* made their bricks in the land of *Ægypt*: after dreſſing the clay, and working it up with water, the laborers place on it a large ſtratum of ſtraw, which is trampled into it and made ſmall by horſes: then more is added, till it arrives at a proper conſiſtency, when it is uſed as a plaiſter, and makes the houſes very warm. The roofs are *ſarked*, *i. e.* covered with inch-and-half deal, ſawed into three planks, and then nailed to the joiſts, on which the ſlates are pinned.

The land proſpect is extremely unpleaſant; for no trees will grow here, in ſpite of all the pains that have been taken: not but in former times it muſt have been well wooded, as is evident from the numbers of trees dug up in all the bogs. The ſame nakedneſs prevales over great part of this coaſt, even far beyond *Bamff*, except in a few warm bottoms.

The corn of this tract is oats and barley; of the laſt I have ſeen very good cloſe to the edges of the cliffs. Rents are paid here partly in caſh, partly in kind; the laſt is commonly ſold to a contractor. The land here being poor, is ſet cheap. The people live hardly: a common food with them is *ſowens*, or the groſſer part of the oatmeal with the huſks, firſt put into a barrel with water, in order to grow ſour, and then boiled into a ſort of pudding, or flummery.

AUG. 11. Croſſed the country towards *Bamff*, over oatlands, a coarſe ſort of downs, and ſeveral black heathy moors, without a ſingle tree for numbers of miles.

CRAIGSTON CASTLE.

See *Craigſton* caſtle, a good houſe, once defenſible, ſeated in a ſnug bottom, where the plantations thrive greatly. Saw here a head of *David Leſly*, an eleve of *Guſtavus Adolphus*: a ſucceſsfull General againſt the royal cauſe; unfortunate when he attempted to ſupport it: loſt the battle of *Dunbar*, being forced to engage contrary to his judgement by the enthuſiaſm of the Preachers: marched with an unwilling army to the fatal battle of of *Worcester*; conscious of its disaffection or its fears, he sunk beneath his apprehensions; was dispirited and confounded: after the fight, lost his liberty and reputation; but was restored to both at the restoration by *Charles* II. who created him Baron of *Newark*. Another head of Sir *Alexander Frazier*, the Knight of *Dores*; both by *Jameson*. Passed by a small ruined castle, in the parish of *Kinedward*, seated on a round hill in a deep glen, and scarce accessible: the antient name of this castle was *Kin*, or *Kyn-Eden*, and said to have been one of the seats of the *Cummins*, Earls of *Buchan*. Ford the *Devron*, a fine river, over which had been a beautifull bridge, now washed away by the floods. Enter *Bamffshire*, and reach its capital

Bamff, pleasantly seated on the side of a hill; has several streets; but that with the town-house in it, adorned with a new spire, is very handsome. This place was erected into a borough by virtue of a charter from *Robert* II. dated Octob. 7: 1372, endowing it with the same privileges and putting it on the same footing with the burgh of *Aberdeen*; but tradition says it was founded in the reign of *Malcolm Canmore*. The harbour is very bad, as the entrance at the mouth of the *Devron* is very uncertain, being often stopped by the shifting of the sands, which are continually changing, in great storms; the pier is therefore placed on the outside. Much salmon is exported from hence. About *Troop* head, some kelp is made; and the adventurers pay the Lord of the Manour 50l. *per ann.* for the liberty of collecting the materials. BAMFF.

Bamff had only one monastery, that of the *Carmelites*, dedicated to the Virgin *Mary*; whose rents, place and lands were bestowed on *King's College* in *Aberdeen* in 1617 by *James* VI.

The Earl of *Finlater* has a houſe, prettily ſeated on an eminence near the town, with ſome plantations of ſhrubs and ſmall trees, which have a good effect in ſo bare a country. The proſpect is very fine, commanding the rich meadows near the town, *Down* a ſmall but well-built fiſhing-town, the great promontory of *Troop-head*, and to the North the hills of *Roſsſhire*, *Sutherland*, and *Cathneſs*.

The houſe once belonged to the *Sharps*; and the violent Arch-biſhop of that name was born here. In one of the apartments is a picture of *Jameſon* by himſelf, ſitting in his painting-room, dreſſed like *Rubens*, and with his hat on, and his pallet in his hand. On the walls are repreſented hung up, the pictures of *Charles* I. and his Queen; a head of his own wife; another head; two ſea views, and *Perſeus* and *Andromeda*, the productions of his various pencil.

DUFF HOUSE. *Duff* Houſe, a vaſt pile of building, a little way from the town, is a ſquare, with a ſquare tower at each end; the front richly ornamented with carving, but, for want of wings, has a naked look: the rooms within are very ſmall, and by no means anſwer the magnificence of the caſe.

In the apartments are theſe pictures: *Frances*, Dutcheſs of *Richmond*, full length, in black, with a little picture at her breaſt; Æt. 57, 1633, by *Vandyck*: was gran-daughter by the father to *Thomas* Duke of *Norfolk*; to *Edward Stafford* Duke of *Buckingham* by the mother. A Lady who attempted the very *climax* of matrimony: firſt married the ſon of a rich vintner; gave hopes after his death to a Knight, Sir *G. Rodney*, who on being jilted by her for an Earl, *Edward* Earl of *Hertford*, wrote to her in his own blood a well-compoſed copy of verſes, and then fell on his ſword: having buried

buried the Earl, gave her hand to *Ludovic* Duke of *Richmond* and *Lenox*, and on his deceaſe ſpread her nets for the *old monarch James* I. Her avarice kept pace with her vanity: when viſited by the great, ſhe had all the parade of officers, and gentlemen who attended: tables were ſpread, as if there had been ample proviſion; but the moment her viſitors were gone, the cloths were taken off, and her train fed with a moſt ſcanty fare. Her pride induced her to draw up an inventory of moſt magnificent preſents ſhe wiſhed the world to believe ſhe had given to the Queen of *Bohemia*; preſents of maſſy plate that exiſted only on paper*. Beſides this ſingular character, are two fine heads of *Charles* I. and his Queen. A head of a *Duff* of *Corſenday*, with ſhort grey hair, by *Coſmo Alexander*, deſendent of the famous *Jameſon*. Near the houſe is a ſhrubbery, with a walk two miles long, leading to the river.

About two miles Weſt of *Bamff*, not far from the ſea, is a great ſtratum of ſand and ſhells, uſed with ſucceſs as a manure. Sea tang is alſo much uſed for corn lands, ſometimes by itſelf, ſometimes mixed with earth, and left to rot: it is beſides often laid freſh on graſs, and anſwers very well. Paſſed by the houſe of *Boyne*, a ruined caſtle, on the edge of a ſteep glen, filled with ſome good aſh and maples. AUG. 12.

Near *Portſoy*, a ſmall town in the pariſh of *Fordyce*, is a large ſtratum of marble, in which *aſbeſtos* has been ſometimes found: it is a coarſe ſort of *Verd di Corſica*, and uſed in ſome houſes for chimney-pieces. *Portſoy* is the principal place in this pariſh, and contains about ſix hundred inhabitants, who carry on a conſiderable

* Vide *Wilſon*'s Life of *James* I. 258, 259.

thread

thread manufacture, and one of snuff: there also belong to the town twelve ships, from forty to a hundred tuns burden; and there are in the parish six fishing boats, each of whose crew consists of six men and a boy. Reach

CULLEN HOUSE.

Cullen House, seated at the edge of a deep glen full of very large trees, which being out of the reach of the sea winds, prosper greatly. This spot is very prettily laid out in walks, and over the entrance is a magnificent arch sixty feet high, and eighty-two in width. The house is large, but irregular. The most remarkable pictures are, a full length of *James* VI. by *Mytens*: at the time of the revolution, the mob had taken it out of *Holy-Rood* House, and were kicking it about the streets, when the Chancellor, the Earl of *Finlater*, happening to pass by, redeemed it out of their hands. A portrait of *James* Duke of *Hamilton*, beheaded 1649, in a large black cloak, with a star, by *Vandyck*. A half-length of his brother, by the same, killed at the battle of *Worcester*. *William* Duke of *Hamilton*, president of the revolution parlement, by *Kneller*. Old Lord *Bamff*, aged 90, with a long white square beard, who is said to have incurred the censure of the church, at that age, for his galantries *.

* Among other pictures of persons of merit, that of the admirable *Crichton* must not be overlooked. I was informed, that there is one of that extraordinary person in the possession of *Alexander Morrison*, Esq; of *Bagnie*, in the county of *Bamff*; it is in the same apartment with some of *Jameson*'s, but seems done by a superior hand: came into Mr. *Morrison*'s possession from the family of *Crichton*, Viscount *Frendraught*, to whom *Crichton* probably sent it from *Italy*, where he spent the last years of his short, but glorious life. Vide Appendix.

Not

Not far from *Cullen* Houſe are the ruins of the caſtle of *Finlater*, ſituated on a high rock projecting into the ſea. It was ſtrengthened in 1455 by Sir *Walter Oglevie*, who had licence from *James* II. to build a tower and fortalice at his caſtle of *Finlater*. It continued in poſſeſſion of the family till it was uſurped by the family of the *Gordons*; but was reſtored to the right heirs about the year 1562, by Queen *Mary*, who for that purpoſe cauſed it to be inveſted both by ſea and land.

The country round *Cullen* has all the marks of improvement, owing to the * indefatigable pains of the late noble owner, in advancing the art of agriculture and planting, and every other uſefull buſineſs, as far as the nature of the ſoil would admit. His ſucceſs in the firſt was very great; the crops of beans, peas, oats, and barley, were excellent; the wheat very good, but, through the fault of the climate, will not ripen till it is late, the harveſt in theſe parts being in *October*. The plantations are very extenſive, and reach to the top of *Binn* hill; but the farther they extend from the bottoms, the worſe they ſucceed.

The town of *Cullen* is mean; yet has about a hundred looms in it, there being a flouriſhing manufacture of linnen and thread, of which near fifty thouſand pounds worth is annually made there and in the neighborhood. Upwards of two thouſand bolls of wheat, barley, oats and meal are paid annually by the tenants to their

* His Lordſhip collected together near 2000 ſouls, to his new town at *Keith*, by *feuing*, i. e. giving in perpetuity, on payment of a ſlight acknowledgement, land ſufficient to build a houſe on, with gardens and back-yard.

landlords, and by them ſold to the merchants and exported: and beſides, the upper parts of the pariſh yield peas, and great quantities of oats, which are ſold by thoſe tenants who pay their rents in caſh.

Near this town the Duke of *Cumberland*, after his march from *Bamff*, joined the reſt of his forces from *Straith-Bogie*, and encamped at *Cullen*.

In a ſmall ſandy bay are three lofty ſpiring rocks, formed of flinty maſſes, cemented together very differently from any ſtratum in the country. Theſe are called the three Kings of *Cullen*. A little farther is another vaſt rock, pierced quite through, formed of pebbly concretions lodged in clay, which had ſubſided in thick but regular layers.

CAIRNS. In this country are ſeveral *Cairns* or Barrows, the places of interment of the antient *Caledonians*, or of the *Danes*, for the method was common to both nations. At *Kil-hillock*, or the Hill of burial, near *Glaſſaugh*, was a very remarkable one demoliſhed about fourteen years ago. The diameter was ſixty feet, the height ſixteen; formed entirely of ſtones brought from the ſhore, as appears by the limpets, muſcles, and other ſhells mixed with them. The whole was covered with a layer of earth four feet thick, and that finiſhed with a very nice coat of green ſod, incloſing the whole. It ſeems to have been originally formed by making a deep trench round the ſpot, and flinging the earth inwards: then other materials brought to complete the work, which muſt have been that of an whole army. On breaking open this *Cairn*, on the ſummit of the ſtony heap beneath the integument of earth was found a ſtone coffin formed of long flags, and in it the complete ſkeleton of a human body,

Urn found near Bamff.

body, lain at full length with every bone in its proper place: and with them a deer's horn, the ſymbol of the favorite amuſement of the deceaſed.

About five years ago another *Cairn* was broke open near the ſame place; and in it was found another coffin about ſix feet long with a ſkeleton, an urn and ſome charcoal: a conſiderable deal of charcoal was alſo met with intermixed every where among the ſtones of the *Cairn*. By this it appears that the mode of interment was various at the ſame period; for one of theſe bodies muſt have been placed entire in its cæmetery, the other burnt and the aſhes collected in the urn.

A third *Cairn* on the farm of *Brankanentim* near *Kil-hillock* was opened very lately; and in the middle was found a coffin only two feet ſquare, made of flag-ſtones ſet on their edge, and another by way of cover. The urn was ſeated on the ground, filled with aſhes, and was ſurrounded in the coffin with charcoal and bones, probably bones belonging to the ſame body, which had not been reduced to aſhes like the contents of the urn.

A fourth urn was diſcovered in a *Cairn* on the hill of *Down*, overlooking the river *Devron* and town of *Bamff*. This was alſo placed in a coffin of flat ſtones, with the mouth downwards ſtanding on another ſtone. The urn was ornamented; but round it were placed three others, ſmaller and quite plain. The contents of each were the ſame; aſhes, burnt bones, flint arrow heads with almoſt vitrified ſurfaces, and a piece of flint of an oval ſhape flatted, two inches long, and an inch and a half thick. There was alſo in the larger urn and one of the leſſer, a ſmall ſlender bone four inches long, and ſomewhat incurvated and perforated at the thicker end:

it is apparently not human; but the animal it belonged to, and the use, are unknown.

The materials of the urns appear to have been found in the neighborhood; and consist of a coarse clay mixed with small stones and sand, and evidently have been only dried and not burnt. By the appearance of the inside of the larger urn, it is probable that it was placed over the bones while they were hot and full of oil; the whole inside being blackened with the steam; and where it may have been supposed to have been in contact with them, the stain pervades the entire thickness. The urn was thirteen inches high.

The urn in the manner it was found; the small bones; and one of the arrow heads (of which no less than thirteen were found in the greatest urn) are engraven from a fine drawing communicated to me by the Rev. Mr. *Laulie*, Minister of *Fordyce*.

Besides is a numerous assemblage of *Cairns* on the *Cotton* hill, a mile South of *Birkenbog*, probably in memory of the slain in the victory obtained in 988, by *Indulphus*, over the *Danes*. The battle chiefly raged on a moor near *Cullen*, where there are similar barrows; but as it extended far by reason of the * retreat of the vanquished, these seem to be flung together with the same design.

Not far from these are two circles of long stones, called *Gael-cross*: perhaps they might have been erected after that battle; and as *Gaul* is the *Erse* word for a stranger or enemy †, as the *Danes* were, I am the more inclined to suppose that to have been the fact.

Nor is there wanting a retreat of the inhabitants in time of war;

* *Buchanan, lib.* vi. *c.* 19.

† Doctor *Macpherson,* p. 240.

for

for round the top of the hill of *Durn* is a triple entrenchment ſtill very diſtinct; the middle of ſtone, and very ſtrong in the moſt acceſſible place: and ſuch faſtneſſes were far from being unneceſſary in a tract continually expoſed to the ravages of the *Danes*.

The vault of the family of *Abercrombies* in this pariſh muſt not be paſſed over in ſilence: it is lodged in the wall of the church, and is only the repoſitory of the ſculls. The bodies are depoſited in the earth beneath; and when the Laird dies, the ſcull of his predeceſſor is taken up and flung into this Golgotha, which at preſent is in poſſeſſion of nineteen.

Some ſuperſtitions ſtill lurk even in this cultivated country. The farmers carefully preſerve their cattle againſt witchcraft by placing boughs of the mountain aſh and honeyſuckle in their cow houſes on the 2d of *May*. They hope to preſerve the milk of their cows, and their wives from miſcarriage by tying red threads about them: they bleed the ſuppoſed witch to preſerve themſelves from her charms: they viſit the well of *Spey* for many diſtempers, and the well of *Drachaldy* for as many, offering ſmall pieces of money and bits of rags. The young people determine the figure and ſize of their huſbands by drawing cabbages blindfold on All-Hallows even; and like the *Engliſh* fling nuts into the fire; and in *February* draw *Valentines*, and from them collect their future fortune in the nuptial ſtate.

AUG. 13.

Paſſed through a fine open country, full of gentle riſings, and rich in corn, with a few clumps of trees ſparingly ſcattered over it. Great uſe is made here of ſtone marle, a gritty indurated marle, found in vaſt ſtrata, dipping pretty much: it is of different colors, blue, pale brown, and reddiſh; is cut out of the quarry, and laid very

STONE MARLE.

very thick on the ground in lumps, but will not wholly dissolve under three or four years. In the quarry is a great deal of sparry matter, which is laid apart, and burnt for lime. Arrive at

CASTLE GORDON.

Castle Gordon, a large old house, the seat of the Duke of *Gordon*, lying in a low wet country, near some large well-grown woods, and a considerable one of great hollies. It was founded by *George* second Earl of *Huntly*; and was originally called the castle of the bog of *Gight*. It inherits at present very little of its former splendor: by accident I met with an old print that shews it in all the magnificence described by a singular traveller of the middle of the last century. '*Bogagieth*,' (says he) 'the Marquiss of *Huntley*'s palace, 'all built of stone facing the ocean, whose fair front (set prejudice 'aside) worthily deserves an *Englishman*'s applause for her lofty and 'majestick towers and turrets, that storm the air; and seemingly 'make dents in the very clouds. At first sight I must confess, it 'struck me with admiration to gaze on so gaudy and regular 'a frontispiece; more especially to consider it in the nook of a 'nation.' *

The principal pictures in *Castle Gordon* are, the first Marquiss of *Huntly*; who on his first arrival at court forgetting the usual obeisance, was asked why he did not bow: he begged his Majesty's pardon, and excused his want of respect by saying he was just come from a place where every body bowed to him. Second Marquiss

* Northern Memoirs, &c. by RICHARD FRANKS, *Philanthropus*. *London* 1694. 12mo. This Gentleman made his journey in 1658, and went through *Scotland* as far as the water of *Brora* in *Sutherland* to enjoy as he traveled, the amusement of angling.

of

OLD CASTLE GORDON?

of *Huntly*, beheaded by the Covenanters. His ſon, the gallant Lord *Gordon*, *Montroſe*'s friend, killed at the battle of *Auldford*. Lord *Lewis Gordon*, a leſs generous warrior; the plague * of the people of *Murray*, (then the ſeat of the Covenanters) whoſe character, with that of the brave *Montroſe*, is well contraſted in theſe old lines:

> If ye with *Montroſe* gae, ye'l get ſic and wae enough;
> If ye with Lord *Lewis* gae, ye'l get rob and rave enough.

The head of the ſecond Counteſs of *Huntly*, daughter of *James* I. Sir *Peter Frazier*, a full length, in armour. A fine ſmall portrait of the *Abbé d' Aubigné*, ſitting in his ſtudy. A very fine head of St. *John* receiving the revelation; a beautifull expreſſion of attention and devotion.

The Duke of *Gordon* ſtill keeps up the diverſion of falconry, and had ſeveral fine Hawks, of the Peregrine and gentle Falcon ſpecies, which breed in the rocks of *Glenmore*. I ſaw alſo here a true Highland gre-hound, which is now become very ſcarce: it was of a very large ſize, ſtrong, deep cheſted, aad covered with very long and rough hair. This kind was in great vogue in former days, and uſed in vaſt numbers at the magnificent ſtag-chaſes, by the powerfull Chieftains. FALCONRY

* Whence this proverb,

> ' The Guil, the *Gordon*, and the Hooded Craw,
> ' Were the three worſt things *Murray* ever ſaw.'

Guil is a weed that infeſts corn. It was from the caſtle of *Rothes*, on the *Spey*, that Lord *Lewis* made his plundering excurſions into *Murray*.

I ſaw

I alſo ſaw here a dog the offſpring of a Wolf and *Pomeranian* bitch. It had much the appearance of the firſt, was very good natured and ſportive; but being ſlipped at a weak Deer it inſtantly brought the animal down and tore out its throat. This dog was bred by Mr. *Brook*, animal-merchant, in *London*, who told me that the congreſs between the wolf and the bitch was immediate, and the produce at the litter was ten.

THE SPEY. The *Spey* is a dangerous neighbor to *Caſtle Gordon*; a large and furious river, overflowing very frequently in a dreadfull manner, as appears by its ravages far beyond its banks. The bed of the river is wide and full of gravel, and the channel very ſhifting.

The Duke of *Cumberland* paſſed this water at *Belly* church, near this place, when the channel was ſo deep as to take an officer, from whom I had the relation, and who was ſix feet four inches high, up to the breaſt. The banks are very high, and ſteep; ſo that, had not the Rebels been providentially ſo infatuated as to neglect oppoſition, the paſſage muſt have been attended with conſiderable loſs.

The ſalmon fiſhery on this river is very great: about ſeventeen hundred barrels full are caught in the ſeaſon, and the ſhore is rented for about 1200l. *per annum*.

AUG. 14. FOCHABERS. Paſſed through *Fochabers*, a wretched town, cloſe to the caſtle. Croſſed the *Spey* in a boat, and landed in the county of *Murray*.

The peaſants' houſes, which, throughout the ſhire of *Bamff*, were very decent, were now become very miſerable, being entirely made

made of turf: the country partly moor, partly cultivated, but in a very ſlovenly manner.

Between *Fochabers* and *Elgin* on the right lies *Innes*, once the ſeat of the very antient family of that name, whoſe annals are marked with great calamities. I ſhall recite two which ſtrongly paint the manners of the times, and one of them alſo the manners of that abandoned Stateſman the Regent Earl of *Morton*. I ſhall deliver the tales in the ſimple manner they are told by the hiſtorian of the houſe.

'This man *Alexander Innes* 20th heir of the houſe (though very 'gallant) had ſomething of particularyty in his temper, was proud 'and poſitive in his deportment, and had his lawſuits with ſeverall 'of his friends, amongſt the reſt with *Innes* of *Pethnock*, which had 'brought them both to *Edinburgh* in the yeir 1576, as I take it, 'qn the laird haveing met his kinſman at the croſs, fell in words 'with him for dareing to give him a citation; in choller either 'ſtabed the Gentleman with a degger or piſtoled him (for it was 'variouſly reported). when he had done, his ſtomach would not 'let him fly but he walked up and doun on the ſpott as if he had 'done nothing that could be quareled, his friends lyfe being a thing 'that he could diſpoſe of without being bound to count for it to 'any oyn. and yn ſtayed till the Earle of *Mortune* who was Regent 'ſent a gaurd and caried him away to the caſtell, but qn he found 'truely the danger of his circumſtance and yt his proud raſh action 'behooved to coſt him his lyfe, he was then free to redeem that at 'any rate and made ane agreement for a remiſſione with the regent 'at the pryce of the barrony of *Kilmalemnock* which this day extends 'to 24 thouſand marks rent yeirly. the evening after the agreement 'was made and writt, being merry with his friends at a collatione 'and talking anent the deirnefs of the ranfome the regent hade made 'him pay for his lyfe, he waunted that hade his foot once loofs he 'would faine fee q[t] the Earle of *Mortune* durft come and poffefs 'his lands: q[ch] being told to the regent that night, he refolved to 'play fuir game with him, and therefore though q[t] he fpoke was 'in drink, the very next day he put the fentence of death in execu-'tione ag[t] him by caufing his head to be ftruck of in the caftle 'and y[n] poffeft his eftate.'

The other relation, ftill more extraordinary, is given in the Appendix.

ELGIN. Dine at *Elgin* *, a good town, with many of the houfes built over piazzas: excepting its great cattle fairs, has little trade; but is remarkable for its ecclefiaftical antiquities. The cathedral had been a magnificent pile, but is now in ruins. *Jonfton*, in his *Encomia Urbium*, celebrates the beauty of *Elgin*, and laments the fate of this noble building:

Arcibus heroum nitidis urbs cingitur, intus
Plebeii radiant, nobiliumque Lares:
Omnia delectant, veteris fed rudera templi
Dum fpectas, lachrymis, Scotia *tinge genas.*

The Weft door is very elegant, and richly ornamented. The choir very beautifull, and has a fine and light gallery running round it;

* *Celticè* Belle ville. In the Appendix is a full and accurate account not only of *Elgin*, but of feveral parts of the county of *Murray*, by the venerable Mr. *Shaw*, Minifter of *Elgin*, aged ninety, and eminent for his knowledge of the antiquities of his country.

and

P. Mazell sculp

ELGIN.

and at the East end are two rows of narrow windows in an excellent gothic taste. The chapter-house is an octagon, the roof supported by a fine single column, with neat carvings of coats of arms round the capital. There is still a great tower on each side of this cathedral; but that in the centre, with the spire and whole roof, are fallen in, and form most awefull fragments, mixed with the battered monuments of Knights and Prelates. *Boethius* says that *Duncan*, who was killed by *Macbeth* at *Inverness*, lies buried here. Numbers of modern tomb-stones also crowd the place; a proof how difficult it is to eradicate the opinion of local sanctity, even in a religion that affects to despise it.

The cathedral was founded by *Andrew de Moray* * in 1224, on a piece of land granted by *Alexander* the II.: and his remains were deposited in the choir under a tomb of blue marble in 1244. The great tower was built principally by *John Innes*, Bishop of this See, as appears by the inscription cut on one of the great pillars: *Hic jacet in Xto Pater et Dominus, Dominus* Johannes de Innes *hujus ecclesiæ episcopus — qui hoc notabile opus incepit et per septennium edificavit* †.

About a mile from hence is the castle of *Spinie*; a large square tower, and a vast quantity of other ruined buildings, still remain, which shews its antient magnificence whilst the residence of the Bishops of *Murray*: the lake of *Spinie* almost washes the walls; is about five miles long, and half a mile broad, seated in a flat country. During winter, great numbers of wild swans migrate hither; and I have been told, that some have bred here. *Boethius* ‡ says they resort here for the sake of a certain herb called after their name, SPINIE.

* *Keith's Bishops of Scotland*. 81.

† M. S. Hist. of the *Innes* family.

‡ *Scotorum* Regni descr. ix.

Not far from *Elgin* is a ruined Chapel, and Preceptory; called *Maiſon dieu.* Near it is a large gravelly cliff, from whence is a beautifull view of the town, cathedral, a round hill with the remains of a caſtle, and beneath is the gentle ſtream of the *Loſſie,* the *Loxia* of *Ptolemy.*

PLUSCAIRDIN PRIORY.

Three miles ſouth is the Priory of *Pluſcairdin,* in a moſt ſequeſtred place; a beautifull ruin, the arches elegant, the pillars well turned, and the capitals rich *.

Croſs the *Loſſie,* ride along the edge of a vale, which has a ſtrange mixture of good corn and black turberies: on the road-ſide is a mill-ſtone quarry.

Arrive in the rich plain of *Murray,* fertile in corn; and the upper parts of the country produce great numbers of cattle. The view of the *Firth* of *Murray,* with a full proſpect of the high mountains of *Roſsſhire* and *Sutherland,* and the magnificent entrance into the bay of *Cromartie* between two lofty hills, form a fine piece of ſcenery.

KINLOSS ABBY.

Turn about half a mile out of the road to the north, to ſee *Kinloſs,* an abby of *Ciſtercians,* founded by *David* I. in 1150. Near this place was murdered by thieves *Duffus,* King of *Scotland:* on the diſcovery of his concealed body it was removed to *Jona,* and interred there with the reſpect due to his merit. The Prior's chamber, two ſemicircular arches, the pillars, the couples of ſeveral of the roofs, afford ſpecimens of the moſt beautifull gothic architecture in all the elegance of ſimplicity, without any of its fantaſtic ornaments. Near the abby is an orchard of apple and pear trees, at leſt coeval with the laſt Monks; numbers lie proſtrate; their venerable branches

* As I was informed, for I did not ſee this celebrated abby.

ſeem

ſeem to have taken freſh roots, and were loaden with fruit, beyond what could be expected from their antique look.

Near *Forres*, on the road-ſide, is a vaſt column, three feet ten inches broad, and one foot three inches thick: the height above ground is twenty-three feet; below, as it is ſaid, twelve or fifteen. On one ſide are numbers of rude figures of animals and armed men, with colors flying: ſome of the men ſeemed bound like captives. On the oppoſite ſide was a croſs, included in a circle, and raiſed a little above the ſurface of the ſtone. At the foot of the croſs are two gigantic figures, and on one of the ſides is ſome elegant fret-work.

GREAT COLUMN.

This is called King *Sueno*'s ſtone; and ſeems to be, as Mr. *Gordon** conjectures, erected by the *Scots*, in memory of the final retreat of the *Danes*: it is evidently not *Daniſh*, as ſome have aſſerted; the croſs diſproves the opinion, for that nation had not then receiv-ed the light of chriſtianity.

On a moor not far from *Forres*, *Boethius*, and *Shakeſpear* from him, places the rencountre of *Macbeth* and the three wayward ſiſters or witches. It was my fortune to meet with but one, which was ſomewhere not remote from the ruins of *Kyn-Eden*: ſhe was of a ſpecies far more dangerous than theſe, but neither *withered*, *nor wild in her attire*, but ſo fair,

She look'd not like an inhabitant o' th' Earth!

Boethius tells his ſtory admirably well: but entirely confines it to the predictions of the three fatal ſiſters, which *Shakeſpear* has ſo finely copied in the IVth ſcene of the 1ſt act. The Poet, in con-

* *Itin. Septentr.* 158.

formity

formity to the belief of the times, calls them witches; in fact they were the *Fates*, the *Valkyriæ** of the northern nations, *Gunna*, *Rota*, and *Skulda*, the handmaids of *Odin*, the arctic *Mars*, and ſtyled the *Chuſers of the ſlain*, it being their office in battle to mark thoſe devoted to death.

> We the reins to ſlaughter give,
> Ours to kill, and ours to ſpare:
> Spite of danger he ſhall live,
> (Weave the crimſon web of war).†

Boethius, ſenſible of part of their buſineſs, calls them *Parcæ*: and *Shakeſpear* introduces them juſt going upon their employ,

> When ſhall we three meet again
> In thunder, lightning, or in rain?
> *When the hurly-burly's done,*
> *When the battle's loſt or won.*

But all the fine incantations that ſucceed, are borrowed from the fancifull *Diableries* of old times, but ſublimed, and purged from all that is ridiculous by the creative genius of the inimitable Poet, of whom *Dryden* ſo juſtly ſpeaks:

> But SHAKESPEAR's magic cou'd not copied be,
> Within that circle none durſt walk but he.

* From *Walur*, ſignifying the ſlaughter in battle, and *Kyria* to obtain by choice: for their office, beſides ſelecting out thoſe that were to die in battle, was to conduct them to *Valhalla*, the Paradiſe of the brave, the Hall of *Odin*. Their numbers are different, ſome make them three, others twelve, others fourteen; are deſcribed as being very beautifull, covered with the feathers of ſwans, and armed with ſpear and helmet. *Vide* Bartholinus *de cauſ. contempt. mortis.* 553, 554, & *notæ vet. Stephanii in Sax. Gramm.* 88. & Torfæus. p. 36.

† *Gray.*

But

We laugh at the magic of others; but *Shakeſpear's* makes us tremble. The windy caps * of King *Eric*, and the vendible knots of wind of the *Finland* † magicians appear infinitely ridiculous; but when our Poet dreſſes up the ſame idea, how horrible is the ſtorm he creates!

Though you *untie* the winds, and let them fight
Againſt the churches; though the yeſty waves
Confound and ſwallow navigation up;
Though bladed corn be lodged and trees blown down;
Though caſtles topple on their warder's heads;
Though palaces and pyramids do ſlope
Their heads to their foundations; though the treaſure
Of nature's genius tumble all together,
Even till deſtruction ſicken, anſwer me
To what I aſk.

Lay at *Forres*, a very neat town, ſeated under ſome little hills, which are prettily divided. In the great ſtreet is the town houſe with a handſome cupolo, and at the end is an arched gateway, which has a good effect. On a hill Weſt of the town are the poor remains of the caſtle, from whence is a fine view of a rich country, interſperſed with groves, the bay of *Findorn*, a fine baſon, almoſt round, FORRES.

* King *Eric* was a great magician, who by turning his cap, cauſed the wind to blow according to his mind.

† Solebant aliquando *Finni*, negotiatoribus in eorum littoribus contraria ventorum tempeſtate impeditis, ventum venalem exhibere, mercedeque oblata, tres nodos magicos non caſſioticos loro conſtrictos eiſdem reddere, eo ſervato moderamine ut ubi primum *diſſolverint*, ventos haberent placidos; ubi alterum, vehementiores; at ubi tertium *laxaverint* ita ſævas tempeſtates ſe paſſuros, &c. *Olaus Magnus* de gent. Sept. 97.

with

with a narrow ſtrait into it from the ſea, and a melancholy proſpect of the eſtate of *Cowbin*, now nearly overwhelmed with ſand. This ſtrange inundation is ſtill in motion, but moſtly in the time of a weſt wind: it moves along the ſurface with an even progreſſion, but is ſtopped by water, after which it forms little hills: its motion is ſo quick, that a gentleman aſſured me he had ſeen an apple-tree ſo covered with it, in one ſeaſon, as to leave only a few of the green leaves of the upper branches appearing above the ſurface. An eſtate of about 300l. *per ann.* has been thus overwhelmed; and it is not long ſince the chimnies of the principal houſes were to be ſeen: it began about eighty years ago, occaſioned by the cutting down the trees, and pulling up the bent, or ſtarwort, which gave occaſion at laſt to the act 15th *G.* II. to prevent its farther ravages, by prohibiting the deſtruction of that plant.

INUNDATION OF SAND.

A little N. E. of the Bay of *Findorn*, is a piece of land projecting into the ſea, called *Brugh* or *Burgh*. It appears to have been the landing place of the *Danes* in their deſtructive deſcents on the rich plains of *Murray*: it is fortified with foſſes; and was well adapted to ſecure either their landing or their retreat.

AUG. 15.

Croſs the *Findorn*; land near a friable rock of whitiſh ſtone, much tinged with green, an indication of copper. The ſtone is burnt for lime. From an adjacent eminence is a pictureſque view of *Forres*. About three miles farther is *Tarnaway* Caſtle, the antient ſeat of the Earls of *Murray*. The hall, called *Randolph*'s Hall, from its founder Earl *Randolph*, one of the great ſupporters of *Robert Bruce*, is timbered at top like *Weſtminſter Hall*: its dimenſions are 79 feet by 35, 10 inches, and ſeems a fit reſort for Barons and their vaſſals. In the rooms are ſome good heads: one of

TARNAWAY CASTLE.

of a youth, with a ribband of ſome order hanging from his neck. *Sir William Balfour*, with a black body to his veſt, and brown ſleeves, a gallant commander on the parlement's ſide in the civil wars; celebrated for his retreat with the body of horſe from *Leſtwithiel* in face of the King's army: but juſtly branded with ingratitude to his maſter, who by his favor to *Sir William* in the beginning of his reign, added to the popular diſcontents then ariſing. The Fair, or *Bonny* Earl of *Murray*, as he is commonly called, who was murdered, as ſuppoſed, on account of a jealouſy *James* VI. entertained of a paſſion the Queen had for him: at leſt ſuch was the popular opinion, as appears from the old ballad on the occaſion:

He was a braw Gallant,
And he played at the Gluve;*
And the bonny Earl of *Murray*,
Oh! he was the Queene's Love.

There are beſides, the heads of his lady and daughter; all on wood, except that of the Earl. To the ſouth-ſide of the caſtle are large birch woods, abounding with Stags and Roes.

AULDEARNE.

Continued my journey weſt to *Auldearne*. Am now arrived again in the country where the *Erſe* ſervice is performed. Juſt beneath the church is the place where *Montroſe* obtained a ſignal victory over the Covenanters, many of whoſe bodies lie in the church,

* For *Glaive*, an old word for a ſword.

'Then furth he drew his truſty *Glaive*,
Quhyle thouſands all arround,
Drawn frae their ſheaths glanſt in the ſun,
And loud the Bougills ſound.'

Hardyknute.

with an inſcription, importing, according to the cant of the time, that they died fighting for their religion and their king. I was told this anecdote of that hero: That he always carried with him a *Cæſar*'s Commentaries, on whoſe margins were written, in *Montroſe*'s own hand, the generous ſentiments of his heart, verſes out of the *Italian* Poets, expreſſing contempt of every thing but glory.

Have a diſtant view of *Nairn*, a ſmall town near the ſea, on a river of the ſame name, the ſuppoſed *Tuaeſis* of *Ptolemy*. Ride through a rich corn country, mixed with deep and black turberies, which ſhew the original ſtate of the land, before the recent introduction of the improved method of agriculture. Reach *Calder*

CAWDOR. Caſtle, or *Cawdor*, as *Shakeſpear* calls it, once the property of its *Thanes*. The antient part is a great ſquare tower; but there is a large and more modern building annexed, with a drawbridge.

All the houſes in theſe parts are caſtles, or at leſt defenſible; for, till the year 1745, the Highlanders made their inroads, and drove away the cattle of their defenceleſs neighbors. There are ſaid to exiſt ſome very old marriage articles of the daughter of a chieftain, in which the father promiſes for her portion, 200 *Scots* marks, and the half of a *Michaelmas moon*, i. e. half the plunder, when the nights grew dark enough to make their excurſions. There is likewiſe in being a letter from Sir *Ewin Cameron* to a chief in the neighborhood of the county of *Murray*, wherein he regrets the miſchief that had happened between their people (many having been killed on both ſides) as his clan had no intention of falling on the *Grants* when it left *Lochaber*, *but only to make an incurſion into* MURRAY-LAND *where every man was free to take his prey*. This ſtrange notion ſeems to have ariſen from the county having been for

ſo

ſo many ages a *Pictiſh* country, and after that under the dominion of the *Danes*, and during both periods in a ſtate of perpetual warfare with the *Scots* and weſtern Highlanders, who (long after the change of circumſtances) ſeem quite to have forgot that it was any crime to rob their neighbors of *Murray*.

Rode into the woods of *Calder*, in which were very fine birch trees and alders, ſome oak, great broom, and juniper, which gave ſhelter to the Roes. Deep rocky glens, darkened with trees, bound each ſide of the wood: one has a great torrent roaring at its diſtant bottom, called the Brook of *Achneem*: it well merits the name of *Acheron*, being a moſt fit ſcene for witches to celebrate their nocturnal rites in.

A JOUG.

Obſerved on a pillar of the door of *Calder* church, a *joug*, i. e. an iron yoke, or ring, faſtened to a chain; which was, in former times, put round the necks of delinquents againſt the rules of the church, who were left there expoſed to ſhame during the time of divine ſervice; and was alſo uſed as a puniſhment for defamation, ſmall thefts, &c.: but theſe penalties are now happily aboliſhed. The clergy of *Scotland*, the moſt decent and conſiſtent in their conduct of any ſet of men I ever met with of their order, are at preſent much changed from the furious, illiterate, and enthuſiaſtic teachers of the old times, and have taken up the mild method of perſuaſion, inſtead of the cruel diſcipline of corporal puniſhments. Science almoſt univerſally flouriſhes among them; and their diſcourſe is not leſs improving than the table they entertain the ſtranger at is decent and hoſpitable. Few, very few of them, permit the bewitchery of diſſipation to lay hold of them, notwithſtanding they allow all the innocent pleaſures of others, which, though not criminal in the layman, they know, muſt bring

SCOTCH CLERGY.

 the

the taint of levity on the churchman. They never ſink their characters by midnight brawls, by mixing with the gaming world, either in cards, cocking, or horſe-races, but preſerve with a narrow income, a dignity too often loſt among their brethren ſouth of the *Tweed.**

The

* THE APOLOGY.

FRIEND. ' YOU, you in fiery purgat'ry muſt ſtay,
' Till gall and ink and dirt of ſcribbling day
' In purifying flames are purg'd away.

TRAVELLER. ' O truſt me dear D*** I ne'er would offend
' One pious divine, one virtuous friend,
' From nature alone are my characters drawn,
' From little *Bob Jerom* to biſhops in lawn;
' O truſt me dear Friend I never did think on
' The Holies who dwell near th' O'erlooker of *Lincoln.*
' Not a prelate or prieſt did e'er haunt my ſlumber,
' Who inſtructively teach betwixt *Tweeda* and *Humber*;
' Nor in South, Eaſt, or Weſt do I ſtigmatiſe any
' Who ſtick to their texts, and thoſe are the MANY.
' But when croſſing and joſtling come queer men of G-d,
' In ruſty brown coats and waiſtcoats of plaid;
' With greaſy cropt hair, and hats cut to the quick,
' Tight white leathern breeches, and ſmart little ſtick;
' Clear of all that is ſacred from bowſprit to poop ſir;
' Who prophane like a pagan, and ſwear like a trooper;
' Who ſhine in the cock-pit, on turf and in ſtable,
' And are the prime bucks and arch wags of each table;
' Who if they e'er deign to thump drum eccleſiaſtic,

' Spout

The *Scotch* livings are from 40l. *per annum* to 150l. *per annum*; a decent houſe is built for the miniſter on the glebe, and about ſix acres of land annexed. The church allows no curate, except in caſe of ſickneſs or age, when one, under the title of helper, is appointed; or, where the livings are very extenſive, a miſſionary or aſſiſtant is allotted; but ſine cures, or ſine-cured preferments, never diſgrace the church of our ſiſter kingdom. The widows and children are of late provided for out of a fund eſtabliſhed by two acts, 17th and 22d *G.* II.* SCOTCH LIVINGS.

'Spout new fangled doctrine enough to make man ſick;
'And lay down a goſpel, but not from their Bibles,
'That good-natur'd vices are nothing but foibles;
'And vice are refining till vice is no more,
'From taking a bottle to taking a *****.
'Then if in theſe days ſuch apoſtates appear,
'(For ſuch I am told are found there and here)
'O pardon dear Friend a well-meaning zeal,
'Too unguardedly telling the ſcandal I feel:
'It touches not you, let the galled jades winch,
'Sound in morals and doctrine you never will flinch.
'O Friend of paſt youth, let me think of the fable
'Oft told with chaſte mirth at your innocent table,
'When inſtructively kind, wiſdom's rules you run o'er,
'Reluctant I leave you, inſatiate for more;
'So, bleſt be the day that my joys will reſtore.'

* An account of the government of the church of *Scotland* was communicated to me by the Reverend Mr. *Brodie*, the late worthy miniſter of *Calder*. Vide Appendix.

Croſs

Crofs the *Nairn*; the bridge large, but the ftream inconfiderable, except in floods. On the Weft is *Kilravoch* Caftle, and that of *Dalcrofs*. Keep due North, along the military road from *Perth*; pafs along a narrow low piece of land, projecting far into the *Firth*, called *Arderfier*, forming a ftrait fcarce a mile over, between this county and that of *Cromartie* *. At the end of this point is *Fort George*, a fmall but ftrong and regular fortrefs, built fince 1745, as a *place d'armes:* it is kept in excellent order; but, by reafon of the happy change of the times, feemed almoft deferted: the barracks are very handfome, and form feveral regular and good ftreets.

FORT GEORGE.

Lay at *Cambeltown*, a place confifting of numbers of very mean houfes, owing its rife and fupport to the neighboring fort.

AUG. 16. CULLODEN.

Paffed over *Culloden Moor*, the place that *North Britain* owes its prefent profperity to, by the victory of *April* 16, 1746. On the fide of the Moor are the great plantations of *Culloden* Houfe, the feat of the late *Duncan Forbes*, a warm and active friend to the houfe of *Hanover*, who fpent great fums in its fervice, and by his influence, and by his perfuafions, diverted numbers from joining in rebellion; at length he met with a cool return, for his attempt to fheath, after victory, the unfatiated fword. But let a veil be flung over a few exceffes confequential of a day, productive of fo much benefit to the united kingdoms.

The young adventurer lodged here the evening preceding the battle; diftracted with the averfion of the common men to difcipline, and the diffenfions among his officers, even when they were at the brink of deftruction, he feemed incapable of acting, could

* Between which plies a ferry-boat.

be

be ſcarcely perſuaded to mount his horſe, never came into the action, as might have been expected from a prince who had his laſt ſtake to play, but fled ingloriouſly to the old traitor *Lovat* *, who, I was told, did execrate him to the perſon who informed him that he was approaching as a fugitive; foreſeeing his own ruin as the conſequence †.

The Duke of *Cumberland*, when he found that the barges of the fleet attended near the ſhore for the ſafety of his perſon, in caſe of a defeat, immediately ordered them away, to convince his men of the reſolution he had taken of either conquering or periſhing with them.

* His Lordſhip was at that time expecting the event of the battle, when a perſon came in and informed him, that he ſaw the Prince riding full ſpeed, and alone.

† Regard to impartiality obliges me to give the following account, very recently communicated to me, relating to the ſtation of the chief on this important day; and that by an eye-witneſs.

The *Scotch* army was drawn up in a ſingle line; behind, at about 500 paces diſtance, was a *corps de reſerve*, with which was the Adventurer, a place of ſeeming ſecurity, from whence he iſſued his orders. His uſual dreſs was that of the Highlands, but this day he appeared in a brown coat, with a looſe great coat over it, and an ordinary hat, ſuch as countrymen wear, on his head. Remote as this place was from the ſpot where the trifling action was, a ſervant of his was killed by an accidental ſhot. It is well known how ſhort the conflict was: and the moment he ſaw his right wing give way, he fled with the utmoſt precipitation, and without a ſingle attendant.

The

The battle was fought contrary to the advice of ſome of the moſt ſenſible men in the rebel army, who adviſed the retiring into the faſtneſſes beyond the *Neſs*, the breaking down the bridge of *Inverneſs*, and defending themſelves amidſt the mountains. They politically urged that *England* was engaged in bloody wars foreign and domeſtic, that it could at that time ill ſpare its troops; and that the Government might, from that conſideration, be induced to grant to the inſurgents their lives and fortunes, on condition they laid down their arms. They were ſenſible that their cauſe was deſperate, and that their ally was faithleſs; yet knew it might be long before they could be entirely ſubdued; therefore drew hopes from the ſad neceſſity of our affairs at that ſeaſon: but this rational plan was ſuperſeded by the favorite faction in the army, to whoſe guidance the unfortunate adventurer had reſigned himſelf.

After deſcending from the Moor, got into a well-cultivated country; and after riding ſome time under low but pleaſant hills, not far from the ſea, reach

INVERNESS.

INVERNESS, finely ſeated on a plain, between the Firth of the ſame name and the river *Neſs*: the firſt, from the narrow ſtrait of *Arderſier*, inſtantly widens into a fine bay, and again as ſuddenly contracts oppoſite *Inverneſs*, at the ferry of *Keſſock*, the paſs into *Roſsſhire*. The town is large and well built, and very populous, being the laſt of any note in *North Britain*. On the North is *Oliver*'s Fort, a pentagon; but only the form remains to be traced by the ditches and banks. Near it is a very conſiderable rope manufacture. On an eminence South of the town is old *Fort George*, which was taken and blown up by the Rebels: it had been no more than a very antient caſtle, the place where *Boethius* ſays that *Duncan* was murdered:

W. Tomkins pinx.t P. Mazell sculp

Invernefs.

murdered: from thence is a moſt charming view of the *Firth*, the paſſage of *Keſſock*, the river *Neſs*, the ſtrange-ſhaped hill of *Tomman heurich*, and various groupes of diſtant mountains.

That ſingular *Tomman* is of an oblong form, broad at the baſe, and ſloping on all ſides towards the top; ſo that it looks like a great ſhip with its keel upwards. Its ſides and part of the neighboring plains are planted, ſo it is both an agreeable walk and a fine object. It is perfectly detached from any other hill; and if it was not for its great ſize, might paſs * for a work of art. The view from it is ſuch, that no traveller will think his labor loſt, after gaining the ſummit.

At *Inverneſs*, and I believe at other towns in *Scotland*, is an officer, called *Dean* of the *Guild*, who, aſſiſted by a council, ſuperintends the markets, regulates the price † of proviſions; and if any houſe falls down, and the owner lets it lie in ruins for three years, the *Dean* can abſolutely diſpoſe of the ground to the beſt bidder.

In this town was a houſe of *Dominicans*, founded in 1233 by *Alexander* II.

Croſs the *Neſs* on a bridge of ſeven arches, above which the tide flows for about a mile.

* Its length at top about 300 yards; I neglected meaſuring the baſe or the height, which are both conſiderable; the breadth of the top only 20 yards.

† Beef, (22 ounces to the pound) 2d. to 4d. Mutton, 2d. to 3d. Veal, 3d. to 5d. Pork, 2d. to 3d. Chickens, 3d. to 4d. a couple. Fowl, 4d. to 6d. apiece. Gooſe, 12d. to 14d. Ducks, 1s. a couple. Eggs, ſeven a penny. Salmon, of which there are ſeveral great fiſheries, 1d. and 1d. halfpenny *per* pound.

Proceed North; have a fine view of the Firth, which now widens again from *Keſſock* into a large bay ſome miles in length. The hills ſlope down to the water-ſide, and are finely cultivated; but the diſtant proſpect is of rugged mountains of a ſtupendous height, as if created as guards to the reſt of the iſland from the fury of the boiſterous North.

Ride cloſe to the water-edge thro' woods of alder; paſs near ſeveral houſes of the *Fraziers*, and reach

CASTLE DUNIE.

Caſtle Dunie, the ſite of the houſe of their chieftain Lord *Lovat*.

The old houſe, which was very mean, was burnt down in 1746; but a neat box, the reſidence of the hoſpitable factor, is built in its ſtead on a high bank well wooded, over the pretty river *Bewley*, or *Beaulieu*. The country, for a certain circuit, is fertile, well cultivated, and ſmiling. The bulk of Lord *Lovat*'s eſtate was in theſe parts; the reſt, to the amount of 500l. *per annum*, in *Straitherick*. He was a potent chieftain, and could raiſe about 1000 men: but I found his neighbors ſpoke as unfavorably of him, as his enemies did in the moſt diſtant parts of the kingdom. His property is one of the annexed eſtates, *i. e.* ſettled unalienably on the crown, as all the forfeited fortunes in the Highlands are: the whole value of which brought in at that time about 6000 l. *per annum*, and thoſe in the Lowlands about the ſame ſum; ſo that the power and intereſt of a poor twelve thouſand *per annum*, terrified and nearly ſubverted the conſtitution of theſe powerfull kingdoms.

FORFEITED ESTATES.

The profits of theſe eſtates are lodged in the hands of Truſtees, who apply their revenue for the founding of ſchools for the inſtruction of children in ſpinning; wheels are given away to poor families, and

and flax-feed to farmers. Some money is given in aid of the roads, and towards building bridges over the torrents; by which means a ready intercourfe is made to parts before inacceffible to ftrangers *. And in 1753, a large fum was fpent on an *Utopian* project of eftablifhing colonies (on the forfeited eftates) of difbanded foldiers and failors: comfortable houfes were built for them, land and money given, and fome lent; but the fuccefs by no means anfwered the intentions of the projectors.

Ford the *Bewley*, where a falmon fifhery, belonging to the *Lovat* eftate, rents at 120l. *per annum*. The country on this fide the river is called *Leirnamonach* †, or the Monk's land, having formerly been the property of the Abby of *Bewley*; and the oppofite fide bears the name of *Airds*, or the Heights. Pafs by fome excellent farms, well enclofed, improved, and planted: the land produces wheat, and other corn. Much cattle are bred in thefe parts, and there are feveral linnen manufactures. AUG. 17. LEIRNAMONACH. AIRDS.

Ford the *Conan* to *Caftle Braan*, the feat of Lord *Fortrofe*; a good houfe, pleafantly fituated on the fide of a hill; commands a view of a large plain, and to the Weft a wild profpect of broken and lofty mountains. CASTLE BRAAN.

There is here a fine full length of *Mary Stuart*, with this infcription: *Maria* D. G. *Scotiæ piiffima regina.* Franciæ *Dotaria. Anno Ætatis Regni* 38. 1580. Her drefs is black, with a ruff, cap,

* The factors, or agents of thefe eftates, are alfo allowed all the money they expend in planting.

† *Lèir*, or *Lether*, land that lies on the fide of a river or branch of the fea; and *Monach*, a monk.

handkerchief, and a white veil down to the ground, beads and prayer-book, and a croſs hanging from her neck; her hair dark brown, her face handſome, and conſidering the difference of years, ſo much reſembling her portrait by *Zucchero*, in *Chiſwick* Houſe, as to leave little doubt as to the originality of the laſt.

A ſmall half length on wood of *Henry Darnly*, inſcribed *Henricus Stuardus* Dominus *Darnly* Æt. IX. M.D.LV. dreſſed in black, with a ſword. It is the figure of a pretty boy.

A fine portrait of Cardinal *Richlieu*. General *Monk*, in a buff coat. Head of Sir *George Mackenzie*. The Earl of *Seaforth*, called, from his ſize, *Kenneth More*. *Frances* Counteſs of *Seaforth*, daughter of *William* Marquiſs of *Powis*, in her robes, with a tawny moor offering her a coronet. *Roger Palmer* Earl of *Caſtlemaine*; diſtinguiſhed by his lady, *Barbara* Dutcheſs of *Cleveland*; and by his ſimple embaſſy to a diſcerning Pope from that bigotted Prince *James* II.

Near the houſe are ſome very fine oaks and horſe-cheſnuts: in the garden, *Turkey* apricots, orange nectarines, and a ſmall ſoft peach, ripe; other peaches, nectarines, and green gages, far from ripe.

DINGWALL. Paſs through *Dingwall*, a ſmall town, the capital of *Roſsſhire*, ſituated near the head of the Firth of *Cromartie*: the Highlanders call it *Inner-Feorain*, *Feoran* being the name of the river that runs near it into the Firth. An antient croſs, and an obeliſk over the burying-place of the Earls of *Cromartie*'s family, were all I ſaw remarkable in it. In the year 1400 *Dingwall* had its caſtle, ſubject to *Donald*, Lord of the Iſles, and Earl of *Roſs*: after that *regulus* was weakened by the battle of *Harlaw*, his territories were invaded; and

and this caſtle reduced to the power of the crown of *Scotland*, by the Duke of *Albany*.

Ride along a very good road cut on the ſide of a hill, with the country very well cultivated above and below, with ſeveral ſmall woods interſperſed near the water's edge. There is a fine view of almoſt the whole bay, the moſt capacious and ſecure of any in *Great Britain*; its whole navy might lie there with eaſe, and ſhips of two hundred tuns may ſail up above two-thirds of its length, which extends thirty miles, from the *Sutters* * of *Cromartie* to a ſmall diſtance beyond *Dingwall:* the entrance is narrow; the projecting hills defend this fine bay from all winds; ſo it juſtly merits the name given it of *Portus ſalutis*.

FIRTH OF CROMARTIE.

FOULES, the ſeat of Sir *Henry Monro*, lies about a mile from the *Firth*, near vaſt plantations on the flats, as well as on the hills. Thoſe on the hills are ſix miles in length, and in a very flouriſhing ſtate. On the back of theſe are extenſive vallies full of oats, bounded by mountains, which here, as well as in the Highlands in general, run from Eaſt to Weſt. Sir *Henry* holds a foreſt from the crown by a very whimſical tenure, that of delivering a ſnow-ball on any day of the year that it is demanded; and he ſeems to be in no danger of forfeiting his right by failure of the quit-rent; for ſnow lies in form of a *glaciere* in the chaſms of *Benwewiſh*, a neighboring mountain, throughout the year.

FOULES.

SINGULAR TENURE.

Continue my journey along the low country, which is rich and well cultivated.

AUG. 18.

* *Sutters*, or Shooters, two hills that form its entrance, projecting conſiderably into the water.

Paſs

Paſs near *Invergordon* *, a handſome houſe, amidſt fine plantations. Near it is the narroweſt part of the Firth, and a ferry into the ſhire of *Cromartie*, now a country almoſt deſtitute of trees; yet, in the time of *James* V. was covered with timber, and over-run with wolves †.

BALLINAGOUAN.

Near the ſummit of the hill, between the Firths of *Cromartie* and *Dornoch*, is *Ballinagouan*, the ſeat of a Gentleman, who has moſt ſucceſsfully converted his ſword into a plough ſhare; who, after a ſeries of diſintereſted ſervices to his country, by clearing the ſeas of privateers, the moſt unprofitable of captures, has applied himſelf to arts not leſs deſerving of its thanks. He is the beſt farmer and the greateſt planter in the country: his wheat and his turneps ſhew the one, his plantations of a million of pines each year the other ‡. It was with great ſatisfaction that I obſerved characters of this kind

* At *Culraen*, three miles from this place, is found, two feet beneath the ſurface, a ſtratum of white ſoapy marle filled with ſhells, and is mnch uſed as a manure.

† Theſe animals have been long extinct in *North Britain*, notwithſtanding M. *de Buffon* aſſerts the contrary. There are many antient laws for their extirpation: that of *James* I. *parlem.* 7. is the moſt remarkable: "The Schireffs & Barons ſuld hunt the wolf four or thrie times in the Zear, betwixt St. *Marks* day & *Lambes*, quhich is the time of their quhelpes, & all tenents ſall riſe with them under paine of ane wadder."

‡ Pine, or *Scotch* fir ſeed, as it is called, ſells from four to ſix ſhillings *per* pound. Rents are payed here in kind: the landlord either contracts to ſupply the forts with the produce of the land, or ſells it to the merchant, who comes for it. The price of labor is 6d. *per* day to the men, 3d. to the women.

very

very frequent in *North Britain*; for during the interval of peace, every officer of any patrimony was fond of retiring to it, aſſumed the farmer without flinging off the gentleman, enjoyed rural quiet; yet ready to undergo the fatigues of war the moment his country clamed his ſervices.

About two miles below *Ballinagouan* is a melancholy inſtance of a reverſe of conduct: the ruins of *New Tarbat*, once the magnificent ſeat of an unhappy nobleman, who plunged into a moſt ungratefull rebellion, deſtructive to himſelf and family. The tenants, who ſeem to inhabit it *gratis*, are forced to ſhelter themſelves from the weather in the very loweſt apartments, while ſwallows make their neſts in the bold ſtucco of ſome of the upper. NEW TARBAT.

While I was in this county, I heard a ſingular but well-atteſted relation of a woman diſordered in her health, who faſted for a ſupernatural ſpace of time; but the length of the narrative obliges me to fling it into the Appendix.

Ride along a tedious black moor to *Tain*, a ſmall town on the Firth of *Dornoch*; diſtinguiſhed for nothing but its large ſquare tower, decorated with five ſmall ſpires. Here was alſo a collegiate church, founded in 1481 by *Thomas* Biſhop of *Roſs*. Captain *Richard Franks*, an honeſt *Cavalier*, who during the uſurpation made an angling peregrination from the banks of the *Trent* to *John a Groat*'s houſe, calls *Tain* 'as exemplary as any place for juſtice, 'that never uſes gibbet or halter to hang a man, but ſacks all their 'malefactors ſo ſwims them to their graves.'* The place appeared very gay at this time; for all the gaudy finery of a little fair was

* Northern Memoirs, &c. by *Richard Franks, Philanthropus. London*, 1694.

displayed

diſplayed in the ſhew of hard ware, printed linnens, and ribbands. Kept along the ſhore for about two miles, through an open corn country; and croſſing the great ferry, in breadth near two miles, thro' a rapid tide, and in a bad boat, land in the county of *Sutherland*, *Cattu* of the Highlanders; and in leſs than an hour reach its capital

DORNOCH. DORNOCH, a ſmall town, half in ruins; once the reſidence of the Biſhops of *Cathneſs*, and, like *Durham*, the ſeat of Eccleſiaſtics: many of the houſes ſtill are called after the titles of thoſe that inhabited them: the Biſhop lodged in the caſtle: the Dean's houſe is at preſent the inn. The cathedral was in form of a croſs; built by *Gilbert Moray*, who died Biſhop of *Cathneſs* in 1245: it is now a ruin, except part, which is the preſent church. * On the doors and window-ſhutters were painted, (as is common in many parts of *North Britain*) white tapdole-like figures on a black ground, deſigned to expreſs the tears of the country for the loſs of any perſon of diſtinction. Theſe were occaſioned by the affecting end of that amiable pair the young Earl and Counteſs of *Sutherland*, who were lovely in their lives, and in their deaths they were not divided, for their happineſs was interrupted by a very ſhort ſeparation; *ſanè ubi idem et maximus et honeſtiſſimus amor eſt, aliquando præſtat morte jungi, quam vita diſtrahi* †.

Ride on a plain not far from the ſea; paſs by a ſmall croſs, called the *Thane*'s, erected in memory of the battle of *Embo* in 1259,

* Sir *Patrick Murray* founded here in 1271 a convent of *Mathurines*.

† Where a mutual and moſt ardent and moſt virtuous affection reigns, it is ſometimes preferable to be united by death, than torn aſunder by life.

between

between *William* Earl of *Sutherland* and the *Danes*, who were overthrown and their General ſlain at this place; and not far from thence the ſpot where an unhappy creature had been burnt, if I miſtake not, in *June* 1727, for the imaginary crime of *witchcraft* *.

Croſs a very narrow inlet to a ſmall bay at *Portbeg*, or the little ferry, in a boat as dangerous as the laſt; for horſes can neither get in or out without great riſque, from the vaſt height of the ſides and their want of ſlips. Keep along the ſhore, paſs by the ſmall village of *Golſpie*, and reach

* This is the laſt inſtance of theſe frantic executions in the North of *Scotland*, as that in the South was at *Paiſly* in 1697, where, among others, a woman, young and handſome, ſuffered, with a reply to her enquiring friends, worthy a *Roman* matron; being aſked why ſhe did not make a better defence on her tryal, anſwered, *My perſecutors have deſtroyed my honor, and my life is not now worth the pains of defending*. The laſt inſtance of national credulity on this head was the ſtory of the witches of *Thurſo*, who tormenting for a long time an honeſt fellow under the uſual form of cats, at laſt provoked him ſo, that one night he put them to flight with his broad ſword, and cut off the leg of one leſs nimble than the reſt; on his taking it up, to his amazement he found it belonged to a female of his own ſpecies, and next morning diſcovered the owner, an old hag, with only the companion leg to this. The horrors of the tale were conſiderably abated in the place I heard it, by an unlucky enquiry made by one in company, *viz.* In what part would the old woman have ſuffered, had the man cut off the cat's tail? But theſe relations of almoſt obſolete ſuperſtitions muſt never be thought a reflection on this country, as long as any memory remains of the tragical end of the poor people at *Tring*, who, within a few miles of our capital, in 1751, fell a ſacrifice to the belief of the common people in witches; or of that ridiculous impoſture in the capital itſelf, in 1762, of the *Cock-Lane* ghoſt, which found credit with all ranks of people.

DUNROBIN. *Dunrobin* Caſtle, the antient ſeat of the Earls of *Sutherland*, founded about the year 1100 by *Robert*, or *Robin*, ſecond Earl of *Sutherland*; ſituated near the ſea, and, as the word *Dun* imports, on a round hill. The few paintings here are, an Earl of *Murray*, an old man, on wood. His ſon and two daughters, by *Co. G.* 1628. A fine full length of *Charles* I. *Angus Williamſon*, a hero of the *clan Chattan*, who reſcued the *Sutherlands* in the time of diſtreſs. A very ſingular picture of the Duke of *Alva* in council, with a cardinal by his ſide, who puts a pair of bellows blown by the Devil into his ear: the Duke has a chain in one hand, fixed to the necks of the kneeling *Flemings*, in the other he ſhews them a paper of recantation for them to ſign; behind whom are the reformed Clergy. The cardinal is the noted *Anthony Perrenot*, cardinal de *Grandville*, ſecretary to *Margaret* of *Auſtria*, Dutcheſs Dowager of *Savoy*, Governeſs of the *Netherlands*; and who was held to be the author, advancer and nouriſher * of the troubles of thoſe countries; and who on his recall into *Spain* was ſuppoſed to be the great promoter of the cruelties exerciſed afterwards by the Duke of *Alva*, the ſucceſſor of his miſtreſs.

The demeſn is kept in excellent order; and I ſaw here (*lat.* 58.) a very fine field of wheat, which would be ripe about the middle of next month.

This was the laſt wheat which had been ſown this year in *North Britain*.

Sutherland is a country abounding in cattle, and ſends out annually 2500 head, which ſold about this time (lean) from 2 l. 10 s.

* *Grimſton's Hiſt. Netherlands.* 344. 349.

to

to 3l. *per* head. Theſe are very frequently without horns, and both they and the horſes are very ſmall. Stags abound in the hills, there being reckoned not leſs than 1600 on the *Sutherland* eſtate, which, in fact, is the greateſt part of the county. Beſides theſe are Roes, Grous, black game and Ptarmigans in plenty, and during winter multitudes of water-fowl on the coaſt.

Not far from *Dunrobin* is a very entire piece of antiquity, of the kind known in *Scotland* by the name of the *Pictiſh* Caſtles, and called here *Cairn Lia'*, or a grey tower: that I ſaw was about 130 yards in circumference, round, and raiſed ſo high above the ground as to form a conſiderable mount: on the top was an extenſive but ſhallow hollow; within were three low concentric galleries, at ſmall diſtances from each other, covered with large ſtones; and the ſide-walls were about four or five feet thick, rudely made. There are generally three of theſe places near each other, ſo that each may be ſeen from any one. Buildings of this kind are very frequent along this coaſt, that of *Cathneſs* and of *Strathnavern*. Others agreeing in external form are common in the *Hebrides*, but differ in their internal conſtruction. In the iſlands they are attributed to the *Danes* *; here, to the *Picts*. Poſſibly each nation might have the ſame mode of building with ſome variation, for I am

PICTISH CASTLES.

* An enquiry is at this time making, by means of a correſpondence in *Copenhagen*, whether any ſuch edifices exiſt at preſent in the *Daniſh* dominions; and what was their ſuppoſed uſe. The reſult will be given in the next volume.

 told

told that ſome are to be ſeen in places where the *Danes* never penetrated. They were probably the defencible habitations of the times. I muſt withdraw my opinion of their having been the *ſuffugia hiemi aut receptacula frugibus*, like thoſe of the antient *Germans*. Such are not uncommon in *Scotland*, but of a form very different from theſe.

AUG. 19. Kept along the ſhore Northward. About a mile from the caſtle are ſome ſmall cliffs of free-ſtone; in one is *Sraith-Leven* Cove, an artificial cave, with ſeats and ſeveral ſhallow circular hollows cut within-ſide, once the retreat of a devout hermit. At ſome diſtance, and near the ſea, are ſmall ſtrata of coal three feet thick, dipping to the Eaſt, and found at the depth of about 14 to 24 yards. Sometimes it takes fire on the bank, which has given it ſo ill a name, that people are very fearfull of taking it aboard their ſhips. I am ſurprized that they will not run the riſque, conſidering the miraculous quality it poſſeſſes of driving away rats wherever it is uſed. This is believed by the good people of *Sutherland*, who aſſured me ſeriouſly of its virtues; and they farther attributed the ſame to the earth and very heath of their county. They add too, that not a rat will live with them, notwithſtanding they ſwarm in the adjacent ſhires of *Roſs* and *Cathneſs* *.

COAL.

In

* Some years ago I bought of the Monks, at the great *Benedictine* convent at *Augſburg*, ſome papers of St. *Ulric*'s earth, which I was aſſured, by *Lutheran* and *Papiſt*, had the ſame rat-expelling quality with that above-mentioned; but whether for want of due faith, or neglect of attending to the forms of the printed proſcriptions given with them, (here copied at full length) I know not, but the audacious

In *Aſſynt*, a part of this county, far Weſt of *Dunrobin*, are large ſtrata of a beautifull white marble, equal, as I was told, to the *Parian*. I afterwards ſaw ſome of the ſame kind found at *Glen-avon* in *Badenoch*.

Croſs the water of *Brora*, which runs along a deep chaſm, over which is a handſome bridge of a ſingle arch. Near is a cave, where the Salmon-fiſhers lie during the ſeaſon: the roof is pierced through to the ſurface, which ſerves for a natural chimney. They take annually about 10 or 12 laſts of fiſh. In a bank not far from the bridge are found abundance of *Belemnitæ*.

The country is very ſandy, and the arable, or cultivated part, very narrow, confined on the Eaſt by the ſea, on the Weſt by lofty black mountains, which approach nearer and nearer to the water, till at length they project into it at the great promontory the *Ord* of *Cathneſs*, the boundary between that county and *Sutherland*; after which the coaſt is bold and rocky, except a ſmall bay or two.

HEMSDALE.

Ford the very dangerous water of *Hemſdale*, rapid and full of great ſtones. Very large Lampries are found here, fiſh deteſted by the Highlanders. Beneath the ſtones on the ſea-ſhore are abundance

cious animals haunt my houſe in ſpite of it:---*Venerabiles Reliquiæ de Terra Sepulchrali, ſive de reſoluta deintùs carne S.* Udalrici *Conf. & Epiſcopi* Auguſtani; *quæ ſi honorificè ad inſtar aliarum Reliquiarum habeantur, & ad Dei laudem, Divìque Præſulis honorem, pium quoddam opus, v. g. Oratio, Jejunium, Eleemoſyna,* &c. *præſtetur, mirum eſt, qua polleant efficaciâ, ad proſcribendos præſertim è domibus, & vicinia Glires, qui ſubſiſtere minimè valent, ubicunque ſimiles Reliquiæ cum fiduciâ fuerint appenſæ, vel aſſervatæ. Idque ex ſpeciali prærogativâ, qua omnipotens Deus inſignia tanti Patroni merita perpetuo miraculo ſtatuit condecorare.*

of

of ſpotted and viviparous Blennies, Father Laſhers, and Whiſtle Fiſh. Mackrel appear here in this month, but without their roes. I thought them far inferior in goodneſs to thoſe of our country. Much Salmon is taken here.

The grey Water-wagtail quits this country in winter; with us it reſides.

Dined at the little village of *Hemſdale*; near which are the ruins of a ſquare tower.

Paſſed through a rich vale full of good barley and oats, between the hill of *Hemſdale* and the *Ord*. Aſcend that vaſt promontory on a good road winding up its ſteep ſides, and impending in many parts over the ſea, infinitely more high and horrible than our *Penmaen Mawr*. Beneath were numbers of Seals floating on the waves, with ſea-fowl ſwimming among them with great ſecurity. Obſerved projecting from one part of the *Ord*, far below, a ſmall and verdant hill, on which, tradition ſays, was fought a ſingle combat between an Earl of *Cathneſs*, and a ſon of the Earl of *Sutherland*, while their two armies looked on from above: the firſt was killed on the ſpot, the laſt died of his wounds.

ORD OF CATHNESS.

Beneath this cape are immenſe caves, the reſort of Seals * and Sea-fowls: the ſides and top are chiefly covered with heath and moraſſy earth, which gives it a black and melancholy look. Ride over ſome boggy and dreary moors. Paſs thro' *Auſdale*, a little

* During ſpring great quantities of Lump-fiſh reſort here, and are the prey of the Seals, as appears from the numbers of their ſkins, which at that ſeaſon float aſhore. The Seals, at certain times, ſeem viſited with a great mortality; for at thoſe times multitudes of them are ſeen dead in the water.

Highland

Highland village. Defcend into a deep bottom covered with alders, willows, birch and wicken trees, to *Langwall*, the feat of Mr. *Sutherland*, who gave me a very hofpitable reception. The country abounds with Stags and Roes, and all forts of feathered game, while the adjacent river brings Salmon almoft up to his door.

LAVELLAN.

I enquired here after the *Lavellan* *, which, from defcription, I fufpect to be the Water Shrew-moufe. The country people have a notion that it is noxious to cattle: they preferve the fkin, and, as a cure for their fick beafts, give them the water in which it has been dipt. I believe it to be the fame animal which in *Sutherland* is called the Water Mole.

AUG. 20.

Proceed on my journey. Pafs near *Berridale*. On a peninfula jutting into the fea is the ruin of the caftle; between it and the land is a deep chafm, where there had been a draw-bridge. On this caftle are ftationed, in the Salmon feafon, perfons who are to obferve the approach of the fifh to the frefh waters.

Near *Clathron* is a druidical ftone fet an end, and of a moft ftupendous fize.

DUNBETH.

Saw *Dunbeth* †, the feat of Mr. *Sinclair*, fituated on a narrow neck of land; on one fide impending over the fea, on the other over a deep chafm, into which the tide flows: a fmall narrow garden, with billows beating on three fides, fills the reft of the land between the houfe and the fea. Numbers of old caftles in this county have the fame tremendous fituation. On the Weft fide of

* *Sibbald Hift. Scotland. Br. Zool. illuft.* cii.

† This caftle was taken and garrifoned by the Marquifs of *Montrofe* in 1650, immediately preceding his final defeat.

this

this houſe are a few rows of tolerable trees; the only trees that I ſaw from *Berridale* to the extremity of *Cathneſs* *. On the right in-land are the ſmall remains of *Knackennan* Caſtle, built by an Earl of *Cathneſs*. From theſe parts is a full view of the lofty naked moun-

SCARABEN. tain of *Scaraben* and *Morven*. The laſt Ptarmigans in *Scotland* are on the firſt; the laſt Roes about *Langwall*, there being neither high hills nor woods beyond. All the county on this ſide, from *Dunbeth* to the extremity, is flat, or at leſt very ſeldom interrupted with hills, and thoſe low; but the coaſts rocky, and compoſed of ſtupendous cliffs.

Refreſhed our horſes at a little inn at the hamlet of *Clythe*, not far from the headland, called *Clytheneſs*. Reach *Thrumſter*, a ſeat of Mr. *Sinclair*'s. It is obſervable, that the names of places in this county often terminate in *ter* and *dale*, which ſavors of *Daniſh* origin.

The *Sinclairs* are very numerous, and poſſeſs conſiderable fortunes in theſe parts; but *Boethius* ſays, that they, the *Fraziers*, *Campbells*, *Boſwels*, and many others, came originally from *France*.

AUG. 21.
WICK.
Paſs through *Wick*, a ſmall burrough town with ſome good houſes, ſeated on a river within reach of the tide; and at a diſtance lies an old tower, called Lord *Oliphant*'s caſtle. In this town lives a weever who weeves a ſhirt, with buttons and button holes entire without any ſeam, or the leſt uſe of the needle: but it is to be fear-ed that he will ſcarce find any benefit from his ingenuity, as he

* But vaſt quantity of ſubterraneous timber in all the moors. Near *Dunbeth* is an entire *Picts* caſtle, with the hollow in the top, and is called the *Bourg* of *Dunbeth*.

cannot

Ipse pinx.t

Fresnick Castle.

P. Mazell sculp.t

cannot afford his labor under five pounds a ſhirt. Somewhat farther, cloſe to the ſea, is *Achringal* tower, the ſeat of Sir *William Dunbar*. Ride over the Links of *Keith*, on the ſide of *Sinclair* bay. Theſe were once a moraſs, now covered with ſand, finely turfed over; ſo in this inſtance the land has been obliged by the inſtability of the ſand. The old caſtle of *Keiſs* is ſeated on a rock, with a good houſe of the ſame name near it.

Near *Freſwick* caſtle the cliffs are very lofty; the ſtrata that compoſe them lie quite horizontally in ſuch thin and regular layers, and ſo often interſected by fiſſures, as to appear like maſonry. Beneath are great inſulated columns, called here *Stacks*, compoſed of the ſame ſort of natural maſonry as the cliffs; many of them are hollowed quite thro', ſo as to form moſt magnificent arches, which the ſea ruſhes thro' with vaſt noiſe and impetuoſity, affording a moſt auguſt piece of ſcenery to ſuch who are ſteady enough to ſurvey it from the narrow and almoſt impending paths.

Freſwick caſtle is ſeated on a narrow rock projecting into the ſea, with juſt room enough for it to ſtand on: the acceſs to it while the draw-bridge was in being, was over a deep chaſm cut thro' the little iſthmus that connected it to the main land. Theſe dreadfull ſituations are ſtrongly expreſſive of the jealous and wretched condition of the tyrant owners. FRESWICK CASTLE.

After riding near *Freſwick* bay, the ſecond ſandy bay in the county, paſs over a very bad moraſs, and after a few miles travel arrive at *Dungſby* bay*, a low tract, conſiſting of oat-lands and DUNGSBY BAY.

* *John a Groat*'s houſe is now known only by name. The proper name of the bay is *Duncan*'s.

grazing land: the *ultima Thule* of Mr. *Wallace*, whoſe deſcription it fully anſwers in this particular.

Quam juxta infames ſcopuli, et petroſa vorago
Aſperat undiſonis ſaxa pudenda vadis *.

The beach is a collection of fragments of ſhells; beneath which are vaſt broken rocks, ſome ſunk, others apparent, running into a ſea never pacific. The contrary tides and currents form here a moſt tremendous conteſt; yet, by the ſkilfulneſs of the people, are paſſed with great ſafety in the narrow little boats I ſaw lying on the ſhore.

The points of this bay are *Dungſby* head and St. *John*'s head, ſtretching out into the ſea to the Eaſt and Weſt, forming a pair of horns; from the reſemblance to which it ſhould ſeem that this country was antiently ſtyled *Cornana*.

ORKNEYS. From hence is a full view of ſeveral of the *Orkney* iſlands, ſuch as *Flota*, *Waes*, *Ronaldſa*, *Swanna*, to the Weſt the *Skerries*, and within two miles of land *Stroma*, famous for its natural mummies,

MUMMIES. or the entire and uncorrupted bodies of perſons who had been dead ſixty years. I was informed that they were very light, had a flexibility in their limbs, and were of a duſky color †. This iſle is

* Quoted by Mr. *Wallace* from the *Iter Balthicum* of *Conradus Celtes*.

† In the *Philoſophical Tranſactions abridged*, viii. 705. is an almoſt parallel inſtance of two corpſes, found in a moor in *Derbyſhire*, that had for 49 years reſiſted putrefaction, and were in much the ſame ſtate as thoſe in *Stroma*. In vol. xlvii. of the *Ph. Tr.* at large, is an account of a body found entire and imputrid at *Staverton* in *Devonſhire*, 80 years after its interment.

fertile

fertile in corn, is inhabited by about thirty families, who know not the uſe of a plough, but dig every part of their corn land.

Dine at the good miniſter's of *Canneſby*. On my return ſaw at a diſtance the *Stacks* of *Dungſby*, a vaſt inſulated rock, over-topping the land, and appearing like a great tower.

Paſſed near the ſeat of a gentleman not long deceaſed; the laſt who was believed to be poſſeſſed of the *ſecond ſight*. Originally he made uſe of the pretence, in order to render himſelf more reſpecta-ble with his clan; but at length, in ſpite of fine abilities, was made a dupe to his own artifices, became poſſeſſed with a ſerious belief of the faculty, and for a conſiderable number of years before his death was made truely unhappy by this ſtrange opinion, which originally aroſe from the following accident. A boat of his was on a very tempeſtuous night at ſea; his mind, filled with anxiety at the danger his people were in, furniſhed him with every idea of the miſfortune that really befell them: he ſuddenly ſtarting up, pronounced that his men would be drowned, for that he had ſeen them paſs before him with wet garments and dropping locks. The event was correſpondent, and he from that time grew confirmed in the reality of ſpectral predictions.

SECOND SIGHT.

There is another ſort of divination, called *Sleinanachd*, or reading the *ſpeal-bone*, or the blade-bone of a ſhoulder of mutton well ſcraped. When Lord *Loudon* was obliged to retreat before the Rebels to the iſle of *Skie*, a common ſoldier, on the very moment the battle of *Culloden* was decided, proclamed the victory at that diſtance, pretending to have diſcovered the event by looking through the bone.

 I heard

I heard of one inſtance of ſecond ſight, or rather of foreſight, which was well atteſted, and made much noiſe about the time the prediction was fulfilled. A little after the battle of *Preſton Pans*, the preſident, *Duncan Forbes*, being at his houſe of *Culloden* with a nobleman, from whom I had the relation, fell into diſcourſe on the probable conſequences of the action: after a long converſation, and after revolving all that might happen, Mr. *Forbes*, ſuddenly turning to a window, ſaid, *All theſe things may fall out; but depend on it, all theſe diſturbances will be terminated on this ſpot.*

GANNETS. Returned the ſame road. Saw multitudes of *Gannets*, or *Soland* Geeſe, on their paſſage Northward: they went in ſmall flocks from five to fifteen in each, and continued paſſing for hours: it was a ſtormy day; they kept low and near the ſhore; but never paſſed over the land, even when a bay intervened, but followed (preſerving an equal diſtance from ſhore) the form of the bay, and then regularly doubled the Capes. I ſaw many parties make a ſort of halt for the ſake of fiſhing; they ſoared to a great height, then darting down headlong into the ſea, made the water foam and ſpring up with the violence of their deſcent; after which they purſued their route.

Swans reſort in *October* to the Lochs of *Hemprigs* and *Waſter*, and continue there till *March*. Abundance of Land-rails are found throughout the county. Multitudes of Sea-fowl breed in the cliffs: among others, the *Lyre*; but the ſeaſon being paſt, I neither ſaw it, nor could underſtand what ſpecies it was *.

* I have ſince learned that it is the Shearwater or *Manks* Petrel of the *Br. Zool.* II. 433.

Went

Went along a fine hard ſand on the edge of *Sinclair* bay. On the South point, near *Noſs-head*, on the ſame rock, are *Sinclair* and *Gernigo* caſtles; but, as if the joint tenants, like beaſts of prey, had been in fear of each other, there was between them a draw-bridge; the firſt too had an iron door, which dropped from above through grooves ſtill viſible: this was inhabited in the year 1603 by a *Sinclair* Earl of *Cathneſs*.

SINCLAIR BAY AND CASTLE.

Should the chapel of St. *Tayre* near this caſtle exiſt, I overlooked that ſcene of cruelty in 1478. The *Keiths* and the *clan Gun* had in that year a feud; but a meeting was fixed at this place for a reconciliation: twelve horſe were to convene on each ſide. The *Cruner*, or chief of the *clan Gun*, and his ſons and neareſt kinſmen, arrived firſt, and were at their prayers in the chapel; when their antagoniſts arrived with twelve horſes, but with two men on each horſe, thinking that to bring no more than the ſtipulated number of horſes was no breach of agreement. Theſe attacked the people in the chapel, and put them all to death, but with great loſs to their own party, for the *Cruner* and his friends ſold their lives dear. I mention this tale to oppoſe the manners of the old *Cathneſians* to thoſe of the preſent hoſpitable and worthy race.

PRODUCE OF CATHNESS.

Cathneſs may be called an immenſe moraſs, mixed with ſome fruitfull ſpots of oats and barley, much coarſe graſs, and here and there ſome fine, almoſt all natural, there being as yet very little artificial. At this time was the hay harveſt both here and about *Dunrobin*: the hay on this rough land is cut with very ſhort ſcythes, and with a briſk and ſtrong ſtroke. The country produces and exports great quantities of *oatmeal*, and much whiſky is diſtilled from the barley: the great thinneſs of inhabitants throughout *Cathneſs* enables.

enables them to ſend abroad much of its productions. No wheat had been raiſed this year in the county; and I was informed that this grain is ſown here in the ſpring, by reaſon of the wet and fury of the winters.

CATTLE. The county is ſuppoſed to ſend out, in ſome years, 2200 head of cattle; but in bad ſeaſons, the farmer kills and ſalts numbers for ſale. Great numbers of ſwine are reared here: they are ſhort, high-backed, long-briſtled, ſharp, ſlender and long-noſed; have long erect ears, and moſt ſavage looks, and are ſeen tethered in almoſt every field. The reſt of the commodities of *Cathneſs* are butter, cheeſe, tallow, hides, the oil and ſkins of ſeals, and the feathers of geeſe.

Here are neither barns nor granaries; the corn is thraſhed out, and preſerved in the chaff in *bykes*, which are ſtacks in ſhape of bee-hives, thatched quite round, where it will keep good for two years.

SALMON. Much Salmon is taken at *Caſtle-hill*, *Dunet*, *Wick*, and *Thurſo*. The miraculous draught at the laſt place is ſtill talked of; not leſs than 2500 being taken at one tide, within the memory of man. At a ſmall diſtance from *Sinclair* caſtle, near *Staxigo* creek, is a ſmall Herring fiſhery, the only one on the coaſt: Cod and other white fiſh abound here; but the want of ports on this ſtormy coaſt is an obſtacle to the eſtabliſhment of fiſheries on this ſide the country.

SEALS. In the month of *November*, numbers of Seals * are taken in the

* Sometimes a large ſpecies twelve feet long has been killed on the coaſt; and I have been informed that the ſame kind are found on the rock *Hiſkir*, one of the Weſtern iſles.

vaſt

vaſt caverns that open into the ſea and run ſome hundred yards under ground. Their entrance is narrow, their inſide lofty and ſpatious. The Seal-hunters enter theſe in ſmall boats with torches, which they light as ſoon as they land, and then with loud ſhouts alarm the animals, which they kill with clubs as they attempt to paſs. This is a hazardous employ; for ſhould the wind blow hard from ſea, theſe adventurers are inevitably loſt *.

Much lime-ſtone is found in this country, which when burnt is made into a compoſt with turf and ſea plants. The tender ſex (I blush for the *Cathneſians)* are the only animals of burden: they turn their patient backs to the dunghills, and receive in their *keiſes*, or baſkets, as much as their lords and maſters think fit to fling in with their pitchforks, and then trudge to the fields in droves of ſixty or ſeventy. The common people are kept here in great ſervitude, and moſt of their time is given to their Lairds, an invincible impediment to the proſperity of the county. SERVITUDE.

Of the ten pariſhes in *Cathneſs*, only the four that lie S. E. ſpeak *Erſe*; all the others ſpeak *Engliſh*, and that in greater purity than moſt part of *North Britain* †.

Inoculation is much practiſed by an ingenious phyſician

* For a fuller account, vide *Br. Zool. illuſtr.* 38.

† I beg leave to refer the reader, for a farther hiſtory of this county, and of *Strathnavern*, to the Appendix; where is inſerted, the obliging communication of the Rev. Mr. *Alexander Pope*, Miniſter of *Edrachilis*, the moſt remote N. W. tract of *North Britain*, which completes the hiſtory of this diſtant part of our iſland.

(Dr.

(Dr. *Mackenzie*, of *Wick)* in this county, and alſo the *Orkneys* *, with great ſucceſs, without any previous preparation. The ſucceſs was equally great at *Sanda*, a poor iſle, where there was no ſort of fuel but what was got from dried cow-dung: but in all theſe places, the ſmall-pox is very fatal in the natural way. Other diſeaſes in *Cathneſs* are colds, coughs, and very frequently palſies.

The laſt private war in *Scotland* was occaſioned by a diſpute relating to this county. The preſent Earl of *Breadalbane*'s granfather married an heireſs of *Cathneſs:* the inhabitants would not admit her title; but ſet up another perſon in oppoſition. The Earl, according to the cuſtom of thoſe ill-governed times, was to aſſert his right by force of arms: he raiſed an army of fifteen hundred men; but the numbers, like thoſe under the conduct of *Gideon*, were thought to be too great: his Lordſhip firſt diſmiſſed five hundred; after that, another five hundred; and with the remainder marched to the borders of *Cathneſs*. Here he thought proper to add ſtratagem to force. He knew that the enemy's army waited for him on the other ſide of the *Ord*. He knew alſo that in thoſe days *whiſky* was the *Nectar* of *Cathneſs:* and in conſequence ordered a ſhip laden with that pretious liquor to paſs round, and wilfully ſtrand itſelf on the ſhore. The directions were punctually obeyed; and the crew in a ſeeming fright eſcaped in the boats to the invading army. The *Cathneſians* made a prize of the ſhip, and indulging themſelves too freely with the freight, became an eaſy prey to the Earl, who

* At this time a perſon was employed in the ſame buſineſs in the *Shetland* iſlands.

attacked

attacked them during their intoxication, and gained the country, which he difpofed of very foon after his conqueft.

I came here too late * to have any benefit from the great length of days; but from *June* to the middle of *July*, there is fcarce any night; for even at what is called midnight the fmalleft print may be read, fo truely did *Juvenal* ftyle thefe people, LONG DAYS.

Minima contentos nocte BRITANNOS.

On my way between *Thrumfter* and *Dunbeth*, again faw numbers of flocks of *Gannets* keeping due North; and the weather being very calm, they flew high. It has not been obferved that they ever return this way in the fpring; but feem to make a circuit of the ifland, till they again arrive at the *Bafs*, their only breeding-place on the Eaftern coaft. AUG. 23. GANNETS.

On defcending a fteep hill is a romantic view of the two bridges over the waters of *Berridale* and *Langwall*, and their wooded glens; and of the caftle of *Berridale* †, over the fea, where the Salmon-fifhers ftation themfelves to obferve the approach of thofe fifh out of the ocean. After a tedious afcent up the King's road of four miles, gain the top of the *Ord*, defcend, and lie at *Hemfdale*. BERRIDALE.

Re-vifit the fame places, till I pafs *Dingwall*. Crofs the *Conan* in a boat, a very beautifull river, not remote from *Caftle Braan*. AUG. 24. TO 29.

* Befides the miffing fo fingular a phænomenon, I found that the bad weather, which begins earlier in the North, was fetting in: I would therefore recommend to any traveller, who means to take this diftant tour, to fet out from *Edinburgh* a month fooner than I did.

† A little up the land is the ruin of *Ach caftle*.

SINGULAR CUSTOMS.

Was in this neighborhood informed of other ſingular cuſtoms of the Highlanders.

On New-year's day they burn juniper before their cattle, and on the firſt *Monday* in every quarter ſprinkle them with urine.

In ſome parts of the country is a rural ſacrifice, different from that before-mentioned. A croſs is cut on ſome ſticks, which is dipped in pottage, and the *Thurſday* before *Eaſter* one of each placed over the ſheep-cot, the ſtable, or the cow-houſe. On the 1ſt of *May* they are carried to the hill where the rites are celebrated, all decked with wild flowers, and after the feaſt is over, re-placed over the ſpots they were taken from; and this was originally ſtyled *Clou-än-Beltein* *, or the ſplit branch of the fire of the rock. Theſe follies are now ſeldom practiſed, and that with the utmoſt ſecrecy; for the Clergy are indefatigable in diſcouraging every ſpecies of ſuperſtition.

In certain places, the death of people is ſuppoſed to be foretold by the cries and ſhrieks of *Benſhi*, or the Fairies wife, uttered along the very path where the funeral is to paſs; and what in *Wales* are called *corps candles*, are often imagined to appear, and foretell mortality.

MARRIAGE CUSTOMS.

The courtſhip of the Highlander has theſe remarkable circumſtances attending it: after privately obtaining the conſent of the Fair, he formally demands her of the father. The Lover and his Friends aſſemble on a hill allotted for that purpoſe in every pariſh, and one of them is diſpatched to obtain permiſſion to wait on the

* *M'Pherſon's introduction*, &c. 166.

daughter:

daughter: if he is fuccefsfull, he is again fent to invite the father and his friends to afcend the hill and partake of a whifky cafk, which is never forgot: the Lover advances, takes his future Father-in-law by the hand, and then plights his troth, and the Fair-one is furrendered up to him. During the marriage ceremony, great care is taken that dogs do not pafs between them, and particular attention is paid to the leaving the Bridegroom's left-fhoe without buckle or latchet, to prevent witches * from depriving him, on the nuptial night, of the power of loofening the virgin zone. As a teft, not many years ago a fingular cuftom prevaled in the *Weftern* Highlands the morning after a wedding: a bafket was faftened with a cord round the neck of the Bridegroom by the female part of the company, who immediately filled it with ftones, till the poor man was in great danger of being ftrangled, if his Bride did not take compaffion on him, and cut the cord with a knife given her to ufe at difcretion. But fuch was the tendernefs of the *Caledonian* fpoufes, that never was an inftance of their neglecting an immediate relief of their good man.

Pafs near the abby † of *Beaulieu*, a large ruin: crofs the ferry, and again reach *Invernefs*.

Made an excurfion ten miles South of *Invernefs* to *Moy-hall*, pleafantly feated at the end of a fmall but beautifull lake of the AUG. 30. MOY-HALL.

* An old opinion. *Gefner* fays that the witches made ufe of toads as a charm, *Ut vim coeundi, ni fallor, in viris tollerent.* Gefner de quad. ovi. p. 72.

† Founded about 1219, by Lord *Patrick Biffett*, for the monks of *Vall'ombrofa.*

ſame name, full of Trout, and *Char*, called in the *Erſe*, *Tarr-dheargnaich*, and in the *Scotch*, Red Weems. This water is about two miles and a half long, and half a mile broad, adorned with two or three iſles prettily wooded. Each ſide is bounded by hills cloathed at the bottom with trees; and in front, at the diſtance of thirty miles, is the great mountain of *Karn-gorm*, patched with ſnow.

This place is called *Starſhnach-nan-gai'el*, or the threſhold of the Highlands, being a very natural and ſtrongly marked entrance from the North. This is the ſeat of the *Clan Chattan*, or the *M'Intoſhes*, once a powerfull people: in the year 1715, fifteen hundred took the field; but in 1745, ſcarce half that number: like another *Abſalom*, their fair miſtreſs was in that year ſuppoſed to have ſtolen their hearts from her *Laird* their chieftain: but the ſevereſt loyaliſt muſt admit ſome extenuation of their error, in yielding to the inſinuations of ſo charming a ſeducer.

CLAN CHATTAN.

Here is preſerved the ſword of *James* V. given by that monarch to the captain of *Clan Chattan*, with the privilege of holding the King's ſword at all coronations: on the blade is the word JESUS. That of the gallant Viſcount *Dundee* is alſo kept here. This antient family was as reſpectable as it was powerfull; and that from very old times. Of this the following relation is ſufficient evidence. In 1341 a *Monro* of *Foulis* * having met with ſome affront from the inhabitants of *Strathardule*, between *Perth* and *Athol*, determined on revenge, collected his clan, marched, made his inroad, and returned with a large booty of cattle. As he paſſed by *Moy-hall*,

* Conflicts of the *Clans*. p. 7.

this

this threſhold of the Highlands, the *Mac-Intoſh* of the time ſent to demand a part of the booty, challenging the ſame as his due by antient cuſtom: *Monro* acquieſced in the demand, and offered a reaſonable ſhare; but not leſs than half would content the chieftain of *Clan Chattan:* this was refuſed; a battle enſued near *Keſſock*; *Mac-Intoſh* was killed; *Monro* loſt his hand, but from that accident acquired the name of *Back-Lawighe:* and thus ended the conflict of *Clagh-ne-herey*.

Boethius relates, that in his time *Inverneſs* was greatly frequented by merchants from *Germany*, who purchaſed here the furs of ſeveral ſorts of wild beaſts*; and that wild horſes were found in great abundance in its neighborhood: that the country yielded a great deal of wheat and other corn, and quantities of nuts and apples. At preſent there is a trade in the ſkins of Deer, Roes, and other beaſts, which the Highlanders bring down to the fairs. There happened to be one at this time: the commodities were ſkins, various neceſſaries brought in by the Pedlars, coarſe country cloths, cheeſe, butter and meal; the laſt in goat-ſkin bags; the butter lapped in cawls, or leaves of the broad *alga* or tang; and great quantities of birch wood and hazel cut into lengths for carts, &c. which had been floated down the river from *Loch-Neſs*.

* *Ad* Neſſæ *lacûs longi quatuor et viginti paſſuum millia, lati duodecim latera, propter ingentia nemora ferarum ingens copia eſt cervorum, equorum indomitorum, capreolorum et ejuſmodi animantium magna vis: ad hæc martirillæ, Fouinæ, ut vulgò vocantur, vulpes, muſtellæ, Fibri, Lutræque incomparabili numero quorum tergora exteræ gentes ad luxum immenſo pretio coemunt.* Scot. Regni Deſcr. ix. Hiſt. Scot. xxx.

The

HIGHLAND DRESS.

The fair was a very agreeable circumſtance, and afforded a moſt ſingular groupe of Highlanders in all their motly dreſſes. Their *brechcan*, or plaid, conſiſts of twelve or thirteen yards of a narrow ſtuff, wrapt round the middle, and reaches to the knees: is often faſtened round the middle with a belt, and is then called *brechcan-feill*; but in cold weather, is large enough to wrap round the whole body from head to feet; and this often is their only cover, not only within doors, but on the open hills during the whole night. It is frequently faſtened on the ſhoulders with a pin often of ſilver, and before with a brotche (like the *fibula* of the *Romans)* which is ſometimes of ſilver, and both large and extenſive; the old ones have very frequently mottos.

The ſtockings are ſhort, and are tied below the knee. The *cuaran* is a ſort of laced ſhoe made of a ſkin with the hairy ſide out, but now ſeldom worn. The *truis* were worn by the gentry, and were breeches and ſtockings made of one piece.

The color of their dreſs was various, as the word *breaccan* implies, being dyed with ſtripes of the moſt vivid hues: but they ſometimes affected the duller colors, ſuch as imitated thoſe of the Heath in which they often repoſed; probably from a principle of ſecurity in time of war, as one of the *Scotch* Poets ſeems to inſinuate.

Virgata gaudent varii quæ eſt veſte coloris,
Purpureum et deamant fere cæruleumque colorem;
Verum nunc plures fuſcum magis, æmula frondi
Quæque erecina adamant, ut ne lux florida veſtis
Splendentis prodat recubantes inque ericetis.

Andreæ Melvini Top ogr. Scotiæ.

The

The *feil-beg*, i. e. little plaid, alſo called *kelt*, is a ſort of ſhort petticoat reaching only to the knees, and is a modern ſubſtitute for the lower part of the plaid, being found to be leſs cumberſome, eſpecially in time of action, when the Highlanders uſed to tuck their *brechcan* into their girdle. Almoſt all have a great pouch of badger and other ſkins, with taſſels dangling before. In this they keep their tobacco and money.

Their antient arms were the *Lochaber* ax, now uſed by none but the town-guard of *Edinburgh*; a tremendous weapon, better to be expreſſed by a figure than words *. ARMS.

The broad-ſword and target; with the laſt they covered themſelves, with the firſt reached their enemy at a great diſtance. Theſe were their antient weapons, as appears by † *Tacitus*; but ſince the diſarming act, are ſcarcely to be met with; partly owing to that, partly to the ſpirit of induſtry now riſing among them, the Highlanders in a few years will ſcarce know the uſe of any weapon.

Bows and arrows were uſed in war as late as the middle of the laſt century, as I find in a manuſcript life of Sir *Ewen Cameron*.

The *dirk* was a ſort of dagger ſtuck in the belt. I frequently ſaw this weapon in the ſhambles of *Inverneſs*, converted into a butcher's knife, being, like *Hudibras*'s dagger,

A ſerviceable dudgeon,
Either for fighting or for drudging.

* *Vide* tab. xii. 1ſt and 2d ed.

† *Simul conſtantia, ſimul arte* Britanni *ingentibus gladiis et brevibus cetris, miſſilia noſtrorum vitare vel excutere.* Vita Agricolæ. c. 36.

The

The dirk was a weapon ufed by the antient *Caledonians*, for *Dio Caffius*, in his account of the expedition of *Severus*, mentions it under the name of Ενχειριδιον *, *Pugio* or *little Dagger*.

The *Mattucafhlafh*, or arm-pit dagger, was worn there ready to be ufed on coming to clofe quarters. Thefe, with a piftol ftuck in the girdle, completely armed the Highlander †.

Fiery-cross. It will be fit to mention here the method the Chieftains took formerly to affemble the clans for any military expedition. In every clan there is a known place of rendezvous, ftyled *Carn a whin*, to which they muft refort on this fignal. A perfon is fent out full fpeed with a pole burnt at one end and bloody at the other, and with a crofs at the top, which is called *Crofh-tàrie*, the crofs of fhame ‡, or the fiery crofs; the firft from the difgrace they would

* *Xiphil. epit. Dionis.*

† *Major*, who wrote about the year 1518, thus defcribes their arms: *Arcum et fagittas, latiffimum enfem cum parvo halberto, pugionem groffum ex folo uno latere fcindentem, fed acutiffimum fub zonâ femper ferunt. Tempore belli loricam ex loris ferreis per totum corpus induunt.* Lib. I. c. viii.

‡ This cuftom was common to the Northern parts of *Europe* with fome flight variation, as appears from *Olaus Magnus*, p. 146, who defcribes it thus: *Bacculus tripalmaris, agiioris juvenis curfu precipiti, ad illum vel illum pagum feu villam hujufmodi edicto deferendus committitur, ut* 3, 4. *vel* 8 *die unus, duo vel tres, aut viritim omnes vel finguli ab anno trilufiri, cum armis et expenfis* 10 *vel* 20 *dierum fub pœna combuftionis domorum (quo ufto baculo) vel fufpenfionis* Patroni, *aut omnium (quæ fune allegato fignatur) in tali ripa, vel campo, aut valle comparere teneantur fubito, caufam vocationis, atque ordinem executionis* Præfecti *provincialis, quid fieri debeat audituri.*

undergo

undergo if they declined appearing; the ſecond from the penalty of having fire and ſword carried thro' their country, in caſe of refuſal. The firſt bearer delivers it to the next perſon he meets, he running full ſpeed to the third, and ſo on. In the late rebellion, it was ſent by ſome unknown diſaffected hand thro' the county of *Breadalbane*, and paſſed through a tract of thirty-two miles in three hours, but without effect.

WOMEN'S DRESS.

The women's dreſs is the *kirch*, or a white piece of linnen, pinned over the foreheads of thoſe that are married, and round the hind part of the head, falling behind over their necks. The ſingle women wear only a ribband round their head, which they call a ſnood. The *tonnag*, or plaid, hangs over their ſhoulders, and is faſtened before with a brotche; but in bad weather is drawn over their heads: I have alſo obſerved during divine ſervice, that they keep drawing it forward in proportion as their attention increaſes; inſomuch as to conceal at laſt their whole face, as if it was to exclude every external object that might interrupt their devotion. In the county of *Breadalbane*, many wear, when in high dreſs, a great pleated ſtocking of an enormous length, called *oſſan preaſſach:* in other reſpects, their dreſs reſembles that of women of the ſame rank in *England:* but their condition is very different, being little better than ſlaves to our ſex.

CHARACTER OF THE HIGHLANDERS.

The manners of the native Highlanders may juſtly be expreſſed in theſe words: indolent to a high degree, unleſs rouſed to war, or to any animating amuſement; or I may ſay, from experience, to lend any diſintereſted aſſiſtance to the diſtreſſed traveller, either in directing him on his way, or affording their aid in paſſing the dangerous torrents of the Highlands: hoſpitable to the higheſt degree,

 and

and full of generosity: are much affected with the civility of strangers, and have in themselves a natural politeness and address, which often flows from the meanest when lest expected. Thro' my whole tour I never met with a single instance of national reflection! their forbearance proves them to be superior to the meanness of retaliation: I fear they pity us; but I hope not indiscriminately. Are excessively inquisitive after your business, your name, and other particulars of little consequence to them: most curious after the politicks of the world, and when they can procure an old newspaper, wlll listen to it with all the avidity of *Shakespear's* blacksmith. Have much pride, and consequently are impatient of affronts, and revengefull of injuries. Are decent in their general behaviour; inclined to superstition, yet attentive to the duties of religion, and are capable of giving a most distinct account of the principles of their faith. But in many parts of the Highlands, their character begins to be more faintly marked; they mix more with the world, and become daily less attached to their chiefs: the clans begin to disperse themselves through different parts of the country, finding that their industry and good conduct afford them better protection (since the due execution of the laws) than any their chieftain can afford; and the chieftain tasting the sweets of advanced rents, and the benefits of industry, dismisses from his table the crowds of retainers, the former instruments of his oppression and freakish tyranny.

HIGHLAND SPORTS.

Most of the antient sports of the Highlanders, such as archery, hunting, fowling and fishing, are now disused: those retained are, throwing the *putting*-stone, or stone of *strength*,

ſtrength *, as they call it, which occaſions an emulation who can throw a weighty one the fartheſt. Throwing the *penny*-ſtone, which anſwers to our coits. The *ſhinty*, or the ſtriking of a ball of wood or of hair: this game is played between two parties in a large plain, and furniſhed with clubs; which-ever ſide ſtrikes it firſt to their own goal wins the match.

The amuſements by their fire-ſides were, the telling of tales, the wildeſt and moſt extravagant imaginable: muſick was another: in former times, the harp was the favorite inſtrument, covered with leather and ſtrung with wire †, but at preſent is quite loſt. Bagpipes are ſuppoſed to have been introduced by the *Danes*; this is very doubtfull, but ſhall be taken notice of in the next volume: the oldeſt are played with the mouth, the loudeſt and moſt ear-piercing of any wind muſick; the other, played with the fingers only, are of *Iriſh* origin: the firſt ſuited the genius of this warlike people, rouſed their courage to battle, alarmed them when ſecure, and collected them when ſcattered. This inſtrument is become ſcarce ſince the abolition of the power of the chieftains, and the more induſtrious turn of the common people. BAGPIPES

The *Trump* or *Jew's Harp* would not merit the mention among the Highland inſtruments of muſick, if it was not to prove

* *Cloch neart.*

† *Major* ſays, *Pro muſicis inſtrumentis et muſico concentu, Lyra ſylveſtres utuntur, cujus chordas ex ære, et non ex animalium inteſtinis faciunt, in qua dulciſſimè modulantur.*

its origin and antiquity: one made of gilt braſs having been found in *Norway* *, depoſited in an urn.

Vocal muſick was much in vogue amongſt them, and their ſongs were chiefly in praiſe of their antient heroes. I was told that they ſtill have fragments of the ſtory of *Fingal* and others, which they carrol as they go along; theſe vocal traditions are the foundation of the works of *Oſſian*.

AUG. 31. Leave *Inverneſs*, and continue my journey Weſt for ſome time by the river-ſide: have a fine view of the plain, the *Tomman*, the town, and the diſtant hills. After a ride of about ſix miles reached *Loch-Neſs* †, and enjoyed along its banks a moſt romantic and beautifull ſcenery, generally in woods of birch, or hazel, mixed with a few holly, whitethorn, aſpin, aſh and oak, but open enough in all parts to admit a ſight of the water. Sometimes the road was ſtrait for a conſiderable diſtance, and reſembled a fine and regular avenue; in others it wound about the ſides of the hills which overhung the lake: the road was frequently cut thro' the rock, which on one ſide formed a ſolid wall; on the other, a ſteep precipice. In many parts we were immerſed in woods; in others, they opened and gave a view of the ſides and tops of the vaſt mountains ſoaring above: ſome of theſe were naked, but in general covered with wood, except on the mere precipices, or where the grey rocks denied vegetation, or where the heath, now glowing with purple bloſſoms, covered the ſurface. The form of theſe hills was very

* Sir *Thomas Brown*'s *Hydriotaphia*. p. 8.

† This beautifull lake has a great reſemblance to ſome parts of the lake of *Lucerne*, eſpecially towards the Eaſt end.

various

various and irregular, either broken into frequent precipices, or towering into rounded ſummits cloathed with trees; but not ſo cloſe but to admit a ſight of the ſky between them. Thus, for many miles, there was no poſſibility of cultivation; yet this tract was occupied by diminutive cattle, by Sheep, or by Goats: the laſt were pied, and lived moſt luxuriouſly on the tender branches of the trees. The wild animals that poſſeſſed this picturesque ſcene were Stags and Roes, black game, and Grous; and on the ſummits, white Hares and Ptarmigans. Foxes are ſo numerous and voracious, that the farmers are ſometimes forced to houſe their Sheep, as is done in *France*, for fear of the Wolves*.

The North ſide of *Loch-Neſs* is far leſs beautifull than the South. In general, the hills are leſs high, but very ſteep; in a very few places covered with bruſh-wood, but in general very naked, from the ſliding of the ſtrata down their ſloping ſides. About the middle is Caſtle *Urquhart*, a fortreſs founded on a rock projecting into the lake, and was ſaid to have been the ſeat of the once powerfull *Cummins*, and to have been deſtroyed by *Edward* I. Near it

CASTLE URQUHART.

* It is to me matter of ſurprize that no mention is made, in the Poems of *Oſſian*, of our great beaſts of prey, which muſt have abounded in his days; for the Wolf was a peſt to the country ſo late as the reign of Queen *Elizabeth*, and the Bear exiſted there at leſt till the year 1057, when a *Gordon*, for killing a fierce Bear, was directed by King *Malcolm* III. to carry three Bears' heads in his banner. Other native animals are often mentioned in ſeveral parts of the work; and in the five little poems on night, compoſitions of as many Bards, every modern *Britiſh* beaſt of chace is enumerated, the howling Dog and howling Fox deſcribed; yet the howling Wolf omitted, which would have made the Bards' night much more hideous.

is

is the broadeſt part of the Loch, occaſioned by a bay near the caſtle.

Above is *Glen-Moriſton*, and Eaſt of that *Straith-Glas*, the *Chiſolm*'s country; in both of which are foreſts of pines, where that rare bird the Cock of the Wood is ſtill to be met with; perhaps in thoſe near *Caſtle Grant?* Formerly, was common throughout the Highlands, and was called *Capercalze*, and *Auercalze*; and in the old law-books, *Capercally*. The variety of the black game, mentioned by M. *Briſſon* under the name of *Coq. de Bruyere piquetè*, was a mixed breed between theſe two birds; but I could not hear that any at preſent were to be found in *North Britain*. *Linnæus* has met with them in *Sweden*, and deſcribes them under the title of *Tetrao cauda bifurca ſubtus albo punctata*. At *Glen-Moriſton* is a manufacture of linnen, where forty girls at a time are taught for three months to ſpin, and then another forty taken in: there are beſides ſix looms, and all ſupported out of the forfeited lands.

Cock of the Wood.

Above is the great mountain *Meal Fourvounich*, the firſt land ſailors make from the Eaſt ſea; on the top is a lake ſaid to be 100 fathoms deep.

I was informed that in that neighborhood are glens and caſcades of ſurpriſing beauty, but my time did not permit me to viſit them.

Dined at a poor inn near the *General*'s *Hut*, or the place where General *Wade* reſided when he inſpected the great work of the roads, and gave one rare example of making the ſoldiery uſefull in time of peace. Near is a fine glen covered at the bottom with wood, through which runs a torrent riſing Southward. The country alſo is prettily varied with woods and corn-fields.

About

Upper Fall of Tyers.

About a mile farther is the fall of *Fyers*, a vaſt cataract, in a darkſome glen of a ſtupendous depth; the water darts far beneath the top thro' a narrow gap between two rocks, then precipitates above forty feet lower into the bottom of the chaſm, and the foam, like a great cloud of ſmoke, riſes and fills the air. The ſides of this glen are vaſt precipices mixed with trees over-hanging the water, through which, after a ſhort ſpace, the waters diſcharge themſelves into the lake.

FALL OF FYERS.

About half a mile South of the firſt fall is another paſſing through a narrow chaſm, whoſe ſides it has undermined for a conſiderable way: over the gap is a true *Alpine* bridge of the bodies of trees covered with ſods, from whoſe middle is an awefull view of the water roaring beneath.

At the fall of *Fyers* the road quits the ſide of the lake, and is carried for ſome ſpace through a ſmall vale on the ſide of the river *Fyers*, where is a mixture of ſmall plains of corn and rocky hills. Then ſucceeds a long and dreary moor, a tedious aſcent up the mountain *See-chuimin*, or *Cummin*'s Seat, whoſe ſummit is of a great height and very craggy. Deſcend a ſteep road, leave on the right *Loch-Taarf*, a ſmall irregular piece of water, decked with little wooded iſles, and abounding with *Char*. After a ſecond ſteep deſcent, reach

Fort Auguſtus *, a ſmall fortreſs, ſeated on a plain at the head of *Loch-Neſs*, between the rivers *Taarf* and *Oich*; the laſt is conſi-

FORT AUGUSTUS.

* Its *Erſe* name is *Kill-chuimin*, or the burial-place of the *Cummins*. It lies on the road to the Iſle of *Skie*, which is about 52 miles off; but on the whole way there is not a place fit for the reception of man or horſe.

derable,

derable, and has over it a bridge of three arches. The fort consists of four bastions; within is the Governor's house, and barracks for 400 men: it was taken by the Rebels in 1746, who immediately deserted it, after demolishing what they could.

LOCH-NESS.

Loch-Ness is twenty-two miles in length; the breadth from one to two miles, except near Castle *Urquhart*, where it swells out to three. The depth is very great; opposite to the rock called the *Horse-shoe*, near the West end, it has been found to be 140 fathoms. From an eminence near the fort is a full view of its whole extent, for it is perfectly strait, running from East to West, with a point to the South. The boundary from the fall of *Fyers* is very steep and rocky, which obliged General *Wade* to make that *detour* from its banks, partly on account of the expence in cutting through so much solid rock, partly through an apprehension that in case of a rebellion the troops might be destroyed in their march, by the tumbling down of stones by the enemy from above: besides this, a prodigious arch must have been flung over the Glen of *Fyers*.

NEVER FREEZES.

This lake, by reason of its great depth, never freezes, and during cold weather a violent steam rises from it as from a furnace. Ice brought from other parts, and put into *Loch-Ness*, instantly thaws; but no water freezes sooner than that of the lake when brought into a house. Its water is esteemed very salubrious; so that people come or send thirty miles for it: old Lord *Lovat* in particular made constant use of it. But it is certain, whether it be owing to the water, or to the air of that neighborhood, that for seven years the garrison of Fort *Augustus* had not lost a single man.

The fish of this lake are Salmon, which are in season from *Christmas* to *Midsummer*, Trouts of about 2 ℔. weight, Pikes and

and Eels. During winter it is frequented by Swans and other wild fowls.

The greateſt riſe of water in *Loch-Neſs* is fourteen feet. The lakes from whence it receives its ſupplies are *Loch-Oich*, *Loch-Garrie*, and *Loch-Quich*. There is but very little navigation on it; the only veſſel is a gally belonging to the fort, to bring the ſtores from the Eaſt end, the river *Neſs* being too ſhallow for navigation.

It is violently agitated by the winds, and at times the waves are quite mountainous. *November* 1ſt, 1755, at the ſame time as the earthquake at *Liſbon*, theſe waters were affected in a very extraordinary manner: they roſe and flowed up the lake from Eaſt to Weſt with vaſt impetuoſity, and were carried above 200 yards up the river *Oich*, breaking on its banks in a wave near three feet high; then continued ebbing and flowing for the ſpace of an hour: but at eleven o'clock a wave greater than any of the reſt came up the river, broke on the North ſide, and overflowed the bank for the extent of 30 feet. A boat near the *General's Hut*, loaden with bruſh-wood, was thrice driven aſhore, and twice carried back again; but the laſt time, the rudder was broken, the wood forced out, and the boat filled with water and left on ſhore. At the ſame time, a little iſle, in a ſmall loch in *Badenoch*, was totally reverſed and flung on the beach. But at both theſe places no agitation was felt on land. ITS AGITATIONS IN 1755.

Rode to the caſtle of *Tor-down*, a rock two miles Weſt of Fort *Auguſtus*: on the ſummit is an antient fortreſs. The face of this rock is a precipice; on the acceſſible ſide is a ſtrong dyke of looſe ſtones; above that a ditch, and a little higher a terraſs ſupported by ſtones: on the top a ſmall oval area, hollow in the middle: SEPT. 1. CASTLE OF TOR-DOWN.

round this area, for the depth of near twelve feet, are a quantity of ſtones ſtrangely cemented with almoſt vitrified matter, and in ſome places quite turned into black *ſcoria:* the ſtones were generally granite, mixed with a few grit-ſtones of a kind not found nearer the place than 40 miles. Whether this was the antient ſite of ſome forge, or whether the ſtones which form this fortreſs * had been collected from the ſtrata of ſome *Vulcano*, (for the veſtiges of ſuch are ſaid to have been found in the Highlands) I ſubmit to farther enquiry.

From this rock is a view of *Ben-ki*, a vaſt craggy mountain above *Glen-Garrie*'s country. Towards the South is the high mountain *Coryarich:* the aſcent from this ſide is nine miles, but on the other the deſcent into *Badenoch* is very rapid, and not above one, the road being, for the eaſe of the traveller, cut into a zigzag faſhion. People often periſh on the ſummit of this hill, which is frequently viſited during winter with dreadfull ſtorms of ſnow.

SEPT. 2. After a ſhort ride Weſtward along the plain, reach *Loch-Oich*, a narrow lake; the ſides prettily indented, and the water adorned with ſmall wooded iſles. On the ſhore is *Glen-Garrie*, the ſeat of Mr. *M'Donald*, almoſt ſurrounded with wood, and not far diſtant is the ruin of the old caſtle. This lake is about four miles long; the road on the South ſide is excellent, and often carried through very pleaſant woods.

GLEN-GARRIE.

LOCH-LOCHY. After a ſmall interval arrive on the banks of *Loch-Lochy*, a fine

* I was informed that at *Ariſaig* is an old caſtle formed of the ſame materials.

piece-

piece of water, fourteen miles long, and from one to two broad. The diſtant mountains on the North were of an immenſe height; thoſe on the South had the appearance of ſheep-walks. The road is continued on the ſide of the lake about eight miles. On the oppoſite ſhore was *Achnacarrie*, once the ſeat of *Cameron* of *Lochiel*, but burnt in 1746. He was eſteemed by all parties the honeſteſt and moſt ſenſible man of any that embarked in the pernicious and abſurd attempt of that and the preceding year, and was a melancholy inſtance of a fine underſtanding and a well-intending heart, over-powered by the unhappy prejudices of education. By his influence he prevented the Rebels from committing ſeveral exceſſes, and even ſaved the city of *Glaſgow* from being plundered, when their army returned out of *England*, irritated with their diſappointment, and enraged at the loyalty that city had ſhewn. The Pretender came to him as ſoon as ever he landed. *Lochiel* ſeeing him arrive in ſo wild a manner, and ſo unſupported, entreated him to deſiſt from an enterprize from which nothing but certain ruin could reſult to him and his partizans. The Adventurer grew warm, and reproached *Lochiel* with a breach of promiſe. This affected him ſo deeply, that he inſtantly went and took a tender and moving leave of his lady and family, imagining he was on the point of parting with them for ever. The income of his eſtate was at that time, as I was told, not above 700l. *per annum*, yet he brought fourteen hundred men into the field.

CAMERON OF LOCHIEL.

The waters of this lake form the river *Lochy*, and diſcharge themſelves into the Weſtern ſea, as thoſe of *Loch-Oich* do through *Loch-Neſs* into the Eaſtern. About the beginning of this lake enter

LOCHABER. *Lochaber* *; ſtop at *Low-bridge*, a poor houſe; travel over a black moor for ſome miles; ſee abundance of cattle, but ſcarce any corn. Croſs

High-bridge, a fine bridge of three arches flung over the torrent *Spean*, founded on rocks; two of the arches are 95 feet high. This bridge was built by General *Wade*, in order to form a communication with the country. Theſe publick works were at firſt very diſagreeable to the old Chieftains, and leſſened their influence greatly; for by admitting ſtrangers among them, their clans were taught that the Lairds were not the firſt of men. But they had another reaſon much more ſolid: *Lochaber* had been a den of thieves; and as long as they had their waters, their torrents and their bogs, in a ſtate of nature, they made their excurſions, could plunder and retreat with their booty in full ſecurity. So weak were the laws in many parts of *North Britain*, till after the late rebellion, that no ſtop could be put to this infamous practice. A contribution, called the *Black-meal*, was raiſed by ſeveral of theſe plundering chieftains over a vaſt extent of country: whoever payed it had their cattle enſured, but thoſe who dared to refuſe were ſure to ſuffer. Many of theſe free-booters were wont to inſert an article, by which they were to be releaſed from their agreement, in caſe of any civil commotion: thus, at the breaking out of the laſt rebellion, a *M'Gregor* †, who had with the ſtricteſt honor (till that event)

BLACK-MEAL.

* So called from a lake not far from Fort *William*, near whoſe banks *Banquo* was ſaid to have been murthered.

† Who aſſumed the name of *Graham*.

preſerved

preserved his friends' cattle, immediately sent them word, that from that time they were out of his protection, and must now take care of themselves. *Barrisdale* was another of this class, chief of a band of robbers, who spread terror over the whole country: but the Highlanders at that time esteemed the open theft of cattle, or the making a *creach* (as they call it) by no means dishonorable; and the young men considered it as a piece of gallantry, by which they recommended themselves to their mistresses. On the other side there was often as much bravery in the pursuers; for frequent battles ensued, and much blood has been spilt on these occasions. They also shewed great dexterity in tracing the robbers, not only through the boggy land, but over the firmest ground, and even over places where other cattle had passed, knowing well how to distinguish the steps of those that were wandering about from those that were driven hastily away by the Free-booters.

From the road had a distant view of the mountains of *Arisaig*, beyond which were *Moydart*, *Kinloch*, &c. At the end of *Loch-Shiel* the Pretender first set up his standard in the wildest place that imagination can frame: and in this sequestered spot, amidst antient prejudices, and prevaling ignorance of the blessings of our happy constitution, the strength of the rebellion lay.

Pass by the side of the river *Lochy*, now considerable. See *Inverlochy Castle*, with four large round towers, which, by the INVERLOCHY. mode of building, seems to have been the work of the *English*, in the time of *Edward* I. who laid large fines on the *Scotch* Barons for the purpose of erecting new castles. The largest of these towers is called, *Cummin*'s. But long prior to these ruins *Inverlochy* had been a place of great note, a most opulent city, remarkable

remarkable for the vaſt reſort of *French* and *Spaniards**, probably on account of trade. It was alſo a ſeat of the Kings of *Scotland*, for here *Achaius* in the year 790 ſigned (as is reported) the league offenſive and defenſive between himſelf and *Charlemagne*. In after-times it was utterly deſtroyed by the *Danes*, and never again reſtored. Reach

Fort William, built in King *William*'s reign; as was a ſmall town near it, called *Maryborough*, in honor of his Queen; but prior to that, had been a ſmall fortreſs, erected by General *Monk*, with whoſe people the famous Sir *Ewen Cameron* † had numerous conteſts. The preſent fort is a triangle, has two baſtions, and is capable of admitting a garriſon of eight hundred men. It was well defended againſt the Rebels in 1746, who raiſed the ſiege with much diſgrace. It was alſo attempted by thoſe of 1715, but without ſucceſs. The fort lies on a narrow arm of the ſea, called *Lochiel*, which extends ſome miles higher up the country, making a bend to the North, and extends likewiſe Weſtward towards the iſle of *Mull*, near twenty-four *Scotch* miles.

THE CHAIN.

This fort on the Weſt, and *Fort Auguſtus* in the centre, and *Fort George* on the Eaſt, form what is called the *chain*, from ſea to ſea. This ſpace is called *Glen-more*, or the great Glen, which, including water and land, is almoſt a level of ſeventy miles. There is, in fact, but little land, but what is divided by firth, loch, or

* *Boethius*. Scot. Regni Deſcr. 4.

† Who is ſaid to have killed the laſt Wolf in *Scotland*, about the year 1680. Memoirs of this celebrated chieftain are given in the Appendix.

river; except the two miles which lie between *Loch-Oich* and *Loch-Lochy*, called *Lagan-achadrom*. By means of *Fort George*, all entrance up the Firth towards *Invernefs* is prevented. *Fort Auguftus* curbes the inhabitants midway, and *Fort William* is a check to any attempts in the Weft. Detachments are made from all thefe garrifons to *Invernefs*, *Bernera* barracks oppofite to the Ifle of *Skie*, and Caftle *Duart* in the Ifle of *Mull* *. Other fmall parties are alfo fcattered in huts throughout the country, to prevent the ftealing of cattle.

Fort William is furrounded by vaft mountains, which occafion almoft perpetual rain: the loftieft are on the South fide; *Benevifh* foars above the reft, and ends, as I was told, in a point, (at this time concealed in mift) whofe height from the fea is faid to be 1450 yards. As an antient *Briton*, I lament the difgrace of *Snowdon*; once efteemed the higheft hill in the ifland, but now muft yield the palm to a *Caledonian* mountain. But I have my doubts whether this might not be rivaled, or perhaps furpaffed, by others in the fame country; for example, *Ben y bourd*, a central hill, from whence to the fea there is a continued and rapid defcent of feventy miles, as may be feen by the violent courfe of the *Dee* to *Aberdeen*. But their height has not yet been taken, which to be done fairly muft be from the fea. *Benevifh*, as well as many others, harbours fnow throughout the year. BENEVISH.

* I was informed that coal has been lately difcovered in this ifland. What advantage may not this prove, in eftablifhments of manufactures, in a country juft rouzed from the lap of indolence!

The

The bad weather which reigned during my ſtay in theſe parts, prevented me from viſiting the celebrated parallel roads in *Glen-Roy*. As I am unable to ſatisfy the curioſity of the Reader from my own obſervation, I ſhall deliver in the Appendix the information I could collect relating to theſe amazing works.

TRADE OF LOCHABER.

The great produce of *Lochaber* is cattle: that diſtrict alone ſends out annually 3000 head; but if a portion of *Inverneſsſhire* is included, of which this properly is part, the number is 10,000. There are alſo a few horſes bred here, and a very few ſheep; but of late ſeveral have been imported. Scarce any arable land, for the exceſſive wet which reigns here almoſt totally prevents the growth of corn, and what little there is fit for tillage ſets at ten ſhillings an acre. The inhabitants of this diſtrict are therefore obliged, for their ſupport, to import ſix thouſand bolls of oatmeal annually, which coſt about 4000l.; the rents are about 3000l. *per annum*; the return for their cattle is about 7500l.; the horſes may produce ſome trifle; ſo that the tenants muſt content themſelves with a very ſcanty ſubſiſtence, without the proſpect of ſaving the leſt againſt unforeſeen accidents. The rage of raiſing rents has reached this diſtant country: in *England* there may be reaſon for it, (in a certain degree) where the value of lands is increaſed by acceſſion of commerce, and by the riſe of proviſions: but here (contrary to all policy) the great men begin at the wrong end, with ſqueezing the bag, before they have helped the poor tenant to fill it, by the introduction of manufactures. In many of the iſles this already ſhews its unhappy effect, and begins to depopulate the country; for numbers of families have been obliged to give up the ſtrong attachment

attachment the *Scots* in general have for their country, and to exchange it for the wilds of *America*.

The houſes of the peaſants in *Lochaber* are the moſt wretched that can be imagined; framed of upright poles, which are wattled; the roof is formed of boughs like a *wigwam*, and the whole is covered with ſods; ſo that in this moiſt climate their cottages have a perpetual and much finer verdure than the reſt of the country.

Salmons are taken in theſe parts as late as *May*; about 50 tons are caught in the ſeaſon. Theſe fiſh never appear ſo early on this coaſt as on the Eaſtern.

Phinocs are taken here in great numbers, 1500 having been taken at a draught. They come in *Auguſt*, and diſappear in *November*. They are about a foot long, their color grey, ſpotted with black, their fleſh red; riſe eagerly to a fly. The fiſhermen ſuppoſe them to be the young of what they call a great Trout, weighing 30 lb. which I ſuppoſe is the *Grey* *.

Left *Fort William*, and proceeded South along the military road on the ſide of a hill, an awefull height above *Loch-Leven* †, a branch of the ſea, ſo narrow as to have only the appearance of a river, bounded on both ſides with vaſt mountains, among whoſe winding bottoms the tide rolled in with ſolemn majeſty. The ſcenery begins to grow very romantic; on the Weſt ſide are ſome woods of birch and pines: the hills are very lofty, many of them taper to a point; and my old friend, the late worthy Biſhop *Pocock*, SEPT. 4.

* *Br. Zool.* III. 248.

† The country people have a moſt ſuperſtitious deſire of being buried in the little iſle of *Mun*, in this Loch.

compared the ſhape of one to mount *Tabor*. Beneath them is *Glen-Co*, infamous for the maſſacre of its inhabitants in 1691, and celebrated for having (as ſome aſſert) given birth to *Oſſian*; towards the North is *Morven*, the country of his hero *Fingal*.

GLEN-CO.

DESCRIPTION OF GLEN-CO.

" The ſcenery * of this valley is far the moſt pictureſque of any in the Highlands, being ſo wild and uncommon as never fails to attract the eye of every ſtranger of the leſt degree of taſte or ſenſibility. The entrance to it is ſtrongly marked by the craggy mountain of *Buachal-ety*, a little Weſt of the *King's houſe*. All the other mountains of *Glen-Co* reſemble it, and are evidently but naked and ſolid rocks, riſing on each ſide perpendicularly to a great height from a flat narrow bottom, ſo that in many places they ſeem to hang over, and make approaches, as they aſpire, towards each other. The tops of the ridge of hills on one ſide are irregularly ſerrated for three or four miles, and ſhot in places into ſpires, which forms the moſt magnificent part of the ſcenery above *Ken-Loch-Leven*. In the middle of the valley is a ſmall lake, and from it runs the river *Coän*, or *Cona*, celebrated in the works of *Oſſian*. Indeed no place could be more happily calculated than this for forming the taſte and inſpiring the genius of ſuch a poet.

ANIMALS.

The principal native animals on the mountains of *Glen-Co* are, Red Deer, *Alpine* Hares, Foxes, Eagles, Ptarmigans, and a few moor-fowl. It is remarkable that the common Hare was never ſeen either here, in *Glen-Creran*, or *Glen-Ety*, till the military roads

* I am indebted to Mr. *John Stuart* of *Killin* for the deſcription of this curious valley, having only had a diſtant view of it.

were

were made. The Partridge is a bird but lately known here, and is ſtill rare. There are neither rats nor vipers.

In *Glen-Co* are ſix farms, forming a rent of 241l. *per annum*; the only crops are oats, bear and potatoes. The increaſe of oats is three bolls and a half from one; of bear four or five. But the inhabitants cannot ſubſiſt upon their harveſt: about three hundred pounds worth of meal is annually imported. They ſell about ſeven hundred pounds worth of black cattle; but keep only ſheep and goats for the uſe of private families: neither butter or cheeſe is made for ſale. The men ſervants are paid in kind; and commonly married. FARMS.

Glen-Co lies in the united pariſh of *Liſmore* and *Appin*, and contains * about four hundred inhabitants, who are viſited occaſionally by a Preacher from *Appin*."

Leave on the left a vaſt cataract, precipitating itſelf in a great foaming ſheet between two lofty perpendicular rocks, with trees growing out of the fiſſures, forming a large ſtream, called the water of *Boan*.

Breakfaſt at the little village of *Kinloch-Leven* on moſt excellent minced ſtag, the only form I thought that animal good in. KINLOCH-LEVEN.

Near this village is a ſingle farm fourteen miles long, which lets for only 35l. *per annum*; and from the nature of the ſoil, perhaps not very cheap.

Saw here a *Quern*, a ſort of portable mill, made of two ſtones about two feet broad, thin at the edges, and a little thicker in the middle. In the centre of the upper ſtone is a hole to pour in the A QUERN.

* Report of the Viſitation, &c. 1760.

corn, and a peg by way of handle. The whole is placed on a cloth; the grinder pours the corn into the hole with one hand, and with the other turns round the upper ftone with a very rapid motion, while the meal runs out at the fides on the cloth. This is rather preferved as a curiofity, being much out of ufe at prefent. Such are fuppofed to be the fame with what are common among the *Moors*, being the fimple fubftitute of a mill.

THE BLACK MOUNTAIN.

Immediately after leaving *Kinloch-Leven* the mountains foar to a far greater height than before; the fides are covered with wood, and the bottoms of the glens filled with torrents that roar amidft the loofe ftones. After a ride of two miles begin to afcend the *black mountain*, in *Argylefhire*, on a fteep road, which continues about three miles almoft to the fummit, and is certainly the higheft publick road in *Great Britain*. On the other fide the defcent is fcarce a mile, but is very rapid down a zigzag way. Reach the *King*'s houfe, feated in a plain: it was built for the accommodation of his Majefty's troops, in their march through this defolate country, but is in a manner unfurnifhed.

PINE FORESTS.

Pafs near *Loch-Talla*, a long narrow piece of water, with a fmall pine wood on its fide. A few weather-beaten pines and birch appear fcattered up and down, and in all the bogs great numbers of roots, that evince the foreft that covered the country within this half century. Thefe were the laft pines which I faw growing fpontaneoufly in *North Britain*. The pine forefts are become very rare: I can enumerate only thofe on the banks of *Loch-Rannoch*, at *Invercauld*, and *Brae-mar*; at *Coygach* and *Dirry-Monach*: the firft in *Straithnavern*, the laft in *Sutherland*. Thofe about *Loch-Loyn*, *Glen-Morifton*, and *Straith-Glas*; a fmall one near *Loch-Garrie*, another

other near *Loch-Arkig*, and a few ſcattered trees above *Kinloch-Leven*, all in *Inverneſsſhire*; and I was alſo informed that there are very conſiderable woods about *Caſtle Grant*. I ſaw only one ſpecies of Pine in thoſe I viſited; nor could I learn whether there was any other than what is vulgarly called the *Scotch Fir*, whoſe ſynonyms are theſe:

Pinus ſylveſtris foliis brevibus glaucis, conis parvis albentibus. Raii hiſt. Pl. 1401. ſyn. ſtirp. Br. 442.

Pinus ſylveſtris. Gerard's herb. 1356. Lin. ſp. Pl. 1418. Flora Angl. 361.

Pin d'Ecoſſe, ou de Geneve. Du Hamel Traité des Arbres. II. 125. No. 5.

Fyrre, Strom. Sondmor. 12.

Moſt of this long day's journey from the *black mountain* was truely melancholy, almoſt one continued ſcene of duſky moors, without arable land, trees, houſes, or living creatures, for numbers of miles. The names of the wild tracts I paſſed through were, *Buachil-ety*, *Corricha-ba*, and *Bendoran*.

The roads are excellent; but from *Fort William* to *Kinloch-Leven*, very injudiciouſly planned, often carried far about, and often ſo ſteep as to be ſcarce ſurmountable; whereas had the engineer followed the track uſed by the inhabitants, thoſe inconveniences would have been avoided.

These roads, by rendering the highlands acceſſible, contributed much to their preſent improvement, and were owing to the induſtry of

MILITARY ROADS.

of our ſoldiery; they were begun in 1723 *, under the directions of Gen. *Wade*, who, like another *Hannibal*, forced his way through rocks ſuppoſed to have been unconquerable: many of them hang over the mighty lakes of the country, and formerly afforded no other road to the natives than the paths of ſheep or goats, where even the Highlander crawled with difficulty, and kept himſelf from tumbling into the far ſubjacent water by clinging to the plants and buſhes of the rock. Many of theſe rocks were too hard to yield to the pick-ax, and the miner was obliged to ſubdue their obſtinacy with gunpowder, and often in places where nature had denied him footing, and where he was forced to begin his labors, ſuſpended from above by ropes on the face of the horrible precipice. The bogs and moors had likewiſe their difficulties to overcome; but all were at length conſtrained to yield to the perſeverance of our troops.

In ſome places I obſerved, that, after the manner of the *Romans*, they left engraven on the rocks the names of the regiment each party belonged to, who were employed in theſe works; nor were they leſs worthy of being immortalized than the *Vexillatio*'s of the *Roman* legions; for civilization was the conſequence of the labours of both.

Theſe roads begin at *Dunkeld*, are carried on thro' the noted paſs of *Killicrankie*, by *Blair*, to *Dalnacardoch*, *Dalwhinie*, and over the *Coryarich*, to *Fort Auguſtus*. A branch extends from thence Eaſtward to *Inverneſs*, and another Weſtward, over *High-bridge*, to *Fort William*. From the laſt, by *Kinloch-Leven*, over the *Black Mountain*, by the King's houſe, to *Tyendrum*; and from thence, by

* Vide *p*. 86.

Glen-

Glen-Urqhie, to *Inveraray*, and ſo along the beautifull boundaries of *Loch-Lomond*, to its extremity.

Another road begins near *Crief*, paſſes by *Aberfeldy*, croſſes the *Tay* at *Tay-bridge*, and unites with the other road at *Dalnacardoch*; and from *Dalwhinie* a branch paſſes through *Badenoch* to *Inverneſs*.

Theſe are the principal military roads; but there may be many others I may have over-looked.

Rode through ſome little vales by the ſide of a ſmall river; and from the appearance of fertility, have ſome relief from the dreary ſcene of the reſt of the day. Reach

Tyendrum, a ſmall village. The inn is ſeated the higheſt of any houſe in *Scotland*. The *Tay* runs Eaſt, and a few hundred yards further is a little lake, whoſe waters run Weſt. A lead-mine is worked here by a level to ſome advantage; was diſcovered about thirty years ago: the veins run S. W. and N. E. TYENDRUM.

Continue my tour on a very fine road on a ſide of a narrow vale, abounding with cattle, yet deſtitute both of arable land and meadow; but the beaſts pick up a ſuſtenance from the graſs that ſprings up among the heath. The country opens on approaching *Glen-Urqhie*, a pretty valley, well cultivated, fertile in corn, the ſides adorned with numbers of pretty groves, and the middle watered by the river *Urqhie*: the church is ſeated on a knowl, in a large iſle, formed by the river: the *Manſe*, or miniſter's houſe, is neat, and his little demeſn is decorated in the moſt advantageous places with ſeats of turf, indicating the content and ſatisfaction of the poſſeſſor in the lot Providence has given him. SEPT. 5. GLEN-URQHIE.

In the church yard are ſeveral grave-ſtones of great antiquity, with figures of a warrior, each furniſhed with a ſpear, or two-hand-

ed

ed ſword: on ſome are repreſentations of the chaſe; on others, elegant fret-work; and on one, ſaid to be part of the coffin of a *M'Gregor*, is a fine running pattern of foliage and flowers, and excepting the figures, all in good taſte.

On an eminence on the South ſide of this vale dwells *M'Nabb*, a ſmith, whoſe family have lived in that humble ſtation ſince the year 1440, being always of the ſame profeſſion. The firſt of the line was employed by the Lady of Sir *Duncan Campbell*, who built the caſtle of *Kilchurn* when her huſband was on a croiſade: ſome of their tombs are in the church yard of *Glen-Urqhie*; the oldeſt has a hammer and other implements of his trade cut on it. At this place I was favored with ſeveral Highland proverbs, inſerted in the Appendix. After breakfaſt, at a good inn near the village, was there preſent at a chriſtening, and became ſponſor to a little *Highlander*, by no other ceremony than receiving him for a moment into my arms: this is a mere act of friendſhip, and no eſſential rite in the church of *Scotland*.

CASTLE OF KILCHURN.

Purſue my journey, and have a fine view of the meanders of the river before its union with *Loch-Aw*: in an iſle in the beginning of the lake is the caſtle of *Kilchurn*, which had been inhabited by the preſent Lord *Breadalbane*'s granfather. The great tower was repaired by his Lordſhip, and garriſoned by him in 1745, for the ſervice of the Government, in order to prevent the Rebels from making uſe of that great paſs croſs the kingdom; but is now a ruin, having lately been ſtruck by lightening.

LOCH-AW.

At a place called *Hamilton*'s Paſs, in an inſtant burſt on a view of the lake, which makes a beautifull appearance; is about a mile broad, and ſhews at leſt ten miles of its length. This water is prettily

Moses Griffiths del. P. Mazell sculp.

KILLCHURN CASTLE.

prettily varied with isles, some so small as merely to peep above the surface; yet even these are tufted with trees; some are large enough to afford hay and pasturage; and in one, called *Inch-hail*, are the remains of a convent*. On *Fraoch-Elan*†, the *Hesperides* of the Highlands, are the ruins of a castle. The fair *Mego* longed for the delicious fruit of the isle, guarded by a dreadfull serpent: the hero *Fraoch* goes to gather it, and is destroyed by the monster. This tale is sung in the *Erse* ballads, and is translated and published in the manner of *Fingal.*

MOUNT CRUACHAN.

The whole extent of *Loch-Aw* is thirty miles, bounded on the north by *Lorn*, a portion of *Argyleshire*, a fertile country, prettily wooded near the water-side. On the N. E. are vast mountains: among them *Cruachan* ‡ towers to a great height; it rises from the lake, and its sides are shagged with woods impending over it. At its foot is the discharge of the waters of this Loch into *Loch-Etive*, an arm of the sea, after a turbulent course of a series of cataracts for the space of three miles. At *Bunaw*, near the north end, is a large salmon-fishery; also a considerable iron-foundery, which I fear will soon devour the beautifull woods of the country.

* The country people are still fond of burying here. Insular interments are said to owe their origin to the fear people had of having their friends corpses devoured by wolves on the main land.

† This island was granted by *Alexander* III. in 1267, to *Gillcrist* M'*Nachdan* and his heirs for ever, on condition they should entertain the King whenever he passed that way.

‡ Or the Great Heap.

SCOTSTOWN. Pafs by *Scotftown*, a fingle houfe. Dine at the little village of *Cladifh*. About two miles hence, on an eminence in fight of the convent on *Inch-hail*, is a fpot, called *Croif-an-t-fleuchd*, or the crofs of bowing, becaufe, in *Popifh* times, it was always cuftomary to kneel or make obeifance on firft fight of any confecrated place *.

Pafs between hills finely planted with feveral forts of trees, fuch as *Weymouth* pines, &c. and after a picturefque ride, reach

INVERARAY *Inveraray* †; the caftle the principal feat of the Dukes of *Argyle*, chief of the *Campbells*; was built by Duke *Archibald*; is quadrangular with a round tower at each corner, and in the middle rifes a fquare one glazed on every fide to give light to the ftaircafe and galleries, and has from without a moft difagreeable effect. In the attic ftory are eighteen good bed-chambers: the ground-floor was at this time in a manner unfurnifhed, but will have feveral good apartments. The caftle is built of a coarfe *lapis ollaris*, brought from the other fide of *Loch-Fine*, and is the fame kind with that found in *Norway*, of which the King of *Denmark*'s palace at *Copenhagen* is built. Near the new caftle are fome remains of the old.

This place will in time be very magnificent: but at prefent the fpace between the front and the water is difgraced with the old town, compofed of the moft wretched hovels that can be imagined. The founder of the caftle defigned to have built a new town on the weft fide of the little bay the houfe ftands on: he finifhed a few houfes, a cuftom-houfe, and an excellent inn: his death interrupted the

* Druidical ftones and temples are called *Clachan*, churches having often been built on fuch places: to go to *Clachan* is a common *Erfe* phrafe for going to church.

† In the Galic, *Inner-aora*.

com-

[M]oses Griffiths del. *P. C. Canot sculp.*

INVERARAY CASTLE.

completion of the plan, which, when brought to perfection, will give the place a very different appearance to what it now bears.

From the the top of the great rock *Duniquaich* is a fine view of the castle, the lawn sprinkled with fine trees, the hills covered with extensive plantations, a country fertile in corn, bordering the Loch, and the Loch itself covered with boats. The trees on the lawn about the castle are said to have been planted by the Earl of *Argyle*: they thrive greatly; for I observed beech from nine to twelve feet and a half in girth, pines nine, and a lesser maple between seven and eight.

But the busy scene of the herring-fishery gave no small improvement to the magnificent environs of *Inveraray*. Every evening * some hundreds of boats in a manner covered the surface of *Loch-Fine*, an arm of the sea, which, from its narrowness and from the winding of its shores, has all the beauties of a fresh-water lake: on the week-days, the chearfull noise of the bagpipe and dance echoes from on board: on the sabbath, each boat approaches the land, and psalmody and devotion divide the day; for the common people of the North are disposed to be religious, having the example before them of a gentry untainted by luxury and dissipation, and the advantage of being instructed by a clergy, who are active in their duty, and who preserve respect, amidst all the disadvantages of a narrow income.

The length of *Loch-Fine* from the eastern end to the point of *Lamond*, is above thirty *Scotch* miles; but its breadth scarce two measured: the depth from sixty to seventy fathoms. It is noted LOCH-FINE.

* The fishery is carried on in the night, the herrings being then in motion.

HERRINGS. for the vaſt ſhoals of herrings that appear here in *July* and continue till *January*. The higheſt ſeaſon is from *September* to *Chriſtmas*, when near ſix hundred boats, with four men in each, are employed. A chain of nets is uſed (for ſeveral are united) of an hundred fathoms in length. As the herrings ſwim at very uncertain depths, ſo the nets are ſunk to the depth the ſhoal is found to take: the ſucceſs therefore depends much on the judgment or good fortune of the fiſhers, in taking their due depths; for it often happens that one boat will take multitudes, while the next does not catch a ſingle fiſh, which makes the boatmen perpetually enquire of each other about the depth of their nets. Theſe are kept up by buoys to a proper pitch; the ropes that run through them faſtened with pegs, and by drawing up, or letting out the rope (after taking out the pegs) they adjuſt their ſituation, and then replace them. Sometimes the fiſh ſwim in twenty fathom water, ſometimes in fifty, and oftentimes even at the bottom.

It is computed that each boat gets about 40l. in the ſeaſon. The fiſh are either ſalted, and packed in barrels for exportation, or ſold freſh to the country people, two or three hundred horſes being brought every day to the water ſide from very diſtant parts. A barrel holds 500 herrings, if they are of the beſt kind; at a medium, 700: but if more, for ſometimes a barrel will hold 1000, they are reckoned very poor. The preſent price 1l. 4s. *per* barrel; but there is a drawback of the duty on ſalt for thoſe that are exported.

The great rendezvous of veſſels for the fiſhery off the weſtern iſles is at *Cambeltown*, in *Cantyre*, where they clear out on the 12th of *September*, and ſometimes three hundred buſſes are ſeen there at a time:

OLD INVERARAY.

time: they muſt return to their different ports by *January* 13th, where they ought to receive the præmium of 2l. 10s. *per* tun of herrings; but it is ſaid to be very ill paid, which is a great diſcouragement to the fiſhery.

The herrings of *Loch-Fine* are as uncertain in their migration as they are on the coaſt of *Wales*. They had for numbers of years quitted that water; but appeared again there within theſe dozen years. Such is the caſe with the lochs on all this weſtern coaſt, not but people deſpair too ſoon of finding them, from one or two unſucceſsfull tryals in the beginning of the ſeaſon; perhaps from not adjuſting their nets to the depth the fiſh happen then to ſwim in: but if each year a ſmall veſſel or two was ſent to make a thorough tryal in every branch of the ſea on this coaſt, they would undoubtedly find ſhoals of fiſh in one or other.

TUNNIES.

Tunnies,* called here *Mackrel-Sture*, are very frequently caught in the herring ſeaſon, which they follow to prey on. They are taken with a ſtrong iron hook faſtened to a rope and baited with a herring: as ſoon as hooked loſe all ſpirit, and are drawn up without any reſiſtance: are very active when at liberty, and jump and frolick on the ſurface of the water.

SEPT. 7.

Croſſed over an elegant bridge of three arches upon the *Aray*, in front of the caſtle, and kept riding along the ſide of the Loch for about ſeven miles: ſaw in one place a ſhoal of herrings, cloſe to the ſurface, perfectly piled on one another, with a flock of Gulls, buſied with this offered booty. After quitting the water-ſide the road is carried for a conſiderable way through the bottoms of naked, deep

* *Br. Zool. illuſtr.* 33.

and gloomy glens. Aſcend a very high paſs with a little loch on the top, and deſcend into *Glen-Crow*, the ſeat of melancholy, ſeldom cheared with the rays of the ſun. Reach the end of *Loch-Long*, another narrow arm of the ſea, bounded by high hills, and after a long courſe terminates in the *Firth* of *Clyde*.

Near this place ſee a houſe, very pleaſantly ſituated, belonging to Colonel *Campbell*, amidſt plantations, with ſome very fertile bottoms adjacent. On aſcending a hill not half a mile farther, appears

REVIEW OF THE LAKES.

LOCH-LOMOND. *North-Britain* may well boaſt of its waters; for ſo ſhort a ride as thirty miles preſents the traveller with the view of four moſt magnificent pieces. *Loch-Aw*, *Loch-Fine*, *Loch-Long*, and *Loch-Lomond*. Two indeed are of ſalt-water; but, by their narrowneſs, give the idea of freſh-water lakes. It is an idle obſervation of travellers, that ſeeing one is the ſame with ſeeing all of theſe ſuperb waters; for almoſt every one I viſited has its proper characters.

Loch-Leven is a broad expanſe, with iſles and cultivated ſhores.

Loch-Tay makes three bold windings, has ſteep but ſloping ſhores, cultivated in many parts, and bounded by vaſt hills.

Loch-Rannoch, is broad and ſtrait, has more wildneſs about it, with a large natural pine wood on its ſouthern banks.

Loch-Tumel is narrow, confined by the ſloping ſides of ſteep hills, and has on its Weſtern limits a flat, rich, wooded country, watered by a moſt ſerpentine ſtream.

The *Loch* of *Spinie* is almoſt on a flat, and its ſides much indented.

Loch-Moy is ſmall, and has ſoft features on its banks, amidſt rude environs.

Loch-

Loch-Neſs is ſtrait and narrow; its ſhores abound with a wild magnificence, lofty, precipitous and wooded, and has all the greatneſs of an *Alpine* lake.

Loch-Oich has lofty mountains at a ſmall diſtance from its borders; the ſhores indented, and the water decorated with iſles.

Loch-Lochy wants the iſles; its ſhores ſlope, and ſeveral ſtraiths terminate on its banks.

Loch-Aw is long and waving: its little iſles tufted with trees, and juſt appearing above the water, its two great feeds of water at each extremity, and its ſingular lateral diſcharge near one of them, ſufficiently mark this great lake.

LOCH-LOMOND.

Loch-Lomond, the laſt, the moſt beautifull of the *Caledonian* lakes. The firſt view of it from *Tarbat* preſents an extenſive ſerpentine winding amidſt lofty hills; on the north, barren, black and rocky, which darken with their ſhade that contracted part of the water. Near this gloomy tract, beneath *Craig Roſton*, was the principal ſeat of the *M'Gregors*, a murderous clan, infamous for exceſſes of all kinds; at length, for a horrible maſſacre of the *Colquhouns**, or *Cahouns*, in 1602, were proſcribed, and hunted down like wild beaſts; their very name ſuppreſſed by act of council; ſo that the remnant, now diſperſed like *Jews*, dare not even ſign it to any deed. Their poſterity are ſtill ſaid to be diſtinguiſhed among the clans in which they have incorporated themſelves, not only by the redneſs of their hair, but by their ſtill retaining the miſchievous diſpoſitions of their anceſtors.

M'GREGORS.

On the weſt ſide, the mountains are cloathed near the bottoms

* Appendix.

with

with woods of oak quite to the water edge; their ſummits lofty, naked and craggy.

On the eaſt ſide, the mountains are equally high, but the tops form a more even ridge parallel to the lake, except where *Ben-Lomond**, like *Saul* amidſt his companions, overtops the reſt. The upper parts were black and barren; the lower had great marks of fertility, or at leſt of induſtry, for the yellow corn was finely contraſted with the verdure of the groves intermixed with it.

GRAMPIAN HILLS.

This eaſtern boundary is part of the *Grampian* hills, which extend from hence through the counties of *Perth*, *Angus*, *Mearns*, and *Aberdeen*. They take their name from only a ſingle hill, the *Mons Grampius* of *Tacitus*, where *Galgacus* waited the approach of *Agricola*, and where the battle was fought ſo fatal to the brave *Caledonians*. Antiquarians have not agreed upon the particular ſpot; but Mr. *Gordon* † places it near *Comrie*, at the upper end of *Straithern*, at a place to this day called *Galgachan Moor*. But to return.

The road runs ſometimes through woods, at others is expoſed and naked; in ſome, ſo ſteep as to require the ſupport of a wall: the whole the work of the ſoldiery: bleſſed exchange of inſtruments of deſtruction for thoſe that give ſafety to the traveller, and a poliſh to the once inacceſſible native.

Two great headlands covered with trees ſeparate the firſt ſcene from one totally different; the laſt is called the Point of *Firkin*. On paſſing this cape an expanſe of water burſts at once on your

* Its height is 3240 feet.

† *Itin. Septent.* 39. The reaſons againſt the opinion of this able antiquary will be given in the other volumes.

eye,

eye, varied with all the ſofter beauties of nature. Immediately beneath is a flat covered with wood and corn: beyond, the headlands ſtretch far into the water, and conſiſt of gentle riſings; many have their ſurfaces covered with wood, others adorned with trees looſely ſcattered either over a fine verdure, or the purple bloom of the heath. Numbers of iſlands are diſperſed over the lake of the ſame elevated form as the little capes, and wooded in the ſame manner; others juſt peep above the ſurface, and are tufted with trees; and numbers are ſo diſpoſed as to form magnificent viſtos between.

Oppoſite *Luſs*, at a ſmall diſtance from ſhore, is a mountainous iſle almoſt covered with wood; is near half a mile long, and has a moſt fine effect. I could not count the number of iſlands, but was told there are twenty-eight: the largeſt two miles long, and ſtocked with Deer.

The length of this charming lake is 24 *Scotch* miles; its greateſt breadth eight: its greateſt depth, which is between the point of *Firkin* and *Ben-Lomond*, is a hundred and twenty fathoms. Beſides the fiſh common to the Lochs are *Guiniads*, called here *Poans*.

At this time were living at the little village of *Luſs* the following perſons, moſt amazing inſtances of cotemporary longevity; and perhaps proofs of the uncommon healthineſs of the place. Theſe compoſe the venerable liſt:

Rev. Mr. *James Robertſon*, Miniſter, aged	90.
Mrs. *Robertſon*, his wife, - - -	86.
Anne Sharp, their ſervant, - - -	94.
Niel Macnaughtan, Kirk-Officer, - -	86.
Chriſtian Gay, his wife, - - -	94.
Walter Maclellan, - - - -	90.

Gg The

The country from *Lufs** to the Southern extremity of the lake continually improves; the mountains fink gradually into fmall hills; the land is highly cultivated, well planted, and well inhabited. I was ftruck with rapture at a fight fo long new to me: it would have been without alloy, had it not been dafhed with the uncertainty whether the mountain virtue, hofpitality, would flourifh with equal vigor in the fofter fcenes I was on the point of entering on; for in the *Highlands* every houfe gave welcome to the traveller.

On the road fide near *Lufs* is a quarry of moft excellent flates. And near the fide of the lake, about a mile or two farther, is a great heap of ftones in memory of St. *Mac-Keffog*, Bifhop and Confeffor, who fuffered martyrdom there A. D. 520, and was buried in *Comftraddan* church.

The vale between the end of the lake and *Dunbarton* is unfpeakably beautifull, very fertile, and finely watered by the great and rapid river *Levin*, the difcharge of the lake, which, after a fhort courfe, drops into the Firth of *Clyde* below *Dunbarton:* there is fcarcely a fpot on its banks but what is decorated with bleacheries, plantations and *villas*. Nothing can equal the contraft in this day's journey, between the black barren dreary glens of the morning ride, and the foft fcenes of the evening, iflands worthy of the retreat of *Armida*, and which *Rinaldo* himfelf would have quitted with a figh.

ENTRANCES INTO THE HIGHLANDS.

Before I take my laft leave of the *Highlands*, it would be proper to obferve that every entrance into them is ftrongly marked by nature.

* A tolerable inn on the borders of the lake.

On

On the South, the narrow and wooded glen near *Dunkeld* inſtantly ſhews the change of country.

On the Eaſt, the craggy paſs of *Bollitir* gives a contracted admiſſion into the *Grampian* hills.

On the North, the mountains near *Loch-Moy* appear very near, and form what is properly ſtyled the threſhold of the country; and on the

Weſt, the narrow road impending over *Loch-Lomond* forms a moſt characteriſtic entrance to this mountainous tract.

But the *Erſe* or *Galic* language is not confined within theſe limits; for it is ſpoken on all ſides beyond theſe mountains. On the Eaſtern coaſt it begins at *Nairn*; on the Weſtern, extends over all the iſles. It ceaſes in the North of *Cathneſs*, the *Orkneys*, and the *Shetland* iſlands *; but near *Loch-Lomond*, is heard at *Luſs*, at *Buchanan*, Eaſt of the lake, and at *Roſeneth*, Weſt of it.

The traveller, who has leiſure, ſhould ride to the eminence of *Millegs*, to ſee the rich proſpect between *Loch-Lomond* and the *Clyde*. One way is ſeen part of the magnificent lake, *Ben-Lomond* and the vaſt mountains above *Glen-Crow*. On the other hand appears a fine reach of the *Clyde* enlivened with ſhipping, a view of the pretty ſeats of *Roſeneth* and *Ardincapel*, and the buſy towns of *Port-Glaſgow* and *Greenock*.

Croſs the ferry over the *Levin* at *Bonnel*, and after a ride of three miles reach

* In the *Shetland iſles* are ſtill ſome remains of the *Norſe*, or old *Norwegian* language.

DUNBARTON. *Dunbarton*, a ſmall but good old town, ſeated on a plain near the conflux of the *Levin* with the Firth of *Clyde*; it conſiſts principally of one large ſtreet in form of a creſcent. On one ſide is the *Tolbooth*, and at the South end the church with a ſmall ſpire ſteeple; it had been collegiate, was founded about 1450 by *Iſabel* Counteſs of *Lenox* and Dutcheſs of *Albany*, and was dedicated to St. *Patrick*, who was born in this county. The waites of the town are bagpipes, which go about at nine o'clock at night and five in the morning.

ITS CASTLE. The caſtle is ſeated a little South of the town on a two-headed rock of a ſtupendous height, riſing in a ſtrange manner out of the ſands, and totally detached from every thing elſe; is bounded on one ſide by the *Clyde*, on the other by the *Levin*. On one of the ſummits are the remains of an old light-houſe, which ſome ſuppoſe to have been a *Roman Pharos*; on the other, the powder magazine: in the hollow between is a large well of water fourteen feet deep. The ſides of the rocks are immenſe precipices, and often over-hang, except on the ſide where the Governor's houſe ſtands, which is defended by walls and a few cannon, and garriſoned by a few invalids. It ſeems to have been often uſed as a ſtate priſon: the Regent *Morton* was ſecured there previous to his tryal. From its natural ſtrength, it was in former times deemed impregnable; ſo that the deſperate but ſucceſsfull ſcalado of it in 1571* may vie with the greateſt attempts of that kind, with the capture of the *Numidian*

* *Robertſon's hiſt. Scotland*, II. 15. *octavo*. *Guthrie's*, VII. 331.

fortreſs,

fortreſs, in the *Jugurthine* war, by *Marius*; or the more horrible ſurprize of *Feſcamp* *, by the gallant *Bois-rosé*.

The *Britons* in very early times made this rock a fortreſs; for it was uſual with them after the departure of the *Romans* to retreat to the tops of craggy inacceſſible mountains, to foreſts, and to rocks on the ſhores of the ſea: but *Boethius* makes the *Scots* poſſeſſed of it ſome ages prior to that, and pretends that it reſiſted all the efforts of *Agricola*, who laid ſiege to it. It certainly may clame a right to great antiquity, for *Bede* declares it to have been the beſt fortified city the *Britons* had during his days. Its antient name was *Alcluid*, or *Arcluid*, or the place on the *Cluid*. But in after-times it acquired the name of *Dun-Britton*, being the laſt place in theſe parts held by the *Britons* againſt the uſurping *Saxons*. In 756, reduced by famine, it was ſurrendered to *Edbert* King of *Northumberland*.

From the ſummits of this rock is a fine view of the country, of the town of *Dunbarton*, the river *Levin*, the Firth of *Clyde* (the *Glota* of *Tacitus*) here a mile broad, and of the towns of *Greenock* and *Port-Glaſgow*, on the oppoſite ſhore. The buſineſs of this country is the ſpinning of thread, which is very conſiderable. There is alſo a great ſalmon-fiſhery: but in this populous country, ſo great is the demand for them that none can be ſpared for curing. *Gilſes* come up the river in *June*, and continue in plenty about twenty days; and many Salmon Trout are taken from *March* to *July*. *Phinocs*, called here Yellow Fins, come in *July*, and continue about the ſame ſpace of time as the Gilſes: the fiſhermen call them the young of ſome great Sea Trout. During *May*, *Parrs* FISH.

* *Sully's Memoirs*, *Vol.* I. *Book* VI.

appear

appear in ſuch numbers in the *Levin*, that the water ſeems quite animated with them. There are beſides in that river, Perch and a few *Poans* *.

SEPT. 8. Paſs by the ruins of *Dunglas* caſtle, near the banks of the *Clyde*, which meanders finely along a rich plain full of barley and oats, and much incloſed with good hedges, a rarity in *North Britain*. At a diſtance are ſome gentle riſings, interſperſed with woods and *villas* belonging to the citizens of *Glaſgow*. Croſs the water of *Kelvin* at the village of *Partic*, and ſoon after reach

GLASGOW. GLASGOW. The beſt built of any modern ſecond-rate city I ever ſaw: the houſes of ſtone, and in a good taſte. The principal ſtreet runs Eaſt and Weſt, and is near a mile and a half long; but unfortunately, is not ſtrait. The *Tolbooth* is large and handſome. Next to that is the Exchange: within is a ſpatious room with full-length portraits of all our monarchs ſince *James* I.; and an excellent one, by *Ramſay*, of *Archibald* Duke of *Argyle*, in a Judge's robe. Before the Exchange is a large equeſtrian ſtatue of King *William*. This is the broadeſt and fineſt part of the ſtreet: many of the houſes are built over piazzas, but too narrow to be of much ſervice to walkers. Numbers of other ſtreets croſs this at right angles, and are in general well built.

MARKET-PLACES. The market-places are great ornaments to this city, the fronts being done in a very fine taſte, and the gates adorned with columns of one or other of the orders. Some of theſe markets are for meal,

* At *Dunbarton* I was informed by perſons of credit, that Swallows have often been taken in midwinter, in a torpid ſtate, out of the ſteeple of the church, and alſo out of a ſand-bank over the river *Endrich*, near *Loch-Lomond*.

greens,

greens, fifh, or flefh. There are two for the laft which have conduits out of feveral of the pillars; fo that they are conftantly kept fweet and clean.

Near the meal-market is a publick granary, to be filled on any apprehenfion of fcarcenefs.

The guard-houfe is in the great ftreet, which is kept by the inhabitants, who regularly do duty. An excellent police is obferved here, and proper officers attend the markets to prevent any abufes.

The old bridge over the *Clyde* confifts of eight arches, and was built 400 years ago by Bifhop *Rea*; two others are now building. The tide flows three miles higher up the country; but at low water is fordable. There is a plan for deepening the channel; for at prefent the tide brings up only very fmall veffels; and the ports belonging to this city lie feveral miles lower, at *Port-Glafgow* and *Greenock*, on the fide of the *Firth*.

Near the bridge is a large alms-houfe, a vaft nailery, a ftone-ware manufacture, and a great porter brewery, which fupplies fome part of uninduftrious *Ireland*. Within fight, on the South fide, are collieries; and much coal is exported into the laft-mentioned ifland, and into *America*.

The great imports of this city are tobacco and fugar: of the former, above 40,000 hogfheads have been annually imported, and moft part of it again exported into *France* and other countries. The manufactures here are linnens, cambricks *, lawns, tapes, TRADE.

* The greateft cambrick manufacture is now at *Paifly*, a few miles from this city.

fuſtians, and ſtriped linnens; ſo that it already begins to rival *Mancheſter*, and has in point of the conveniency of its ports, in reſpect to *America*, a great advantage over it.

COLLEGE. The College is a large building, with a handſome front to the ſtreet, reſembling ſome of the old colleges in *Oxford*. *Charles* I. ſubſcribed 200l. towards this work, but was prevented by the troubles from paying it; but *Cromwel* afterwards fulfilled the deſign of the royal donor. It was founded in 1450, by *James* II. Pope *Nicholas* V. gave the *bull*, but Biſhop *Turnbull* ſupplied the money. There are about 400 ſtudents belonging to the college, who lodge in the town: but the Profeſſors have good houſes in the college. Young gentlemen of fortune have private tutors, who have an eye to their conduct; the reſt live entirely at their own diſcretion.

The library is a very handſome room, with a gallery round it, ſupported by pillars. That beneficent nobleman the firſt Duke of *Chandos*, when he viſited the college, gave 500l. towards building this apartment.

Meſſrs. *Robert* and *Andrew Foulis*, printers and bookſellers to the univerſity, have inſtituted an academy for painting and engraving; and like good citizens, zealous to promote the welfare and honor of their native place, have at vaſt expence formed a moſt numerous collection of paintings from abroad, in order to form the taſte of their *eleves*.

The printing is a very conſiderable branch of buſineſs, and has long been celebrated for the beauty of the types and the correctneſs of the editions. Here are preſerved in caſes numbers of monumental

and

and other ſtones *, taken out of the walls on the *Roman* ſtations in this part of the kingdom; ſome are well cut and ornamented: moſt of them were done to perpetuate the memory of the *vexillatio*, or party, who performed ſuch or ſuch works; others in memory of officers who died in the country.

The cathedral is a large pile, now divided into two churches: beneath, and deep under ground, is another, in which is alſo divine ſervice, where the congregation may truely ſay, *clamavi e profundis:* the roof is fine, made of ſtone, and ſupported by pillars; but the beauty much hurt by the crowding of the pews. Near this is the ruin of the caſtle, or Biſhop's palace. CHURCHES.

The new church is a very handſome building, with a large elegant porch; but the outſide is much disfigured by a ſlender ſquare tower with a pepper-pox top: and in general, the ſteeples of *Glaſgow* are in a remarkable bad taſte, being, in fact, no favorite part of architecture with the church of *Scotland*. The inſide of that juſt ſpoken of is moſt neatly finiſhed, ſupported by pillars, and very prettily ſtuccoed: it is one of the very few exceptions to the ſlovenly and indecent manner in which Preſbytery keeps the houſes of GOD: reformation in manners of religion ſeldom obſerves mediocrity: here it was outrageous; for a place of worſhip commonly neat was deemed to ſavor of popery: but, to avoid the imputation of that extreme, they run into another; for in many parts of *Scotland* our LORD ſeems ſtill to be worſhipped in a ſtable, and often in a very wretched

* Several have been engraven by the artiſts of the academy. The Provoſt of the Univerſity did me the honor of preſenting me with a ſet.

one. Many of the churches are thatched with heath, and in ſome places are in ſuch bad repair as to be half open at top; ſo that the people appear to worſhip, as the *Druids* did of old, in open temples.

SEPT. 10. Went to ſee *Hamilton* Houſe, twelve miles diſtant from *Glaſgow*: ride through a rich and beautifull corn country, adorned with ſmall woods, gentlemen's ſeats, and well watered. Hereabout I ſaw the firſt muddy ſtream ſince I had left *Edinburgh*; for the Highland rivers running generally through a bed of rock, or pure gravel, receive no other teint, in the greateſt floods, than the brown cryſtalline tinge of the moors, out of which they riſe.

BOTHWELL BRIDGE. See on the Weſt, at a little diſtance from the road, the ruins of *Bothwell* caſtle, and the bridge, remarkable for the Duke of *Monmouth*'s victory over the Rebels in 1679. The church was collegiate, founded by *Archibald* Earl of *Douglas*, 1398, and is, as I heard*, oddly incruſted with a thin coat of ſtone.

HAMILTON. *Hamilton* Houſe, or Palace, as it is called here, is ſeated at the end of a ſmall town; is a large diſagreeable pile of building, with two deep wings at right angles with the centre. The gallery is of great extent, and furniſhed (as well as ſome other rooms) with moſt excellent paintings: that of *Daniel* in the Lion's den, by *Rubens*, is a great performance: the fear and devotion of the Prophet is finely expreſſed by his uplifted face and eyes, his claſped hands, his ſwelling muſcles, and the violent extenſion of one foot: a Lion looks fiercely at him with open mouth, and ſeems only reſtrained by the Almighty power from making him fall a victim to his

* Biſhop *Pocock*'s *manuſcript Journal.*

hunger;

hunger; and the ſignal deliverance of *Daniel* is more fully marked by the number of human bones ſcattered over the floor, as if to ſhew the inſtant fate of others, in whoſe favor the Deity did not interfere.

The marriage-feaſt, by *Paul Veroneſe*, is a fine piece; and the obſtinacy and reſiſtance of the intruder, who came without the wedding garment, is ſtrongly expreſſed.

The treaty of peace between *England* and *Spain*, in the reign of *James* I. by *Juan de Pantoxa*, is a good hiſtorical picture. There are ſix Envoys on the part of the *Spaniards*, and five on that of the *Engliſh*, with their names inſcribed over each: the *Engliſh* are the Earls of *Dorſet*, *Nottingham*, *Devonſhire*, *Northampton*, and *Robert Cecil*.

Earls of *Lauderdale* and *Lanerk* ſettling the covenant, both in black, with faces full of puritanical ſolemnity.

Several of the Dukes of *Hamilton*. *James* Duke of *Hamilton*, with a blue ribband and white rod. His ſon, beheaded in 1649. His brother, killed at the battle of *Worceſter*. The Duke who fell in the duel with Lord *Mohun*.

Fielding, Earl of *Denbigh* *; his hair grey, a gun in his hand, and attended by an *Indian* boy. It ſeems perfectly to ſtart from the canvaſs, and the action of his countenance looking up has

* The perſon who ſhewed the houſe called him Governor of *Jamaica*; but that muſt be a miſtake. If any errors appear in my account of any of the pictures, I flatter myſelf it may be excuſed; for ſometimes they were ſhewn by ſervants; ſometimes the owners of the houſe were ſo obliging as to attend me, whom I could not trouble with a number of queſtions.

matchleſs ſpirit. His daughter, and her huſband the Marquiſs of *Hamilton.*

Old Duke of *Chatelherault*, in black, with an order about his neck.

Two half-lengths in black; one with a fiddle in his hand, the other in a groteſque attitude; both with the ſame countenances; good, but ſwarthy; miſtakenly called *David Rizzo*'s; but I could not learn that there was any portrait of that unfortunate man.

Maria Dei Gratia Scotorum Regina, 1586. *Æt.* 43. a half-length; a ſtiff figure, in a great ruff, auburne hair, oval but pretty full face, of much larger and plainer features than that at Caſtle *Braan*, a natural alteration from the increaſe of her cruel uſage, and of her ill health; yet ſtill with a reſemblance to that portrait. It was told me here, that ſhe ſent this picture, together with a ring, to the Duke of *Hamilton*, a little before her execution.

A head, ſaid to be *Anna Bullen*, very handſome, dreſſed in a ruff and kerchief edged with ermine, and in a purple gown; over her face a veil, ſo tranſparent as not to conceal

The bloom of young deſire and purple light of love.

Earl *Morton*, Regent of *Scotland.*

The rough reformer *John Knox.*

Lord *Belhaven*, author of the famous ſpeech againſt the union.

Philip II. at full length, with a ſtrange figure of Fame bowing at his feet with a label and this motto, *Pro merente adſto.*

CHATELHÉRAULT.

About a mile from the houſe, on an eminence above a deep wooded glen, with the *Avon* at its bottom, is *Chatelherault*; ſo called from the eſtate the family once poſſeſſed in *France:* is an elegant banqueting

banqueting houſe, with a dog-kennel, gardens, &c. and commands a fine view of the country. The park is now much incloſed: but I am told that there are ſtill in it a few of the breed of the wild cattle, which *Boethius** ſays were peculiar to the *Caledonian* foreſt, were of a ſnowy whiteneſs, and had manes like lions: they were at this time in a diſtant part of the park, and I loſt the ſight of them. WILD CATTLE.

I regret alſo the not being able to viſit the falls of the *Clyde* near *Lanerk*, which I was informed were very romantic, conſiſting of a ſeries of cataracts of different heights from ten to fifteen feet, ſome falling in ſheets of water, others broken, and their ſides bounded by magnificent rocks covered with trees.

Returned to *Glaſgow*.

SEPT. 11.

Croſſed the country towards *Sterling*. Paſſed through the village of *Kylſithe*, noted for a victory gained by *Montroſe* over the Covenanters. Thro' a bog, where numbers of the fugitives periſhed, is now cutting part of the canal that is to join the Firths of *Forth* and *Clyde*. Saw the ſpot where the battle of *Bannockbourne* was fought, in which the *Engliſh* under *Edward* II. had a ſhamefull defeat. *Edward* was ſo aſſured of conqueſt that he brought with him *William Baſton*, a *Carmelite*, and famous poet, to celebrate his victory; but the monarch was defeated, and the poor bard taken and forced by the conqueror, *invitâ minerva*, to ſing his ſucceſs, which he did in ſuch lines as theſe: KYLSITHE.

* *Gignere ſolet ea ſylva boves candidiſſimos in formam Leonis jubam habentes, cætera manſuetis ſimillimos verò adeo feros*, &c. Deſcr. Regni Scotiæ, fol. xi.

Hic

Hic capit, hic rapit, hic terit, hic ferit, ecce dolores;
Vox tonat; æs ſonat; hic ruit; hic luit; arcto modo res.
Hic ſecat; hic necat; hic docet; hic nocet; iſte fugatur:
Hic latet, hic patet; hic premit, hic gemit; hic ſuperatur.

At this place that unfortunate monarch *James* III. was defeated by his rebellious ſubjects; in his flight fell down from his horſe, and bruiſed by his fall was drawn into a neighboring mill, and ſoon after aſſaſſinated by a Prieſt called in to receive his confeſſion and afford him ſpiritual aſſiſtance.

ST. NINIAN. Went through the ſmall town of St. *Ninian* *, a mile South of *Sterling*. The church had been the powder-magazine of the Rebels, who, on their return, blew it up in ſuch haſte, as to deſtroy ſome of their own people, and about fifteen innocent ſpectators.

STERLING. *Sterling* and its caſtle, in reſpect of ſituation, is a miniature of *Edinburgh*; is placed on a ridged hill, or rock, riſing out of a plain, having the caſtle at the upper end on a high precipitous rock. Within its walls was the palace of ſeveral of the *Scotch* Kings, a ſquare building, ornamented on three ſides with pillars reſting on groteſque figures projecting from the wall, and on the top of each pillar is a ſtatue, ſeemingly the work of fancy. Near it is the old parlement houſe, a vaſt room 120 feet long, very high, with a timbered roof, and formerly had a gallery running round the inſide. Below the caſtle are the ruins of the palace belonging to the Earls

* Apoſtle of the *Picts*, ſon of a prince of the *Cumbrian Britains*, converting the *Picts* as far as the *Grampian* hills. Died 432.

of

Tomkins pinx.t P. Mazell sculp.t

Sterling Castle.

of *Mar*, whoſe family had once the keeping of this fortreſs. There are ſtill the *Erſkine* arms and much ornamental carving on parts of it. The town of *Sterling* is incloſed with a wall; the ſtreets are irregular and narrow, except that which leads to the caſtle. Here, and at the village of *Bannockbourne*, is a conſiderable manufacture of coarſe carpets.

From the top of the caſtle is by far the fineſt view in *Scotland*. To the Eaſt is a vaſt plain rich in corn, adorned with woods, and watered with the river *Forth*, whoſe meanders are, before it reaches the ſea, ſo frequent and ſo large, as to form a multitude of moſt beautifull peninſulas; for in many parts the windings approximate ſo cloſe as to leave only a little iſthmus of a few yards. In this plain is an old abby, a view of *Alloa*, *Clackmannan*, *Falkirk*, the Firth of *Forth*, and the country as far as *Edinburgh*. On the North, the *Ochil* hills, and the moor where the battle of *Dumblain* was fought. To the Weſt, the ſtraith of *Menteith*, as fertile as the Eaſtern plain, and terminated by the Highland mountains, among which the ſummit of *Ben-Lomond* is very conſpicuous.

The *Sylva Caledonia*, or *Caledonian* Foreſt, begun a little North of *Sterling*, and paſſing through *Menteith* and *Straithern*, extended, according to *Boethius*, as far as *Athol* on one ſide, and *Lochaber* on the other. It is very ſlightly mentioned by the antients *; but the ſuppoſed extent is given by the *Scottiſh* hiſtorian.

FALKIRK.

Lie at *Falkirk*, a large ill-built town, ſupported by the great fairs for black cattle from the Highlands, it being computed that

* By *Pliny*, *lib.* iv. *c.* 16. and *Eumenius*, in his Panegyric on *Conſtantius*, *c.* 7.

24,000

24,000 head are annually ſold here. There is alſo a great deal of money got here by the carriage of goods, landed at *Carron* wharf, to *Glaſgow*. Such is the increaſe of trade in this country, that about twenty years ago not three carts could be found in the town, and at preſent there are above a hundred that are ſupported by their intercourſe with *Glaſgow*.

In the church-yard, on a plain ſtone, is the following epitaph on *John de Graham*, ſtyled the right hand of the gallant *Wallace*, killed at the battle of *Falkirk* in 1298: *

Here lies Sir *John* the *Grame* both wight and wiſe,
Ane of the chief reſkewit *Scotland* thriſe.
Ane better knight not to the world was lent
Nor was gude *Grame* of trueth, and of hardiment.
Mente manuque potens, et VALLÆ *fidus Achates*
Conditur hic Gramus *bello interfectus ab* Anglis.
22 *Julii*. 1298.

Near this is another epitaph, occaſioned by a ſecond battle of *Falkirk*, as diſgracefull to the *Engliſh* as the other was fatal to the *Scots*: the firſt was a well diſputed combat; the laſt, a pannic on both ſides, for part of each army flew, the one Weſt, the other Eaſt, each carrying the news of their ſeveral defeats, while the total deſtruction of our forces was prevented by the gallant behaviour of a brigadier, who with two regiments faced ſuch of the rebels as kept the field, and prevented any further advantages. The epitaph

* Fought between *Falkirk* and *Carron* works, at a place called to this day *Graham*'s Moor.

I allude

I allude to is in memory of Sir *Robert Monro* *, the worthy chieftain of that loyal clan, a family which loſt three brothers the ſame year in ſupport of the royal cauſe. Sir *Robert* being greatly wounded in the battle was murthered in cool blood, by the Rebels, with his brother Dr. *Monro*, who with fraternal piety was at that time dreſſing his wounds: the third was aſſaſſinated by miſtake for one who well deſerved his death for ſpontaneous barbarities on High-

* Conditur heic quod poterit mori
ROBERTI MONRO *de Foulis*, Eq. Bar.
Gentis ſui Principis
Militum Tribuni:
Vita in caſtris curiaque *Britannica*
Honeſtè productâ
Pro Libertate religione Patriæ
In acie honeſtiſſimé defunctâ
Prope FALKIRK *Jan.* xviii. 1746. Æt. 62.
Virtutis conſiliique fama
In *Montanorum* cohortis Præfectura
Quamdiu prælium FONTONÆUM memorabitur
Perduratura;
Ob amicitiam et fidem amicis
Humanitatum clementiamque adverſariis
Benevolentiam bonitatemque omnibus,
Trucidantibus etiam,
In perpetuum deſideranda.
DUNCANUS MONRO *de Obſdale*, M. D. Æt. 59.
Frater Fratrem linquere fugiens,
Saucium curans, ictus inermis
Commoriens cohoneſtat Urnam.

landers approaching according to proclamation to ſurrender their arms.

I have very often mentioned fields of battles in this part of the kingdom; ſcarce a ſpot has eſcaped unſtained with gore; for had they no publick enemy to contend with, the *Scots*, like the *Welſh* of old, turned their arms againſt each other.

IRON FOUNDERIES.

Carron iron-works lie about a mile from *Falkirk*, and are the greateſt of the kind in *Europe*: they were founded about eight years ago, before which there was not a ſingle houſe, and the country a mere moor. At preſent, the buildings of all ſorts are of vaſt extent, and above twelve hundred men are empioyed. The iron is ſmelted from the ſtone, then caſt into cannon, pots, and all ſorts of utenſils made in founderies. This work has been of great ſervice to the country, by teaching the people induſtry and a method of ſetting about any ſort of labor, which before the common people had ſcarce any notion of.

Carron wharf lies on the *Forth*, and is not only uſefull to the works, but of great ſervice even to *Glaſgow*, as conſiderable quantities of goods deſtined for that city are landed there. The canal likewiſe begins in this neighborhood, which, when effected, will prove another benefit to theſe works.

ARTHUR'S OVEN.

At a ſmall diſtance from the founderies, on a little riſing above the river *Carron*, ſtood that celebrated antiquity called *Arthur*'s Oven, which the ingenious Mr. *Gordon* * ſuppoſes to have been a

* *Itin. Septentr. p.* 24. *tab.* iv. As the book is very ſcarce, I have taken the liberty of having that plate copied into this work.

ſacellum,

ſacellum, or little chapel, a repoſitory for the *Roman Inſignia*, or ſtandards: but, to the mortification of every curious traveller, this matchleſs edifice is now no more; its barbarous owner, a *gothic* knight, cauſed it to be demoliſhed, in order to make a mill-dam with the materials, which, within leſs than a year, the *Naiades*, in reſentment of the ſacrilege, came down in a flood and entirely ſwept away.

Saw near *Callendar*-Houſe ſome part of *Antoninus*'s Wall, or, as it is called here, *Graham*'s Dyke *. The *vallum* and the ditch are here very evident, and both are of a great ſize, the laſt being forty feet broad and thirteen deep; it extended from the Firth of *Forth* to that of *Clyde*, and was defended at proper diſtances by forts and watch-towers, the work of the *Roman* legions under the command of *Lollius Urbicus*, in the reign of *Antoninus Pius*. According to Mr. *Gordon*, it began at old *Kirk Patrick* on the Firth of *Clyde*, and ended two miles Weſt of *Abercorn*, on the Firth of *Forth*, being in length 36 miles, 887 paces. SEPT. 12. GRAHAM'S DYKE.

Paſſed thro' *Burrowſtoneſs*, a town on the Firth, inveloped in ſmoke from the great ſalt-pans and vaſt collieries near it. The town-houſe is built in form of a caſtle. There is a good quay, much frequented by ſhipping; for conſiderable quantities of coal

* So called from *Graham*, who i ſaid to have firſt made a breach in this wall ſoon after the retreat of the *Romans* out of *Britain*. Vide *Boethius*, cxxxi.

are ſent from hence to *London*; and there are beſides ſome *Greenland* ſhips * belonging to the town.

Ride near *Abercorn*, called by *Bede* the monaſtery of *Abercurnig*; of which no mention is made in the accounts of the *Scotch* religious houſes: nor has there been for many centuries the leſt remains; for *Buchanan* ſays that none of any kind were to be met with even in his time; except the ruins of a tower belonging to the *Douglaſes*.

HOPETON-HOUSE.

Reach *Hopeton*-Houſe, the ſeat of the Earl of *Hopeton*; a houſe begun by Sir *William Bruce*, and finiſhed by Mr. *Adams*: is the handſomeſt I ſaw in *North Britain*: the front is enriched with pilaſters; the wings at ſome diſtance joined to it by a beautifull colonade: one wing is the ſtables, the other the library. In the laſt is a ſingle piece of lead ore weighing five tuns, got out of his Lordſhip's mines at the *Lead-hills*.

The great improvements round the houſe are very extenſive; but the gardens are ſtill in the old taſte: trees and ſhrubs ſucceed here greatly; among others were two *Portugal* laurels thirty feet high. Nothing can equal the grandeur of the approach to the houſe, or the proſpect from it. The ſituation is bold, on an eminence, commanding a view of the Firth of *Forth*, bounded on the North by the county of *Fife*; the middle is chequered with iſlands, ſuch as

* This year the whale-fiſhery began to revive; which for a few years paſt had been ſo unſucceſsfull, that ſeveral of the adventurers had thoughts of diſpoſing of their ſhips. Perhaps the whales had till this year deſerted thoſe ſeas; for *Marten*, p. 185 of his voyage to *Spitzbergen*, remarks, "That theſe animals, either weary "of their place, or ſenſible of their own danger, do often change their har"bours."

Garvey,

Garvey, *Inch Keith* *, and others; and to the South-Eaſt is a vaſt command of *Eaſt Lothian*, and the terminating object the great conic hill of *North Berwick*.

The whole ride from *Sterling* to *Queen's-Ferry* (near *Hopeton-*Houſe) is not to be paralleled for the elegance and variety of its proſpects: the whole is a compoſition of all that is great and beautifull: towns, villages, ſeats, and antient towers, decorate each bank of that fine expanſe of water the *Firth*; while the buſy ſcenes of commerce and rural œconomy are no ſmall addition to the ſtill life. The lofty mountains of the Highlands form a diſtant but auguſt boundary towards the North-Weſt; and the Eaſtern view is enlivened with ſhips perpetually appearing or vaniſhing amidſt the numerous iſles.

Paſs by *Queen's-Ferry*; fall into the *Edinburgh* road, and finiſh, this evening, in that capital, a moſt agreeable and proſperous Tour. It was impoſſible not to recall the idea of what I had ſeen; to imagine the former condition of this part of the kingdom, and to compare it with the preſent ſtate, and by a ſort of ſecond-ſight make a probable conjecture of the happy appearance it will aſſume in a

* This iſle is oppoſite *Leith*. By order of council, in 1497, all venereal patients in the neighborhood were tranſported there, *Ne quid detrimenti res publica caperet*. It is remarkable, that this diſorder, which was thought to have appeared in *Europe* only four years before, ſhould make ſo quick a progreſs. The horror of a diſeaſe, for which there was then ſuppoſed to be no cure, muſt have occaſioned this attention to ſtop the contagion; for even half a century after, one of the firſt monarchs of *Europe*, *Francis* I. fell a victim to it. The order is ſo curious that we have given it a place in the Appendix.

very

very few years. Nor could I forbear repeating the prophetic lines* of *Aaron Hill*, who seemed seized with a like *rêverie :*

Once more! O North, I view thy winding ſhores,
Climb thy bleak hills and croſs thy duſky moors.
Impartial view thee with an heedfull eye,
Yet ſtill by nature, not by cenſure try.
England thy ſiſter is a gay coquet,
Whom art enlivens, and temptations whet:
Rich, proud, and wanton, ſhe her beauty knows,
And in a conſcious warmth of beauty glows:
Scotland comes after like an unripe fair,
Who ſighs with anguiſh at her ſiſter's air;
Unconſcious, that ſhe'll quickly have her day,
And be the toaſt when *Albion*'s charms decay.

SEPT. 18. After a few days experience of the ſame hoſpitality in *Edinburgh* that I had met with in the Highlands, I continued my journey South, through a rich corn country, leaving the *Pentland* hills to the Weſt, whoſe ſides were covered with a fine turf. Before I reached *Crook*, a ſmall village, the country grew worſe: after this it aſſumed a Highland appearance, the hills were high, the vales narrow, and there was beſides a great ſcarcity of trees, and hardly any corn; inſtead, was abundance of good paſturage for ſheep, there being great numbers in theſe parts, which ſupply the North of *England*. The roads are bad, narrow, and often on the edges

* Written on a window in *North Britain*.

of precipices, impending over the river *Tweed*, here an inconſidera-ble ſtream. Reach

MOFFAT, a ſmall neat town, famous for its ſpaws; one ſaid to be uſefull in ſcrophulous caſes, the other a chalybeate, which makes this place much reſorted to in ſummer. Doctor *Walker*, miniſter of the place, ſhewed me in manuſcript his natural hiſtory of the *weſtern iſles*, which will do him much credit whenever he favors the world with it. MOFFAT.

Here the unfortunate nobleman Lord Viſcount *Kenmure* ſet up the Pretender's ſtandard on the 12th of *October* 1715, in fatal compliance with the importunities of the diſaffected Lowlanders.

The country between *Moffat* and *Lockerby* is very good, a mixture of downs and corn-land, with a few ſmall woods: the country grows quite flat and very unpleaſant: but inceſſant rains throughout my journey from *Edinburgh*, rendered this part of my tour both diſagreeable and unedifying. Croſs a ſmall river called the *Sark*, which divides the two kingdoms, and enter CUMBERLAND.

About three miles farther croſs the *Eſk* over a handſome ſtone-bridge, and lie at the ſmall village of *Longtown*. The country is very rich in corn, but quite bare of trees, and very flat. Near this village, at *Netherby*, are the ruins of a *Roman* ſtation, where ſtatues, weapons and coins are often dug up.

I had not leiſure to remark the ſeveral antiquities that Mr. *Graham* is poſſeſſed of: but out of them ſelect the following, engraven in the annexed plate, and in the tail piece to the concluding page.

No. I. is a figure in a dreſs with cloſe ſleeves, not unlike in the body

body to a carter's frock, or what *Montfaucon* calls *ſagum clauſum**, reaching down to the heels. On one ſide is a boar, on the other a wheel, and beneath that an altar: in the left hand is part of a *cornucopia*. The figure is evidently *Gauliſh*, but the hiſtory is obſcure: the boar is often an emblem of *Caledonia*: the wheel a known type of Fortune: it is alſo a concomitant of two *Saxon* Deities †, of the idol of the *Sun* and of *Seater*; and I would chuſe to derive it from *Germany* or *Gaul* rather than from *Rome*. It ſeems a Deity of ſome barbarous nation, but it is a difficult taſk to aſſign it to any one in particular. The *Gauls* and *Germans* were neighbors; they might in ſome inſtances have the ſame objects of worſhip. As the *Roman* armies were latterly compoſed of different *Gauliſh* and foreign nations, their Deities were introduced and intermixed with thoſe of the *Romans*, a moſt ſuperſtitious people, ready and accuſtomed to adopt thoſe of every country. We need not wonder at the variety of figures found in this country, for it appears from an inſcription ‡ that there had been at *Cambeck* a *Temple of every nation*, a latitudinarian Pantheon, ſo that every religion enjoyed a liberty of conſcience.

I conjecture that this figure was the *mater Deûm*, the mother of the gods of ſome *Gauliſh* or *German* nation, probably engraven after their intercourſe with the *Romans*, for there appears a mixture of

* III. part 1. tab. xlvii.

† *Verſtegan*. 69. 78. *Wormii Mon. Dan*. p. 16.

‡ The inſcription runs thus------B. V. *omnium Gentium* Templum olim vetuſtate conlabſum JUL. PITIANUS P. P reſtituit.

emblem.

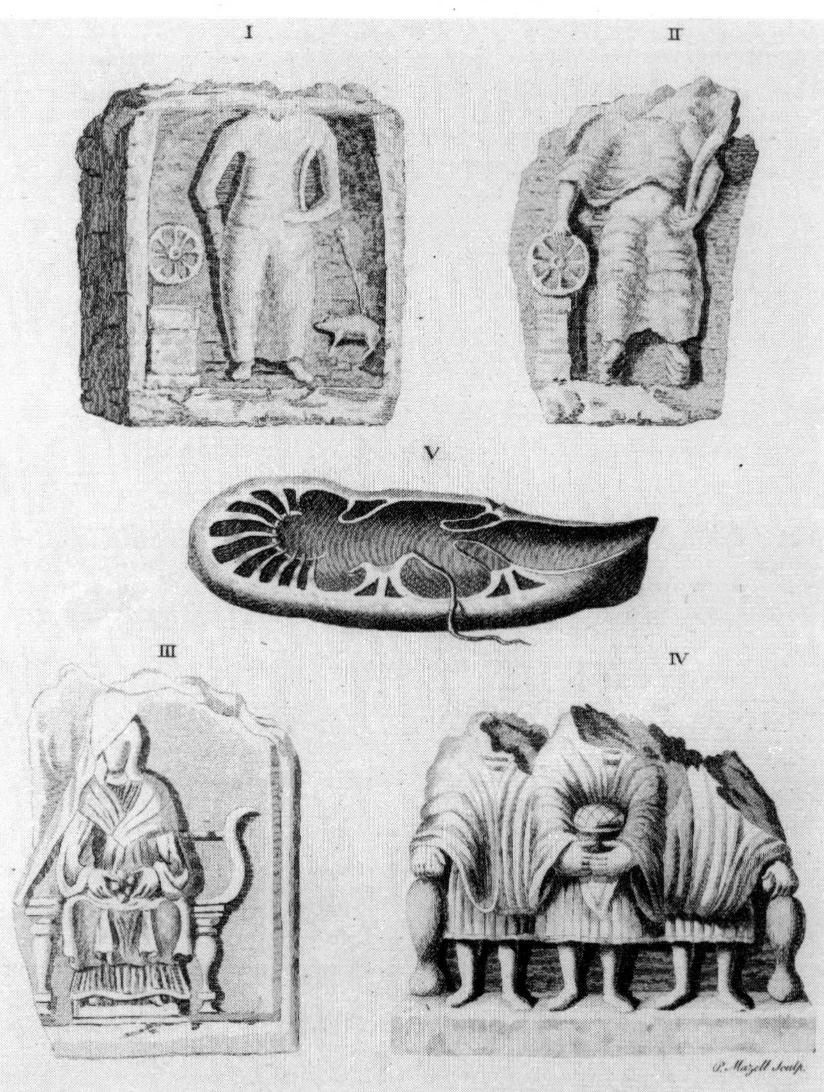

ANTIQUITIES AT NETHERBY.

emblem. *Cybele* or the mother of the gods is often engraven with a *cornucopia:* and *Tacitus** mentions a *German* people that worſhipped this goddeſs, and uſed the boar as the emblem of their ſuperſtition: which was an amulet, a charm againſt all dangers. They ſeldom made uſe of iron weapons, but often of clubs. It appears to me that what riſes above the boar is intended for an inſtrument of that kind. The figure is deprived of its head; I cannot purſue my compariſon with this deity any farther.

No. II. is a ſecond headleſs figure reſembling the former, only that a ſort of ſhort cloſe mantle covers the ſhoulders and breaſt. It has the wheel, altar, and *cornucopia*; but beneath the feet appear the *crupezia*, ſuch as are beneath the feet of the celebrated ſtatue of the dancing *Fawn.*

No. III. is a figure ſitting in a chair (with large elbows), cloathed in garments much plaited and folded: on the lap are apples or fruits. *Nehalenia*, a *Zeland* goddeſs, is repreſented in this attitude†, and her lap thus filled: the habit differs, but this deity might have been adopted by another nation, who dreſſed her according to its own mode.

No. IV. is a curious groupe of three figures ſtanding with their backs to a long ſeat with elbows. They are habited in a looſe *ſagum* or *ſaic*, as the *Britons* name it, reaching but little below the knees: that in the middle is diſtinguiſhed by a pointed flap, and a veſſel filled whether with fruits or corn is not very evident. Theſe may perhaps be the *Deæ matres* of the barbarous nations, and

* De moribus *Germanorum*. c. 45.

† *Montfaucon*. II. part ii. p. 443.

introduced here by ſome of the *German* levies; there having been found in *Britain* three altars dedicated to them by the *Tungrian* cohort. They were local deities, protectreſſes of certain towns and villages among the *Gauls* * and *Germans*, by whom they were tranſported into *Britain*, which is acknowledged in two inſcriptions, where they are called *tranſmarinæ.* If they were rural deities the contents of the cup is very apt. I may remark that the antients in general were fond of the number THREE; and the *Gauls* † are known to groupe their deities very frequently in triplets; a number the moſt complete as it regards *Beginning*, *Middle*, and *End.*

The Vth figure is a ſpecies of ſhoe in all probability belonging to the natives of this iſland; and was found in a moor in *Cumberland.* It is formed of one piece of leather; and nicely adapted to the foot. The *cuoranen* till very lately worn by the Highlanders was of this nature; the *mockaſins* of the *North American* nations are not much diſſimilar: ſo exactly does neceſſity operate in diſtant countries in producing the ſame inventions.

The 1ſt figure in the tail piece is dreſſed in its *ſagum.* On the right is a veſſel ſtanding on two high legs or ſupports. The figure ſeems going to fling in what it holds in one hand: the other leans on ſomething that reſembles an ear of corn. This probably is a rural deity of ſome barbarous nation.

No. II. is a victory treading with one foot on a globe: in one hand a mural crown; in the other a palm branch. Beneath the

* *Archaelogia.* Vol. III.

† *Gordon.* tab. xxxvi. xxxix. and xl. *Keyſler Antiq. Celt.* tab. xv.

crown,

crown, Vic. Aug. or *Victoria Augusti*. Mr. *Horsley*, who has engraven this stone, supposes it to belong to the emperor *Commodus*.

No. III. is also engraven by the same gentleman. The upper figure is that of a *Sea Goat*, a *chimera*; the other he styles a *Pegasus*, and has given it more exact representation of wings than are found on the sculpture.

Sept. 20. Carlisle.

Cross the *Eden* to *Carlisle*, a pleasant city, surrounded with walls, like *Chester*, but they are very dirty, and kept in very bad repair. The castle is antient, but makes a good appearance at a distance: the view from it is fine, of rich meadows, at this time covered with thousands of cattle, it being fair-day. The *Eden* here forms two branches, and insulates the ground; over one is a bridge of four, over the other one of nine arches. There is besides a prospect of a rich country, and a distant view of *Cold-fells*, *Cross-fells*, *Skiddaw*, and other mountains.

The cathedral * is very imperfect, *Cromwel* having pulled down part to build barracks with the materials. There remains some portion that was built in the *Saxon* times, with very massy pillars and round arches. The rest is more modern, said to have been built in the reign of *Edward* III. who had in one part an apartment to lodge in. The arches in this latter building are sharp pointed: the East window remarkably fine.

The manufactures of *Carlisle* are chiefly of printed linnens, for which near 3000 l. *per annum* is paid in duties. It is also

* Begun by *Walter*, deputy of these parts, under *William Rufus*; but the new choir was not founded till about 1354.

noted for a great manufacture of whips, which employs numbers of children.

Salmons appear in the *Eden* in numbers ſo early as the months of *December* and *January*; and the *London*, and even *Newcaſtle* markets, are ſupplied with early fiſh from this river: but it is remarkable that they do not viſit the *Eſk* in any quantity till *April*, notwithſtanding the mouths of both theſe waters are at a ſmall diſtance from each other. I omitted in its proper place an account of the *Newcaſtle* fiſhery, therefore inſert here the little I could collect relating to it. The fiſh ſeldom appear in the *Tyne* till *February*: there are about 24 fiſheries on the river, beſides a very conſiderable were, and the whole annual capture amounts to about 36,000 fiſh. I was informed that once the fiſh were brought from *Berwick* and cured at *Newcaſtle*; but at preſent, notwithſtanding all goes under the name of *Newcaſtle* Salmon, very little is taken there, in compariſon of what is caught in the *Tweed*.

The country near *Carliſle* conſiſts of ſmall encloſures; but a little farther on, towards *Penrith*, changes into coarſe downs. On the Eaſt, at a diſtance, are ridges of high hills running parallel to the road, with a good incloſed country in the intervening ſpace. Above *Penrith* is a rich incloſed tract, mixed with hedge-row trees and woods. On the South-Weſt, a proſpect of high and craggy mountains. After I left *Lockerby*, Nature, as if exhauſted with her labors in the lofty hills of *Scotland*, ſeemed to have lain down and repoſed herſelf for a conſiderable ſpace; but here began to riſe again with all the ſublimity of *alpine* majeſty.

PENRITH.

PENRITH is an antient town, ſeated at the foot of a hill: is a great thoroughfare for travellers; but has little other trade, except

tanning

tanning and a ſmall manufacture of checks. In the church-yard is a monument of great antiquity, conſiſting of two ſtone pillars eleven feet ſix inches high, and five in circumference in the lower part, which is rounded; the upper is ſquare, and tapers to a point: in the ſquare part is ſome fret-work, and the relievo of a croſs; and on the interior ſide of one is the faint repreſentation of ſome animal. Both theſe ſtones are mortiſed at their lower part into a round one: they are about fifteen feet aſunder; the ſpace between them is incloſed on each ſide with two very large but thin ſemicircular ſtones; ſo that there is left a walk between pillar and pillar of two feet in breadth. Two of theſe leſſer ſtones are plain, the other two have certain figures at preſent ſcarce intelligible.

ANTIENT COLUMNS.

Theſe ſtones ſeem to have been monumental, and are evidently chriſtian, as appears by the croſs on the capital: fable ſays that they were to perpetuate the memory of *Ceſarius*, a hero of gigantic ſtature, whoſe body extended from ſtone to ſtone: but it is probable that the ſpace marked by theſe columns contained ſeveral bodies, or might have been a family ſepulchre. I muſt here obſerve that ſince the publication of the former editions of this book I have had opportunity of re-examining theſe ſtones, and comparing them with Doctor *Todd*'s figures engraven in my XIIIth plate: and am convinced that they are entirely fictitious; and ſuch is the opinion of ſome gentlemen of the place whom I conſulted on the occaſion.

Not far from theſe pillars is another called the *Giant's thumb*, five feet eight inches high, with an expanded head perforated on both ſides; from the middle the ſtone riſes again into a leſſer head rounded at top, but no part has a tendency to the figure of a croſs, being

being in no part mutilated; ſo that it is difficult to judge the uſe or deſign of this pillar *.

CHURCH. The church is very neat: the galleries ſupported by twenty ſtones each ten feet four inches high, and four feet two in circumference. On one of the walls is this melancholy record of a peſtilence that waſted the country in the latter end of the reign of Queen *Elizabeth*:

> A. D. M. D X C VIII ex gravi peſte quæ regionibus hiſce incubuit, obierunt apud *Penrith* 2260. *Kendal* 2500 *Richmond* 2200. *Carliſle* 1196. †
>
> Poſteri
>
> avortite vos et vivite

On conſulting a very old regiſter kept in this pariſh it appears that the plague raged here for fifteen months; from the 22[d] *Sept*[r] 1597 to 5th *Jan* 1598. and that only 680 perſons were buried in the pariſh during that time. It ſeems therefore probable that *Penrith* muſt have been the centre of ſome particular diſtrict, and that the numbers recorded on the wall muſt comprehend all that died within that ſpace. *Penrith* now contains about 2000 ſouls. At a medium, 63 have died annually the laſt ten years, or 630 in the whole. In the ten years preceding the peſtilence there were

* *Vide* tab. iii of the 1ſt and 2d editions.

† It broke out in *Carliſle* *Oct*. 3d. That city in all probability was much more populous than *Penrith*, but being on the borders of *Scotland*, no notice of any deaths was taken except thoſe in the city and places quite adjacent.

only

only 686 funerals; ſo that there was no great difference between the number of inhabitants at that and the preſent time. Some centuries previous to this *Penrith* had another viſitation of the ſame nature. When the *Scots* under the Earl of *Douglas* in 1380 made an inroad into *Cumberland*, they ſurprized this place at the time of the fair *, and returned with immenſe booty; but ſuffered ſeverely in conſequence, for they introduced into their country the plague contracted in this town, which ſwept away one third of the inhabitants of *Scotland* †.

CASTLE.

The caſtle is at the ſkirts of the town, and now very ruinous. It appears not to have been of a high antiquity; for in a compromiſe of certain differences between *Henry* III. and *Alexander* King of *Scotland*, it was ſtipulated that *Henry* ſhould grant to *Alexander* 200 librates of land in *Northumberland* or *Cumberland*, if ſo much of *Henry*'s land could be found in any of the places where no caſtle was ſituated; and *Penrith* was part of this grant. *Richard* Duke of *Glouceſter*, afterwards *Richard* III. reſided frequently at this caſtle, and either was the founder or repaired it greatly, for there is no mention of it before his time. The ſeignory of *Penrith* ‡ was part of the great eſtate he had with his Dutcheſs: by his reſidence here and his magnificent mode of living he gained great popularity in the North, and he ſeemed to depend greatly on the troops from that part, for he cauſed five thouſand to march from thence to *London* to ſupport his coronation.

* *Hollinſhed*. 428.

† *Guthrie's Hiſt. Scotl.* III. 123.

‡ *Buck's Life of Richard* III.

The

The caſtle was diſmantled by *Cromwel*, but it does not appear in any hiſtory to have ſuſtained a ſiege.

Full many a gem of pureſt ray ſerene,
The dark unfathom'd caves of ocean bear:
Full many a flower is born to bluſh unſeen,
And waſte its ſweetneſs in the deſert air.

For in this town lives Miſs *Calvin*, of exquiſite ſkill in painting of plants and flowers with equal elegance and accuracy: a heaven-born genius, obſcure and unknown!

SEPT. 21. Croſs over the *Eimot* at *Yeoman*'s bridge, and enter WESTMORELAND. At a ſmall diſtance beyond the bridge near the road ſide is the circle called *Arthur*'s round table, conſiſting of a high dike of earth, and a deep foſs within ſurrounding an area twenty-nine yards in diameter. There are two entrances exactly oppoſite to each other; which interrupt the ditch, in thoſe parts filled to a level with the middle. Some ſuppoſe this to have been deſigned for tilting matches, and that the champions entered at each opening. Perhaps that might have been the purpoſe of it; for the ſize forbids one to ſuppoſe it to be an encampment.

ARTHUR'S ROUND TABLE.

MAYBOROUGH.

A little to the North of this, on the ſummit of a ſmall hill, is *Mayborough*, a vaſt circular dike of looſe ſtones: the height and the diameter at the bottom is ſtupendous: it ſlopes on both ſides, and is entirely formed of pebbles, ſuch as are collected out of rivers. There is an entrance on the Eaſt ſide leading into an area eighty-eight yards in diameter. Near the middle is an upright ſtone nine feet eight inches high, and ſeventeen in circumference in the thickeſt part.

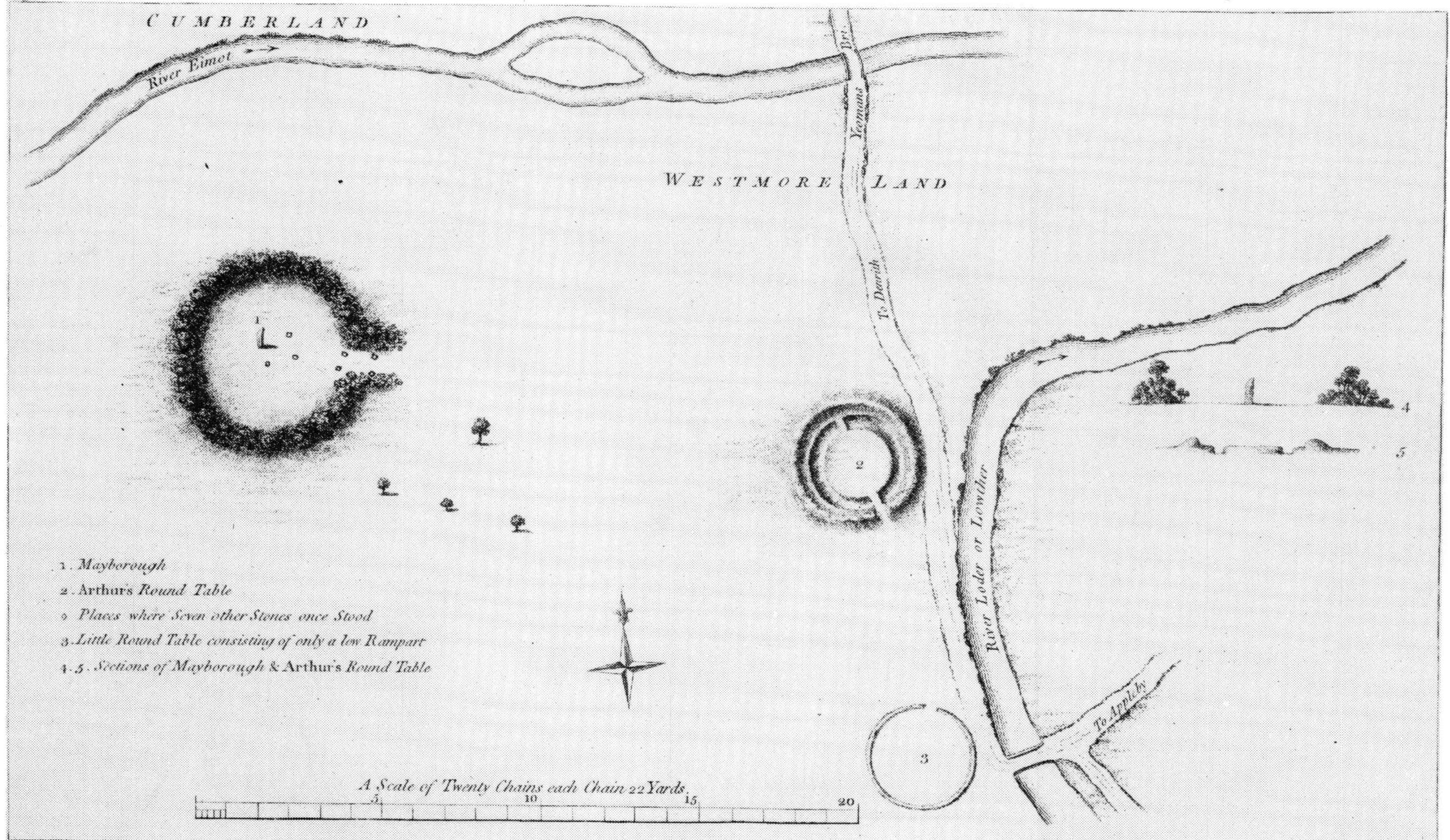
CUMBERLAND
River Eimot
Bri.
Yeomans
WESTMORE LAND
To Penrith
River Loder or Lowther
To Appleby
1
2
3
4
5
1. Mayborough
2. Arthur's Round Table
∘ Places where Seven other Stones once Stood
3. Little Round Table consisting of only a low Rampart
4. 5. Sections of Mayborough & Arthur's Round Table
A Scale of Twenty Chains each Chain 22 Yards
5
10
15
20

Moses Griffith del.

P. Mazell sculp.

SHAP ABBY.

part. There had been three more placed ſo as to form (with the other) a ſquare. Four again ſtood on the ſides of the entrance, viz. one on each exterior corner; and one on each interior: but excepting that at preſent remaining, all the others have long ſince been blaſted to clear the ground.

The uſe of this accumulation ſeems to have been the ſame with that called *Bryn-gwyn* at *Trer Dryw* in *Angleſea* *, a ſupreme conſiſtory of *druidical* adminiſtration, as the *Britiſh* names import. That in *Angleſea* is conſtructed in the ſame manner with this: but at preſent there are no remains of columns in the interior part. Tradition is entirely ſilent about the origin of this place: nothing can be collected from the name which is *Saxon*, and given long after its conſtruction.

Almoſt oppoſite to *Mayborough* on the *Cumberland* ſide of the *Eimot* is a vaſt *cairn* or tumulus, compoſed of round ſtones, and ſurrounded with large grit ſtones of different ſizes, ſome a yard ſquare; which all-together form a circle ſixty feet in diameter.

CLIFTON MOOR.

Croſs the *Lowther* or *Loder*, and in about three or four miles diſtance paſs *Clifton Moor*, where the Rebels in 1745 ſacrificed a few men to ſave the reſt of their army. Reach

SHAP PRIORY.

Shap or *Heppe*, a long village with the ruins of the Priory of *Premonſtrenſian canons* and its beautifull tower placed in a ſequeſtered bottom to the North-Weſt of the road. The religious of this houſe were originally placed at *Preſton* in *Kendal* by *Thomas* ſon of *Goſpatric*; and afterwards removed to this valley, which in old times was called the valley of *Mary Magdalene*, and was granted to

* *Mona Antiqua*. 2d ed. 90.

them by *Robert de Vetevipont* in the thirteenth year of King *John*. *Heppe* took its name from *Matthew de Heppe*, the firſt owner of the lands *.

Rows of stones.

On the common near the road ſide about half a mile beyond the village are certain large circles, and ovals formed of ſmall ſtones: and parallel to the road commences a double row of granites of immenſe ſizes, croſſed at the end by another row, all placed at ſome diſtance from each other. This alley I may call it, extended once above a mile; paſſing quite through the village; perſons now living remember to have ſeen ſome ſtones that formed part of the lines, but now blaſted in order to clear the ground. The ſpace between the lines at the South end is eighty-eight feet: they converge towards each other, for near *Shap* the diſtance decreaſes to fifty-nine feet; and it is probable that they met and concluded in a point forming a wedge. That this monument was *Daniſh* may be inferred from the cuſtom of the *Northern* nation of arranging their recording ſtones in forms that they ſeemed to determine ſhould be expreſſive of certain events: thoſe that were placed in a ſtrait and long order commemorated the emulations of champions: ſquares ſhewed equeſtrian conflicts: circles, the interments of families: wedge-ſhaped, a fortunate victory †. Succeſs might have attended the Northern invaders in this place, which gave riſe to their long arrangement: the fall of ſome conſanguineous heroes in the action cauſed the gratefull tribute of the ſtoney circles.

* *Dugdale Monaſt.* II. 595.

† *Olaus Magnus* de Gent. Septentr. lib. 1. c. 18.

Paſs

Paſs over *Shap* fells, more black, dreary and melancholy than any of the Highland hills, being not only barren, but deſtitute of every picturefque beauty. This gloomy ſcene continues for ſeveral miles: leave on the right the narrow valley of *Long Sladale*, and at a diſtance the mountain of *Kenmoor* fell, famous for its ſlate quarries. The proſpect grows more chearful within a ſmall diſtance of

KENDAL, a large town, ſeated in a beautifull valley prettily cultivated, and watered by the river *Ken* or *Kent*. The principal ſtreet is above a mile long, running North and South: the houſes old and irregular, moſtly of wood plaiſtered. Yet the whole has an air of neatneſs and induſtry without the leſt oſtentation of wealth; none appear meanly poor, or inſultingly rich. The number of inhabitants is about ſeven thouſand; chiefly engaged in manufactures of linſies, worſted ſtockings woven and knit, and a coarſe ſort of woollen cloth called *cottons* ſent to *Glaſgow*, and from thence to *Virginia* for the uſe of the *Negroes*. The carding and the frizing mills, the raſping and cutting of logwood by different machines are well worth ſeeing: and the tenter fells all round the town where the cloth is ſtretched, ſhew the extent of the manufactures, which employ great quantities of wool from *Scotland* and *Durham*. KENDAL: MANUFACTURES.

Yet the place labors under great diſadvantages: the country near it yields no corn except oats: the fuel is in general peat; for the coals being brought from *Wigan* and other diſtant places, coſt nineteen ſhillings *per* tun: yet notwithſtanding, it has flouriſhed in manufactures from the time of *Richard* the Second to the preſent: *Cambden* honors it with this encomium, *Lanificii Gloria, et Induſtria præcellens*.

 The

CHURCH.

The church is large, divided into five iſles. The moſt remarkable tomb is one in the altar form of black marble, with various arms on the ſide and end, ſuppoſed to be that of *William Parr*, anceſtor of *William Parr* Marquiſs of *Northampton*, and his ſiſter Queen *Catherine*, wife to *Henry* VIII.

CASTLE.

The ruins of the caſtle are on the ſummit of a round hill on the Weſt ſide of the town. It is of great antiquity; but the founder is not known. It appears to me to have been built on an artificial mount raiſed on the top of the hill, with a deep foſs round the baſe. The Barony of *Kendal* was granted by *William* the Conqueror to *Ivo de Talebois*, one of his followers, whoſe deſcendents frequently reſided in the caſtle. From them it paſſed by marriage to the *Roſſes*, and from them to the *Parrs*: and when in their poſſeſſion *Catherine* afterwards Queen of *England* was born here; a lady who had the good fortune to deſcend to the grave with her head, in all probability merely by outliving her tyrant. It does not appear that this caſtle ſuſtained any ſiege: but in 1174 the *Scots* under *Duncan* Earl of *Fife* entered and plundered the town, broke open the churches, put all the inhabitants to the ſword ſparing neither age nor ſex*.

WATER-CROOK; THE OLD CONCANGIUM.

Take a very pleaſant walk to *Water-Crook*, a mile diſtant, along the ſides of the *Ken*. This had been the *Concangium* of the *Notitia*, a ſtation on the Eaſt ſide of the river, whoſe veſtiges are almoſt worn away by the plough. Altars, coins, and other antiquities have been found here. I ſaw in the walls of the barn of the farm houſe, the monumental inſcription preſerved by Mr. *Horſely*, p. 300.

* *Holinſhed's Chron.* 91.

ſuppoſed

ſuppoſed by him to have been in memory of two freed-men; and that there was added the penalty of a fine on any who preſumed to bury in that ſepulchre. Here is preſerved an altar un-inſcribed, but ornamented with beautifull feſtoons: and I alſo ſaw the remains of the ſtatue ſuppoſed of *Bacchus* or *Silenus*.

Croſs the river, and walk over ſome fine meadows. Paſs by ſome large round hillocks, one appearing artificial: aſcend to gain the heights above the town: leave below me near the ſkirts a well called the *Anchorite*'s, probably from ſome hermitage once in its neigborhood. Reach *Caſtle law* hill, a great artificial mount above the town, and oppoſite to the caſtle. The ſummit is flat: juſt within its verge is a circular ditch; and another tranſverſe probably the place of the foundation of a tower. Round the baſe is a deep foſs and high dike, and on the Eaſt ſide of the dike two baſtions to give it additional ſtrength. Immediately below is a ſpot called *battle place*, but tradition does not preſerve the reaſon of the name.

Croſs the *Ken*, and in an hour and a half, North of *Burton*, enter LANCASHIRE. Reach its capital, *Lancaſter*, a large and well-built town, ſeated on the *Lune*, a river navigable for ſhips of 250 tuns as high as the bridge. The cuſtom-houſe is a ſmall but moſt elegant building, with a portico ſupported by four ionic pillars, on a beautifull plain pediment. There is a double flight of ſteps, a ruſtic ſurbaſe and coins; a work that does much credit to Mr. *Gillow*, the architect, an inhabitant of this town. LANCASTER.

The church is ſeated on an eminence, and commands an extenſive but not a pleaſing view. The caſtle is entire, the courts of

juſtice

juſtice are held in it; and it is alſo the county jail. The front is very handſome, conſiſts of two large angular towers, with a handſome gateway between.

Eleven miles farther is the village of *Garſtang*, ſeated on a fertile plain, bounded on the Eaſt by the *fells*, on the Weſt by *Pelling* moſs, which formerly made an eruption like that of *Solway*. The adjacent country is famous for producing the fineſt cattle in all the county. A gentleman in that neighborhood has refuſed 30 guineas for a three year old cow: calves of a month old have been ſold for 10; and bulls from 70 to 100 guineas, which have afterwards hired out for the ſeaſon for 30; ſo notwithſtanding his misfortune, well might honeſt *Barnaby* celebrate the cattle of this place.

> Veni *Garſtang* ubi nata
> Sunt Armenta fronte lata.
> Veni *Garſtang*, ubi malè
> Intrans forum beſtiale,
> Fortè vacillando vico
> Huc et illuc cum amico,
> In Juvencæ dorſum rui
> Cujus cornu læſus fui.

A little to the Eaſt is a ruined tower, the remains of *Grenehawgh* caſtle, built as *Cambden* ſuppoſes, by *Thomas Stanley* firſt Earl of *Derby*, to protect himſelf from the outlawed nobility, whoſe eſtates had been granted him by *Henry* VII.

Haſtened

Haſtened through *Preſton*, *Wigan*, *Warrington*, and *Cheſter*, and finiſhed my journey with a rapture of which no fond parent can be ignorant, that of being again reſtored to two innocent prattlers after an abſence equally regretted by all parties. SEPT. 22.

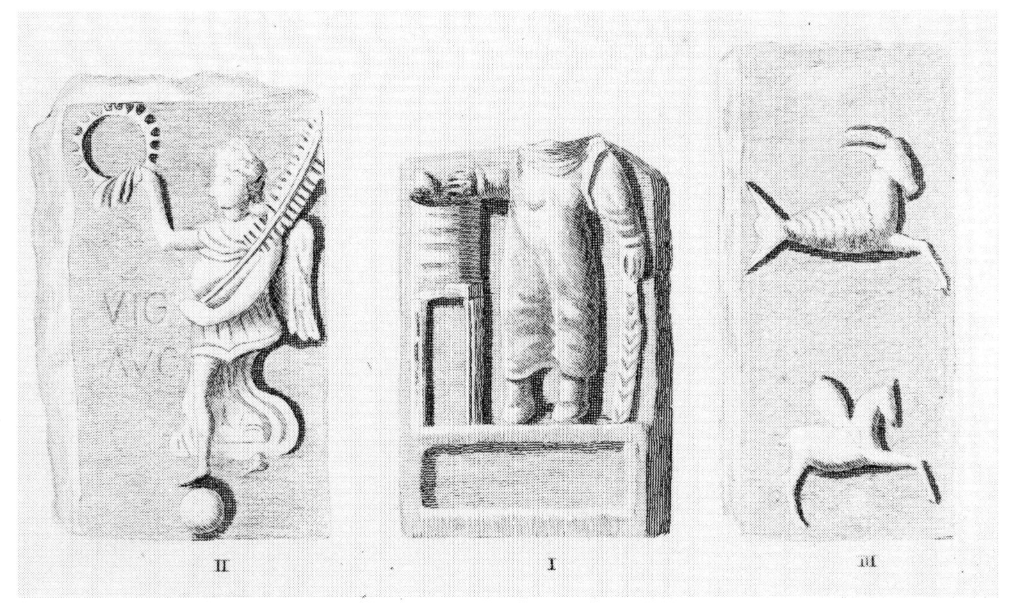

II I III

APPENDIX.

NUMBER I.

OF SCOTCH PINES;

By JAMES FARQUHARSON, Eſq. of INVERCAULD.

IT is generally believed that there are two kinds of fir trees, the produce of *Scotland*, viz. the red or reſinous large trees, of a fine grain, and hard ſolid wood: the other, a white wooded fir with a much ſmaller proportion of reſin in it, of a coarſer grain, and a ſoft ſpungy nature, never comes to ſuch a ſize, and much more liable to decay. At firſt appearance, this would readily denote two diſtinct ſpecies, but I am convinced that all the trees in *Scotland*, under the denomination of *Scotch* fir, are the ſame; and

 that

that the difference of the quality of the wood, and ſize of the trees, is entirely owing to circumſtances, ſuch as the climate, ſituation, and ſoil they grow in. Theſe fineſt fir trees, appear in the moſt mountainous parts of the Highlands of *Scotland*, in glens or on ſides of hills generally lying to a Northerly aſpect, and the ſoil of a hard gravelly conſiſtence, being the natural produce of theſe places; the winged ſeeds are ſcattered in quantities by the winds, from the cones of the adjacent trees, which expand in *April* and *May*, with the heat of the ſun; theſe ſeedlings when young, riſe extremely cloſe together, this makes them grow ſtraight, and free from ſide branches of any ſize, to the height of 50 or 60 feet before they acquire the diameter of a foot: even in this progreſs to height, they are very ſlow, occaſioned by the poorneſs of the ſoil, and the numbers on a ſmall ſurface, which I may ſay makes them in a conſtant ſtate of war for their ſcanty nouriſhment, the ſtronger and talleſt by degrees overtopping the weaker, and when the winds blow they laſh againſt one another, this aſſiſts in beating off any horizontal branches that might damage the timber with knots, as well as by degrees cruſhes the overtopped trees. In ſuch ſtate of hoſtility they continue ſtruggling until the maſter trees acquire ſome ſpace around them; then they begin to ſhoot out in a more buſhy manner at the top, gradually loſing their ſpiral form, increaſing afterwards more in ſize of body than height, ſome acquiring four feet diameter, and above ſixty feet of height to the branches fit for the fineſt deal board. The growth is ſtill extremely ſlow, as is plainly proved by the ſmallneſs of the grain of the wood, which appears diſtinctly in circles, from the centre to the bark. Upon cutting a tree overcloſe at the root, I can venture to point out the exact age, which in theſe old firs comes to an amazing number of years. I lately pitched upon on a tree of two feet and a half diameter, as this is near the ſize of a planted fir of fifty years of age mentioned, and I counted exactly two hundred and fourteen circles or coats, which makes this natural fir above four times the age of the planted one. Now as to planted firs, theſe are raiſed firſt in dreſſed ground from the ſeed, where they ſtand two ſeaſons or more, then are planted out in the ground they are to continue in at regular diſtances, have a clear circumference round them for extending both roots and branches; the one gives too quick nouriſhment to the tree which ſhoots out in luxuriant growths, and the other allows many of the branches to ſpread horizontally, ſpoiling the timber with knots; beſides, this quick growth occaſions theſe thick yearly circular coats of wood, which form a coarſe grain, of a ſpungy ſoft nature. The juices never after ripen into a proportional quantity their reſinous preſervative balm: ſo that the plantations decay before the wood acquires age, or a valuable ſize, and the timber when uſed in work has neither ſtrength, beauty, nor duration. I believe the climate has likewiſe a great ſhare in forming the nature of the beſt wood, which I account for in the following manner. The moſt mountainous parts of the Highlands, particularly the Northerly hanging ſituations, where theſe fine fir trees are, have a much ſhorter time of vegetation than a more Southerly expoſure, or the lower open countries, being ſhaded by high hills from the rays of the ſun even at mid-day for months together, ſo that with regard to other vegetables nature viſibly continues longer in a torpid ſtate there than in other places of the ſame latitude. This dead ſtate of nature for ſo long a time yearly appears to me neceſſary to form the ſtrength and health of this particular ſpecies of timber. No doubt they may at firſt ſhow a gratefulneſs for better ſoil and more ſun by ſhooting out ſpontaneouſly, but if the plant or tree is ſo altered by this luxury that it cannot attain any degree of perfection fit for the purpoſes intended, the attempt certainly proves in vain.

From what is ſaid above, it is not at all my intention to diſſuade from planting *Scotch* fir, but to encourage thoſe that have the proper ſoil and ſituation to do ſo, being of opinion that where theſe circumſtances agree, and there, planting not in lines, but irregularly and thicker than common, the trees will come to be of equal ſize and value with the natural ones. In confidence of this, I have planted ſeveral millions on the ſides of hills out of reach of ſeed from the natural firs.

NUM-

NUMBER II.

OF ELGIN AND THE SHIRE OF MURRAY;

By the Rev. Mr. SHAW, Minifter of ELGIN.

THE parifh of ELGIN can afford little matter for anfwering Mr. *Pennant*'s quæries, and therefore I extend my view thro' the whole province or country of *Murray*, extending by the coaft from the river of *Spey* to the Eaft, to the river of *Beauly* to the Weft, which is the boundary of the province of *Rofs*: and extending to the South-Weft as far as the North end of *Loch-Lochy*, and comprehending the countries of *Strathfpey*, *Badenoch*, *Strathern*, *Strath-nairn*, and *Strath-verick*, all which were the feats of the antient *Moravienfes*. I fhall make my anfwers to the quæries in order, and advance nothing but what confifts with my perfonal knowledge, or for which I have unqueftionable authority.

I. This province is naturally divided by the rivers of *Spey*, *Loffey*, *Findern*, *Nairn*, *Nefs*, and *Beauly*. The river of *Spey* rifing on the borders of *Lochaber* is more than fixty *Scotch* miles, or a hundred *Englifh*

English in length, but too rapid to be navigable. Upon this river great floats of fir and birch wood are carried down to the firth; the float is guided by a man ſitting in a *Courach*, of which *Solinus*, Cap. 22. ſays of the *Iriſh*, "*Navigant vimineis alveis, quos circumdant ambitione tergorum bubulorum*," a ſhort but exact deſcription of the *Courach*. It is in ſhape oval, about 4 feet long and three broad, a ſmall keel from head to ſtern, a few ribs croſs the keel, and a ring of pliable wood round the lip of it, the whole covered with the rough hide of an ox or a horſe. The rower ſits on a tranſverſe ſeat in the middle, and holds in his hand a rope, the end of which is tied to the float, and with the other hand he manages a paddle, and keeps the float in deep water and brings it to ſhore when he pleaſes. The rivers of *Loſſey*, *Findern* and *Nairn* have nothing remarkable in them, but the river of *Neſs* is obſervable on the following accounts, viz. It runs from *Loch-Neſs*, a lake 23 miles long, and from 2 to 3 broad; this Loch is fed by a river running from *Loch-Eoch*, into which a river falls from *Loch-Garrie*, into which a river enters from *Loch-Queich*: *Loch-Neſs* and the river running from it never freeze, but the water is warm in the keeneſt froſt. There are many other lakes in this province, of which one called the lake *Dundelchack* is remarkable: the inhabitants of the neighborhood told me that this lake is never covered with ice before the month of *January*, but in that month and *February* one night's ſtrong froſt covers it all over with ice: this lake ſtands in the pariſh of *Durris*, within two miles of *Loch-Neſs*. On the Eaſt ſide of *Loch-Neſs*, a large mile above the Loch, is the water fall of *Fober*, where the river *Feach Len* falls over a ſteep rock about 80 feet in height; and the water breaking upon the ſhelves, rarifies like a fog. In this province are ſeveral chalybeat

chalybeat mineral ſprings, as at *Tinland* in *Lanbride* pariſh, at *Auchterblare* in *Duthel* pariſh, at *Relugas* in *Edenkeely* pariſh, at *Muretoun* in *Inverneſs* pariſh.

II. In the pariſh of *Drainie* there is a large cave open to the ſea, of a conſiderable length, breadth and height. There are many natural caves in the hills, within which hunters, herds and thieves take ſhelter in time of ſtorm: there is an artificial cave in the lands of *Raits* in *Badenoch*, in which fugitives and thieves were wont to reſt; but it is now demoliſhed in part. Of the mountains in this province I ſhall name but two or three: the *Carngorm* in *Strathſpey* is remarkable for its height, and for the ſtones found upon it; I have ſeen theſe ſtones of blue, green, yellow, and amber colors; ſome ſo large as to make big ſnuff boxes or ſmall cups; ſome of a hexagonal or pentagonal figure, and tapering to a point at each end. Theſe are now well known to the curious, and to jewellers. Another mountain is *Benalar* in *Badenoch*, which I imagine is the higheſt ground in *Scotland*, for waters running from it fall into the ſea at *Dundee*, at *Inverlochy*, and at *Garmoch* in *Murray*. On the Weſt ſide of *Loch-Neſs* there is a hill called *Meafuarvoney*: Mr. *Gordon* the Geographer was impoſed upon by being told that it is two miles perpendicular above the lake, and that on the top of it there is a ſmall lake which could never be ſounded, and communicates with *Loch-Neſs:* but I can aſſure you it is not near one mile above the Loch, and there is no ſuch lake on the top of it. For picturesque ſcenes, worth drawing, I know none except *Loch-Neſs*, with the rocks, woods, caſcades of rills of water, and ſome plots of corn land, on both ſides of the Loch, which make a delightfull ſcene to one ſailing the Loch in the King's Yacht, or in a barge.

barge. Poſſibly Mr. *Pennant* would get drawings of the remains of the cathedral church in *Elgin*, and of ſome old caſtles.

III. No earthquake, I can learn, was ever felt in this province. No whirlwind any way remarkable: there are ſeveral echoes, but ſcarcely worth the mentioning. About the year 1733 or 4, flaſhes of lightning ſo ſtruck the houſe of *Innes* near *Elgin*, as by entering into creviſes in the wall to drive out ſome big ſtones, likewiſe to rent a conſiderable long vault, and to toſs a large cap-ſtone above forty yards from the houſe, as the late Sir *Harry Innes* of that ilk told me.

IV. The common diſeaſes in our country are fevers, rheums, cold, ſcrofula, hyſteric and hypocondriac; bites of ſerpents, and mad dogs. Our natural phyſicians cure fevers, by making the patient drink plentifully of barley water or wangreſs, and when the fever riſes high the patient drinks a large draught of cold water which brings out a profuſe ſweat, that ends in a criſis. For rheums, they twice a day bath the part affected, pouring cold water upon it, and after it is dried, rubbing it till it is warm, and covering it with plaiding or flannel. For colds, they keep bed for two days, drinking warm, and if they ſweat not, they take the cold bath in a river or brook, which produces ſweat. The ſcrofula they find incurable, but in young perſons, by waſhing often with lime water, it cures in a few years. Hyſterics and hypocondriacs, in my opinion, are the effects of tea, coffee, ſloth and lazineſs, but theſe diſeaſes are never known in our highlands. When one is bit by a ſerpent or ſnake, if he can reach the wound, he ſucks the blood, covers the wound, and often foments the part wounded, and members round it, with a decoction of the buds and leaves of aſh trees. When one is bit

by

by a mad dog, as often happens in the highlands, he with a razor immediately cuts out the flesh of the part wounded, sucks the blood in plenty, and covers the wound with a handful of cobwebs: or if he has not courage to cut out the flesh, and thereby to prevent the poison from mixing with the blood, he causes the wound to be well sucked and then foments it with warm oil or melted butter. I have seen these cures performed with remarkable success. We have had, fifty years ago, a terrible disease called the *Civans*, which broke out into blotches in several parts of the body, and often turned into a gangrene in the face: this disease was brought by the military returning from *Flanders*, and was cured only by a plentiful salivation with mercury, but now we are happily free from it.

V. In the parish of *Elgin*, *William Calanch* a farmer died about the year 1740, at the age of about 119 years; we have had many who lived to an 100 years; we have some who have two thumbs on each hand, or two great toes on each foot.

VI. and VII. In this town of *Elgin* the number of inhabitants increases, occasioned by strangers living in the borough and many poor people coming from the country into it. But in the parish to landward the number appears to decrease, by reason of tenants taking up larger farms than formerly: the number now is above 5000.

VIII. The corns raised in this province are wheat, barley, oats, peas and beans, and rye. Of these in good years we have enough to serve the country, and to export above 20,000 bolls, besides serving the Highland countries. Our manufactures are linnen in considerable quantities, wool and common stuffs, and now at *Inver-*

neſs a flouriſhing ſail manufactory, and a ropery. Our fiſhery is conſiderable, for of white or ſea fiſh there is great plenty to ſerve the country and towns, and ſometimes to export a little. And our ſalmon on the rivers of *Spey*, *Findern*, *Neſs* and *Beauly*, ſerves the towns and country, and we export annually to the value of about 12,000l.

IX. Near the frith, the farmers manure with ſea ware or weeds, which produces richly; in other parts they uſe marle, lime, dung of cattle, and in the Highlands *tathing*, i. e. keeping their cattle in ſummer and autumn within pinfolds on barren or reſted ground, that by their dung they may enrich the ſoil; and in many parts they uſe green earth mixed with the dung of black cattle and horſes.

X. We cultivate ſome hemp, much flax, of which we not only make linnen for home conſumption, and have three bleaching fields within the province, beſides private bleaching, but we ſell great quantities of linnen yarn to the merchants of *Glaſgow* and others. We likewiſe cultivate potatoes in great plenty to ſerve the country.

XI. From the lowlands of the province few or no cattle are ſent out of the country, but from the highland glens and valleys, ſeveral hundreds of black cattle, ſome horſes, but no ſwine, are annually ſold into *England* and the Southern counties of *Scotland*.

XII. There are in this province ſeveral ſmall mounts or *motes* of which I cannot determine whether any of them be artificial or not: they generally ſtand about 40 paces one from another; I ſhall name only the following, viz. Near the town of *Elgin* are two little mounts called the ſhooting buts, and two of the ſame kind are near the Kirk of *Petty*. I am inclined to think, that before the inventi-

on

on of fire arms, these were marks for shooting at with bows and arrows: but that in time of *Druidism*, they were the seats on which the *Druids* met to determine questions in law and property; and they are in the *Galic* language called *Tomavoed*, i. e. the Court hill; and in the South they are called *Laws*, as *North Berwick Law*, *Largo Law*, &c. I may add the *Omnis terra* or *Mote hill* at *Scoon*. We have few military entrenchments worth the mentioning, as the *Romans* encamped little, if at all, so far North. *Druidical* circles have been very frequent in this province. The stones were generally about four feet in length, and eighteen inches in breadth: for the most part, the stones are removed by the country people, and I shall name but one or two, viz. At *Stonny field* near *Inverness*, there was a large circle about thirty feet diameter, some of the stones as yet stand. In *Durris* at the North end of *Loch-Ness* is a *Druid* temple of three concentric circles: in all of these druidical circles, there was an altar stone at the centre, but that at *Durris* is taken away, and near the centre is a hollowed stone, which either was a laver to wash in, or a bason to receive the blood of the sacrifice. Besides circles, there were many *Druidical* cairns in this country, on which at their solemn festivals, they offered their sacrifices; these cairns were about five feet high, and about thirty feet in circumference, and hedged around with stones pitted in the earth to prevent the falling out of the stones of the cairn: such a cairn stands in the parish of *Alves*, four miles from *Elgin*; another in the parish of *Birney*, two miles from that town; and two or three near *Avemore*, in the parish of *Duthel* in *Strathspey*. From these circles and cairns many churches are to this day called CLACHAN, i. e. a Collection of Stones; and as they stood in time of *Druidism* in groves and

 woods,

woods, a church in *Wales* was called LHAN, probably from *Lhuin* a grove. There is within a half-mile to the Eaſt of the town of *Forres*, an obeliſk called *Sevens*'s ſtone. The height of it cannot now with certainty be known, it is ſaid to be twelve feet ſunk in the corn field. When ſome years ago it was likely to fall, the Counteſs of *Murray* cauſed it to be erected, and much ſunk to prevent falling: it is about 23 feet above ground, about 4 feet broad: what is above ground is viſibly divided into ſeven parts, whereof the loweſt is almoſt hid by the ſtones ſupporting it; the ſecond diviſion contains many figures, but much defaced; in the third compartment, are figures of men, and ſome of beaſts with human heads; the fourth contains enſigns and military weapons; and in the fifth, ſixth and ſeventh, the figures are ſcarce diſcernible: on the reverſe, there is a croſs, beneath which are two human figures of a gothic form: this ſeems to be a monument of a battle fought in that place, by K. *Malcolm* the II. of *Scotland* againſt the *Danes*, about the year 1008. There are about two or three obeliſks of 6 or 7 feet height below the Kirk of *Alves*, probably, as monuments of ſkirmiſhes and the burying of men of ſome figure.

XIII. In this province we had two biſhopricks, one abby, three priories, one præceptory, and ſeveral convents. The firſt biſhoprick was that of *Murthlack*, now *Mortlich*, erected by K. *Malc*. II. *An*. 1010, when he had given a total defeat to the *Danes* in that valley: the dioceſe conſiſted only of three pariſhes, and after three biſhops had ſerved there it was tranſlated to *Aberdeen*, *An*. 1142. As an account of it will be fully given by others, I inſiſt not further.

The ſecond biſhoprick was that of *Murray*. In the fourth century

tury the biſhop affected a pre-eminence over his fellow preſbyters, and an equality in many things to ſovereign princes: as princes had their thrones, were crowned, wore crowns, had their palaces, their miniſters of ſtate, their privy council, and their ſubjects; ſo biſhops had a ſolium, a conſecration, a mitre, palaces, dignified clergy, chapter, and inferior clergy. The epiſcopal biſhoprick of *Murray*, was in my opinion erected by K. *Alex*. I.; and the biſhops of it were, in ſucceſſion,

(1.) *Gregorius*, who is a witneſs in a charter of K. *Dav*. I. to *Dumfermline*, confirming K. *Alexander*'s charter to that abby; there he is called *Gregorius Moravienſis Epiſcopus:* and in the foundation charter of the priory of *Schoon*, *An*. 1115, *Gregorius Epiſcopus* is a witneſs, who probably was the ſame with the formerly mentioned.

(2.) *William* was made apoſtolic legate *An*. 1159, and died 1162. I find not what time he was conſecrated.

(3.) *Felix*, is a witneſs in a charter by K. *William*, *Wilielmo filio freſken*, *de terris*, *de Strablock*, *Roſoil*, *Inſhkele*, *Duffus Machare*, *et Kintray*. He died about *An*. 1170.

(4.) *Simeon de Toney*, Monk of *Melroſe*, elected 1171, and died *An*. 1184, he was buried in *Birney*.

(5.) *Andrew*, conſecrated *An*. 1184, and died *An*. 1185.

(6.) *Richard*, conſecrated *Idi. Martii*, *An*. 1187, by *Hugo* biſhop of St. *Andrew*'s, and died *An*. 1203, and was buried in *Spynie*.

(7.) *Bricius*, brother of *William* lord of *Douglas*, and prior of *Leſſmahego*, elected *An*. 1203, and died *An*. 1222, and was buried at *Spynie*. He had repreſented to the pope that the former biſhops had no fixed ſee, or cathedral, ſome reſiding at *Birney*, ſome at *Kinnedar*, and ſome at *Spynie*; and he obtained that *Spynie* ſhould

be

be the bishop's see: he appointed the dignified clergy and canons, and founded a college of canons, eight in number.

(8.) *Andrew* (son of *William Murray* of *Duffus*) Dean of *Murray*, consecrated *An.* 1223. He founded the cathedral church at *Elgin*, added 14 canons to the college, and assigned manses and prebends for them, and for the dignified clergy, and died *An.* 1242.

Here it will be proper to give some account of the cathedral church at *Elgin*, for it does not appear that *Briceus* built any church at *Spynie*. Bishop *Andrew* was not pleased with the situation of *Spynie* for a cathedral, and therefore petitioned the pope that because of the distance from the burgh of *Elgin*, which would divert the canons from their sacred functions to go and buy provisions in the burgh, that he might allow the cathedral to be translated to the *Ecclesia sanctæ Trinitatis prope Elgin:* Pope *Honorius* granted his request, and by his bull dated 4to. *Idum*. *Aprilis* 1224 empowered the Bishop of *Cathness*, and the Dean of *Rosemarky*, to make the desired translation. These met at the place desired, on the 14 of the kalends of *August*, *An.* 1224: and finding it "*in commodum Ecclesiæ*," declared the church of the holy Trinity to be the cathedral church of the diocese of *Murray* in all times coming: it is said that bishop *Andrew* laid the foundation stone of the church on the same day above-mentioned, but it does not appear what the form or dimensions of that first church were.

(9.) *Simon* Dean of *Murray* succeeded and died 1252, and was buried in the choir of the cathedral near to bishop *Andrew*.

(10.) *Archibald* Dean of *Murray*, consecrated *An.* 1253, and died *December* 5th, *An.* 1298, and was buried in the choir. This bishop having no palace built one at *Kinnedar*, and lived there. In his time

time *William* Earl of *Roſs* having done great harm to the parſon of *Petty*, was obliged to do pennance, and for reparation, gave the lands of *Catboll* in *Roſs* to the biſhops of *Murray* in perpetuum.

(11.) *David Murray*, conſecrated at *Avignon* in *France*, by *Boneface* VIII. *anno* 1299, and died *January* 20th, *anno* 1325.

(12.) *John Pilmore*, conſecrated 3[ti]. *Kal. Aprilis*, *anno* 1326, and died at *Spynie* on *Michaelmas* eve, 1362.

(13.) *Alexander Bar*, *Doctor decretorum*, conſecrated by *Urban* V. *An.* 1362, died at *Spynie*, *May* 1397. In his time, viz. *An.* 1390, *Alexander Stewart* (ſon of king *Robert* II.) Lord *Badenoch*, commonly called the *Wolf* of *Badenoch*, keeping violent poſſeſſion of the biſhop's lands in that country, was excommunicated in reſentment, in the month of *May*, *An.* 1390. He with his followers burnt the town of *Forres*, with the choir of that church, and the Arch-Deacon's houſe; and in *June* that year burnt the town of *Elgin*, the church of *St. Giles*, the hoſpital of *Maiſon-Dieu*, the cathedral church, with eighteen houſes of the canons in the college of *Elgin*. For this he was made to do pennance, and upon his humble ſubmiſſion, he was abſolved by *Walter Trail* biſhop of *St. Andrews*, in the black-friars church of *Perth* (being firſt received at the door, barefoot, and in ſackcloth, and again before the high altar in preſence of the king and his nobles) on condition that he would make full reparation to the biſhop and church of *Murray*, and obtain abſolution from the Pope. Biſhop *Bar* began the rebuilding of the church, and every canon contributed to it, as did every pariſh in the dioceſe.

(14.) *William Spynie*, Chanter of *Murray*, D. I. C. conſecrated at *Avignon* by *Benedict* the IX. *Sept.* 13th, 1397, and died *Aug.* 20th,

An.

An. 1406. He carried on the reparation of the cathedral, but the troubles of the times caused it to make slow advances. On *July* 3, *An.* 1402, *Alexander* III. son of the Lord of the Isles, plundered *Elgin*, burnt many houses, and spoiled the houses of the canons: he was excommunicated, and offered a sum of gold, as did every one of his captains, and he received absolution: this money was applied for erecting a cross and a bell in that part of the canonry which lies next the bridge of *Elgin*.

(15.) *John Innes*, Parson of *Duffus*, Archdeacon of *Cathness*, and L.L. D. was consecrated by *Benedict* the XIII. *Jan.* 23d. *An.* 1406, and died *April* 25th, *An.* 1414, and was buried in his own isle in the cathedral, where his statue at large still remains with this inscription, " *Hic jacet reverendus in Christo Pater & Dominus* " D. Joannes Innes de Innes, *hujus ecclesiæ Episcopus, qui hoc* " *notabile opus incepit, et per Septennium ædificavit.*" He built that isle and a part of the great steeple or tower. After his death, the chapter met and all were sworn that on whomsoever the lot should fall to be bishop, he should annually apply one third of his revenues until the building of the cathedral should be finished.

(16.) *Henry Leighton*, parson of *Duffus*, and L. L. D. was consecrated in *Valentia* by *Benedict* XIII. *March* 8th, *An.* 1415: he diligently carried on the building, and finished the great tower, and was translated to *Aberdeen An.* 1425. The cathedral church having been completely finished in the time of this bishop, I shall here describe that edifice, which was all in the gothic form of architecture. It stood due East and West, in the form of a passion or *Jerusalem* cross: the length of it 264 feet: the breadth 35 feet: the length of the traverse 114 feet. The church was ornamented with

with five towers, whereof two parallel towers ſtood on the Weſt end, one in the middle, and two at the Eaſt end: the two Weſt towers ſtand entire in the ſtone work, and are each 84 feet high: what the height of the ſpires was I do not find; probably they were of wood, and fell down long ſince. The great tower in the centre of the nave ſtood on two arched pillars croſſing at top, and was, including the ſpires, 198 feet in height: the two turrets in the Eaſt end are ſtill entire, and each has a winding ſtair-caſe leading to a channel or paſſage in the walls round the whole church. The height of the ſide walls is 36 feet. The great entry was betwixt the two towers in the Weſt end: this gate is a concave arch, 24 feet broad in baſe, and 24 in height, terminating in a ſharp angle: on each ſide of the valves in the ſweep of the arch are 8 round, and 8 fluted pilaſters, 6½ feet high, adorned with a chapiter, from which ariſe 16 pilaſters that meet in the key of the arch. Each valve of the door was 5 feet broad, and about 10 feet high. To yield light to this large building, beſides the great windows in the porticos, and a row of windows in the wall above, each 6 feet high, there was above the gate a window of an acute angled arch 19 feet broad in baſe, and 27 in height: and in the Eaſt end between the turrets, a row of five parallel windows, each 2 feet broad and 10 high: above theſe five more each 7 feet high, and over theſe a circular window near 10 feet diameter: the grand gate, the windows, the pillars, the projecting table, pedeſtals, cordons, are adorned with foliage, grapes, and other carvings. The traverſe, in length as above, ſeems to have been built by the families of *Dunbar* and *Innes*, for the North part of it is called the *Dunbar's* iſle, and the South part the *Innes'* iſle.

The chapter houſe, in which the biſhop's privy council met, ſtands on the North ſide of the choir: it is a curious piece of architecture communicating with the choir by a vaulted veſtry. The houſe is an exact octagon, 34 feethigh, and the diagonal breadth within walls 37 feet: it is almoſt a cube, arched and vaulted at top, and the whole arched roof ſupported by one pillar in the centre of the houſe. Arched pillars from every angle terminated in the grand pillar, which is 9 feet in circumference, cruſted over with 16 pilaſters, and 24 feet high: adorned with a chapiter, from which ariſe round pillars that ſpread along the roof, and join at top; and round the chapiter are engraven the arms of ſeveral biſhops. There is a large window in each of ſeven ſides, the eighth ſide communicating, as was ſaid, with the choir; and in the North wall are five ſtalls cut in nitches for the biſhop's miniſters of ſtate, viz. the dean, chanter, arch deacon, chancellor, and treaſurer, the *Dean*'s *Stall* raiſed a ſtep higher than the other four. This ſtructure of the cathedral came to decay in the manner following, viz. The regent earl of *Murray* being obliged to levy ſome forces, and being ſtraitned in money, appointed by his privy council *February* 14, 1567, 8, the ſheriffs of *Aberdeen* and *Murray*, with other gentlemen, to take the lead, thatch or covering off the cathedrals of *Aberdeen* and *Murray*, and to ſell it for paying the troops, which was done, and ſhipped for *Holland*; but the ſhip ſoon after launched in the ſea, ſunk with the lead, which it is thought was done by a ſuperſtitious *Roman* catholic, who was captain of it. Of this whole edifice, the chapter houſe, the walls of the choir, the Weſtern ſteeples and the Eaſtern turrets remain as yet entire, but the ſide walls of the nave and the traverſe are moſt part fallen,

fallen, and *Peace Sunday*, *An.* 1711, the great tower or ſteeple in the middle fell from the foundation.

The cathedral ſtood within the precinct of the college, near the river ſide of *Loſſey:* this precinct was walled round with a ſtrong ſtone wall, and was about 1000 yards in circumference, a part of the walls ſtill remains entire; it had four gates, every one of which probably had (as is apparent the Eaſtern had) an iron gate, a port-cullis, and a porter's lodge: within the precinct the dignified clergy and all the canons had houſes and gardens, and without the precinct, towards the town of *Elgin*, there was a ſmall burrow with a croſs, where the church men purchaſed their proviſions. The biſhop's place ſtood at *Spynie*, a large mile from *Elgin:* when it ſtood entire, it was the moſt ſtately I have ſeen in any dioceſe in *Scotland.* The area of the buildings was an oblong ſquare of 60 yards; in the South-Weſt corner ſtood a ſtrong tower vaulted, the wall 9 feet thick, with an eaſy winding ſtair-caſe, a cape houſe at top, with a battlement round it. In the other three corners are ſmall towers with narrow rooms. In the South ſide of the area, there was a chapel and tennis court: and in other parts were ſtables and all neceſſary offices. The gate, or entry, was in the middle of the Eaſt wall, ſecured by aniron grate and a port-cullis: over the gate ſtand the arms of biſhop *John Innes*, and the initial letters of his name, which affords a conjecture, that he was the firſt who built any part of this court. Around the palace was a ſpacious precinct, with gardens, and walks, and which now pay twelve pounds ſterling to the crown. The lands of *Spynie* and the precinct were granted by the crown to one gentleman after another, till the revolution, and ſince that time, the precinct continues in the crown, and the lands belong to Mr. *Brodie* of *Spynie*,

 now

now of *Brodie:* but the iron grate, the roof, the joiſts, and all the timber work were carried off by the former leſſees, and now all is in decay.

The dioceſe of *Murray* compriſed the counties of *Murray* and *Nairn*, and the greateſt part of the counties of *Bamff* and *Inverneſs*, and had 56 paſtoral charges. What the revenue of this biſhoprick was before the reformation cannot now be well known; for *Patrick Hepburn*, the laſt popiſh biſhop, fewed and ſold at leaſt a third part of the lands of the biſhoprick, including what he was obliged to give to the Regent of *Scotland*, *An.* 1568, for harbouring his intercommuned uncle *James* Earl of *Bothwell*, who married our unfortunate Q. *Mary*, *An.* 1563, when an account of all dignified clergy's revenues was called in by the parliament, the revenues of the biſhoprick of *Murray*, as then given up, were as follows; viz. In money, £1649 : 7 : 7, *Scots*: wheat, 10 bolls: barley, 77 chalders, 6 bolls, 3 firlots, and two pecks: oats, 2 chalders, 8 bolls: ſalmon, 8 laſts: poultry, 223. Beſides the emoluments of the regality of *Spynie*, and of the commiſſaries of *Spynie* and *Inverneſs*, and the great teinds of the pariſh of *Elgin*, and of *St. Andrew's* in *Murray*, *Ogſton*, *Laggon*, and the biſhop's ſhare of the revenues of the common kirks.

The only abby we had was that at *Kinloſs*, which ſtood in what is now called the pariſh of that name. It was founded by K. *David* I. 10mo *Kal. Januarii*, *An.* 1150. The abbot was mitred, and had a ſeat in parliament: the monks were of the *Ciſtercian* order, called *Monachi Albi.* K. *David* endowed it, as did K. *William*, with many lands. *Aſelinus* was the firſt abbot, and *Robert Reid* was the laſt. The revenues of the abby, *An.* 1561, were found to be, in money,

money, £1152 : 1 : 0, *Scots:* barley and meal, 47 chalders, 11 bolls, 1 firlot, and 3 pecks: oats, 10 bolls, 3 firlots: wedders, 34: geese, 41: capons, 60: and poultry, 125. The abbot had a regality within the abby lands: Mr. *Edward Bruce* was made commendator, and afterwards lord of *Kinloss*, *An.* 1604: from whom *Alexander Brodie* of *Lethen* purchased the lands of *Kinloss*, and the superiority of the other abby lands. The ruins of the building are so small, that it cannot be known what it was when entire; for, *An.* 1651 and 1652, the stones of it were sold and carried to build *Cromwel's* fort at *Inverness*, and nothing now remains but confused ruins.

The oldest priory we had in this province was at *Urquhart*, three miles East of *Elgin.* It was founded by K. *David* I. *An.* 1125, in honor of the Trinity. It was a cell of *Dumfermline* with *Benedictine* monks. K. *David* endowed it liberally. The revenues thereof were not given up in *An.* 1563, and so I can give no account of them. The priory lands were erected into a regality, but no vestige of the buildings now remains. In 1565, *Alexander Seton* was made commendator, and 1591, created Lord *Urquhart*, and *An.* 1605 Earl of *Dumfermline*; but the honors being forfeited in 1690, *Seton* of *Barns* claimed the lordship, and about *An.* 1730 it was purchased by the family of *Gordon.*

The next priory was at *Pluscarden*, founded by K. *Alexander* II. *An.* 1230, and named *Vallis Sancti Andreæ.* It was planted by *Monachi Vallis Caulium.* None but the prior and procurator were allowed to go without the precinct; the monks becoming vicious were expelled, and other monks brought from *Dumfermline.* The lands of this priory were very considerable, and they had a *Grangia* and

and a cell of monks at *Grange hill.* The revenue of this priory, given up *An.* 1563, was, in money, £525 : 10 : 1½, *Scots:* wheat, 1 chalder, 1 boll, 2 firlots: malt, meal and barley, 51 chalders, 4 bolls, 3 firlots, 1 peck: oats, 5 chalders, 13 bolls: dry multures, 9 chalders, 11 bolls: ſalmon, 30 laſts. The buildings ſtood 4 miles S. W. from the town of *Elgin*, in a warm valley called the glen of *Pluſcarden.* The walls of the precinct make a large ſquare, and are pretty entire. The church ſtands about the middle of the ſquare, a fine edifice in the form of a croſs, with a ſquare tower all of hewen aſhlar. The oratory and refectory join to the South end of the church, under which is the dormitory. The chapter houſe is of curious work, an octagonal cube, vaulted roofs ſupported by one pillar, all as yet entire. They had a regality in the priory lands, and a diſtinct regality in *Grange hill*, called the regality of *Stanefore-noon.* At the reformation Sir *Alexander Seton* was, *An.* 1565, made commendator. The lands of *Pluſcarden* and *Old Milns* near *Elgin* paſſed through ſeveral hands, and are now the property of *James* Earl of *Fife.*

The third priory was at *Kinguſie*, founded by *George* Earl of *Huntly*, about *An.* 1490. Of what order the monks were, or what were the revenues of the priory, I have not learned. The few lands belonging to it being the donation of the family of *Huntly*, were at the reformation re-aſſumed by them, and continue to be their property.

There were likewiſe within this province ſeveral convents of religious orders. In the town of *Elgin* were *Grey Friars*, *Black Friars*, *Red Friars*, *Templars Houſes*, and a Nunnery of the religious of *St.*

Catherine

Katherine of *Sienna.* There were other convents at *Forres* and *Invernefs.*

Clofe by the town of *Elgin* ftood the præceptory of *Maifon Dieu.* It was a hofpital for entertaining ftrangers, and maintaining poor infirm people. The buildings are now gone to ruins. They had confiderable lands in the parifhes of *Elgin*, *Lanbride*, *Knockando*, and *Dundurkus*, all which were by K. *James* VI. and *Charles* I. granted to the town of *Elgin*, and now hold few of them.

In this province we had four royal forts; the firft ftood on a round hill that overlooks the town of *Elgin*; and fome of the walls, all of run lime, do as yet remain. The Earls of *Murray* fince the year 1313 were conftables of it, and had confiderable lands for their falary. Their office continued till 1748, when heritable offices were annexed to the crown, and now they have no more but the hill called *Lady hill*, which yields a fmall rent annually. Another fort ftood in the town of *Nairn*, but no veftiges of it now remain. Mr. *Campbell* of *Calder* (and formerly the *Thanes* of that ilk) was conftable, and in 1748 was paid a compenfation for that office. The third fort was at *Invernefs*, of which the Earls of *Rofs* were formerly conftables; and after their forfeiture, the Earl of *Huntly* obtained the office of conftable, with very confiderable lands as falary, and continued to be conftable till 1629. I need not here fpeak of *Cromwel*'s fort at *Invernefs*, of which no doubt others will give a full account. The fourth fort was at *Urquhart*, on the Weft fide of *Loch-Nefs*: the buildings were pretty large, and in a great part as yet ftand. In the time of *David* II. *Alexander Boes* was governor of this fort; afterwards, *Chifolm* of that ilk was governor: but fince the middle of century fifteenth I do not find it had any governor,

vernor, and now the lands of *Urquhart* are the property of Sir *Ludowick Grant* of *Grant*. Befides thefe forts we had many old caftles within this province commonly called *Fortalicia.* One ftood at *Duffus*, three miles North of *Elgin*, and was the feat of the chief of the *Moravienfes* as early as the eleventh century. The caftle ftood on a green mote, on the bank of the Loch of *Spynie:* it was a fquare, the wall about 20 feet high, and 5 feet thick, with a parapet, a ditch, and a draw bridge: within the fquare were buildings of timber for accommodating the family, and alfo neceffary offices. The walls are as yet pretty entire. Such *Fortalices* were alfo at *Balveny* in the parifh of *Murtlich*, at *Abernethy* in that parifh, at *Lochindorb* in the parifh of *Cromdil*, at *Raet* in *Nairn* parifh, and at *Ruthven* in *Kingufie* parifh. All which were large fquares, and many rooms built with timber within the walls.

I fhall give no account of the modern forts of *Fort George* at *Ardirfeir*, or *Fort Auguftus* at the South end of *Loch-Nefs*, and fhall only defcribe a promontory in the parifh of *Duffus*, four miles from *Elgin*. Our hiftorians call it *Burgus*, it juts into the frith, and rifes above low water about fixteen yards. To the Weft and North it is a perpendicular rock, to the Eaft the afcent is fteep but graffy, to the South towards land the afcent is more eafy. The area on the top is near a rectangular figure, in length about 100 yards, and in breadth about 50. After the *Danes* had defeated the *Scots* army at *Forres* about *An.* 1008, they fent for their wives and children, and made this promontory an *afylum* to them and a place of arms. It was at top furrounded with a ftrong rampart of oaken logs, of which fome are as yet digged up: by a trench cut on the South fide they brought the fea round the promontory, and within this,

this, had other trenches, and they fortified it to the Eaſt. The trenches are now filled up. After the battle of *Mortlich* in the year 1010, the *Danes* abandoned it, and left the country of *Murray*. To return.

(17.) *Columba Dunbar* ſucceeded, and died *An.* 1435.

(18.) *John Wincheſter*, L. B. and chaplain to king *James* II. was conſecrated, 1438, and died 1458. In 1452, the king erected the town of *Spynie* into a free burgh of barony, and erected all the lands of the biſhoprick into the regality of *Spynie*.

(19.) *James Stewart*, dean, conſecrated 1458, died *An.* 1460.

(20.) *David Stewart*, parſon of *Spynie*, ſucceeded in 1461, built the high tower of the palace, and died *An.* 1475.

(21.) *William Tulloch*, tranſlated from *Orkney*, *An.* 1477, was Lord Privy Seal, and died 1482.

(22.) *Andrew Stewart*, Dean of *Murray* and Privy Seal, ſucceeded, *An.* 1483, and died 1498.

(23.) *Andrew Foreman*, commendator of *Dry Burgh*, ſucceeded, *An.* 1501, and was tranſlated to *St. Andrew's*, *An.* 1514.

(24.) *James Hepburn* ſucceeded, and died *An.* 1524.

(25.) *Robert Shaw*, ſon of *Sauchy* and abbot of *Paiſly*, was conſecrated 1525, and died 1528.

(26.) *Alexander Stewart*, ſon of the Duke of *Albany*, ſucceeded, and died *An.* 1535.

(27.) *Patrick Hepburn*, uncle to *James* Earl of *Bothwell*, and commendator of *Scoon*, was conſecrated *An.* 1537. He dilapidated, fewed, or ſet in long leaſes a great part of the church lands, and died *An.* 1573, on the 20th *June*.

I have ſeen ſeveral catalogues of the popiſh biſhops of *Murray*, both printed and manuſcript, but all imperfect; comparing theſe with the writings of Sir *James Dalrymple*, Sir *Robert Sibbald*, Biſhop *Keith*, the chartulary of *Murray*, and the chronicle of *Mel Roſs*, the above catalogue may I think be depended upon. To return to the quæries.

XIV. There are in this province manuſcript hiſtories of ſeveral families, which might be of ſome ſervice in compiling a general hiſtory; as of the families of *Dunbar*, *Innes*, *Brodie*, *Calder*, *Kilravock*, *M'Intoſh*, and *Grant*. With regard to antient weapons, I have ſeen in the houſe of *Grant*, of *Kilravock*, and in other houſes, ſteel helmets, habergeons, and coats of mail, and of buff leather. Adder ſtones, glaſs beds, &c. are but amulets not worth regarding.

XV. I know not one picture worth regarding, except a picture of the Virgin *Mary* in the houſe of *Caſtle Grant*.

XVI. No battle in the pariſh of *Elgin*, but many within this province, as at *Forres*, about *An.* 1008, betwixt the *Scots* and *Danes*; at *Mortlich*, *An.* 1010, between the ſame; at *Spey*-mouth, *An.* 1078, the King againſt the *Moravienſes*; again, *An.* 1110, againſt the ſame people; and, *An.* 1160, on the *Muir of Urquhart*, king *Malcolm* IV. againſt the ſame *Moravienſes*; at *Ceanlochlochie*, *An.* 1544, betwixt the *Fraziers* and *M'Donalds*; at *Glenlivot*, *An.* 1594, the King againſt the Earls of *Huntly*, *Errol*, and *Angus*; at *Auldearn*, *An.* 1645, the Covenanters againſt *Montroſe*; at *Cromdel*, *An.* 1690, the King's troops againſt the Highlanders; and at *Culloden*, *An.* 1745, the Duke of *Cumberland* againſt the Rebels.

XVII. *Druidiſm* having been the form of religion in this country before Chriſtianity, the people ſtill retain ſome ſuperſtitious cuſtoms

toms of that Pagan religion. As *Bel-tein:* on the firſt of *May* the herds of ſeveral farms gather dry wood, put fire to it, and dance three times Southways about the pile. In the middle of *June* farmers go round their corn with burning torches, in memory of the *Cerealia.* On *Hallow* even they have ſeveral ſuperſtitious cuſtoms. At the full moon in *March* they cut withes of the miſletoe or ivy, make circles of them, keep them all year, and pretend to cure hecticks and other troubles by them. And at marriages and baptiſms they make a proceſſion around the church, *Deaſoil,* i. e. ſunways, becauſe the ſun was the immediate object of the *Druids'* worſhip.

XVIII. Their ſports are hunting, firing at marks, foot-ball, club-ball, &c. And the only annual feſtival they obſerve is *Chriſtmas*; ſpent more as the *Saturnalia* were of old, than as *Chriſt*'s birth ought to be.

XIX. We have no true marle in this country, nor any *aſbeſtus:* but we have granite, talcum, lapis ſpecularis, and at *Stadtfield* within four miles of *Elgin* there was lately found lead ore, and in *Glengarry* they have for ſeveral years had an iron forge and made pigs of iron; likewiſe about 40 years ago a company from *England* ſet up a mill and forge for iron in *Abernethy* in *Strathſpey*, and made very good bars of iron, but through their own extravagance they abandoned it. There is through all this province great plenty of iron ore. I have often ſeen the *ignis fatuus*, which is a piece of rotten birch wood, lying in a mire, and ſhining in a dark night, like a flame of firs: likewiſe *ignis lambens*, which is an unctuous vapour falling upon a man's wig, or mane of a horſe, which ſhines bright, but by a ſlight rub it is extinguiſhed.

XX. Great plenty of the particulars in the 20th quæry may be found on the ſea coaſt in this province; if any will take the trouble to collect them.

XXI. I know no ſpecies of wood remarkable, and peculiar to this province, except *Red Saugh*, or ſallow, which is no leſs beautifull than mahogany, and is much more firm and tough, and not ſo brittle; it receives a fine poliſh, and in color reſembles light-colored mahogany; it grows in rocks, and is very rare. But we have great foreſts of firs and birches: and as the *Grampian* hills divide in *Athol* into one branch running Northward, and another Eaſtward; in the former branch are great woods of fir and birch in *Breadalbane*, *Rannoch*, *Strathſpey*, *Badenoch*, *Glen-moriſton*, *Strathglaſs*, and *Strath-carron* in *Sutherland*; and in the other branch are ſuch foreſts in *Brae-mar*, *Glen-muik*, *Glen-tanner*, &c. I am inclined to think that theſe are the remains of the antient *Sylva Caledonia*. Among other vegetables, we have in great plenty, in the heaths and woods, the following berries, viz. wild raſps, wild ſtrawberries, blueberries, bugberries, *uva urſæ*, &c. And we have one root I cannot but take notice of, which we call *Carmele*: it is a root that grows in heaths and birch woods to the bigneſs of a large nut, and ſometimes four or five roots joined by fibres; it bears a green ſtalk, and a ſmall red flower. *Dio*, ſpeaking of the *Caledonians*, ſays, "*Certum cibi* "*genus parant ad omnia, quem ſi ceperint quantum eſt unius fabæ* "*magnitudo, minime eſurire aut ſitire ſolent.*" *Cæſar de Bel. Civ.* lib. 3tio. writes, that *Valerius*'s ſoldiers found a root called CHARA, "*quod admiſtum lacte multam inopiam levabat, id ad ſimilitudinum panis efficiebant.*" I am inclined to think that our *Carmele* (i. e. ſweet root) is *Dio*'s *Cibi genus*, and *Cæſar*'s *Chara*: I have often

ſeen

ſeen it dried, and kept for journeys through hills where no proviſions could be had: I have likewiſe ſeen it pounded and infuſed, and when yeſt or barm is put to it, it ferments, and makes a liquor more agreeable and wholeſome than mead. It grows ſo plentifully, that a cart load of it can eaſily be gathered, and the drink of it is very balſamic.

XXII. Sea fowl in this province reſort in winter to lakes and lochs, as Loch of *Spynie*, *Loch-Neſs*, *Loch-Nadorb*, &c. Eagles and Falcons breed in high rocks and inacceſſible mountains, as *Scorgave* in *Rothemurchus*. There are ſome ſpecies of fowls, if not peculiar to this province, at leaſt rare in other countries: ſuch as, the *Caperkyly*, as large as the domeſtick *Turkey*; it frequents the fir woods, and perches in the top of very tall trees, but the hen breeds in the heath. Another fowl is the *Black Cock*, which frequents birch woods in hills, is of the ſize of a capon, of a ſhining blue color: it is by ſome authors called *Gallus Scoticanus*. A third fowl is *Tarmagan*, of the ſize of a Partridge, haunts the high rocky hills, is of a color ſpotted brown and white. Theſe three fowls are very harmleſs, and make delicious food.

N. B. In anſwering quæry IV. it is omitted that our natural phyſicians, when they find a toe or a finger hurt, and beginning to corrupt, they ſtrike it off with a chizzel, and ſere the wound with a hot iron, and ſoon cure it. Inſtead of bleeding by lancets, they ſcarify the fleſh about the ancle, and they take blood from the naſal vein by cleaving the quill of a hen and binding it into four branches, and ſcarifying the noſtrils thereby. For vomits, they uſe a decoction of groundſill, of the bark of the ſervice tree, and a decoction of Holborn ſaugh; and for purgatives, the decoction of ſervice bark

bark and a decoction of mugwort boiled in new whey. In anſwering quæry I. I omitted to ſay, that the river of *Bewly* was antiently called *Farar:* it riſes in the hills towards *Glenelg*, and runs through *Glenſtrathfarar*; and I am inclined to think that in *Ptolemy*'s Geographical Tables the *Murray* frith is called *Æſtuarium Vararis* from the river *Farar* (changing the *F* into *V*) that falls into the head of it. And the river was called *Bewly* when, *An.* 1230, a priory of the monks *Vallis Caulium* was ſettled there, who called their ſeat *Beaulieu*, i. e. *Bello loco*; and then the old name of *Farar* was diſcontinued, except among the Highlanders.

The Admirable CRICHTON.

NUMBER III.

THE LIFE OF JAMES CRICHTON, OF CLUNIE; COMMONLY CALLED THE ADMIRABLE CRICHTON.

THIS compilation was ſome years ago printed at *Aberdeen*. I have had opportunity of comparing it with moſt of the authorities quoted in ſupport of the hiſtory of ſo extraordinary a perſon, and find them uſed with judgement and fidelity. Excepting a few notes, I preſent it to the readers in the ſtate I found it: and ſhall only acquaint them that the life of this Glory of *North Britain* may be found in the 81ſt Number of the *Adventurer*, treated in a more elegant, but far leſs comprehenſive manner.

THIS gentleman was deſcended from a very antient family; his father *Robert Crichton* of *Clunie* and *Eliock*, was one of thoſe who commanded Queen *Mary*'s army at the battle of *Langſide* in the year 1568. He was born at *Clunie* *, his paternal inheritance,

* The preſent houſe of *Clunie* ſtands in an iſland in a lake of the ſame name. But the old houſe or caſtle ſtood on one ſide of the water: and its place is diſtinguiſhed by nothing but a mound and imperfect moat.

in

in the ſhire of *Perth*, in the year 1551. He was taught his grammar at the ſchool of *Perth*, and his philoſophy at the univerſity of *St. Andrews* * under Mr. *John Rutherford* †. He had hardly attained to the 20th year of his age, when he had run through the whole circle of the ſciences, and could ſpeak and write to perfection in ten different languages; but this was not all, for he had likewiſe improved himſelf to the utmoſt degree in riding, dancing, ſinging, and playing upon all ſorts of inſtruments.

Having thus accompliſhed himſelf at home, his parents ſent him abroad to accompliſh him further by travelling. And coming to *Paris*, it is not to be imagined what conſternation he raiſed in that famous univerſity; as we have it from an eye-witneſs, who gives us this account of it ‡: " There came," ſays he, " to the college of " *Navarre*, a young man of 20 years of age, who was perfectly " well ſeen in all the ſciences, as the moſt learned maſters of the " univerſity acknowleged: In vocal and inſtrumental muſick none " could excel him, in painting and drawing in colors none could " equal him; in all military feats he was moſt expert, and could " play with the ſword ſo dexterouſly with both his hands that no " man could fight him; when he ſaw his enemy or antagoniſt, he " would throw himſelf upon him at one jump of 20 or 24 feet

* Vid. Ald. Manut. Epiſt. Ded. Paradox. Cicer; Dict. Critiq. & Hiſtor. par M. *Bayle*; Dempſter Hiſt. Eccleſ. p. 1876. Joan. imperialis Muſ. Hiſtor. p. 241. Sir *Thomas Urquhart*'s Vindication of the *Scots* Nation, &c.

† *Aldus* calls *Crichton* firſt couſin to the King, and ſays that he was educated along with his Majeſty under *Buchanan*, *Hepburn*, *Robertſon*, and *Rutherford*.

‡ Steph. Paſch. Diſquiſ. lib. 5. cap. 23.

" diſtance:

" diſtance: He was a maſter of arts, and diſputed with us in the
" ſchools of the college upon medicine, the civil and canon law,
" and theology; and although we were above fifty in number, be-
" ſides above three thouſand that were preſent; and ſo pointedly
" and learnedly he anſwered to all the queſtions that were propoſed
" to him, that none but they that were preſent can believe it. He
" ſpake *Latin*, *Greek*, *Hebrew*, and other languages moſt politely:
" he was likewiſe an excellent horſeman, and truely if a man ſhould
" live an hundred years without eating, drinking or ſleeping, he
" could not attain to this man's knowledge, which ſtruck us with a
" panick fear; for he knew more than human nature could well
" bear; he overcame four of the doctors of the church; for in
" learning none could conteſt with him, and he was thought to be
" *Antichriſt*."

Sir *Thomas Urquhart* of *Cromarty* giving an account of this diſpute, ſays, that *Crichton*, when he came to *Paris*, cauſed ſix programs on all the gates of the ſchools, halls and colleges belonging to the univerſity, and on all the pillars and poſts before the houſes of the moſt renowned men for literature in the city, inviting all thoſe who were well verſed in any art or ſcience, to diſpute with him in the college of *Navarre*, that day ſix weeks, by nine of the clock in the morning, where he ſhould attend them, and be ready to anſwer to whatever ſhould be proponed to him in any art or ſcience, and in any of theſe twelve languages, *Hebrew*, *Syriack*, *Arabick*, *Greek*, *Latin*, *Spaniſh*, *French*, *Italian*, *Engliſh*, *Dutch*, *Flemiſh* or *Sclavonian*, and that either in verſe or proſe, at the diſcretion of the diſputant; and during all this time inſtead of making a cloſs application to his ſtudies, he minded nothing, but hunting, hawking, tilting, vaulting, riding of a well managed horſe, toſſing the pike, handling the muſket, and other military feats, or in houſe games, ſuch as balls, concerts of muſick vocal and inſtrumental, cards, dice, tennis, and the other diverſions of youth; which ſo provoked the ſtudents of the univerſity, that they cauſed write beneath the program that was fixt on the *Sorbonne* gate, "If you would "meet with this monſter of perfection, to make ſearch for him ei- "ther in the tavern or bawdy-houſe, is the readieſt way to find "him." Yet upon the day appointed he met with them in the college of *Navarre*, and acquit himſelf beyond expreſſion in that diſpute, which laſted from nine till ſix of the clock at night: At length, the *Præſes* having extolled him highly, for the many rare and wonderfull endowments that God and nature had beſtowed upon him, he roſe from his chair, and accompanied by four of the moſt eminent profeſſors of the univerſity, gave him a diamond ring and a purſe full of gold, as a teſtimony of their love and favor, which ended with the acclamations and repeated huzza's of the ſpectators. And ever after that he was called, The Admirable *Crichton*. And my author ſays, that he was ſo little fatigued with that day's diſpute, that the very next day he went to the *Louvre*, where he had a match of tilting, an exerciſe in great requeſt in thoſe days, and in the preſence of ſome princes of the court of *France*, and a great many ladies, he carried away the ring fifteen times on end, and broke as many lances on the *Saracen*.

The learned M. *du Launy*, in his hiſtory of the college of *Navarre*, finding the hiſtory of this diſpute recorded in a MS. hiſtory of the college of *Navarre*, and the like account of a *Spaniard* in *Trithemius*, confounds the two together, and robs our author of the glory of this

this action, and places it in the year 1445, whereas it should be in the year 1571, as we have reason to believe, from the authority of those that were cotemporary with him, and knew him, and have recorded this of him; but we need not be surprized at M. *du Launy*'s denying him the glory of this action, when we find M. *Baillet*, another learned *Frenchman*, denying there ever was such a man as our author *, notwithstanding that *Aldus Manutius* dedicates his book of *Cicero*'s paradoxes to him in the year 1581, and that the most of the eminent men in *Italy* in that age were acquainted with him, as we shall show in the remaining part of the history of his life. About two years after his dispute at *Paris*, *Trajano Boccalini* in his advertisements from Parnassus, tells us, that he came to *Rome*, *Boccalini* being then at *Rome*, himself, and by a placad which he affixed upon all the eminent places of the city, he challenged all the learned men in *Rome*, in the following terms, *Nos Jacobus Crichtonus Scotus, cuicunque rei propositæ ex improviso respondebimus.* That is to say, he was ready to answer to any question that could be proposed to him, without being previously advertised of it. Upon which the wits put a paper in *Pasquin*'s † hand, endeavouring to ridicule him; but that noways discouraging him, he came at the time and place appointed by his placad, and in the presence

* Hist. des Enf. Celeb.

† The pasquinade was to this effect, written beneath the challenge, *And he that will see* it *let him go to the signe of the* Faulcon *and* it *shall be shewn*. This, says *Boccalini*, made such an impression on *Crichton*, that he left the place where he was so grosly affronted as to be put on a level with jugglers and mountebanks.

of

of the pope, many cardinals, biſhops, doctors of divinity, and profeſſors in all the ſciences; he gave ſuch ſurprizing inſtances of his univerſal knowlege, that they were no leſs ſurprized with him, than they had been at *Paris*.

From *Rome* he goes to *Venice*, where he contracted an intimate friendſhip with *Aldus Manutius*, *Laurentius Maſſa*, *Speron Speronius*, and ſeveral other learned men, to whom he preſented ſeveral poems in commendation of the city and univerſity, and among the reſt, one to *Aldus Manutius*, which we have ſtill extant in the *Delitiæ Poetarum Scotorum* *. This poem gave him a very agreeable ſurprize, being preſented by a ſtranger, whom he judged by the performance to be a perſon of an extraordinary genius; but when he came to diſcourſe with him, he was ſtruck with admiration, and finding him known in every thing, he brought him to the acquaintance of all the people of learning or note that were in *Venice*, and all of them were ſo ſurprized with him, that they thought him, as he really was, the wonder of the world, and never ſpoke of him but with admiration; at length being brought before the doge and ſenate, he made a handſome ſpeech to them, which being accompanied with all the graces and beauties of eloquence and nature † that appeared in his perſon in their utmoſt luſtre, he received the thanks of the ſenate, and nothing was talked through the whole city, but of this prodigy of nature. Having ſtayed for ſome time at *Venice*, he went to *Padua* to viſit the learned men that were at that famous univerſity; and he had no ſooner arrived there, but

* Delitiæ Poet. Scot. ubi ſupra.

† Joan. Imperial. ubi ſupra.

there

there was a meeting of all the learned men in the city, in the houſe of *Jacobus Moyſius Cornelius*, to wait upon him, and converſe with him: He opened the aſſembly with an extemporary poem in praiſe of the city, univerſity, and the aſſembly that had honored him with their preſence at that time; and after ſix hours of a diſpute, which he ſuſtained againſt them, in whatever they could propoſe to him in all the ſciences, he concluded with an extemporary oration in praiſe of ignorance, that *Aldus Manutius* * ſays that they all thought that they were in a dream, and that he had almoſt perſuaded them that it was better to be ignorant, than learned and wiſe. Some time after this he fixed a paper on the gates of St. *John* and St. *Paul*'s churches, wherein he offered to prove before the univerſity, that there was an infinite number of errors in *Ariſtotle*'s philoſophy, which was then only in vogue, and in all his commentaries, both in theological and philoſophical matters, and to refute the dreams of ſeveral mathematicians: He likewiſe made an offer to diſpute in all the ſciences, and to anſwer to whatever ſhould be propoſed to him, or objected againſt him, either in the common logical way, or by numbers and mathematical figures, or in a hundred ſorts of verſes as they pleaſed.

Aldus Manutius, who was preſent at this diſpute, ſays †, that he performed all that he had promiſed, to their greateſt amazement: And he tells us likewiſe of another diſpute that he had before a great concourſe of people in the biſhop of *Padua*'s houſe, without mentioning the occaſion or particulars of it; but *Joannes Imperialis*

* Aldus Man. Præf. in Cicer. Parad.

† Ubi ſupra.

tells us *, that he was informed by his father, who was preſent at this diſpute, that it was with one *Archangellus Mercenarius*, a famous philoſopher, upon philoſophical ſubjects, in which he acquitted himſelf ſo well, that his adverſary owned before the aſſembly that he had overcome him.

From *Venice* he went to *Mantua*; at this time there was a gladiator at *Mantua*, who had foiled in his travels the moſt famous fencers in *Europe*, and had lately killed in that city three perſons who had entered the liſts with him; the Duke of *Mantua* was highly offended that he had granted this fellow his protection, ſince it had ſuch a fatal conſequence: *Crichton* being informed of this, offered his ſervice to the Duke, to rid not only his dominions, but *Italy* of this murtherer, and to fight him for fifteen hundred piſtoles: though the Duke was unwilling to expoſe ſuch a fine gentleman as our author, to ſuch an hazard, yet relying upon the report of his performances in all warlike atchievements, it was agreed to; and the time and place being appointed, the whole court were witneſs to the performance. In the beginning of the combat, *Crichton* was upon the defenſive, and the *Italian* attacked him with ſuch vigor and eagerneſs, that he began to grow faint, having overacted himſelf; then our author attacked him with ſuch dexterity and vigor, that he run him through the body in three different places, of which he immediately died. The huzza's and acclamations of the ſpectators were extraordinary upon this occaſion, and all of them acknowleged, that they had never ſeen art grace nature, nor nature ſecond the precepts of art, with ſo much livelineſs as

* Ubi ſupra.

they had ſeen that day; and to crown the glory of this action, *Crichton* beſtowed the prize of his victory upon the widows who had loſt their huſbands in fighting with this gladiator.

Theſe, and his other wonderfull performances, moved the Duke of *Mantua* to make choice of him for preceptor to his ſon *Vincent de Gonzagua*, a prince of a riotous temper, and diſſolute life. The court was highly pleaſed with the Duke's choice, and for their diverſion he compoſed a comedy, wherein he expoſed and ridiculed * all the weakneſſes and failures of the ſeveral employments that men betake themſelves to; which was looked upon as one of the moſt ingenious ſatires that ever was made upon mankind; but that which was moſt wonderfull and aſtoniſhing was, that he himſelf perſonated the divine, philoſopher, lawyer, mathematician, phyſician, and ſoldier, with ſuch an inimitable grace, that every time he

* The unhappy effect that this humour had on two maids of honor is admirably told by Sir *Thomas Urquhart*, a ſecond *Rabelais*, and the beſt tranſlator of that extravagant author.

" They heard in him alone the promiſcuous ſpeech of fifteen ſeveral actors, by " the various raviſhments of the excellencies whereof, in the frolickneſs of a jo- " cound ſtraine beyond expectation, the logof-aſcinated ſpirits of the beholding " hearers and auricularie ſpectators, were ſo on a ſudden ſeazed upon in their " riſible faculties of the ſoul, and all their vital motions ſo univerſally affected in " this extremitie of agitation, that, to avoid the inevitable charmes of his intoxi- " cating ejaculations, and the accumulative influences of ſo powerfull a tranſporta- " tion, one of my *Lady Dutcheſs* chief maids of honour, by the vehemencie of the " ſhock of thoſe incomprehenſible raptures, burſt forth into a laughter, to the " rupture of a veine in her body; and another young lady, by the irreſiſtible " violence

he appeared upon the theatre, he ſeemed to be a different perſon; but from being the principal actor of a comedy, he became the wofull ſubject of a moſt lamentable tragedy, being moſt barbarouſly murthered by his pupil, which happened thus:

One night as he was walking alongſt the ſtreets in the time of the carnaval, and playing upon his guitarre, he was attacked by half a dozen of people in maſks; but they found that they had not an ordinary perſon to deal with, for they were not able to ſtand their ground againſt him, and having diſarmed the principal perſon amongſt them, he pulled off his maſk, and begged his life, telling him, that he was the prince his pupil. *Crichton*, who immediately knew him, fell down upon his knees, and told him, that he was ſorry for his miſtake, and that what he had done was only in his own defence, and that if he had any deſign upon his life, he might always be maſter of it; and then taking his own ſword by the point, he

" violence of the pleaſure unawares infuſed, where the tender receptibilitie of her " too too tickled fancie was left able to hold out, ſo unprovidedly was ſurpriſed, " that, with no leſs impetuoſitie of ridibundal paſſion then (as hath been told) " occaſioned a fracture in the other young ladie, ſhe, not able longer to ſupport " the well beloved burden of ſo exceſſive delight, and intranſing joys of ſuch " *Mercurial* exhilarations through the ineffable extaſie of an over maſterd appre- " henſion, fell back in a ſwoon, without the appearance of any other life into " her, then what by the moſt refined wits of theological ſpeculators is conceived " to be exerced by the pureſt parts of the ſeparated *entelechies* of bleſſed Saints in " their ſublimeſt converſations with the celeſtial hierarchies: this accident procured " the incoming of an apothecarie with reſtoratives, as the other did that of a ſur- " geon with conſolidative medicaments."

Vindication of the honour of *Scotland*, &c. p. 111, 112.

he preſented him with it; which the prince taking in his hand, and not being able to overcome his paſſion for the affront that he thought he had ſuſtained, in being foiled with all his attendants, he immediately run him through the heart.

What moved the prince to this ungenerous and brutal action, is variouſly conjectured; for ſome think that it was jealouſy, ſuſpecting that he was more in favors with a young lady whom he paſſionately loved than he was. Others ſay, that it was only to try his valor, and the effect of a drunken ramble; but whatever was the cauſe of it, 'tis certain that thus he died, in the beginning of the month of *July*, in the year 1583, in the thirty-ſecond year of his age, or, as *Imperialis* ſays, in the twenty-ſecond.

His death was extraordinarily lamented by all the learned men in *Europe*, and from theſe *Italian* writers, who knew, and were cotemporary with him, it is, that I have moſt of all that I have ſaid of him. *Joannes Imperialis*, a doctor of medicine of *Vicenza* in *Italy*, who has wrote our author's life, and who could not but know the truth of all, or moſt of what he has ſaid of him, ſince he lived upon the places in which they were acted, and who had them from his father, who was an eye and ear witneſs to them, ſays*, "That he "was the wonder of the laſt age, the prodigious production of na- "ture, the glory and ornament of *Parnaſſus* in a ſtupendious and "an unuſual manner, and as yet in the judgement of the learned "world, the *Phœnix* of literature, and rather a ſhining particle of "the Divine Nature and Majeſty, than a model of what human "nature and induſtry can attain to. And what can be more,"

* Muſæum Hiſtor. p. 241.

continues he*, " above our comprehension, than in the 21st year " of his age to be master of ten languages, and to be perfectly well " seen in philosophy, mathematicks, theology, the belles-letters, " and all the other sciences; besides, was it ever heard of in the " whole compass of this globe, that one with all this, should be " found expert to admiration, in fencing, dancing, singing, riding, " and the other exercises of the gymnastick art? besides all this, he " is said to have been one of the most beautifull, and one of the " handsomest gentlemen the world ever saw, so that nature had " taken as much care about his body, as she had done about his " mind; and in one word, he was the utmost that man could come " to." M. *Bayle* says †, that he was one of the greatest prodigies of wit that ever lived; and *Fælix Astolfus* that he had such a prodigious memory ‡ that he retained more books upon his mind, than any of his age had read; *Plures libros memoriter tenebat quam quisquam ea ætate legerat.*

And Sir *Thomas Urquhart* of *Cromarty*, having insisted on all the particulars of our author's life in a fustian and bombastical strain, tells us, that in the comedy which he composed, and was an actor in before the court of *Mantua*, in the fifth and last act, he himself personated no less than 15 different characters of persons and employments in their different habits.

And in his character of him, he tells us, that he gained the esteem of all kings and princes, by his magnanimity and knowledge; of all

* Musæum Histor. Imper. Joa. ibidem, Venetiis apud Juntas 1650, in 4to.

† Bib. Crit.

‡ Officina Hist. p. 102.

noblemen

noblemen and gentlemen, by his courtlinefs and breeding; of all knights, by his honorable deportment and pregnancy of wit; of all the rich, by his affability and good fellowfhip; of all the poor, by his munificence and liberality; of all the old, by his conftancy and wifdom; of all the young, by his mirth and gallantry; of all the learned, by his univerfal knowlege; of all the foldiers, by his undaunted valor and courage; of all the merchants and artificers, by his upright dealing and honefty; and of all the fair fex, by his beauty and handfomnefs; in which refpect, he was a mafter-piece of nature. "The reader," fays he, "perhaps will think this wonderfull, and fo would I too, were it not that I know, as Sir *Philip Sidney* fays, that a wonder is no wonder in a wonderfull fubject, and confequently not in him, who for his learning, judgement, valor, eloquence, beauty and good fellowfhip, was the perfecteft refult of the joint labors of *Pallas*, *Apollo*, *Mars*, *Mercury*, *Venus* and *Bacchus*, that hath been fince the days of *Alcibiades*; and he was reported to have been enriched with a memory fo prodigious, that any fermon, fpeech, harangue, or other manner of difcourfes of an hour's continuance he was able to recite without hefitation, after the fame manner of gefture and pronunciation in all points, wherewith it was delivered at firft; and of fo ftupendious a judgement, that nothing efcaped his knowledge": And for the truth of all this, he appeals to above two thoufand witneffes, that were ftill alive, and had known him. And fpeaking of his death, which he attributes to an amour, he tells us, that it was in the 32d year of his age; that the whole court went in mourning for him; that the epitaphs and elegies that were compofed upon his death, if collected, would exceed the bulk of *Homer*'s works, and that his picture was ſtill to be ſeen in the moſt of the bed-chambers and galleries of the *Italian* nobility, repreſenting him upon horſeback, with a lance in the one hand, and a book in the other *.

Dempſter, who was cotemporary with him, and a profeſſor of the civil law at *Bononia* in *Italy*, agrees as to the moſt of what we have ſaid of him; but he tells us †, that he was for ſome time at *Geneva*, as he was on his travels to *Italy*, and that they offered him a conſiderable ſalary, if he would remain with them; but that he refuſed it, and that no man offered to detract from his juſt praiſes, but *Trajano Boccalini*; but that he being a perſon of no erudition, it was rather a glory than any diſgrace upon him to be ſo treated by a perſon of his character. Yet the ſame *Dempſter* blames our author very much, not for his boaſting of the endowments of his mind, but for his affirming that he was deſcended from the royal family of *Scotland*. Many poems and epitaphs were compoſed upon him, but I ſhall only inſert that of our countryman, Dr. *John Johnſton*, in his inſcriptions upon our heroes, who makes him die in the year 1581.

* The print prefixed to this life was taken from a picture in poſſeſſion of Lord *Eliock*, Lord of Seſſions, copied from an original belonging to Mr. *Graham* of *Airth*. I am told that there is a very fine portrait of this celebrated perſon the property of Mr. *Morriſon* of *Bogny*, which was ſent from *Italy* by *Crichton* a ſhort time before he was killed.

† Hiſt. Eccleſ. Gen. Scot. ubi ſupra.

JACOBUS CRITONIUS CLUNIUS.

Musarum pariter ac Martis Alumnus, omnibus in ſtudiis, ipſis etiam Italis admirabilis, Mantuæ a Ducis Mantuani nocturnis inſidiis occiſus eſt, Anno Chriſti 1581.

ET genus & cenſum dat Scotia, Gallia pectus
Excolit: admirans Itala terra virum,
Ambit, & eſſe ſuum vellet; gens æmula vitam
Abſtulit; an ſatis hoc dicat ut illa ſuum
Mantua habet cineres ſcelus execrata nefandum,
At tumuli tanto gaudet honore tamen.

I know nothing of this author that is extant, but two poems, one in praiſe of the city of *Venice*, and the other addreſſed to *Aldus Manutius* *. Both which are in the firſt volume of the *Delitiæ Poetarum Scoticorum*.

* *Crichton* replies to one of the *Naiads* of the *Po* who appeared to him on his arrival at *Venice*:

---------------- Fateor me candide *Naias*
Promeritum quæcunque fero: nec turpis egeſtas
Infandumve ſcelus ſervi mea pectora vexat.
At me quis miſerum magna cognoſcit in urbe
Aut quis ad æquoreas flentem ſolatur arenas?

The *Naid* directs him to *Aldus*:

Hunc pete namque regens filo veſtigia cæca
Diriget ille tuos optato in tramite greſſus.
Inde via pendet. ſequere hunc quæcunque jubentem.
Sic te Diva monet ſævam quæ Gorgona geſtat,
Quæ plerumque tuis preſens erit optima votis.

Dempſter

Dempſter gives us the following catalogue of his works, where it plainly appears, that he makes three books out of that placad which he affixed upon the gates of St. *John* and St. *Paul's* churches in *Padua*.

The Catalogue of his Works.

I. ODÆ ad Laurentium Maſſam plures.

II. Laudes Patavinæ, Carmen extempore effuſum, cum in Jacobi Moyſii Cornelii domo experimentum ingenii coram tota Academiæ frequentia non ſine multorum ſtupore faceret.

III. Ignorationis Laudatio, extemporale Thema ibidem redditum poſt ſex horarum diſputationes, ut præſentes ſomnia potius fovere quam rem ſe veram videre affirmarint, ait Manutius.

IV. De appulſu ſuo Venetias. Delitiæ Poet. Scot. Vol. I. p. 268.

V. Odæ ad Aldum Manutium. Del. Poet. Scot. Vol. I. p. 269.

VI. Epiſtolæ ad Diverſos.

VII. Præfationes ſolemnes in omnes ſcientias ſacras & profanas.

VIII. Judicium de Philoſophis.

IX. Errores Ariſtotelis.

X. Armis an Literæ præſtant, Controverſia oratoria.

XI. Refutatio Mathematicorum.

XII. A Comedy in the Italian Language.

NUM-

NUMBER IV.

OF THE MURDER OF A LAIRD OF INNES, AS RELATED IN THE OLD ACCOUNT.

JOHN Lord *Innes*, having no children, ſettles his eſtate upon his next heir and couſin *Alexander Innes* of *Cromy*, and ſeems to ſuffer him to enjoy his title and poſſeſſions in his life time. *Robert Innes* of *Innermarky*, another cadet of the family, is diſguſted to ſee *Innes* of *Cromy* endowed with ſo much power and preferred to him. He alarms Lord *John*, and makes him repent ſo far of what he had done, that he joins in conſpiracy with *Innermarky* to aſſaſſinate his couſin *Alexander*. The author ſays, "*John* being brought over to his minde (viz. *Innes's* of *Innermarky*) there wanted nothing but a conveniency for putting y^r^ purpoſe to execution, which did offer itſelf in ye month of *Apryle* 1580, at q^ch^ tyme *Alex^r^* being called upon ſome buſines to *Aberdeen* was obliged to ſtay longer there then he intended, by reaſone that his only ſone *Robert* a youth of 16 yeirs of age hade fallen ſick at the college, and his father could not leave the place untill he ſaw q^t^ became of him. He hade tranſported him out

out of the old toune, and hade brought him to his own lodgeing in the new toun; he hade alſo ſent ſeveral of his ſervants home from tyme to tyme to let his Lady know the reaſone of his ſtay, by means of theſe ſervants it came to be known perfectly at *Kinnardy* in q[t] circumſtance *Alexander* was at *Aberdeen*, q[r] he was lodged, and how he was attended, which invited *Innermarky* to take the occaſione. Wherefore getting a conſiderable number of aſſiſtants with him, he hade Laird *John* ryde to *Aberdeen*: they enter the toun upon the night, and about middnight came to *Alexander*'s lodgeing.

The outer gate of the cloſs they found oppen, but all the reſt of the doors ſhutt; they wer afraid to break up doors by violence, leaſt the noiſe might alarm the neighbourheed, but choiſed rather to ryſe ſuch a cry in the cloſs as might obleidge thoſe who wer within to oppen the door and ſee q[t] it might be. The feuds at that tyme betwixt the familys of *Gordone* and *Forbes* wer not extinguiſhed, therfor they ryſed a cry, as if it hade been upon ſome out fall among theſe people, crying *help a Gordon, a Gordon*, which is the gathering word of the friends of y[t] familie.

Alexander, being deeply intereſted in the *Gordon*, at the noiſe of the cry ſtarted from his bedd, took his ſword in his hand and oppened a back door that led to y[e] court below, ſtept down three or four ſteps and cryed to know q[t] was the matter. *Innermarky* who by his word knew him, and by his whyt ſhirt decerned him perfectly, cocks his gun and ſhootts him through the body in ane inſtant. As many as could get about him fell upon him and butchered him barbarouſly. *Innermarky* perceaveing in the mean tyme y[t] Laird *John* ſtood by, as either relenting or terified, held the bloody dagger to his throatt that he hade newly taken out of the murthured body,

body, ſwearing dreadfully y^t he would ſerve him the ſame way if he did not as he did, and ſo compelled him to draw his dagger and ſtab it up to the hilts, in the body of his neareſt relatione, and the braveſt that boare his name. After his example all who wer ther behooved to doe the lyke, that all might be alyke guilty; yea in proſecutione of this, it has been told me that Mr. *John Innes*, afterwards *Coxtoune*, being a youth than at ſchooll, was ryſed out of his bedd and compelled by *Innermarky* to ſtab a daggar unto the dead body, that the more might be under the ſame condemnatione; a very crafty cruelty.

The next thing looked after was the deſtructione of the ſick youth *Robert*, who hade lyein y^t night in a bedd by his father, but upon the noyſe of q^t was done, hade ſcrambled from it, and by the help of one *John* of *Culdreaſons*, or rather of ſome of the people of the houſs, hade got out at ane unfrequented bak door into the garden, and from y^t into a neighbour's houſs, q^r he hade ſhaltered; the LORD in his providence preſerveing him for the executing vengence upon theſe murthurers for the blood of his father.

Then *Innermarky* took the dead man's ſignet ring, and ſent it to his wife, as from her huſband, by a ſervant whom he hade purchaſed to that purpoſe, ordering her to ſend him ſuch a particular box q^{ch} contained the bond of *Tailie*, and all y^t had followed thereupon betwixt him and Laird *John*, whom the ſervant ſaid he hade left w^t his m^r at *Aberdeen*: and y^t for diſpatch he hade ſent his beſt hors with him, and hade not taken leaſure to writ, but ſent the ring. Though it troubled the woman much to receave ſuch a blind meaſage, yet her huſband's ring, his own ſervant and his horſs, prevailed ſo with her, togither with the man's impportunity to be gone, that ſhee delivered to him q[t] he ſought, and let him go.

There happened to be then about the houſs a youth related to the family, who was courious to go to the lenth of *Aberdeen*, and ſee the young Laird who hade been ſick, and to whom he was much adicted. This youth hade gone to the ſtable to interceed with the ſervant that he might carrie him behind him, and in his diſcourſs hade found the man under great reſtraint and confuſion of minde, ſometyme ſayeing he was to go no further than *Kinnardy* (which indeed was the truth) and at oy[r] tymes that he behooved to be immediatly at *Aberdeen*.

This brought him to be jealous, though he knew not q[t], but further knowledge he behooved to have, and therfor he ſtept out a little beyond the entry, watching the ſervant's comeing, and in the by going ſudently leapt on behind him, and would needs either go alonges with him, or have a ſatisfieing reaſone, why he refuſſed him.

The conteſt became ſuch betwixt them, that the ſervant drew his durk to ridd him of the youth's trouble, q[ch] the other wrung out of his hands, and down right killed him w[t] it, and brought back the box wth the writs and horſs to the houſ of *Innes* (or *Cromie*, I know not q[ch]).

As the lady is in a confuſione for q[t] hade fallen out, ther comes aneother of the ſervants from *Aberdeen*, who gave ane account of the ſlaughter, ſo that ſhee behooved to conclude a ſpeciall hand of providence to have been in the firſt paſage. Her next courſs was to ſecure her huſband's writts the beſt ſhe could, and flee to her friends for ſhalter, by whos means ſhe was brought w[t] all ſpeed to the

the king, befor whom ſhee made her complaint. And q^t is heir ſet doun is holden by all men to be true matter of fact.

The Earle of *Huntly* imediatly upon the report of the ſlaughter concerned himſelf becauſs of his relatione to the dead, and looked out for his ſon, whom he inſtantly carried to *Edinburgh*, and put him for ſhalter into the family of the Lord *Elphinſtoune*, at that tyme Lord high Treaſurer of the kingdome.

Innermarky and Laird *John*, after the ſlaughter, came back to the Lord *Saltoun*'s houſs, who leived then at *Rothimay*, and is thought to have been in the knowledge of q^t they hade been about, for certaine it is they wer ſupported by the *Abernethys*, ay untill the law went againſt them. From *Rothymay* they went with a conſiderable party of horſs, and repoſceſt Laird *John* in all the parts of the eſtate of *Innes*. And *Innermarky*, to make the full uſe of q^t he hade ſo boldly begun, did upon the ſeventein *Maii* 1580, which was 5 weeks after the ſlaughter, take from Laird *John* a new diſpoſitione of the eſtate of *Innes*.

By what is ſaid *Innermarky* may appeir to have been a man full of unrighteouſneſs, craft and cruelty; yet ſome ſay for alleviatione of his fact, that he having his chieff's favour hade got the firſt diſpoſition of his eſtate failieing airs of himſelf, but that *Cromy* had taken a poſterior right and hade ſupplanted *Innermarky*, for q^{ch} he in revenge had killed him, &c. But falſneſs of the allegance (mean as it is) is plaine paſt contradictione, from the above narraitted writ, q^{ch} was given to *Innermarky* but 40 days after the ſlaughter of *Cromy*.

For two full yeirs *Iunermarky* and *John* had poſſeſt the eſtate of *Innes*, ſtrenthening themſelfs with all the friendſhip they could ac-

 quyre,

quyre; but being in end declaired out lawes, in the 3^d^ yeir *Robert* Laird of *Innes*, the son of *Alex^r^*, came North with a commission against them and all others concerned in the slaughter of his father. This *Robert* was a young man weill endued w^t^ favour and understanding, which hade ingadged the Lord Treasurer so far to wedd his interest, that he first weded the young man to his daughter, and then gott him all the assistance requisit to possess him of his estate, q^ch^ was no sooner done but he led wast the possessions of his enemies; burning and blood shed was acted by both partys with animously enough.

In the mean tyme Laird *John* had run away to seek some lurking place in the South, q^r^ he was discovered by the friends of the Lord *Elphinstoune*, and by them taken and sent North to the Laird *Robert*, who did not put him to death, but took him bound to various sorts of performances, as appears by the contract betwixt them in *Anno* 1585: one gross was, y^t^ he should deliver up the chartor chist, and all the old evidents, q^ch^ he and *Innermarky* had seased, and which I doubt if ever he faithfully did, els this relation hade been with less pains and mor fully instructed.

As to *Innermarky*, he was forced for a while to take the hills, and when he wearied of that, he hade a retreat of a difficult access within the houss of *Edinglassy*, q^r^ he sleeped in little enough security; for in *September* 1584, his houss was surprysed by Laird *Robert*, and that reteiring place of his first entred by *Alexander Innes*, afterwards of *Cotts*, the same who some yeirs befor had killed the servant who came from *Innermarky* with the false tokin for ye writs, and who all his lyfe was called *Craigg in peirill*, for venturing upon *Innermarky* then desperat, and whos cruelty he helped to repay it in in its own coine; ther was no mercy for him, for ſlaine he was, and his hoar head cut off and taken by the widdow of him whom he hade ſlain, and caried to *Edinburgh* and caſten at the King's feett, a thing too maſculine to be commended in a woman.

NUMBER V.

OF CATHNESS, STRATHNAVER, AND SUTHERLAND;

By the Rev. Mr. ALEXANDER POPE, Minifter of REAY.

AS the *Picts* poffeffed the Northern parts of *Scotland* of old, as they did the moft fertile parts of the South, and were expelled in the year 839, we have very little of their hiftory: what preferves the remembrance of that people is only the round buildings wherein they dwelt, of which there are numbers over all the North, particularly *Sutherland*, *Cathnefs*, and *Orkney*.

It is obfervable in thefe buildings, that there is no mortar of any kind, neither clay or lime; nor had they any notion of cafting an arch. They confift of the beft ftones they could find, well laid and joined; the wall was fometimes 14 feet thick, and the great room, which was quite round, 22 feet diameter; the perpendicular wall 12 feet high; and the roof was carried on round about with long ftones, ſtones, till it ended in an opening at the top, which ſerved both for light and a vent to carry off the ſmoke of their fire. Where the ſtones were long and good, they had ſmall rooms for ſleeping in the thickneſs of their wall. The door or entry was low, 3 feet for ordinary, ſhut up by a large broad ſtone. There is one of them entire in the pariſh of *Loth*, which the Biſhop of *Oſſory* viſited and examined. It is the only one that is ſo, as far as I could find, excepting one at *Suiſgil* in the pariſh of *Kildonnan*. It is to be obſerved that where the ſtones were not flat and well bedded, for fear the outer wall ſhould fail, they built great heaps of ſtones to ſupport it, ſo that it looks outwardly like a heap without any deſign, which is the caſe at *Loth beg* in the pariſh of *Lothis*. At the deſire of the Biſhop of *Oſſory* I meaſured ſeveral of them, and ſaw ſome quite demoliſhed. We found nothing in them but hand-mills, or what the Highlanders call *Querns*, which were only 18 inches diameter, and great heaps of deer bones and horns, as they lived much more by hunting than any other means.

From the extirpation of the *Picts* to the year 1266, *Scotland* was harraſſed by invaſions from the *Norwegians* and *Danes*, particularly the North part; for *Harold* the fair, King of *Norway*, ſeized *Orkney* in the latter end of the 9th century. From *Norway*, ſwarms came to *Orkney*, and the paſſage being ſo ſhort, all the North of *Scotland* was continually in arms. As nothing can be expected in that period but fighting, bloodſhed and rapine, we cannot look for improvements of any kind, and for that reaſon it is needleſs to attempt any particular hiſtory of it. It is true, *Torfæus* gives us ſome account of that time, which is all that we have.

As

As to the family of *Sutherland*, they have possessed that country since the expulsion of the *Picts*, and have continued as Thanes and Earls to this time. That they are originally of *German* extraction, is evident from their arms. Doctor *Abercrombie*, in his History of the *Scots* Heroes, mentions *Donald* Thane of *Sutherland* married to a niece of King *Kenneth* II. May that good family continue and prosper.

Lord *Reay*'s family derive their original from *Ireland*, in the 12th century, when King *William the Lion* reigned. The occasion of their settling in the North is mentioned by *Torfæus*, as captains of a number of warriors to drive the *Norwegians* out of *Cathness*.

The *Sinclairs* Earls of *Cathness* are only of a late date. The family of *Roslin* is their original in *Scotland*: but their coming into *England* is as early as the year 1066: for I find them mentioned among the commanders in the army of *William* the Conqueror, in the roll of *Battel abby*. They were first Earls of *Orkney*, then Earls of *Cathness*, and still continue in the person of *William Sinclair* of *Ratter*, who carried the peerage before the *British* parliament this present year 1772.

As for the history of these parts, I shall begin with

EDRACHILIS.

This parish, which belongs to the family of *Reay*, is all forest and rocks, little arable, and scarcely any plain ground, excepting the town of *Scoury*. The pasture is fine, and plenty of red deer, but the country at some distance looks as if one hill was piled upon another.

another. The firth that runs far into the land abounds with good fiſh, and herring in their ſeaſon.

Torfæus mentions a bloody battle fought in this firth, at a place called *Glen du*, by two pirates; one of them he calls *Odranus Gillius*, the other *Suenus*, wherein the latter was victorious. There is likewiſe a tradition of ſome bloody engagements betwixt the *Mackays* and *Macleods*.

PARISH OF DIURNESS.

This pariſh was of old a graſs room or ſhealing to the Biſhop of *Cathneſs*, and was diſpoſed of to the family of *Sutherland* by Bp. *Andrew Stuart*, and the family of *Sutherland* gave it to Lord *Reay*'s family. Two pieces of antiquity are to be ſeen in this pariſh: 1ſt. *Dornadilla*'s tower or hunting-houſe, which ſtands in *Strathmore*; a very ſtrange kind of building, well worth the ſeeing *. It is certain that the fineſt paſture is in the hills of *Diurneſs*, which rendered it the beſt foreſt in *Scotland* of old. Our antient *Scots* Kings hunted there frequently, and it appears that this was a cuſtom as far back as the time of King *Dornadilla*. 2d. There is on the ſide of a hill called *Bui ſpinunn*, a ſquare piece of building, about 3 feet high and 12 ſquare, well levelled, called *Carn nri*, or King's carn, which probably was the place where his Majeſty ſat or ſtood, and ſaw the ſport, as he had from hence an extenſive proſpect. *Torfæus* mentions that one *Suenus* from *Orkney* waited on the King of *Scotland*

* A further account of this tower will be given in the Tour and Voyage of 1772.

as he was diverting himſelf in the hunting ſeaſon in the hills of *Diurneſs*. This ſhould be in the days of *Malcolm* II.

At *Loch-eribol*, on the North ſide, there is a plain rock which is ſtill called *Lech vuaies*, where they ſay that *Hacon*, King of *Norway*, ſlaughtered the cattle he took from the natives in his return to *Orkney*, after the battle of *Largis* in the year 1263. *Torfæus* gives a journal of that expedition, and mentions King *Hacon*'s landing there. But there is a tradition that a party of *Norwegians*, venturing too far into that country, were cut to pieces; and that the place is called *Strath urradale*, from the name of the *Norwegian* commander: a cuſtom very common of old.

The greateſt curioſity in this pariſh is a cave called *Smow*. It is a ſtupendous arch or vault, and runs under ground ſo far that the extremity of it was never found. *Donald* Lord *Reay*, the firſt of that family, made an attempt, and we are told he proceeded very far, meeting with lakes, and paſſing through them in a boat: but, after all, was obliged to ſatisfy himſelf with ſeeing a part.

Here are ſeveral caves that run far under ground, but *Smow* is the moſt remarkable. I am told that of late they have diſcovered, in the manor or mains of *Diurneſs*, a hole of great depth: it was of old covered with large ſtones, but theſe it ſeems have mouldered away. So that it is the conjecture of many, that there are numbers of cavities of great extent, under ground, in this pariſh.

This pariſh is all upon the lime ſtone, and abounds in marble; the part called ſtrictly *Diurneſs*, is a plain, the ſoil good, and the graſs incomparable, therefore capable of the higheſt improvement. The lakes are ſtored with the fineſt fiſh, and full of marle. The hills afford the beſt paſturage for ſheep, and the ſeas are well ſtored with

with fiſh. But the great diſadvantage to this country is, that it is expoſed to the North-Weſt ſtorms, which drive the ſand upon it, and have by that means deſtroyed ſeveral good farms, and threaten more harm daily.

In this pariſh is a firth, called *Loch-Eribol*; *Torfæus* calls it *Goas-fiord*, or the firth of *Hoan*, an iſland oppoſite to it. This is one of the fineſt and ſafeſt roads for ſhipping in *Europe*; the navy of *Great Britain* can enter into it at low water, and find good anchoring. It is a loſs that this incomparable bay has not been ſurveyed, and the different anchoring places marked. It would be a mighty bleſſing to mariners, being ſo near *Cape wrath*, one of the moſt ſtormy capes in the world. For it would be a ſafe retreat to veſſels, in time of ſtorm, either ſailing towards the cape, or to thoſe that had the misfortune to receive any damage off it. *Cape wrath* is alſo in the pariſh of *Diurneſs*.

PARISH OF TONGUE.

The antiquities of this pariſh are few. There is an old *Daniſh* building upon the ſummit of a hill, called *Caſtel varrich*, or *Barr* caſtle: for the *Danes* or *Norwegians* poſſeſſed that country for ſome time. *Tongue* is the ſeat of Lord *Reay*'s family. This pariſh is rather better for paſture than tillage, but what corn ground they have is extremely good. Of old there was a fine foreſt in it, and there is ſtill plenty of deer. The anceſtors of Lord *Reay*'s family drove the *Danes* from theſe parts.

In this pariſh is a loch, called *Loch-Hacon*; in it an iſland, called *Illan Lochan Hacon*, in which there is the ruin of a ſtone building

 with

with an artificial walk in it, called *Grianan*, becauſe dry and expoſed to the ſun. From which it appears that Earl *Hacon*, who poſſeſſed *Orkney* and *Cathneſs*, had a hunting houſe in this iſland, and lodged there, with his warriors, in the hunting ſeaſon. The ſea coaſt, for the greateſt part, is all rock, of a rough granite, or what we call *whin*. Here is a promontory or cape, called *Whiten head*, very ſtormy when it is a hard gale.

There was formerly a chapel in an iſland near *Skerray*; the common people call it the Iſle of *Saints*; it goes by the name of *Iſland comb*.

Another iſland, called *Illan na nroan*, all a high rock, but good land, and plenty of water and moſs. It might be rendered impregnable. Both theſe iſlands are in the pariſh of *Tongue*. I have been in *Illan comb*; if the ſand had not over-run a part, it would be a charming place.

A bloody battle was fought in this pariſh, of old, by one of the anceſtors of Lord *Reay*, againſt one *Angus Murray*, a *Sutherland* man, wherein the *Sutherland* men were cut to pieces. The field of battle is called *Drim na coub*. And in the ſame place there was a ſkirmiſh betwixt Lord *Reay*'s men, and a number of *Frenchmen* that were on board the *Hazard* ſloop of war, in 1746: ſome of the *French* were killed, and the reſt taken priſoners.

This pariſh is remarkable for an excellent ebb, where they have the fineſt cockles, muſcles, ſpout fiſh, and flounders or floaks; which is a great bleſſing to the poor, and no ſmall benefit to the rich. And in the firth of *Tongue* there is a fine iſland, abounding with rabbets, called *Rabbet Iſle*. It has many lochs, or freſh water lakes, full of the fineſt trout and ſalmon.

PARISH

Parish of FAR.

The whole of theſe four pariſhes was of old called *Strathnaver*, from the river *Naver*, which was ſo called, as ſome think, from the name of one of King *Kenneth* the Second's warriors. It is a noble body of water, well ſtored with ſalmon, having many fruitfull and beautifull villages on the banks of it, and is ſo inhabited for 18 miles.

At a place called *Langdale* there were noble remains of a *Druidical* temple, being a circle of 100 feet diameter, and ſurrounded with a trench, ſo that the earth formed a bank; in the midſt of it a ſtone was erected like a pillar, where the *Druid* ſtood and taught. The country people have now trenched or delved that ground, and ſown it with corn. There was in that town a large round building, and a place where they buried of old.

This pariſh is of great extent, rather a country for paſture than tillage. A great battle was fought of old at a place called --------, *Harald* or *Harald*'s field or plain, betwixt *Reginald* King of the Iſles, and *Harald* Earl of *Orkney* and *Cathneſs*. *Harald* was well drubbed; the field of battle is full of ſmall carns, where the ſlain are buried, and ſome large ſtones erected like pillars ſhew where perſons of note were interred. *Torfæus* tells a long ſtory about this affair; it ſeems that they had bloody ſkirmiſhes at --------, and near the manſe of *Far*, as appears from the number of cairns in both theſe places. There is a moſt curious ſepulchral monument in the church yard of *Far*, which may be of that date; it is of hard hill granite, well cut, conſidering the æra of it. But what the meaning of the ſculpture is, we know not. Only we may gueſs, that the perſon for whoſe ſake

ſake it was erected, was a Chriſtian, becauſe of the croſs upon the ſtone; and that he was a warrior, becauſe we ſee a ſhield or target upon it. I have taken a draught of it.

In this pariſh, in old times, was a chapel at a town called *Skail*, upon the river *Naver*; another in the extremity thereof, at *Moudale*; and another at *Strathie*, the moſt beautifull and fertile part of the pariſh.

Betwixt *Far* and *Kirtomy*, in this pariſh, is a moſt ſingular curioſity, well worth the pains of a traveller to view, being the remains of an old ſquare building or tower, called *Borve*, ſtanding upon a ſmall point joined to the continent by a narrow neck of land not ten feet wide. This point or head is very high, conſiſting of rock, and ſome gravel on the top; on both ſides is very deep water, and a tolerable harbour for boats. This tower ſeems to be built by the *Norwegians*; and the tradition is, that one *Thorkel*, or *Torquil*, a warrior mentioned by *Torfæus*, was the perſon that built it. They ſpeak likewiſe of a lady that was concealed there, ſhe is ſaid to be an *Orkney* woman, and *Thorkel* was an *Orkney* man. But what is moſt curious, is, that through the rock upon which the tower ſtands, there is a paſſage below of 200 feet in length, like a grand arch or vault, through which they row a boat. The writer has been one of a company that rowed through it. The paſſage is ſo long, that when you enter at one end, you fancy that there is no poſſibility to get out at the other, *et vice verſa*. How this hard rock was thus bored or excavated, I cannot ſay; but it is one of the moſt curious natural arches, perhaps, in the known world.

In

In this pariſh there is alſo a promontory, called *Strathy head*; *Ptolemy* the Geographer calls it *Vervadrum*, as he calls *Cape wrath*, *Tarvedrum*, and *Dungſbey head*, *Berubium*. Theſe three promontories run in a line, from N. W. to North, and jut far out into the ſea, having moſt rapid tides upon them. In *Strathy head* is a ſtately cave, called *Uai nei*, or cave where they find driven wood or timber. The entrance into this cave is very grand, the natural rock almoſt forming itſelf like the ſway of an arch: the writer hereof has admired the beauty of it. This promontory is the fineſt paſture for ſheep and goats in the North of *Scotland*.

To the North-Eaſt of *Strathy* there is a ſtone erected near the highway, with a croſs upon it, which ſhews its antiquity as a ſepulchral monument. Erected ſtones were the diſtinguiſhing marks of the graves of perſons of note in time of Paganiſm. And after Chriſtianity was planted in this kingdom, the diſtinction of Pagan from Chriſtian was, that a croſs was cut upon the ſepulchral monuments of the latter. I have ſeen many with this diſtinguiſhing badge.

No doubt there are mines in this country, if perſons of ſkill examined our ſhores and rocks; as yet no pains have been taken. I have been told that there is at *Loch-Eribol* plenty of iron ſtone, and ſomething like a tin mine. As I do not underſtand theſe things, I chuſe to paſs them over. As for ſea-fiſh and ſhells, we have none extraordinary. It is true, in *Cathneſs*, *John a Groat*'s buckies are very curious and beautifull, of which we ſhall take notice in the pariſh of *Canneſbey*.

PARISH

APPENDIX.

PARISH OF REAY.

Some part of this pariſh lies in the ſhire of *Sutherland*, but the greateſt part in that of *Cathneſs*; that part in *Sutherland* is called *Strath-Halladale*, from *Halladha* Earl of *Orkney*, a *Norwegian*, ſlain in battle in the beginning of the 10th century. The field of battle is full of ſmall cairns, or heaps of ſtone. The commander in chief, and principal warriors ſlain in that action, are buried in a place apart from the field of battle; I have frequently ſeen the place. The tradition is, that *Halladha* is buried in a ſpot encloſed with a circular trench 10 or 12 feet wide, and that his ſword lies by his ſide. There was a ſtone erected in the middle of this circle, part of which ſtill remains. Near the field of battle ſtands a little town, called *Dal Halladha*, or *Halladha*'s field. A river runs through *Strath-Halladale*, which is rather paſture ground on the ſides of it, for the eleven miles it is inhabited.

The boundary betwixt *Sutherland* and *Cathneſs*, to the North, is called *Drim Halliſtin*. *Cathneſs* is a flat plain country, having few hills; the ſoil good, and producing great quantities of corn in fruitfull ſeaſons; it lies upon quarries of a black ſlate kind, and perhaps no country on earth excells it for ſmooth thin flags or ſlates of great dimenſions. As theſe flags may be ſeen in all parts of the country, it is needleſs to deſcribe them. The ſoil not being deep, and the country flat, renders our highways very deep in winter, and very dry in ſummer. That part of the pariſh of *Reay* in the ſhire of *Cathneſs*, is excellent corn ground through the whole of it. It appears that many battles have been fought in it in former times, but we have no tradition concerning them. In later times ſome bloody

bloody ſkirmiſhes happened betwixt *M'Kay* of *Strathnaver*, and *Keith* Earl *Mareſchal*; and alſo betwixt the *Cathneſs* and *Strathnaver* people.

The following chapels ſtood in this pariſh of old; St. *Mary*'s at *Lybſter*; St. *Magnus*'s at *Shebſter*; one at *Shail*, another at *Baillie*, and a third in *Shurerie*; beſides the pariſh kirk, dedicated to St. *Colman*, at *Reay*. There is an old caſtle at *Dunreay*, and modern houſes both at *Bighouſe* and *Sandſide*.

Lead mines are frequent in *Cathneſs*; but the country is ſo flat, that there is no working them for water. The moſt promiſing mine is at *Sandſide*, being in the face of a rock near the ſea. It might prove of value, if proper pains were taken to work it. The highway runs near it.

It ſeems that the *Saxons*, in the 5th century, plagued this country; and it is probable that *Thurſo* is ſo called from *Horſa*, the *Saxon* general, who landed in the river of *Thurſo*, or *Inver-Horſa*, the landing place of *Horſa*. And when the *Saxons* plundered *Cathneſs*, it ſeems they had a bloody conflict with the natives. In this pariſh there is a place called *Tout Horſa*, or *Horſa*'s grave, where they ſay that ſome great warrior was ſlain and buried; in the place is a great ſtone erected. Probably he was one of *Horſa*'s captains. This is the tradition.

PARISH OF THURSO.

Thurſo, or *Inver-Horſa*, ſo called from the *Saxon* general, is a town of an old date; we find mention made of it as a populous place in the 11th century, and from it the pariſh is denominated.

Formerly a ſtrong caſtle ſtood in it, called *Caſtrum de Thorſa*; but no veſtige of it is now extant. The Earls of *Cathneſs* had a fine ſquare at *Thurſo Eaſt*, now demoliſhed. The Biſhop of *Cathneſs* had a ſtrong caſtle at *Scrabſter*, near *Thurſo*, called the caſtle of *Burnſide*, built in the 13th century, by *Gilbert Murray*, Biſhop of *Cathneſs:* the ruins are ſtill extant. Another caſtle ſtood at *Ormly*, near *Thurſo*; lately demoliſhed. At *Murkil*, to the Eaſt of *Thurſo*, there were great buildings of old; it was a ſeat of the late Earl of *Cathneſs*, and at *Hamer* he had a modern houſe. An old tower, ſtill extant, ſtands at *Brines*, three miles Weſt of *Thurſo*.

As for chapels and places of worſhip, one ſtood at *Croſs Kirk*, one at *Brines*, another at *Gwic*, and a ſmall chapel ſtood in the parks of *Thurſo Eaſt*, where Earl *Harold* the younger was buried. The walls are fallen down; but Mr. *Sinclair* of *Ulbſter*, very generouſly, is determined to encloſe that ſpot, becauſe that young nobleman is interred there. The church of *Thurſo* was the Biſhop's chapel; and when he reſided in *Cathneſs*, he often preached there. I was told by the late Earl of *Cathneſs*, that there was a nunnery in antient times near his ſeat at *Murkil*. The country people call the place the *Gloſters*; but no veſtige of the building is extant, excepting the remains of the garden wall, which encloſed a rich ſpot of ground. *Torfæus* ſays that a Queen of *Norway* lived ſometime at *Murkil*. He relates that *Harold* the bloody, ſon to King *Harold* the fair, was baniſhed for his cruelty, with his Queen; and that his brother *Hacon* ſucceeded to the throne: but after *Harold* the bloody was ſlain in *England*, his Queen returned to *Orkney*, and reſided ſome time at *Murkil* in *Cathneſs*.

The

The ſame author mentions great battles fought in this pariſh; one in the 11th century, on the plains of *Thurſo Eaſt*, betwixt *Thorfinnus* Earl of *Orkney*, and one *Karl* or *Charles*; he calls him King of *Scotland*, or a General of the *Scots* army. Another bloody battle at *Claredon*, near *Thurſo Eaſt*, betwixt the Earls *Harold* the elder and younger. I have already told that Earl *Harold* the younger is buried near the field of battle, and a chapel erected over his grave, which is now to be encloſed by Mr. *Sinclair* of *Ulbſter*, a moſt promiſing youth.

The Biſhop of *Cathneſs*, ſince the reformation, lived in a ſmall houſe at *Scrabſter*, which is ſtill extant, and belongs to the crown. He had a graſs room in the *Highlands*, called *Dorary*, where ſtood a chapel, called *Gavin's Kirk*, or *Temple Gavin*; the walls are ſtill ſtanding. The river of *Thurſo* abounds with ſalmon, ten and eleven laſts of fiſh have been caught.

PARISH OF OLRIG.

A fine corn country, two miles and a half in length, and a mile broad, or thereabouts. Nothing memorable in it.

PARISH OF DUNNET.

The Northerly winds have covered a great part of this pariſh with ſand; a large tract of ground is ruined, and not likely to be recovered. In this pariſh ſtands *Dunnet head*, or what *Ptolemy* calls *Berubium*, a large promontory, with a moſt terrible tide on the point of it. A hermit in antient times lived upon it, the ruins of his cell are extant. It is a fine ſheep paſture. The pariſh itſelf is an excellent corn country. At *Ratter* is the ſeat of the preſent Earl of *Cathneſs*.

Parish of CANNESBEY.

Is a fine corn country. Here was the antient reſidence of one of the Governors of *Cathneſs*, under the *Norwegian* Lords that held *Orkney* and *Cathneſs*. They dwelt at *Dungſbey*, and their office was called the *Præfectura de Dungalſbæis*. *Torfæus* mentions bloody battles fought betwixt the *Scots* and *Norwegians*, near *Dungiſby*, in the 10th century. And *Ewin*, King of *Scotland*, fought an army of *Orkney* men, at *Huna* in this pariſh, and deſtroyed their King and his army. Here was, formerly, beſides the pariſh church, a chapel at *St. John*'s *head*, near *Mey*, and another at *Freſwick*.

At *Mey* there is a beautifull, ſtrong caſtle, belonging to Sir *John Sinclair*. Here a kind of coal is found, like the *Lanſtaffen* coal in *Wales*. At *Freſwick* ſtands a large modern houſe, the ſeat of Mr. *John Sinclair*. And there is a ſtrong old caſtle, built on a high rock joined to the continent by a narrow neck of land, to the South of *Freſwick*. *Torfæus* calls it *Lambaburgum* ſive *caſtrum agnorum*. It ſuſtained a memorable ſiege in the 12th century. In later times it was poſſeſſed by *Mouat* of *Bucholly*. The common people call it *Buccle*'s caſtle, a corruption of *Bucholli*e's caſtle. In *Dungiſby*, the rapid tides of the *Pentland* throw up vaſt quantities of moſt beautifull ſea ſhells, abundance of which are carried South for ſhell work. They are called *John a Groat*'s buckies. The town and ferry belonged of old to a gentleman of the name of *Groat*.

An

An iſland belongs to this pariſh, called *Stroma*, in which there is a vault where they bury, built by one *Kennedy* of *Carnmuch*. The coffins are laid on ſtools above ground. But the vault being on the ſea edge, and the rapid tides of the *Pentland* firth running by it, there is ſuch a ſaltiſh air continually, as has converted the bodies into mummies; inſomuch, that one *Murdo Kennedy*, ſon of *Carnmuch*, is ſaid to beat the drum on his father's belly.

PARISH OF WICK.

An excellent corn country, and a fruitfull ſea; 2000 barrels of herrings were caught here in the year 1771. There was a chapel near Caſtle *Sinclair*, called *St. Tay*, another at *Ulbſter*, and a third at *Kilmiſter*. The caſtle of *Girnigo* is the oldeſt building in this pariſh. I cannot find out by whom it was erected. It is probable ſome ſtrong building ſtood here before the preſent ruinous houſe was erected. It ſtands on a rock in the ſea. Near it ſtood Caſtle *Sinclair*, built by *George* Earl of *Cathneſs*; a grand houſe in thoſe days. Not far from it ſtood the caſtle of *Akergil*, built by *Keith* Earl *Mareſchal*: but this place is now rendered a moſt beautifull and convenient ſeat, by Sir *William Dunbar* of *Hemprigs*, the proprietor. In the old tower is the largeſt vault in the North of *Scotland*, beautified with elegant lights and plaiſtering, by Sir *William*; ſo that it is now the grandeſt room in all this part of the country.

The town of *Wick* is a royal burgh, now riſing ſince the herring fiſhery has proſpered. To the South of it ſtands an old tower, called Lord *Olifant*'s caſtle. A copper ore was diſcovered there,

and

and wrought for ſome time, but I do not find they have proceeded in it.

In this pariſh there is a haven for fiſhing boats, called *Whaligo*, which is a creek betwixt two high rocks. Though the height of one of theſe rocks is ſurprizing, yet the country people have made ſteps by which they go up and down, carrying heavy burdens on their back; which a ſtranger, without ſeeing, would ſcarcely believe. This is a fine fiſhing coaſt.

There was a battle fought at Old *Namarluck*, in 1680, betwixt the Earl of *Cathneſs*, and Lord *Glenurchy*.

PARISH OF LATHRONE.

Eighteen miles long; partly paſture, partly corn ground. It has a chapel at *Eaſter Clyth*, and another at the water of *Dunbeath*, beſides the pariſh kirk.

At the loch of *Stemſter*, in this pariſh, ſtands a famous *Druidical* temple. I have viewed the place: the circle is large, above 100 feet diameter; the ſtones are large and erect; and to ſhew that the planetary ſyſtem was obſerved by them, they are ſet up in this manner, 1: 2: 3: 4: 5: 6: 7. Then the ſame courſe begins again; 1: 2: 3: 4: &c. Few of the ſtones are now fallen. Near the temple there is a ruin, where the *Arch-Druid*, it ſeems, reſided. I find no ſuch large *Druid* temples in the country; as for ſmall ones, they are generally found in many places.

Upon a rock in the edge of the ſea, in *Eaſter Clyth*, there is an old building, called *Cruner Gunn*'s caſtle. This gentleman of the name of *Gunn*, was *Coronator* or Juſticiary of *Cathneſs*: he was baſely

basely murthered, with several gentleman of the name, and of other names, in the kirk of *St. Teay*, near Castle *Sinclair*, by *Keith* Earl *Mareschal*. The story is told at full length in the history of the family of *Sutherland*. This happened in the 15th century. At *Mid Clyth* there was a large house, built by Sir *George Sinclair* of *Clyth*. At *Nottingham* there is an elegant new house, built by Capt. *Sutherland* of *Farse*: near this is the parish kirk. There is a strong old castle at *Dunbeath*; and near *Langwall* is a strong old ruin, said to be *Ronald Cheir*'s castle; he lived in the 14th century, and was a great hunter of deer, as will be told when we come to speak of the parish of *Halkirk*. He had a third part of *Cathness* in property: his great estate was divided betwixt his two daughters; one of which became a nun, the other married the ancestor of the Lord *Duffus*.

There is an old building at *Lathrone*, called *Harold* tower, said to have been built by wicked Earl *Harold*, in the 12th century.

We read of bloody encounters in this parish, betwixt the *Cathness* men, and *Hugo Freskin* Earl of *Sutherland*: and likewise many conflicts betwixt the two countries in after-times. *Torfæus* says that King *William the Lion* marched into *Cathness* with a great army, and encamped at *Ousdale*, or *Eiskensdale*. This expedition of his Majesty's, was to drive out wicked Earl *Harold* the elder, who had slain *Harold* the younger. The King seized *Cathness* as a conquest, then Earl *Harold* submitted himself to him.

Parish of LOTH.

A fine corn country; much harrassed of old by the *Danes*, or *Norwegians*.

Norwegians. In it are St. *Ninian*'s chapel at *Navidale*, *John the Baptiſt*'s at the river *Helmiſdale*, St. *Inan*'s at *Eaſter Gartie*, and St. *Trulleu*'s at *Kintradwel*, beſides the pariſh kirk. The caſtle of *Helmiſdale* was built by Lady *Margaret Baillie*, Counteſs of *Sutheeland*: and there was a ſquare or court of building at *Craiag*, erected by Lady *Jane Gordon*, Counteſs of *Sutherland*; no veſtige of it now extant.

There is fine fiſhing in the rivers of *Helmiſdale* and *Loth*. The latter has a very high cataract, where the water pours from a high rock, and falls into a terrible gulph below. If this could be removed, this river would afford excellent ſalmon fiſhing. The hills in this pariſh were of old famous for hunting. At --------- there is a hunting houſe, probably built by the *Picts*, conſiſting of a great number of ſmall rooms, each compoſed of three large ſtones. Theſe buildings prove that a tribe lived here in the hunting ſeaſon. Near it ſtands a large *Pictiſh* caſtle, called *Carn Bran*. It ſeems that this *Bran*, or *Brian*, was ſome great man in thoſe days, and that all theſe accommodations were of his building. The quarry from whence the ſtones were carried to build this caſtle, is ſtill to be ſeen, and the road for their carriage viſible, being like a ſpiral line along the ſide of the hill.

I read of no battles in this pariſh: ſome bloody conflicts are told us, and theſe are to be ſeen in the hiſtory of the family of *Sutherland*. Near the miln of *Loth beg* is the entire *Picts* houſe, which the Biſhop of *Oſſory* entered. There is a fine caſcade as you travel along the ſhore under *Loth beg*, which makes a charming appearance when there is any fall of rain, or in time of a keen froſt.

PARISH

Parish of CLYNE.

Partly corn ground, and partly fit for paſture. There was a chapel at *Dol*, called *St. Mahon*. No conſiderable buildings in this pariſh. *Sntherland* of *Clyne* had a good houſe; and *Nicolas* Earl of *Sutherland* had a hunting ſeat in the Highlands, called *Caſtle Uain*, but now demoliſhed.

There is a tradition that a battle was fought at *Kilalmkill*, in this pariſh, wherein the country people routed the *Danes*. The common marks of a battle are viſible there, viz. a number of ſmall cairns. Another bloody battle was fought at *Clyne Milton*, betwixt the *Sutherland* and *Cathneſs* men; the ſlaughter was great, and the cairns, ſtill to be ſeen there, cover heaps of ſlain.

The river of *Brora* affords a fine ſalmon fiſhery: it falls into the ſea at *Brora*. Within two large miles is the loch of that name, which abounds with ſalmon. From the loch the river lies to the Weſt; and at a place called *Achir-na-kyl*, is a moſt charming caſcade: here alſo they fiſh for pearls. On the top of a ſmall hill, near the houſe of *Clyne*, is a lime-ſtone quarry; and in the heart of the ſtone, all ſorts of ſea ſhells known in theſe parts are found. They are freſh and entire, and the lime ſtone within the ſhell reſembles the fiſh. The Biſhop of *Oſſory* employed men to hew out maſſes of the rock, which he broke, and carried away a large quantity of ſhells. Near the bridge of *Brora* there is a fine large cave, called *Uai na Calman*. The Biſhop of *Oſſory* admired it, and ſaid there were ſuch caves about *Bethlehem* in *Paleſtine*. The coal work and ſalt work are obvious here. But at *Strathleven*, near the ſea,

 there

there is a hermit's apartment, cut artificially in the natural rock, well worth a viſit from any curious traveller.

I need not mention the artificial iſland in the loch of *Brora*, made by the old Thanes of *Sutherland*, as a place of refuge in dangerous times. Near that loch ſtands a high hill or rock, called *Creig baw ir*, on the ſummit of which there is great ſpace. This rock is fortified round; and as the neck that joins it to another rock is ſmall, it ſeems that when they were invaded by enemies, they fled to this ſtrong hold, and drove their cattle likewiſe into it for ſafety. Others ſay it was a place for keeping of a watch.

Parish of GOLSPIE.

This is a fine corn country. The pariſh kirk was of old at *Culmalie*; and at *Golſpie* the family of *Sutherland* had a chapel of eaſe, dedicated to *St. Andrew* the Apoſtle. In this pariſh ſtands the ſeat of the Earls of *Sutherland*, at *Dunrobin*; but during the *Daniſh* wars, they lived at a greater diſtance from the ſea. This pariſh affords no other great buildings; nor is there any tradition concerning any battles fought in it: ſmall ſkirmiſhes have happened here; particularly in the year 1746, when the Earl of *Cromarty* was taken priſoner. Moſt remarkable is the devaſtation done by ſand; large tracts of corn ground have been quite ſpoiled thereby, and more miſchief is threatened yearly.

Parish of DORNOCH.

In this pariſh ſtands the cathedral church of *Cathneſs*. The *Norwegians*

Norwegians having murthered Biſhop *John* at *Scrabſter*, and Biſhop *Adam* at *Halkirk*, in the year 1222; *Gilbert Murray*, the ſucceeding Biſhop, built the cathedral at *Dornoch*, which was, when entire, a neat compact building. It was burnt in troubleſome times, and never fully repaired. The Biſhop had a ſummer reſidence at *Skibo*; but in winter he lived in his caſtle at *Dornoch*, the ruins of which are to be ſeen. There was a ſtately fabrick of a church, built in that town in the 11th century, by St. *Bar*, Biſhop of *Cathneſs*; but Bp. *Murray* thought it too ſmall: it ſtood where the council houſe now ſtands. We are told that the dioceſe of *Cathneſs* was not divided into pariſhes till the days of Bp. *Murray*; and that he tranſlated the Pſalms and Goſpels into the *Iriſh* language, or *Scots Galic*. The dignified clergy had houſes and glebes in *Dornoch*; theſe made up his chapter when there was occaſion to call one. It is a loſs that we have none of their records; nor indeed is it a great wonder, conſidering the daily invaſions of the *Danes*, which ended not till 1266.

In Bp. *Murray*'s time, there was a bloody battle fought at *Hilton*, near *Embo*; he and *William* Earl of *Sutherland* fought there againſt the *Danes*, and cut them to pieces. The *Daniſh* General was killed, and lies buried in *Hilton*. There was a ſtone erected over his grave, which the common people called *Ree* croſs, or croſs in *Ri*, or King's croſs, fancying that the King of *Norway* was there buried. A Brother of the Biſhop was alſo killed in this battle; his body lies in a ſtone coffin in the Eaſt iſle of the cathedral, above ground, near the font. The hewn ſtone erected to the Eaſt of *Dornoch*, is a trophy of this victory. It has the Earl of *Sutherland*'s arms on the North ſide, ſtill very viſible, and the Biſhop of *Cathneſs*'s arms on the South ſide, but the heat of the ſun has quite deſtroyed the ſculpture.

The driving of ſand is very hurtfull to this pariſh, and threatens ſtill more harm. The only old buildings in it, excepting thoſe already mentioned, is *Skibo*. *Hugo Freſkin*, Earl of *Sutherland*, gave theſe lands to Bp. *Gilbert Murray*, then Archdeacon of *Murray*, in 1186. It paſſed through ſeveral hands, till at laſt it came to Lord *Duffus*'s, and now it returns to the family of *Sutherland*. It was a great pile of building, ſurrounded with a rampart. The preſent modern houſe is ſtill habitable. The ſituation is moſt beautifull, and a fine houſe there would have a noble effect. *Cyder hall* is only a modern houſe. The plantations here, and at *Skibo*, are the moſt thriving in this pariſh. At the latter place a houſe was lately built in a very elegant taſte. *Embo* is an old building, the ſeat of the Knights of *Embo*. It is a pity that it has neither plantations nor policy about it.

PARISH OF CREICH.

Has no great buildings in it. *Pulcroſſi* is the beſt. The great cataract at *Invershin* is a grand ſight. Such a large body of water pouring down from a high rock, cannot miſs affording entertainment. The river of *Shin* abounds with large ſalmon, and ſturgeons are often ſeen there. In the 11th or 12th century lived a great man in this pariſh, called *Paul Meutier*. This warrior routed an army of *Danes* near *Creich*. Tradition ſays that he gave his daughter in marriage to one *Hulver*, or *Leander*, a *Dane*; and with her, the lands of *Strabobee*; and that from that marriage are deſcended the

the *Clan Landris*, a brave people, in *Rossshire*. The gentlemen of the name of *Gray* possessed *Mertil-Creich*, of an old date; and at *Mrydol* there was a good house and orchard, which I believe are still extant. I find no other *memorabilia* in the parish of *Creich*.

PARISH OF LARG.

The most remarkable thing in it is *Loch-Shin*, which is computed to be 18 miles long, with fine pasture ground on each side of it. What skirmishes have happened in this parish are mentioned in the history of the family of *Sutherland*.

PARISH OF ROGART.

Consists of good pasture and good corn land. A bloody battle was fought here, near *Knochartol*, in the days of Countess *Elizabeth*. Tradition says, that upon the field of battle such a number of swords were found, that they threw numbers of them into a loch; and that in dry summers, they still find some of them. There is a place in this parish called *Moriness*, and *Ptolemy* the Geographer places there a people called the *Morini*. He also calls the river *Helmisdale*, *Ileas*; and the natives call it in the *Galic*, *Illie*, *Avin Illie*, *Bun Illie*, *Stra Illie*.

PARISH OF KILDONNAN.

Consists of a valley, divided into two parts by the river *Helmisdale*, or *Illie*, only fit for pasture. The parish kirk is dedicated to St.

St. *Donan.* A tribe lived here called *Gunns*, of *Norwegian* extraction: they have continued here upwards of 500 years, and contributed to extirpate the *Danes* out of *Sutherland.* They were in all times *Satellites* to the Earls of *Sutherland.* Their chieftain is lately dead, and reprefented by two boys; it were to be wifhed that fome generous perfon would take care of their education. The moft remarkable piece of hiftory relating to this parifh, is what *Torfæus* mentions, viz. That *Helga* Countefs of *Orkney*, and her fifter *Frauhaurk*, lived at *Kinbrafs*, and fupported a grand family there. This lady had a daughter called *Margaret*, who was educated in thefe defarts, and there married *Maddadius* Earl of *Athole*, uncle's fon to King *David* I. of *Scotland.* Thefe buildings were burnt, and reduced to heaps, fo that we cannot difcern what their model has been; at prefent, they are called *Carn fhuin.* And *Torfæus* fays that one *Suenus* burnt and demolifhed them.

What fmall fkirmifhes have happened in this parifh, are not worth mentioning, excepting what *Torfæus* mentions relative to *Kinbrafs*, betwixt *Suenus* an *Orkney* man, and *Aulver Rofta*, captain of a guard, which an old wicked lady, called *Frauhaurk*, kept to defend her. This lady, we are told, had ordered a party to go and murder *Olafus*, the father of *Suenus*, at *Dungfbey*, which party *Aulver* commanded. They came to *Dungfbey*, and burnt that brave man, and fix more with him, in his own houfe. Luckily the lady of the houfe was abfent, being invited to an entertainment in the days of *Chriftmas.* Her fon *Gunnius*, the anceftor of the *Gunns*, was with her, and *Suenus* was alfo abfent. After many years *Suenus* comes with a party, attacks *Aulver*, and after a fmart engagement defeats him, fo that he fled, and as many as could made their

their escape with him. *Suenus*, after this, burns *Frauhaurk*, and all her family, and made a heap of the buildings. And though the ruins are great, yet no man can tell of what kind they were; that is, whether round like the *Pictish* houses, or not. This happened in the 12th century.

PARISH OF HALKIRK.

Partly corn land, partly pasture. Many places of worship have been in this parish; such as the parish kirk of *Skinnan*, the hospital of St. *Magnus* at *Spittal*, the walls of the church belonging to it being still extant. The chapel of *Olgrim beg*. The chapel of St. *Troston*, at *Westfield*. The chapel of St. *Queran*, at *Strathmore*. Another chapel at *Dilred*. And as the Bishop of *Cathness* lived of old at *Halkirk*, his chapel was called St. *Kathrin*, of which there is no vestige left but a heap of rubbish.

The *Norwegian* Lords that were superiors of *Cathness*, built the castle of *Braal*. Here lived Earl *John*, who is said to have caused the burning of the Bishop of *Cathness*. This Bishop, whose name was *Adam*, lived near the place where the minister's house stands, too near the bloody Earl. It is said he was severe in exacting tithes, which made the country people complain: whereupon the Earl told them that they should take the Bishop and boil him. Accordingly they went on furiously, and boiled the Bishop in his own house, together with one *Serlo* a monk, his companion, in the year 1222. King *Alexander* II. came in person to *Cathness*, and, it is said, executed near 80 persons concerned in that murder. The Earl fled, but

but was afterwards pardoned by the King. However, ſome time after, he was killed in the town of *Thurſo*, by ſome perſons whom he deſigned to murder. At *Braal* there was a fine garden, beſide which they catch the firſt ſalmon from the month of *November* to the month of *Auguſt*. The ſituation is moſt beautifull, very wéll adapted for the ſeat of a great man. The caſtle of *Dilred* was built by *Sutherland* of *Dilred*, deſcended from the family of *Sutherland*. It is a ſmall building on the top of a rock. His ſon, *Alexander Sutherland*, forfeited his eſtate; and theſe lands were given to the anceſtor of Lord *Reay*, but now belong to Mr. *Sinclair* of *Ulbſter*.

Up the river ſtands an old ruin, called Lord *Chein*'s, or *Ronald Chein*'s, hunting houſe. He was the *Nimrod* of that age, ſpending a great part of his time in that exerciſe. The houſe ſtood at the outlet of a loch, called *Loch-more*, the ſource of the river of *Thurſo*, which abounds with ſalmon. *Ronald Chein* had a cruive on this river, with a bell ſo conſtructed, that when a fiſh tumbled in the cruive the bell rang. The tradition is, that all theſe Highlands were then foreſt and wood, but now there is ſcarely any wood. This loch is about half a mile long, and near that in breadth, and is the beſt fiſh pond in *Britain*; many laſts are caught every year on the ſhore of this loch, by the country people. Sixty nets are for ordinary ſhot on it in a night, and fiſh in every one. Many gentlemen clame a property in it, for which cauſe it is a common good tó the country in general.

There is in the town of *North Calder* an old ruin, called *Tulloch hoogie*. *Torfæus* ſays that *Ronald* Earl of *Orkney* was treacherouſly murdered there by a ruffian he calls *Thiorbiornus Klerkus*, and a ſmart ſkirmiſh enſued. *Thiorbiornus* fled, and being hotly purſued,

was

was burnt in a houſe where he took ſhelter, and eight more with him. This was in the 12th century. Two battles were fought by the *Danes* in the dales of the pariſh of *Halkirk.* One at *Toftin-gale*, the grave of the foreigners. A *Scots* nobleman, whom *Torfæus* calls *Comes Magbragdus*, commanded on one ſide; and a *Norwegian*, called *Liotus*, on the other. *Liotus* was mortally wounded, and buried at *Sten-hou*, near the kirk of *Watten.* The other battle was fought at *Halſary.* The large ſtones erected at *Rangag* and thereabout, are ſepulchral monuments, where perſons of note are buried. There was a battle fought in the 16th century, by the *Gunns* and others, at a place called *Blarnandoſs*, near *Harpiſdale*, wherein the *Gunns* were routed. The beautifull river of *Thurſo* runs through this pariſh, and numbers of ſalmon are caught in it. *Pictiſh* houſes are very numerous along the ſhore, but all fallen down. It is a moſt beautifull pariſh, and muſt have of old abounded with game and fiſh, which invited people to ſettle in it. Mr. *Sinclair* of *Ulbſter*, is proprietor of one half of it.

PARISH OF BOWAR.

Here the Archdeacon of *Cathneſs* reſided. The Pope of *Rome* was, of old, patron. I have in my poſſeſſion, two preſentations from his Holineſs to the Archdeacon of *Bowar.* It was antiently a very extenſive pariſh, but now *Watten* is part of it. I know of no other place of worſhip, beſides the pariſh kirk, excepting the chapel of *Dun*, where a clergyman officiated, before the erection of the pariſh of *Watten.* I know of nothing memorable concerning it. If there ever were any grand buildings in it, no veſtiges of them now remain. *Torfæus* mentions a great man that lived here in the 12th century, named *Maddan:* one of whose sons was stiled *Magnus* the Generous, the other Count *Ottar* of *Thurso*. His daughter *Helga* married *Harold* the Orator, Earl of *Orkney*. Another married *Liotus*, a noble *Dane*, that lived in *Sutherland*. And the third was married to a *Dane* that lived in --------- in *Orkney*.

PARISH OF WATTEN.

A country fit for both tillage and pasture. The chapel of *Dun* stands now in it. Here are no buildings but of modern date. The only memorable thing in this parish is the grave of *Liotus*, Earl of *Orkney*. At *Sten-hou*, near the kirk of *Watten*, stands a great rock upon a green spot of ground, which is said to be the sepulchral monument of this Earl. The Monkish tradition is, that St. *Magnus* converted a dragon into this stone. This is as true as what they relate of his crossing the *Pentland* firth upon a stone, and that the print of the Saint's feet is visible on the same stone in the kirk of *Burrich*, in *South Ronaldsha* in *Orkney*.

N. B. In the history of the family of *Sutherland*, mention is made of one Sir *Paul Menzies*, Provost of *Aberdeen*, who discovered a silver mine in *Sutherland*, and found it to be rich, but death prevented his working it. It seems he covered the place where he found it, and no person of skill has observed it since that time. It is probable that *Creig nargod* is the place where this mine may be, and that this discovery was the cause of this appellation; for I can see no other reason for that name or designation. Persons of skill ought to examine these bounds. *Creign airgid*, or the silver hill, is above *Cullmalie*.

NUM-

NUMBER VI.

THE LIFE OF SIR EWEN CAMERON, OF LOCHIEL.

THIS memoir, ſo deſcriptive of the manners of the times, and the wild war carried on between the Hero of the piece, and *Cromwel*'s people, was communicated to me by a Gentleman of *Lochaber*. It merits preſervation not ſolely on account of its curioſity; but that it may prove an inſtructive leſſon to the preſent inhabitants of that extenſive tract, by ſhewing the happineſs they may enjoy in the preſent calm, after the long ſtorm of war and aſſaſſination their forefathers were curſed with.

SIR *Ewen Cameron* was born in *February*, 1629. He lived with his foſterfather for the firſt ſeven years, according to an old cuſtom in the Highlands, whereby the principal gentlemen of the clan are entitled to the tuition and ſupport of their chief's children during the years of their pupillarity. The foſterfathers were alſo frequently at the charge of their education during that period; and when the pupils returned home, these fathers gave them a portion equal to what they gave their own children; as the portion consisted in cattle, before they came to age it increased to a considerable height.

Before his years of pupillarity expired, he was put under the charge and management of the Marquiss of *Argyle*, the same who was executed soon after the Restoration. The Marquiss, intending to bring him up in the principles of the Covenanters, put him to school at *Inverara*, under the inspection of a Gentleman of his own appointment. But young *Lochiel* preferred the sports of the field to the labours of the school. *Argyle* observing this, brought him back to himself, and kept a watchfull eye over him, carrying him along with him wherever he went.

After the defeat of the Royalists at *Philiphaugh*, in 1645, it happened that as the Parliament sat at *St. Andrew's*, on the trial of the prisoners of distinction there seized, *Lochiel*, who went there with the Marquiss, found means to pay a visit to Sir *Robert Spotswood*, one of the prisoners, a few days before his execution. Then and there it was he received the first intelligence concerning the state and principles of parties in *Scotland*. Sir *Robert*, happy to see his young visitant, the son of his old acquaintance *John Cameron*, took the opportunity to relate in an eloquent manner, the causes of the present rebellion, and its history from its first breaking out, with a view of the tempers and characters of the different factions that had conspired against the Crown. He explained the nature of our constitution, insisted much on the integrity and benevolence of the King, but inveighed bitterly against his *Scotch* enemies; and concluded with expressing his astonishment how *Lochiel*'s friends could

put

put him under the charge of *Argyle*, and conjuring him to abandon that party as ſoon as he could. This diſcourſe had ſuch an impreſſion on the mind of *Lochiel*, that it continued all his life time.

Some time after, *Argyle* addreſſed his pupil in a different tone, but had little influence over him: he never could be ſatisfied why ſo many brave fellows were executed, as he heard no confeſſions of guilt, as thieves and robbers are wont to make; but dying with the courage and reſolution of Gentlemen. After this, *Lochiel* was anxious to return to his country, inflamed with a deſire of exerting himſelf in the Royal cauſe, and of joining *Montroſe* for that end. Upon the application of his uncle *Breadalbine*, and the *Camerons*, *Argyle* parted with his pupil; and he returned to *Lochaber*, to head his clan in the 18th year of his age.

An opportunity of acting the Chief ſoon occurred. *Glengary* and *Reppoch*, Heads of two numerous tribes of the *M'Donalds*, refuſed to pay *Lochiel* certain taxations for ſome lands they held of him: *Lochiel* armed a body of the *Camerons*, with a view to compel them; *Glengary* and *Reppoch*, finding him thus bold and reſolute, thought proper to ſettle their affairs amicably, and gave him no further trouble for the future. By ſuch determined conduct, *Lochaber* enjoyed a profound peace for ſome little time, while the whole of *Scotland* beſides was a ſcene of war and bloodſhed.

In 1651, *Lochiel* was honored with a letter from King *Charles* II. inviting him and his clan to uſe and put themſelves in arms, for the relief of their country and ſovereign; in conſequence of which, early in ſpring 1652, after collecting his men, he was the firſt who joined *Glencairn*, who had juſt then ſet up the Royal ſtandard in the Highlands. In the different encounters his Lordſhip and the

Royaliſts

Royaliſts had with *Lilburne*, *Morgan*, and others, *Lochiel* diſplayed more conduct and vigor than could be expected from one ſo young, and as yet unexperienced in the art of war. He diſtinguiſhed himſelf in a particular manner in a ſkirmiſh which happened between *Glencairn* and Col. *Lilburne*, at *Brea-mar*, where he was poſted at a paſs, which he defended with great ſpirit, till *Glencairn* and his army retreated to a place of ſecurity. *Lilburne*, in the mean time, getting between *Lochiel* and the army, and finding it impoſſible to draw out the General to an engagement, made a violent attack upon *Lochiel*: *Lochiel*, after making a bold reſiſtance for ſome time, at laſt retreated gradually up the hill, with his face to the enemy, who durſt not purſue him, on account of the ruggedneſs of the ground, and the ſnow that then covered it. *Glencairn*'s army was at this time full of factions and diviſions; occaſioned by the number of independent chiefs and gentlemen in his army, who would not condeſcend to ſubmit to one another, either in opinion or action. *Lochiel* was the only perſon of diſtinction that kept himſelf diſengaged from theſe factions; for in order to avoid them, he always choſe the moſt diſtant parts, where his frequent ſucceſſes had endeared him to the General, who recommended him in a ſtrong manner to the King, as appears by the following Letter his Majeſty ſent him.

" To our truſty and well beloved the Laird of *Lochiel*.

" *CHARLES* R.

" Truſty and well beloved, we greet you well. We are inform-
" ed by the the Earl of *Glencairn* with what notable courage and
" affection to us you have behaved yourſelf at this time of tryal,
" when

"when our intereſt and the honour and liberty of your country "is at ſtake; and therefore we cannot but expreſs our hearty ſenſe "of ſuch your good courage, and return you our princely thanks "for the ſame; and we hope all honeſt men who are lovers of us "and their country will follow your example, and that you will "unite together in the ways we have directed, and under that au- "thority we have appointed to conduct you for the proſecution of "ſo good a work, ſo we do aſſure you we ſhall be ready, as ſoon "as we are able, ſignally to reward your ſervice, and to repair the "loſſes you ſhall undergoe for our ſervice, and ſo we bid you fare- "well. Given at *Chantilly*, *Nov.* 3. 1653. In the fifth year of "our reign."

When General *Middleton* came from *Holland*, 1654, to take the command of the King's troops in *Scotland*, *Lochiel* joined him with a full regiment of good men, while many of the other heads of clans made their peace with General *Monk*, who had marched into the Highlands at the head of a ſmall army, giving another compoſed of horſe and foot to General *Morgan*. Many trifling conflicts enſued between theſe two Generals and the Highlanders; but *Lochiel* being of the party who had oppoſed *Morgan*, an active and brave officer, run ſeveral hazards, and encountered many difficulties; but his preſence of mind and reſolution never forſook him.

Monk left no method unattempted to bribe him into a ſubmiſſion. Theſe propoſals were ſo engaging, that many of his friends importuned him to accept of them; but he deſpiſed them all, and would not ſubmit. *Monk* finding all his attempts ineffectual, reſolved to plant a garriſon at *Inverlochy*, where *Fort William* now ſtands, in order to keep the country in awe, and their chief at home. *Lochiel* being informed of this deſign, thought

thought the moſt adviſable plan would be to attack the enemy on their march from *Inverneſs*, imagining they would come from that place or that way; but the ſudden arrival of the *Engliſh* at ſea diſconcerted all his meaſures. They brought with them ſuch plenty of materials, and were in the neighborhood of ſo much wood, that in a day's time after their landing, Col. *Bigan* their commander and the governor of the new fort to be erected, had ſecured his troops from all danger.

Lochiel ſaw all their motions from a neighboring eminence, and ſeeing it impracticable to attack them with any probability of ſucceſs, retired to a place three miles Weſtward, to a wood on the North ſide of *Lochiel*, called *Achdalew*; from this he could have a full view of his enemy at *Inverlochy*. All his men he diſmiſſed to remove their cattle farther from the enemy, and to furniſh themſelves with proviſions: excepting about 38 perſons whom he kept as a guard. He alſo had ſpies in and about the garriſon, who informed him of all their tranſactions. Five days after their arrival at *Inverlochy*, the governor diſpatched 300 of his men on board of two veſſels which were to ſail Weſtward a little, and to anchor on each ſide of the ſhore near *Achdalew*. *Lochiel* heard their deſign was to cut down his trees and carry away his cattle, and was determined if poſſible to make them pay well for every tree and every hide; favored by the woods, he came pretty cloſe to the ſhore, where he ſaw their motions ſo perfectly that he counted them as they came out of the ſhip, and found the number of the armed exceed 140, beſides a number of workmen with axes and other inſtruments.

Having fully ſatisfied himſelf, he returned to his friends, and aſked their opinion. The younger part of them were keen for attacking; but

but the older and the more experienced remonſtrated againſt it, as a moſt raſh and hazardous enterpriſe. *Lochiel* then enquired of two of the party who had ſerved for ſome time under *Montroſe*, if ever they ſaw him engage on ſo diſadvantageous terms; they declared they never did. He, however, animated by the ardor of youth, or promted by emulation, (for *Montroſe* was always in his mouth) inſiſted in a ſhort but ſpirited harangue, that if his people had any regard for their King or their Chief, or any principle of honor, the *Engliſh* ſhould be attacked: "for," ſays he, "if every man kills his man, which I hope you will do, I will anſwer for the reſt." Upon this, none of his party made further oppoſition, but begged that he and his brother *Allan* ſhould ſtand at a diſtance from the danger. *Lochiel* could not hear with patience the propoſal with regard to himſelf, but commanded that his brother *Allan* ſhould be bound to a tree, and that a little boy ſhould be left to attend him; but he ſoon flattered or threatned the boy to diſengage him, and ran to the conflict.

The *Camerons* being ſome more than thirty in number, armed partly with muſquets, and partly with bows, kept up their pieces and arrows till their very muzzles and points almoſt touched their enemies' breaſts, when the very firſt fire took down above 30. They then laid on with their ſwords, and laid about with incredible fury. The *Engliſh* defended themſelves with their muſquets and bayonets with great bravery, but to little purpoſe. The ſkirmiſh continued long, and obſtinate: at laſt the *Engliſh* gave way, and retreated towards the ſhip, with their faces to the enemy, fighting with aſtoniſhing reſolution. But *Lochiel*, to prevent their flight, commanded two or three of his men to run before, and from behind a buſh to make a noiſe, as if there was another party of Highlanders to intercept their retreat. This took ſo effectually, that they ſtopped, and animated by rage, madneſs, and deſpair, they renewed the ſkirmiſh with greater fury than ever, and wanted nothing but proper arms to make *Lochiel* repent of his ſtratagem. They were at laſt, however, forced to give way, and betake themſelves to their heels; the *Camerons* purſued them chin deep in the ſea; 138 were counted dead of the *Engliſh*, and of the *Camerons* only 5 were killed.

In this engagement, *Lochiel* himſelf had ſeveral wonderfull eſcapes. In the retreat of the *Engliſh*, one of the ſtrongeſt and braveſt of the officers retired behind a buſh, when he obſerved *Lochiel* purſuing, and ſeeing him unaccompanied with any, he leaped out, and thought him his prey. They met one another with equal fury. The combat was long, and doubtfull. The *Engliſh* Gentleman had by far the advantage in ſtrength and ſize; but *Lochiel* exceeding him in nimbleneſs and agility, in the end tript the ſword out of his hand: upon which, his antagoniſt flew upon him with amazing rapidity; they cloſed, and wreſtled till both fell to the ground in each other's arms. The *Engliſh* Officer got above *Lochiel*, and preſſed him hard; but ſtretching forth his neck by attempting to diſengage himſelf, *Lochiel*, who by this time had his hands at liberty, with his left hand ſeized him by the collar, and jumping at his extended throat, he bit it with his teeth quite through, and kept ſuch a hold of his grip, that he brought away his mouthfull; this, he ſaid, was the *ſweeteſt bite he ever had in his life time.* Immediately afterwards, when continuing the purſuit after that encounter was over, he found his men chin deep in the ſea; he quickly followed them, and obſerving a fellow on deck aiming his piece at him, plunged into the ſea, and eſcaped,

escaped, but so narrowly that the hair on the back part of his head was cut, and a little of the skin ruffled. In a little while a similar attempt was made to shoot him: his fosterbrother threw himself before him, and received the shot in his mouth and breast, preferring his Chief's life to his own.

In a few days afterwards, resolving to return to Gen. *Middleton*, he ordered all his men to assemble and join him; but while he waited for their return, he cut off another party of the garrison soldiers who were marching into the country, at *Auchentore*, within half a mile of the fort, killed a few, and took several prisoners. His former engagements with the General obliged him at last to join, which he did, with a great number of his clan; but was not long with him when he had certain information that the Governor of *Inverlochy* availed himself of *Lochiel*'s absence, by making his troops cut down the woods, and collect all the provisions in the country. His return to *Lochaber* being necessary, *Middleton* agreed to it, upon condition he would leave the greatest part of his men behind him. This he did, and set out privately for his country with only 150 men. He soon found his information was too true: in order to obtain redress, he posted his men, early in the morning of the day after his arrival, in different parts of a wood called *Stronnevifs*, within a mile of the garrison, where the soldiers used to come out every morning, to cut and bring in wood. Four or five hundred came in the ordinary manner. *Lochiel*, observing them from a convenient part of the wood where he rested, gave the signal at a proper time. His men soon made the attack, the enemy were soon routed, and a great slaughter made; 100 fell upon the spot, and the pursuit was carried on to the very walls of the garrison. It is remarkable, that not an officer eſcaped, they being the only active perſons that made reſiſtance. Thus continued *Lochiel* for ſome time a peſt to the garriſon, frequently cutting off ſmall detachments, partly by ſtratagem, partly by force; but his name carried ſo much terror with it, that they gave him no opportunity for ſome time of doing them much harm.

Gen. *Middleton* being at this time extremely unſucceſsfull in ſome of his adventures, particularly in an action ſome of his troops had lately with Major Gen. *Morgan*, at *Lochgarry*, where they were totally defeated, ſent an expreſs to *Lochiel*, ſupplicating his preſence, that meaſures might be concerted how to conclude the war in an honorable manner. *Lochiel* reſolved to go at the head of 300 men, and made the proper preparations for his journey with all imaginable ſecrecy; yet the Governor gets notice of his intended expedition, and orders *Morgan* if poſſible to intercept him. *Middleton* was at *Brae-mar*, in the head of *Aberdeenſhire*, between which place and *Lochaber* there is a continued range of hills for upwards of 100 miles. Over theſe did he travel, ſleeping in ſhellings, (huts which the herds build for ſhelter when in the mountains) on beds of hedder with their crops turned upwards, without any covering but his plaid. In the courſe of this expedition, he was like to be ſurprized by the activity of *Morgan* once and again; but getting up to the tops of the mountains, he always eſcaped the enemy, but frequently not to their profit, as his men often run down the hill, and after diſcharging a few pieces or arrows among them, would as eaſily aſcend.

Soon after his junction with *Middleton*, the war was given over, and *Middleton* retired to *France*, having preſented *Lochiel* with a

moſt

moſt favorable declaration, ſigned at *Dunvegan*, in *Sky*, *March* 31. 1655. But though the war was thus given over in general, and many of the nobility and heads of clans had ſubmitted to *Monk*, upon getting their eſtates reſtored, *Lochiel* ſtill ſtood out, not able to bear the inſolence of the troops quartered in a garriſon ſo near him. For the Governor, encouraged by the departure of *Middleton*, and taking the advantage of *Lochiel's* abſence in *Sky*, uſed to allow his officers to go out frequently in hunting parties, well guarded with a good number of armed men, deſtroying the game. *Lochiel*, on his return, having learned this, ſoon put a ſtop to their inſolence; for convening a party of the *Camerons*, he watched one day at a convenient place, while he ſaw one of theſe hunting parties coming towards the hill whereon he ſat, and having divided his men, and given them proper inſtructions, the attack was made with ſucceſs: moſt of the party were ſlain, and the reſt taken priſoners. The loſs of ſo many officers afforded new matter of grief and aſtoniſhment to the Governor, and prompted him to make ſome attempts to obtain redreſs, but they were all in vain. He, however, by this time became acquainted with the ſituation and manners of the country, and procured a number of mercenary deſperadoes around him, who gave him exact intelligence of whatever happened. This obliged *Lochiel* to flit his quarters to a farther diſtance from the fort, while he employed ſuch of his clan as continued faithfull, as counter-ſpies near the garriſon; and by their means, the reſolutions and plans of the Governor were not only made public, but many of his ſpies were detected and apprehended, whom *Lochiel* ordered to be hung up, without any ceremony or form of trial.

Soon

Soon after his encounter with the hunting party, an expreſs came to him from the Laird of *M'Naughtin*, a true Royaliſt in *Cowal*, a country oppoſite to *Inverara*, in *Argyleſhire*, acquainting him, that there were in that country three *Engliſh*, and one *Scotch* Colonel, with other Officers, who were deputed by Gen. *Monk* to ſurvey the forts and forfeited places in that part of the Highlands; and that it was poſſible to ſeize them with a few ſtout fellows. *Lochiel*, rejoiced at this intelligence, picked out 100 choice *Camerons*, with whom he marched for *Cowal*, ſtill keeping the tops of the mountains, leſt his deſigns ſhould be diſcovered and publiſhed. There he met his friend *M'Naughtin*, who informed him that the Officers lay at a certain inn, well guarded with armed ſoldiers. Upon which, he gave the proper orders to his men, who executed them with ſo much expedition and ſkill, that the officers, ſervants, and ſoldiers were all apprehended, and carried, almoſt without halting, to a place of ſecurity, before they well knew where they were. This place was a ſmall iſland in *Loch-Ortnick*, a freſh water lake 12 miles in length, about 10 miles North of *Inverlochy*.

The priſoners, though terrified at firſt, were ſoon undeceived. The horrible executions which *Lochiel*'s men made in the ſeveral rencounters they were engaged in, made his enemies believe him to be cruel and ſanguinary in his diſpoſition; but the gentle treatment, and the great civility the priſoners met with, ſoon convinced them of the contrary: he omitted nothing that could contribute to their happineſs; but particularly he propoſed and exhibited ſeveral hunting matches, which gave them great ſatisfaction. During their impriſonment, they took the liberty now and then to repreſent to

Lochiel

Lochiel the expediency and the prudence of a treaty with the General. He at firft rejected the motion, and fcorned the advice; but being often repeated, he began to give way to their reafonings, but ftill faid, that no wife man fhould truft his fafety in the hands of their pretended Protector, whofe whole life was a continued fcene of ambition, rebellion, hypocrify, and cruelty; and that though he was able to do little for the fervice of the King or his country, yet would he always preferve his confcience and honor unftained, till perhaps a more favorable opportunity of reftoring the King might offer. Thefe conferences being often renewed, brought *Lochiel* to declare himfelf in a more favorable manner. For the truth is, that he diffembled his fentiments at firft, wanting nothing fo much as an honorable treaty; for his country was impoverifhed, and his people almoft ruined. He ftill, however, protefted, that before he would confent to difarm himfelf and his clan, abjure his King, and take oaths to the Ufurper, he would live as an outlaw and fugitive, without regard to confequences. To this it was anfwered, that if he only fhewed an inclination to fubmit, no oath fhould be required, and he fhould have his own terms.

In confequence of this affirmation, *Lochiel*, with the advice of his friends, made out a draught of his conditions, which were tranfmitted to Gen. *Monk*, by Col. *Campbel*, one of the prifoners, he having given his word of honor he would foon return. Upon receipt of this, the General made out a new fet of articles, of much the fame nature with the draught fent, which he returned to *Lochiel*, fignifying to him, if he agreed thereto they would ftand good, otherwife not. After making fome fmall alterations, *Lochiel* confented, and the Marquifs of *Argyle* became his guarantee. This treaty was burned

burned in a houſe of *Lochiel's*, which was conſumed by accident. However, the moſt material articles are preſerved in *Monk's* letters to him, and are as follows.

'No oath was required of *Lochiel* to *Cromwel*, but his word of 'honor to live in peace. He and his clan were allowed to keep 'their arms as before the war broke out, they behaving peaceably. 'Reparation was to be made to *Lochiel* for what wood the Governor 'of *Inverlochy* cut on his grounds. A free and full indemnity was 'granted him for all riots, depredations, and crimes committed by 'him or his men preceding the preſent treaty. Reparation was to 'be made to the tenants for all the loſſes they ſuſtained from the 'garriſon ſoldiers. The tithes, ceſs, and other public burdens 'which had not been paid during the wars, were remitted, on con-'dition they ſhould be paid afterwards, with ſeveral others of the 'like nature.' All that was demanded by *Monk* of *Lochiel*, was, that he and his clan ſhould lay down their arms in name of King Charles II. before the Governor of *Inverlochy*, and take them up again in name of the States, without mentioning the Protector; that he would afterwards keep the peace, pay publick burdens, and ſuppreſs tumults, thefts, and depredations.

Theſe articles being agreed to, and ſubſcribed by *Monk* and *Lochiel*, the priſoners were diſcharged, but *Lochiel* begged they would honor him with their preſence at the ceremony of laying down their arms, which they complied with. Having convened a reſpectable number of his clan, he ranged them into companies, under the command of the Captains of their reſpective tribes, and put himſelf at their head. In this manner he marched to *Inverlochy*, in the ſame order as if going to battle, pipes playing, and colors flying.

The

The Governor drew out the ſoldiers, and put them in order on a plain near the fort; placing them in two lines oppoſite to the *Camerons*. *Lochiel* and the Governor firſt ſaluted each other as friends. The articles of the treaty were then read, and the ceremony of laying down and taking up the arms performed. Both parties afterwards partook of a ſplendid entertainment, prepared by the Governor for the occaſion, to the great ſatisfaction of all preſent. Thus did *Lochiel*, the only Chief in the Highlands that continued to ſupport the Royal cauſe after it was agreed the war ſhould be given over, at laſt ſubmit in an honorable way. *Monk* ſent him a letter of thanks for his chearful compliance, dated at *Dalkeith*, 5. *June* 1655.

During the remaining part of *Oliver*'s life, and the reigns of King CHARLES II. and JAMES II., *Lochiel* lived chiefly at home, in a broken kind of tranquillity, occaſioned by the diſtractions of the times, and the pretenſions of neighboring Chiefs and Lairds to parts of his eſtate: but he always ſhewed ſo much prudence and courage on every emergency, as gained him the friendſhip of the great, and the eſteem of all. He was held in particular favor by the two brothers CHARLES and JAMES, and received from them many marks of their royal regard. It may not be unworthy the attention of the curious to narrate the following incident.

Lochiel and the Laird of *M'Intoſh* had a long diſpute concerning ſome lands in *Lochaber*. *M'Intoſh* claimed them in conſequence of a grant of them he had from the *Lord of the Iſles*, afterwards confirmed by K. *David Bruce*: *Lochiel*'s plea was perpetual poſſeſſion. The conteſt was often renewed, both at the law courts and by arms. Many terms of accommodation were propoſed to the contending parties, but in vain. King CHARLES II. himſelf would needs be the mediator; but nothing but ſuperior force would prevail. In 1665, *M'Intoſh*, with his own clan and the *M'Pherſons*, convened an army of 1500 men, with which he ſets out for *Lochaber*. *Lochiel*, aided by the *M'Gregors*, raiſes 1200, 900 of which were armed with guns, broad ſwords and targets, and 300 with bows and arrows. (It is remarked, this was the laſt conſiderable body of bowmen that ever was ſeen in the Highlands.) Juſt as they were in view of one another, and almoſt ready to fight, the Earl of *Breadalbane*, who was Couſin German to both, arrived at the head of 300 men, and immediately ſent for the two Chiefs. He declared whoever ſhould oppoſe the terms he was to offer, he ſhould join the contrary party with all his power, and be his foe while he lived. Accordingly propoſals of agreement were made, and ſubmitted to by both parties. *Lochiel* continued in poſſeſſion of the lands; for which a ſum of money was given to *M'Intoſh*, to renounce all claims for the future. The articles of agreement were ſigned 20th *September* 1665, about 360 years after the commencement of the quarrel; and next day the two Chiefs had a friendly meeting, and exchanged ſwords. The leading Gentlemen of both clans performed the ſame friendly ceremony.

It muſt appear ſtrange, that now not a bow is to be ſeen in the Highlands, nor any propenſity towards that kind of armour. One might imagine, when the diſarming act took place, bows and arrows would have been a good ſubſtitute for guns; and, if I recollect rightly, there is no prohibition of bows in the act.

At the revolution, Sir *Ewen*, who was always prepoſſeſſed in favor of the hereditary right, and particulary for JAMES, whoſe friendſhip

friendſhip he had often experienced, was reſolved to ſupport his cauſe, as far as he could, at all hazards. In this reſolution he was confirmed by a letter he had from JAMES, dated 29 *March* 1689, then in *Ireland*, ſolliciting his aid, and that of his friends. Upon receipt of this letter, he viſited all the neighboring Chiefs, and wrote to thoſe at a diſtance, communicating to them the King's letter, and calling a general meeting to concert what meaſures ſhould be taken. They aſſembled on *May* 13th, near his houſe, and mutually engaged to one another to ſupport his Majeſty's intereſt againſt all invaders. When Viſcount *Dundee* got a commiſſion from King JAMES to command his troops in *Scotland*, *Lochiel* joined him with his clan, notwithſtanding that Gen. *M'Kay* made him great offers, both in money and titles, to abandon JAMES's intereſt.

He made a diſtinguiſhed figure at the ſkirmiſh of *Killikrankie*, under Lord *Dundee*, againſt Gen. *M'Kay*, though then above the age of ſixty-three. He was the moſt ſanguine man in the council for fighting; and in the battle, though placed in the centre oppoſite to Gen. *M'Kay*'s own regiment, yet ſpoke he to his men one by one, and took their ſeveral engagements either to conquer or die. Juſt as they began the fight, he fell upon this ſtratagem to encourage his men: He commanded ſuch of the *Camerons* as were poſted near him to make a great ſhout, which being ſeconded by thoſe who ſtood on the right and left, run quickly through the whole army, and was returned by the enemy. But the noiſe of the muſquets and cannon, with the echoing of the hills, made the Highlanders fancy that their ſhouts were much louder and briſker than that of the enemy; and *Lochiel* cried out, "Gentlemen, Take courage, the day

" is ours: I am the oldeſt Commander in the army, and have al-
" ways obſerved ſomething ominous and fatal in ſuch a dull, hollow, " and feeble noiſe as the enemy made in their ſhout, which prognoſti- " cates that they are all doomed to die by our hands this night; " whereas ours was briſk, lively, and ſtrong, and ſhews we have " vigor and courage." Theſe words, ſpreading quickly through the army, animated the troops in a ſtrange manner. The event juſtified the prediction: the Highlanders obtained a complete victory. The battle was fought, 1689. *Lochiel* continued for ſome time with that army; but being diſſatisfied with the conduct of *Cannon*, and ſome of the principal Officers, retired to *Lochaber*, leaving his ſon in his place during the reſt of the campaign.

When terms of ſubmiſſion were offered by King WILLIAM to the outſtanding Chiefs, though many were glad to accept of them, yet *Lochiel* and a few others were determined to ſtand out, untill they had King JAMES's permiſſion, which was at laſt obtained, and only a few days before King WILLIAM's indemnity expired.

There is nothing elſe memorable, in the publick way, in the life of Sir *Ewen Cameron*. He outlived himſelf, becoming a ſecond child, even rocked in a cradle; ſo much were the faculties of his mind, and the members of his body, impaired. He died *A. D.* 1718.

NUM-

NUMBER VII.

OF THE MASSACRE OF THE *COLQUHOUNS*.

IN the Baronage of *Scotland*, by Sir *Robert Douglas*, it appears that in the years 1594 and 1595, the clan of *Macgregors*, with ſome of their lawleſs neighbors, came down upon the low country of *Dumbartonſhire*, and committed vaſt outrages and depredations, eſpecially upon the territories of the *Colquhouns*. The then *Humphry Colquhoun* raiſed his vaſſals and followers to oppoſe them, and was joined by many of the Gentlemen in the neighborhood. Both parties met in *Glenfrone*, where a bloody conflict enſued. They fought with great obſtinacy till night parted them, and many brave men were killed on both ſides, but the *Colquhouns* appear to have been worſted. The Laird of *Colquhoun* eſcaped, and retired to a ſtrong caſtle; but being cloſely purſued by a party of the enemy, they broke into the caſtle, and found him in a vault, where they inſtantly put him to death with many circumſtances of cruelty.

In

In the year 1602, in the month of *February*, it was that this *Humphry Colquhoun* was ſlain; at which time the young Noblemen and Gentlemen who were at ſchool at *Dumbarton*, came as ſpectators to ſee the battle of *Glenfrone*, but were not ſuffered to approach near the danger, but were ſhut up in a barn by the *Colquhouns* for ſafety. The *Macgregors* prevailing, are ſaid afterwards to have barbarouſly put them all to death: upon which, an Act of Parliament was made, forfeiting the eſtate, and extirpating the whole clan and name of the *Macgregors*. This Act was again renewed in King *William*'s reign.

NUM-

NUMBER VIII.

ITINERARY.

Miles.

DOWNING,

21 Chefter, *Deonna*, *Devana*, PTOL. *Deva*, ANTON. RAV. CHOROG. *Deva*, *colonia legio cretica vicefima valeria victrix*, R. C.

18 Northwich, *Condate*, R. C.

8 Knutsford,

12 Macclesfield,

10 Buxton,

13 Middleton,

11 Chefterfield,

16 Workfop,

12 Tuxford,

8 Dunham Ferry, on the Trent, *Trivona fl.* R. C.

10 Lincoln,

Miles.

10 Lincoln, *Lindum*, Ptol. Anton. Rav. Chorog. R. C.
6 Waſhenbrough and back to Lincoln,
12 Spittle,
12 Glanford Bridge,
12 Barton,
Humber River, *Abus*, Ptol. R. C.
8 Hull,
8 Burton Conſtable,
22 Burlington Quay,
Its bay, *Gabrantuicorum portuoſus ſinus*, Ptol. *Portus fælix*, R. C.
5 Flamborough Head, *Brigantum extrema*, R. C.
10 Hunmanby,
10 Scarborough,
13½ Robin Hood's Bay,
6½ Whitby,
13 Skellin Dam,
9 Giſborough,
12 Stockton,
Tees River, *Tiſis fl.* R. C. Its mouth, *Dunum ſinus*, Ptol.
20 Durham,
Were River, *Vedra fl.* R. C.
6 Cheſter-le-Street, *Epiacum*, R. C.
9 Newcaſtle, *Pons Aelii*, Notit. Imp.
Tyne River, *Vedra fl.* Ptol. *Tina fl.* R. C.
14 Morpeth,
9 Felton,

10 Alnwick,

Miles.

10 Alnwick, *Alauna*, Rav. Chorog.

16 Belford,

16 Berwick, *Tueſſis*, Rav. Chorog.

Tweed River, *Alaunus*, Ptol. *Tueda*, R. C.

SCOTLAND.

16 Old Cambus,

10 Dunbar, *Ledone*, Rav. Chorog. *Dun* a ſmall hill, and *bar* a point of any thing.

6 North Berwick,

14 Preſton Pans,

8 Edinburgh,

9 South Ferry,

Firth of Forth, *Boderia*, Ptol. *Bodotria*, Taciti. R. C.

2 North Ferry,

Fife County, *Horoſtii*, R. C. *Caledonia*, Taciti.

15 Kinroſs,

20 Rumbling Brig, Caſtle Campbell, and back to Kinroſs,

13 Caſtle Dupplin, *Duabliſis*, Rav. Chorog.

8 Perth, *Orrea*, R. C.

Tay River and its mouth, *Taus*, Taciti. *Tava Æſt.* Ptol. R. C.

1 Scone,

1 Lunkerty,

13 Dunkeld,

20 Taymouth,

Miles.

15 Carrie on Loch-Rannoch,
20 Blair,
35 Through Glen-Tilt to Invercauld,
18 Tulloch,
15 Kincairn,
9 Banchorie,
18 Aberdeen,
Dee River, *Diva fl.* Ptol. R. C.
Ythen River, *Ituna fl.* R. C.
25 Bowneſs,
27 Craigſton Caſtle,
9 Bamff,
Devron River, *Celnius fl.* R. C.
8 Cullen,
12 Caſtle Gordon,
Spey River, *Celnius fl.* Ptol. *Tueſſis*, R. C.
8 Elgin, *Alitacenon*, Rav. Chorog.
10 Forres,
11 Tarnaway Caſtle, Calder, Fort George,
Firth of Murray, *Tuæ. Æſt.* Ptol. *Varar Æſt.* R. C.
12 Inverneſs, *Pteroton*, *caſtra alata*, R. C.
10 Caſtle Dunie,
18 Dingwall, Foules,
Firth of Cromartie, *Loxa fl.* R. C.
Roſsſhire, *Creones*, R. C. The ſame writer places at *Channery* in this county, *Aræ finium Imp. Rom.*
15 Ballinagouan,

6 Tain,

Miles.

6 Tain, *Caſtra alata*, Ptol.

9 Dornoch. Its Firth, *Vara Æſt.* Ptol. *Abona fl.* R. C.

Sutherland County, *Logi*, R. C.

9 Dunrobin Caſtle,

18 Hemſdale,

Ord of Cathneſs, *Ripa alta*, Ptol.

Cathneſs County, *Carnabii*, *Cattini*, R. C. *Virubium promontorium*, R. C.

8 Langwall,

15 Clythe; Clytheneſs, *Vervedrum prom.* R. C.

8 Thrumſter,

3 Wick,

Wick River, *Ilea fl.* Ptol.

16 Duncan's or Dungſby Bay, and John a Groat's Houſe,

Dungſby Head, *Berubium promontorium*, Ptol. *Caledonia extrema*, R. C.

Stroma Iſle, *Ocetis Inſula*, R. C.

2 Caneſby, and back the ſame road to

137 Inverneſs,

Inverneſs County, *Caledonii*, R. C.

17 General's Hut,

15 Fort Auguſtus,

Loch Lochy, *Longus fl.* R. C.

28 Fort William, R. C. places *Banatia* near it.

14 Kinloch-Leven,

9 King's Houſe,

19 Tyendrum,

Miles.

12 Dalmalie,

16 Inveraray,

22 Tarbut,

Loch-Lomond, *Lincalidor Lacus*, R. C.

8 Lufs,

12 Dunbarton, *Theodofia*, R. C.

Firth of Clyde, *Glota*, TACITI. *Clotta Æft.* R. C.

15 Glafgow, *Clidum*, RAV. CHOROG.

24 Hamilton, and back to Glafgow,

13 Kylfithe,

18 Sterling,

8 Falkirk,

Calendar,

15 Hopeton Houfe,

11 EDINBURGH,

18 Lenton,

18 Bild,

18 Moffat,

18 Lockerby,

ENGLAND.

21 Longtown in Cumberland,

Netherby, *Caftra exploratorum*, ANTON. *Aefica*, RAV. CHOROG.

9 Carlifle, *Lugavallium*, ANTON.

18 Penrith, *Bereda*, RAV. CHOROG.

11 Shap

Miles.

11 Shap in Weftmoreland,
15 Kendal, *Concangium*, NOTIT. IMP.
11 Burton, *Coccium*, R. C.
11 Lancafter, *Longovicus*, NOTIT. IMP.
Lune River, *Alanna fl.* R. C.
11 Garftang,
11 Prefton,
18 Wigan,
13 Warrington,
21 Chefter,
21 Downing in Flintfhire.

THE antient names of places marked R. C. are borrowed from the late Dr. *Stukeley*'s account of *Richard* of *Cirencefter*, with his antient Map of *Roman Brittain* and the Itinerary thereof, publifhed in 1757. The reft from Mr. *Horfly*'s Remarks on *Ptolemy*, *Antonine's Itinerary*, *Notitia imperii*, and *Ravennatis Britanniæ Chorographia*.

INDEX.

I N D E X.

THE ARTICLES marked thus * are ADDITIONS to the former EDITIONS.

A.

Page

*ABERCROMBIES, their Golgotha, - 141
Aberdeen, New, - - 121
--------- Old, - - 125
Advocate's Library in *Edinburgh*, - 52
**Alcluid*, - - 229
Alnwick Castle, - - 32
Alum Works in *Yorkshire*, - 22
Amber, - - 15
*Apology to the *English* Clergy, - 154
Appenines of *England*, - - 27, 28
Argentine, *Struan*'s favorite fountain, - 103
Arthur's Oven, - - 242
*-------- Round Table, - - 256
Athol House, - - 104
Augustus, Fort, - - 199
Auldearne, - - 153

Avosetta,

INDEX.

Page

Avosetta, - - 12
Aw, Loch, - - 216

B.

Bagpipes, - - 195
**Balfour*, Sir *William*, his picture and character, 153
Bamborough Castle, well regulated charity there, 33, 34
Bamff, - - 133
Bannockbourne, battle of, - 237
Bass Isle, - - 47
Beggars, few in *Scotland*, - 89
Belford, - - 33
Bel-tein, a singular superstition, - 97, 186, 291
Benevish, higher than *Snowdon*, - 207
Berridale, - - 175, 185
Berwick on *Tweed*, its Salmon fishery, - 39, 40
-------- North, - - 49
Birch tree, its great use, - 116
Birds, of *Lincolnshire*, - - 11
--------- *Flamborough* Head, - 17
--------- *Farn* Islands, - - 38
Birnam Wood, - - 80
Black meal, a forced levy so called, - 204
Blair House, - - 104
Bodotria of *Tacitus*, - - 43
Bollitir, Pass of, - - 118
Botanic Garden at *Edinburgh*, - 59
**Bowar* Parish, - - 345
Bowness Castle, its strange situation, - 129
Braan Castle, - - 163
Brae-mar, - - 109
Bran, fine cascade on the, - 81

Brotche,

Page

Brotche, - - 91
*Buckingham, Henry Stafford Duke of, his fate, 3
Bulfinch, Greater, - 116
Bullers of Buchan, - - 131
*Burgh, the, in Murray, a Danish strength, 152, 288
Burlington Quay and Abby, - 16
Burrowstoness, - - 243
Buxton, its salubrious waters, - - 5

C.

Cairns, curious near Bamff, - 138, 140
Calder, or Cawdor Castle, - - 154
Cambus, Old, - - 43
Cameron of Lochiel, amiable character of, - 203
* ------- Sir Ewen, his life, - - 347
Campbell Castle, - - 71
*Cannesbey Parish, - - 332
*Cant, Andrew, his epitaph, - 122
Carlisle, - - - - 251
Carron Iron Works, - - 242
*Carmele, the orobus tuberosus, - - 292
Cathness, - - 174, 181
* -------- account of, by the Rev. Mr. Pope, - 318
Cattle, Wild, - - 237
Cawdron Lin, a cataract there, - 70
*Cerealia, imitation of the antient, - 291
Chain, the, what, - - 206
Chester, its singular streets, - 1
------- Cathedral, - - ibid.
------- Hypocaust, - - 2
Chesterfield, - - 7
Chester-le-Street, - - 30

Churches,

Page

Churches, flovenly in *Scotland*, - 233
* *Clagh-na-herey*, conflict at, - - 189
Clan-Chattan. or *M'Intofhes*, - 188
Clergy, *Scotch*, commendable conduct of, - 155
* *Clyne* Parifh, - - 337
Coal of *Sutherland*, its miraculous quality, - 172
Coble, a fmall boat, - - 36
Cock of the Wood, - - 198
Cokin, its romantic fituation, - - 29
Columnar rocks at *Dunbar*, - - 44
Coldingham Moor and Abby, - - 42
* *Colquhouns*, Maffacre of, - - 365
Coranich, or howling at funerals, - - 99
Coryarich Hill, - - - 202
Cottages, wretched in the Highlands, - 117
Craigfton Caftle, - - 132
Crane, now unknown in *England*, - 13
* *Creich* Parifh, - - 340
* CRICHTON, the Admirable, his life, - - 295
* *Cromar*, diftrict in *Aberdeenfhire*, - - 119
Cromartie, Firth of, - - 165
Crows, *Royfton*, or Hooded, - - 85
* *Culbleen* Hill, - 119
Cullen Houfe and Town, - - 133
------ fingular rocks near, - - 138
Culloden Houfe and Moor, - - 158
Cuftoms, fingular ones in the Highlands, - 95
Cuthbert's, St. Ducks, - - 37

D.

* *Dalmore*, fine Pine foreft, - - 109
Days, long in *Cathnefs*, - 185

Page

Dalkeith, Pictures there, - - 63, 64
Dean of *Guild*, what, - - 161
* *Deæ matres*, - - 248, 249
* *Deasoil*, a superstitious rite, - 291
Delamere Forest, - - 2
* *Desmond*, Countess of, her history, - 73
Dingwall Town, - - 164
* *Diurness* Parish, - - 321
Dogger Bank, great Fishery near, - 20
* *Don*, its Bridge, by whom built, - - 128
Dornoch, - - - 168
* ------- Parish, - - 338
* *Drugon*, the *Flandrian*, his story, - 15
Dunbar, - - 44
* ------- Earl of, his monument and character, - 46
* ------- Battles of, - - 46, 47
Dunbarton Castle and Town, - 228
Dunbeth Castle, - - 175
Dungsby Bay, - - - 177
Dunie Castle, - - - 162
Dunkeld, - - 80, 81
* *Dunnet* Parish, - - 331
Dunrobin Castle, - - 170
Dunsinane, - - 80
Dupplin, Pictures there, - 72, 73
Durham, - - 28

E.

Eagles, - - - 85
* *Edrachilis* Parish, - - 320
Eider Ducks, - - 36

Edinburgh,

Page

Edinburgh, its lofty situation, - 49
----------- inconveniences, - - 50
----------- Reservoir, - - 51
----------- University, - - 56
Elf-shots, what, - - 101
Elgin, a good town, - - 146
------ its Cathedral, - - *ibid.*
*------ history of, by the Rev. Mr. *Shaw*, - 269
Erse language, where spoken, - 227

F.

Fairies, belief in, - - 101
Falcons, - - - 143
Falkirk, great Cattle fairs there, - - 239
-------- Battles of, - - - 240
* *Far* Parish, - - 325
Farn Islands- - - 36
Faskally, its beauties, - - 105
Fasting Woman, extraordinary case of, - 167
Fen, East, its fish and birds, - 10, 11, 12
Fiery cross, what, - - 192
Finchal Monastery, - - 30
Fine, Loch, its Herring fishery, - 219, 220
* *Finlater*, Castle of, - - 137
Flamborough Head, its birds, - 16, 17
Flixton, - - 18
Fochabers, - - 144
Forfeited estates, how applied, - 162
Forres, great column near, - - 149
Foss-dyke, - - - 7
Foulis, Messrs. their Academy, - 232
Fraoch-Helan, the *Hesperides* of the Highlands, - 217

Page

Freeburgh Hill, a large *Tumulus*, - 26
Freſwick Caſtle, horrid ſituation of, - 177
Funeral cuſtoms, - - 99
Furvie, overwhelmed with ſand, - 129
Fyers, Fall of, - - 199

G.

Gannet, - - 48, 180
Garſtang, - - 262
Geeſe, how often plucked, - - 9
Geneological Picture, curious at *Taymouth*, - 87
George, Fort, Old, - - 160
-------------- New, - - 158
Giſborough, - - 23
Glaſgow, its magnificence, - - 230
Glen-Co, - - - 210
* ------- deſcribed, - - *ibid.*
* *Glen-Muik*, fine cataract, - - 119
Glen-Roy, ſtrange roads there, - - 208
Glen-Tilt, a dangerous Paſs, - 108
Glen-Urquhie, - - - 215
Godric, St. his auſterities, - - 30
* *Golſpie* Pariſh, - - - 338
Gordon Caſtle, - - 142
Gowrie's Conſpiracy, - - 77
Graham, *John de*, his epitaph, - - 240
Graham's Dyke, - - - 243
Grampian Hills, - - 224
Granite Quarries at *North Ferry*, - - 67
------------------- *Aberdeen*, - - 125
Gre-hound, the Highland, - - 143

Groat's

Page

Groat's, John a, house, - - 177
Gull, *Arctic*, - - - 66

H.

* *Halkirk* Parish, - - 343
Halydon Hill, Battle of, - - 41
Hamilton, Pictures there, - - - 234
Hares, White, - - - - 84
Heronry, a great, - - 13
Herring fishery, - - - 220
Herriot's Hospital, - - 56
High-bridge, - - - 204
Highlands, awefull entrances into, - 226
Highlanders, dress of the men, - - 190
-------------------------- women, - 193
------------ arms, - - - 191
------------ character of, - - 193
------------ sports and amusements of, - 194
Hilda, St. - - - 25
Holy-Rood House, Pictures there, - - 53
Hopeton House, - - - 244
Hornsea, - - - 15
Huntings, magnificent in old times, - 106, 110

I.

* *James* III. where killed, - - 238
Jameson, the Painter, - - - 87
--------- fine Picture of his at *Taymouth*, - - *ibid.*
--------- other Pictures of his, - - 133, 134
Jet, where found, - - - 24
* *Jew*'s Harp, found in an urn, - - 195

* *Innes*.

Page

* *Innes* Family, tragical relation of, - - 145
* ---------------------------------- another, - 311
Inoculation, practiſed as far as *Shetland,* - - 184
Inveraray Town and Caſtle, - - - 218
Invercauld, its magnificent ſituation, - - 113, &c.
Inverlochy Caſtle, - - - 206
Invernеſs, - - - 160
--------- Fair, - - 189
Joug, what, - - - 155
Itinerary, - - - - 367

K.

Kendal, great Woollen Manufacture there, - 259
* ------ Caſtle, - - - 260
Kilchurn Caſtle, - - - 216
* *Kildonnan* Pariſh, - - 341
Killicrankie, Paſs of, - 105
* *Kinguſie* Priory, - - - 286
Kinloch-Leven, - - - 209, 211
Kinloſs Abby, - - 148, 284
Kinmore Church, decent congregation there, - 88
Kinroſs, - - - 67
Kittiwake, a ſort of Gull, - - 130
Kylſithe battle, - - - 237

L.

Labor, its price in *Scotland,* - - 72, 117
Lakes, review of, - - - 222
Lancaſter, - - - 260
* *Larg* Pariſh, - - - 341
Late wake, a ſtrange funeral cuſtom, - - 99

* *Lathrone*

Page

* *Lathrone* Parifh, - - - 334
Lavellan, the Water Shrew-Moufe, - - 175
* *Legh*, *Perkin a*, his epitaph, - - - 4
Leith, - - - - 60
* *Lefley*, General, his character, - - 132
Lincoln, its beautifull Cathedral, - - 8
Livings, *Scotch*, value of, - - - 157
Lochaber, - - - - 204, 208
Lochiel, his feat, - - - 203
Loch-Leven, - - - 68
------------ its Fifh and Birds, - - 70
* ------------ fiege of its Caftle, - - - 69
Loch-Lomond, its charms, - - - 223
Loncarty, Battle of, - - - - 79.
* Longevity, great inftances of, - - - 225
Loffie River, - - - - 148
* *Loth* Parifh, - - - - 335
Lothian, Eaft, its fertility, - - - 43

M.

Macclesfield, - - - 3
Mac-Gregors, a murderous clan, - - - 223
Mackrel-Sture, - - - 221
Mac-Nabbs, an antient family of Smiths, - - 216
Marble, White, - - - 173
Marriage Cuftoms, fingular, - - 186
* *Mayborough*, a curious antiquity, - - 257
Michaelmas Moon, what, - - - 154
Moffat, - - - - 243
Moncrief, Hill of, its fine view, - - 74
Monro, Sir *Robert*, his epitaph, - - 241
Morpeth, - - - - 33

* *Morvern*,

Page

* *Morvern*, high hill in *Aberdeenſhire*, - - 120
Mountain, the Black, - - - 212
Moy-hall, - - - - 188
Mummies, Natural, - - 178
* *Murray*, County of, its hiſtory, - - 269
-------- Earl of, the bonny, - - 153
* -------- Biſhoprick of, - - 284

N.

Nairn, - - - - 154
* *Nehalennia*, the Goddeſs, - - 249
Neſs, Loch, - - - 196, 200
------------ Agitations of, in 1755, - 200
* *Netherby*, Antiquities there, - - 247
Newbottle, Pictures there, - - - 61
Newcaſtle on Tyne, - - - 31
------------------- its Salmon fiſhery, - - 252
Ninian's, St. Church blown up, - - - 238
Northwich, - - - 3

O.

Ochil Hills, - - - - 71
Officers, Half-pay, their laudable purſuits in *North Britain*, 166
* *Olrig* Pariſh, - - - 331
Ord of *Cathneſs*, a high promontory, - - 174
Orkney Iſles, - - - 178
Ouzels, Ring, - - - 85

P.

* *Pananich* Spaw, - - - 119

* Pardon

Page

*Pardon for ſins, its price, - - 4
Pearls, - - - - 76
Penrith, the Pillars at, - - - 253
* ------ Caſtle, - - - - 255
Perth, a fine town, - - - 75
------ its trade, - - - 76
Phinocs, a ſpecies of Trout, - - - 209
Pictiſh Caſtles, - - - - 171
* ------ Houſes, - - - - 318
*Pines, Obſervations on their Growth, - - 265
Pine Foreſts. - - - - 109, 115, 213
Pines, vaſt plantations of, - - 166
*Plague at *Penrith*, - - - 254
Preſton Pans, battle of, - - 49
**Pluſcarden* Abby, - - - 285
Proverbs, *Erſe*, - - - 216
Proviſions, prices of, at *Edinburgh*, - - 68
---------------------- at *Aberdeen*, - - 125
---------------------- at *Inverneſs*, - - 161
Ptarmigans, - - - 85

Q.

Quern, a hand-mill, - - - 211

R.

Rannoch, Loch, Pine foreſt near, - - 93
Rats, will not live in *Sutherland*, - - 172
Rents, how paid in the Highlands, - - 117, 166
------- raiſing of, ill effects of, - - 208
**Richmond*, *Frances* Dutcheſs of, her character, - 134
Roads, the Military, - - 213, 214
Robin Hood's Bay, - - - 22, 24
Roe-Bucks, - - - 94
**Rogart* Pariſh, - - - 341
Royſton Crows, - - - 85

Page

Rumbling Brig near *Glen-Devon*, - - 70
---------------- near *Dunkeld*, - - - 81
* *Ruthven*, General, his picture and character, - 62

S.

Sacrament, sometimes indecently received in *North Britain*, - 89
Sailors and Soldiers, attempt to colonize, - - 102
Salmon fisheries, antient laws to preserve, - - 128
----------------- in *England*, - - - 40
----------------- in *Scotland*, - - 144, 183
Salt pits at *Northwich*, - - - 3
Sand, inundations of, - - - 129, 152
Scarborough, - - - 18
------------ its Fisheries, - - 19, 20
Scone, - - - - 78
Scotland, unpromising entrance into, - - 42
Seals, - - - 182
Second sight, - - - 179
Sheelings, or Summer Dairies, - - 109
* *Skipsey* Castle, - - - - 15
* *Shap* Abby, - - - - 257
* ---- curious range of stones, - - - 258
* Shoe, antient, - - - 250
Slain's Castle, - - - 129
Snow flake, - - - 115
Soland Geese, *vide* Gannet.
* *South Ferry*, its fine view, - - 65
Spalding, - - - 13
Spectre story, - - - 96
Spey, a violent river, - - 144
Spinie Castle and Lake, - - - 147
Stags, - - - - 106
Sterling, - - - 238

Stuart,

Page

Stuart, Mary, Pictures of, - - 123, 163, 236
Stocking Trade in *Aberdeen*, - - 149
Stockton, - - - - 27
Strath-Earn, - - - 72
* *Strathnaver*, its history, - - 318
Stroma Isle, - - - 178
Struan, *Robertson* of, a Poet, - - 95
Swineshead Abby, - - - 14
Sutherland, - - - 168
* ---------- history of, by the Rev. Mr. *Pope*, - 318
Sybilla, Queen, where buried, - - 89
Sylva Caledonia, - - - 239

T.

* *Tain*, capital punishment once used there, - 167
Tantallon Castle, - - - 47
Tarnaway Castle, - - - 152
------------------ Pictures there, - - 153
Tay, Loch, - - - 84
------------ never frozen till the year 1771, - *ibid.*
------------ Isle, and Convent on it, - - 89
Tay-bridge, Inscription on it, - - 86
Tay-mouth, its beauties, - - - 82
* *Tayre*'s, St. Chapel, cruel massacre there, - 181
Theft of Cattle, once held not dishonorable, - 205
* *Thurso* Parish, - - - 329
* *Tongue* Parish, - - - 323
Tordown Castle, its singular cement, - - 201
Tumel, the Falls of, - - - 103
----- Lake, - - - 104
Tunny, - - - 221
Turner, Dr. *William*, the Naturalist, - 32
Tweed, - - - 39
Tyendrum, the highest seated house in *Scotland*, - 215

U.

Page

Ulric, St. his earth, - - 172
*Urns, - - - 139
Urquhart Caſtle, - - 197, 287
--------- Priory, - - - 285

V.

Venereal patients, where formerly confined, - 245

W.

*War, laſt private in *Scotland*, - - 184
**Water-Crook*, the old *Concangium*, - - 260
**Watten* Pariſh, - - - 346
Were, its fiſh, - - - 29
Whitby, - - - - 25
Wick, - - - - 174
* ---- Pariſh, - - - - 333
William, Fort, - - - 206
Witches, where burnt, - - - 58, 169
--------- *Macbeth*'s, - - - 149
--------- of *Thurſo*, - - - 169
*Wolf of *Badenoch*, - - - 279
Wolves, how long exiſting in *Scotland*, - - 206
Women, the common, hardly treated in *North Britain*, 131, 183

Y.

Yew tree, a great, - - 90
**Yorke* Caſcade, - - - 105
Ythen River, - - - 128

THE END.